M000239000

Cultural Adaptations

Cultural Adaptations

Tools for Evidence-Based Practice With Diverse Populations

Edited by
Guillermo Bernal and
Melanie M. Domenech Rodríguez

American Psychological Association
Washington, DC

Copyright © 2012 by the American Psychological Association. All rights reserved. Except as permitted under the United States Copyright Act of 1976, no part of this publication may be reproduced or distributed in any form or by any means, including, but not limited to, the process of scanning and digitization, or stored in a database or retrieval system, without the prior written permission of the publisher.

Published by
American Psychological Association
750 First Street, NE
Washington, DC 20002
www.apa.org

To order
APA Order Department
P.O. Box 92984
Washington, DC 20090-2984
Tel: (800) 374-2721; Direct: (202) 336-5510
Fax: (202) 336-5502; TDD/TTY: (202) 336-6123
Online: www.apa.org/pubs/books
E-mail: order@apa.org

In the U.K., Europe, Africa, and the Middle East, copies may be ordered from
American Psychological Association
3 Henrietta Street
Covent Garden, London
WC2E 8LU England

Typeset in Goudy by Circle Graphics, Inc., Columbia, MD

Printer: United Book Press, Inc., Baltimore, MD
Cover Designer: Naylor Design, Washington, DC

The opinions and statements published are the responsibility of the authors, and such opinions and statements do not necessarily represent the policies of the American Psychological Association.

Library of Congress Cataloging-in-Publication Data

Cultural adaptations : tools for evidence-based practice with diverse populations / edited by Guillermo Bernal and Melanie M. Domenech Rodríguez.
     p. cm
  Includes bibliographical references and index.
   ISBN 978-1-4338-1151-7 (alk. paper) — ISBN 1-4338-1151-0 (alk paper) 1. Social psychology. I. Bernal, Guillermo, II. Domenech Rodríguez, Melanie M.
   HM1033.C8495 2012
   302—dc23
                                    2012004884

British Library Cataloguing-in-Publication Data
A CIP record is available from the British Library.

Printed in the United States of America
First Edition

DOI: 10.1037/13752-000

To a past generation, especially Jorge Alberto and Maria Elena, my parents, and Alfonso Bernal del Riesgo, my uncle, a lifelong advocate of rooting psychotherapy in culture. To my generation, Jorge Luis, Eduardo, and Mariela, my brothers and sister. From all of them I learned much about adaptation and cultures. This work is my hope for benefit to future generations.

—Guillermo Bernal

To Elba Rosa and Juan José, who raised me as a child. To María Luisa and Ana Cecilia, who are a raising me as a parent. To my mentors and my students, who have raised me as a scholar. All inhabit this work; may it be worthy.

—Melanie Domenech Rodríguez

CONTENTS

CONTRIBUTORS

Hortensia Amaro, PhD, Department of Counseling and Applied Educational Psychology, Department of Health Sciences, and Institute on Urban Health Research, Bouvé College of Health Sciences, Northeastern University, Boston, MA

Marc S. Atkins, PhD, Department of Psychiatry, University of Illinois at Chicago

Manuel Barrera Jr., PhD, Department of Psychology, Arizona State University, Tempe

Guillermo Bernal, PhD, Institute for Psychological Research, University of Puerto Rico, Río Piedras

Karen Bonilla-Silva, PhD, Institute for Psychological Research University of Puerto Rico, Río Piedras

Charlotte Brown, PhD, Western Psychiatric Institute and Clinic, University of Pittsburgh School of Medicine, Pittsburgh, PA

Kyaien O. Conner, PhD, MPH, MSW, Western Psychiatric Institute and Clinic, University of Pittsburgh School of Medicine, Pittsburgh, PA

Dharma E. Cortés, PhD, Department of Psychiatry, Cambridge Hospital/Harvard Medical School, Cambridge, MA

Jacqueline S. Gray, PhD, Center for Rural Health and Department of Pathology, School of Medicine and Health Sciences, University of North Dakota, Grand Forks

Jill S. Hill, PhD, Department of Counseling and Clinical Psychology, Teachers College, Columbia University, New York, NY

Wei-Chin Hwang, PhD, Department of Psychology, Claremont McKenna College, Claremont, CA

Anna S. Lau, PhD, Department of Psychology, University of California, Los Angeles

Ané M. Maríñez-Lora, PhD, Department of Psychiatry, University of Illinois at Chicago

Michelle McMurray, MSW, LSW, Western Psychiatric Institute and Clinic, University of Pittsburgh School of Medicine, Pittsburgh, PA

Guerda Nicolas, PhD, Department of Educational and Psychological Studies, University of Miami, Coral Gables, FL

John C. Norcross, PhD, ABPP, Department of Psychology, University of Scranton, Scranton, PA

Diego Osuna, MD, MPH, Kaiser Permanente Colorado, Denver

Mae Lynn Reyes-Rodríguez, PhD, Department of Psychiatry, University of North Carolina, Chapel Hill

Melanie M. Domenech Rodríguez, PhD, Department of Psychology, Utah State University, Logan

Emily Sáez-Santiago, PhD, Institute for Psychological Research, University of Puerto Rico, Río Piedras

María R. Scharrón-del-Río, PhD, Department of School Psychology, Counseling, and Leadership, School of Education, Brooklyn College, City University of New York, Brooklyn

Billie Schwartz, MA, Department of Educational and Psychological Studies, University of Miami, Coral Gables, FL

Lisa A. Strycker, MA, Oregon Research Institute, Eugene

Deborah J. Toobert, PhD, Oregon Research Institute, Eugene

Joseph E. Trimble, PhD, Department of Psychology, Western Washington University, Bellingham

Fabiana Wallis, PhD, Center for Trauma Recovery, Portland, OR

FOREWORD

JOHN C. NORCROSS

Since the earliest days of modern psychotherapy, every half-conscious practitioner has realized that treatment should be tailored to the individuality of the patient and the singularity of his or her context. William Osler (1906), the father of modern medicine, said, "It is sometimes much more important to know what sort of a patient has a disease than what sort of disease a patient has."[1] The mandate for individualizing psychotherapy was embodied in Gordon Paul's 1967 iconic question: "*What* treatment, by *whom*, is most effective for *this* individual with *that* specific problem, and under *which* set of circumstances?"[2]

Alas, empirical research in psychotherapy did not keep pace with the clinical realization that each client, each culture, may deserve a new treatment. The vast majority of the matching research tried to discover particular therapies for particular disorders, largely ignoring the person and the culture. The research suggests that Treatment X for Disorder Y is certainly useful for select diagnoses; however, only matching psychotherapy to a disorder is

---

[1]Osler, W. (1906). *Aequanimitas*. New York, NY: McGraw-Hill.
[2]Paul, G. (1967). Strategy of outcome research in psychotherapy. *Journal of Consulting Psychology, 31*, 109–118.

incomplete and not always effective. Every half-conscious practitioner also recognizes that what works for one person suffering from, say, depression, may not work for another depressed person with a differing personality, culture, coping style, or stage of change. The elusive grail has been to adapt psychotherapy to the patient's disorders *and* transdiagnostic characteristics in ways that are both clinically practical and demonstrably effective.

The American Psychological Association's (APA's) Task Force on Evidence-Based Practice, on which I was honored to serve, tried to chart a path by expanding the process of evidence-based practice to include the individuality and humanity of the client. Before that, most of health care adhered to the Institute of Medicine definition of *evidence-based practice* (EBP) as the integration of best research evidence with clinical expertise and patient values. APA, by contrast, defined EBP as the integration of the best available research with clinical expertise in the context of patient characteristics, culture, and preferences. Thus, the patient assumes a more active, prominent position, and the APA definition deliberately invokes cultural responsiveness. Put bluntly, clinical practice without attending to culture cannot be characterized as EBP.

In this generous, groundbreaking volume, editors Guillermo Bernal and Melanie Domenech Rodríguez compile the best available research and clinician expertise on cultural adaptations in psychotherapy. Their own seminal meta-analysis of 65 experimental studies, entailing 8,620 clients, proves that cultural adaptations work better than traditional (nonadapted) therapies. The results showed a definite advantage ($d = .46$) in favor of clients receiving culturally adapted treatments. But Bernal, Domenech Rodríguez, and the contributors to this volume take us even further: They show us how to actualize this superior effectiveness by tailoring treatment to culture in various ways, such as incorporating cultural content/values into treatment, using the client's preferred language, and matching clients with therapists of similar ethnicity/race. In doing so, they also show us that culturally adapted therapies improve access to health care, reduce health disparities, and enhance the health of the population in general.

In working with racial and ethnic minority patients, psychotherapists frequently confront a clinical dilemma: Should we use a research-supported treatment even if it has not been validated on patients of the same race, ethnicity, or culture as my patient? Fidelity to a research-supported treatment offers the promise that it "works" but not necessarily with that person or population. Or, should we use a treatment preferred by the patient and in accord with her cultural convictions even if it has not been extensively tested in randomized clinical trials? Flexibility to the patient's preferences and culture offers the promise that it "fits" but not necessarily of research support.

Dynamic tension occurs in resolving the conflict between fidelity and fit, both essential elements of EBP. We seek fidelity to a manualized treatment that has been found efficacious in controlled research. At the same time, we seek fit in adapting the service to accommodate the needs of the specific client. Errors in either direction can portend failure: Practitioners can become overly cautious in protecting fidelity by adhering rigidly to a manualized protocol and minimizing cultural differences, or they can become overly flexible in readily adapting a treatment without or in disregard of the research evidence.

Contributors to *Cultural Adaptations: Tools for Evidence-Based Practice With Diverse Populations* are acutely responsive to the dialectic between fit and fidelity. Indeed, culturally responsive therapies simultaneously embrace both. Cultural adaptations represent the *ideal cases*, in that the pillars of the EBP trinity—research support; clinical expertise; and patient characteristics, culture, and preferences—converge or agree. We can enjoy, at once, the nomothetic benefits of leveraging controlled research with the idiographic sensitivity of tailoring treatment to the patient's culture, characteristics, and preferences. In other words, this book remarkably balances fidelity with fit. Practitioners, educators, and researchers alike will marvel at the impressive results of research-supported cultural adaptations, as I certainly have done.

This book's editors and contributors also wisely eschew the pernicious polarization between the treatment method and the therapeutic relationship. Much of my own work over the past decade concerns the power of nourishing the relationship in psychotherapy—which, come to think of it, is quintessentially cultural. This volume prizes the curative value of therapeutic relationships without demeaning or devaluing the treatment method. The contributors strike a perfect balance in that cultural adaptations are presented as both technical and interpersonal, both instrumental and interpersonal, both technical and relational in the tradition of evidence-based practice.

In the end, *Cultural Adaptations* masterfully reconciles or perhaps transcends many of the bifurcations that have bedeviled our field: research versus practice, fidelity versus fit, treatment method versus therapeutic relationship, nomothetic versus idiographic. I am excited to be practicing during the era when we have learned to create a new psychotherapy for each patient in ways that improve treatment outcomes and reduce health disparities. And I am privileged to write this Foreword for a book that shows us how to tailor psychotherapy to the individuality of the clients and the singularity of her culture. It's probably premature to declare that the holy grail of psychotherapy has been found, but with this volume we definitely know where it is located and how we can reach it.

ACKNOWLEDGMENTS

At the turn of the 20th century, the poet Antonio Machado bade Spaniards to engage the present and look to the future with these words: "Caminante, son tus huellas el camino, y nada más; caminante, no hay camino, se hace camino al andar" (Traveler, your footsteps pave the way, nothing more; traveler, there is no road, the road is made by walking). The poem speaks to each individual traveler, implying solitude, yet at this juncture we are most struck by the realization that we walk alongside many; the road has been paved by incalculable numbers of footsteps. We want to acknowledge our fellow travelers. We are thankful for the company, the help, and the inspiration every step of the way.

We are most grateful to the contributors who believed in the idea of an edited volume on cultural adaptations. Despite occasional inclement weather, bumps in the road, and unexpected delays in our journey, our colleagues stayed the course—committed to the importance of this project. We are thankful for their collegiality, support, and outstanding contributions.

The support of friends and colleagues was invaluable. At the University of Puerto Rico, Blanca Ortiz Torres, Jeannette Rosselló, Wanda Rodríguez, and Alfonso Martínez Taboas have provided a lifetime of support and encouragement. Current and former protégés, such as Janet Bonilla, María Scharrón-del-Río,

Julio Santana Mariño, Yovanska Duarté, Emily Sáez Santiago, Carmen Rivera-Medina, and Eduardo Cumba, have been a source of inspiration. At Utah State University, Ana Baumann Walker, Melissa Donovick, Elisaida Méndez Rodríguez, Jesús Rodríguez, Audrey Schwartz, and Kee Straits made contributions to shaping, building, and furthering this work. They have all become treasured colleagues. Beyond our ivory towers, collaborations with esteemed colleagues like Rubén Parra-Cardona, Nancy Amador Buenabad, and Elizabeth Wieling have also furthered our work in cultural adaptations. It has been a joy to walk together on this path.

We each started our professional journey with noteworthy help from our mentors. Guillermo Bernal first learned the joys and challenges of research as an undergraduate from Leonard Jacobson. While in graduate school, his systemic view unfolded under the guidance of Stuart Golan and Harold Raush. Later, during his clinical internship, Ivan Boszormenyi-Nagy, Gerald Zuk, and Braulio Montalvo were influential in developing an appreciation of the complexities of relationships and intergenerational networks. As a new faculty member in the multicultural context of San Francisco, Guillermo joined up with peer-mentors such as Ricardo Muñoz, Eliseo Pérez-Stable, and James Sorensen in the struggle to treat and conduct research with persons and families from diverse language, racial, and ethnic backgrounds.

For Melanie Domenech Rodríguez, Marion Forgatch literally reached out across the room with a *Parenting Through Change* manual and essentially asked, "What needs to happen to it to make it work for Latinos?" She not only opened a door but also offered a seat at the table—stimulating an intellectually generous conversation on theory, methods, and clinical practices—and a keen editorial eye. Above all, she has offered true kinship. The path to reach Marion was first paved by Michael Slater, who ignited Melanie's passion for research and singlehandedly steered her to the field of psychology, and later by Fred Beauvais, Ernie Chavez, Ana Mari Cauce, and the Family Research Consortium–III faculty, all of whom ensured that she stay the course, weaving scientific rigor with social justice.

Much of the work reported in these pages would not have been possible without the support of seemingly invisible individuals who helped pave the way with training and research support. The early research on cultural adaptations was supported by funds from the National Institute on Mental Health and the National Institute on Drug Abuse. Individuals such as Cheryl Boyce, Ernest Márquez, Willo Pequenat, Delores Perron, LeShawndra Price, Sherman Ragland, David Stoff, and Ellen Stover helped us a great deal in setting the foundations for establishing a new avenue of research. Their energy, dedication, and courage have inspired us.

We are indebted to the friends, colleagues, and students at the University of Puerto Rico who provided the important support structure that enabled us to move forward in editing chapters, coordinating with authors, and writing our own chapters. We are especially grateful to Luz Mireya González, Lizzie Bultrón, Ada Rivera, Wilmarie Santiago, and Fermarie Villegas.

At APA Books, we are thankful to Susan Reynolds for warmly encouraging us to engage with this project. Peter Pavilionis, Daniel Brachtesende, Neelima Charya, and Ron Teeter provided the structure and editorial skills to ensure that our message would be as clear as possible. The impact of their work should not be underestimated.

This volume is a mile marker on a road that we hope will lead us all toward improved science and practice in the mental health fields. In these pages there is ample evidence of an otherwise unnamed culture: scientific culture. We hold scientific cultural beliefs (e.g., theories) and engage in specific scientific cultural practices (e.g., treatments, research methods) that have been passed through generations via significant rituals (e.g., classroom teaching, apprenticeships, graduation). These scientific cultural beliefs and practices stand to grow and evolve over time, as many cultures do, shedding archaic components, retaining relevant components, and integrating new beliefs and practices based on new wisdom and experiences. We are humbled to have the opportunity to contribute to a piece of this process in the evolution of our science.

I
FOUNDATIONS

1

CULTURAL ADAPTATION IN CONTEXT: PSYCHOTHERAPY AS A HISTORICAL ACCOUNT OF ADAPTATIONS

GUILLERMO BERNAL AND
MELANIE M. DOMENECH RODRÍGUEZ

Cultural adaptations of psychological treatments have emerged from nearly 3 decades of debate as to the role of culture in psychotherapy. Critiques were voiced as to the relevance of contemporary psychology and psychotherapy to ethnocultural groups (ECGs), which eventually gave way to the early calls for the consideration of sensitivity to culture, ethnicity, and language. These were followed by concerns regarding significant numbers of participants from diverse cultures and contexts in research that were followed by policy changes (e.g., National Institutes of Health [NIH], 1994) and increases in treatment research with diverse ECGs. The field of cultural adaptation brings together the best of the multicultural and the evidence-based movements in the service of offering psychological treatments that are based on the best available research and that consider culture and context in a thoughtful, documented, and systematic way. Growing evidence shows that culturally adapted treatments work (Benish, Quintana, & Wampold, 2011; T. B. Smith, Domenech Rodríguez, & Bernal, 2011). However, the field has yet to achieve a convergence of cultural adaptation frameworks and is missing detailed examples to guide those wishing to engage in adaptations. This book seeks to address both gaps.

PSYCHOTHERAPY AND ITS CULTURAL ATTACHÉS

The relationship between culture and psychotherapy is complex and multifaceted, as is the definition of *culture* (Betancourt & Lopez, 1993; Triandis, 2007). We consider culture as an intergenerationally transmitted system of meanings shared by a group or groups of people. Culture may have concrete products (e.g., tools, sculptures, art, buildings) and subjective elements (e.g., social norms, beliefs, values, behavior). Depending on psychotherapy traditions, culture can be invisible or simply absent, or so intertwined as to be inseparable. On this broad spectrum, psychotherapy has been described as culturally embedded, culturally influenced, culturally related (Tseng, 1999), and historically situated (Cushman, 1995). Psychotherapy has also been described as culturally adapted, anchored, appropriate, centered, competent, congruent, informed, relevant, responsive, and sensitive. All of these terms imply different degrees of intensity in the relationship between culture and psychotherapy. The term *embedded* implies the strongest relationship, as psychotherapy is viewed as an integral part of the context (Wampold, 2001). The terms *centered* and *anchored* imply that a culture that is distinct from the culture of psychotherapy is used to modify the elements of treatment with the goal of aligning the therapy to the culture of the target population (P. B. Pedersen, 1997). The terms *sensitive, congruent, informed, relevant,* and *responsive* imply distinct efforts at modifying psychotherapy to the culture of a particular population with varying gradations of intensity or influence. Finally, the term *culturally adapted* refers to systematic changes made to a protocol so that features of the culture and language of particular groups are considered as part of the treatment (Bernal, Jiménez-Chafey, & Domenech Rodríguez, 2009).

Yet if psychotherapy is viewed as a cultural phenomenon that emerged at a particular point in history and is evolving over time, the issue at hand is not so much the influence of culture on psychotherapy but the effort to make visible the culture within models of psychotherapy and to carefully examine the challenges involved in transporting and adapting these models to other cultural and linguistic groups. This chapter frames cultural adaptations within the historical context of the field of psychotherapy. We review how psychotherapies have been adapted historically in response to social, political, and geographical shifts. We then provide a brief review of the emergence of cultural adaptations in the context of evidence-based treatments (EBTs), followed by examples of psychotherapy adaptations.

HISTORICAL ADAPTATIONS TO PSYCHOTHERAPY

There are multiple definitions of *psychotherapy* and over 400 different types of psychotherapies (Garfield, 1992). Psychotherapy may be broadly defined as the coming together of a therapist and a client to identify a solution to the client's problem(s) that is considered to be mental in nature or, simply, to promote better mental health of the client (Tseng, 1999). More specifically, it can be defined as the systematic use of the interpersonal relationship to affect changes in the person's cognition, feelings, and behavior (Strupp, 1989). Psychotherapy has also been much more specifically defined in terms of propositional and procedural models (Ford & Urban, 1998) and the epistemological assumptions underlying such models. Structurally, psychotherapy is a service offered by professionals from different disciplines (e.g., medicine, nursing, psychology, social work, counseling). Socially, psychotherapy is a system of treatment influenced by the values and norms of each discipline, intended to benefit the public (e.g., clients, families, schools, courts), and monitored by the individuals who establish the mental health public policy, such as governmental agencies and insurance companies (Strupp & Howard, 1992). Regardless of the focus or scope of definitions, the interpersonal relationship and verbal interactions are understood to be necessary components of therapeutic/psychological change (Freedheim, 1995). Yet it is only relatively recently that definitions of psychotherapy have explicitly included culture and context.

Forces in Psychotherapy

Psychoanalytic theory and its related offshoots, broadly known as *psychodynamic* theories, are considered the first wave or force in psychotherapy theories. These were followed by cognitive and behavioral theories as the second force. Interestingly, it appears that behavioral interventions were conducted as early as 1896 (Freedheim, 1995) in the United States, in Lightner Witmer's clinic, thought to be the first psychological clinic established in the world. The influence of Witmer's work and that of other behavioral scholars was not strongly apparent in the field of psychology until decades later. This second force in psychology was homegrown, although Witmer trained in Germany prior to his work in the United States and the work of the Russian physiologist Ivan Pavlov strongly informed behaviorism. However, many of the notable behaviorists (Hull, Skinner, Thorndike, Tolman, Watson) were U.S.-born and conducted their work in the United States. Behavioral approaches evolved from simple reward systems to talking, or couch therapy, with Wolpe's (1958) systematic desensitization approach (developed in South Africa), which was later followed by social learning approaches using behavior modeling (Bandura, 1989). Cognitive approaches to psychotherapy were also developed by Aaron Beck, Albert Ellis, and George Kelly. Despite their conceptual differences, both psychodynamic and behavioral approaches to psychotherapy were inextricably linked to traditions of observation, documentation, and replication to support or refute their utility. Psychotherapy practice has been linked to research from its inception.

The third force in psychology combines humanistic and existential orientations and applies them to psychotherapy. While humanistic and existential approaches were advanced by U.S.-based psychologists (e.g., Carl Rogers, Rollo May, Abraham Maslow, and most recently Irvin Yalom), it is important to note that these approaches were built on the foundations of existential theory, which was developed by notable philosophers in France (Sartre), Germany (Heidegger, Nietzsche), Denmark (Kierkegaard), and Austria (Frankl).

Multiculturalism represents a fourth force in psychotherapy (P. Pedersen, 1988, 1989, 1990; Ponterotto & Casas, 1991; Sue, Bingham, Porche-Burke, & Vasquez, 1999), based on changing demographics that resulted in a new social context, increasingly diverse in terms of race, ethnicity, language, and culture. Multicultural psychologists question the universality of psychotherapy approaches developed from specific cultural perspectives and particularly stemming from theories and procedures developed from and for primarily privileged sectors of society (L. Smith, 2005). Critiques of these approaches began to evolve, highlighting a need for alternative ways of working with specific ECGs including African Americans, Latinos/as, American Indians, and Asian Americans. For example, as early as the 1980s within the family therapy movement, texts on ethnicity were published (McGoldrick, Giordano, & Pearce, 1982), and within the ethnic minority movement, key articles and texts began to emerge (P. Pedersen, 1988; Ponterotto & Casas, 1991; Sue et al., 1999) that provided the conceptual basis for modifying or developing treatments and services, considering language, culture, and context.

The multicultural movement challenged the claim of universality of contemporary theories and models of psychotherapy, questioning their ecological and social validity for diverse cultural and linguistic groups. Criticisms ranged from observations that conventional treatments did not consider basic elements of the social context, such as poverty, to claims that culture and language of different societal sectors seemed to be ignored. Yet cultural invisibility cannot be assumed to imply absence. The historical accounts in this chapter show that indeed, psychotherapy has been transformed and adapted, in part, by changing cultures and contexts.

Changes and Adaptations

The earliest tailoring of psychotherapy treatments can be described in terms of changes to the *structure* (from the couch to the chair) and *intensity* (from four to five sessions per week to one per week) as psychoanalysis was transformed into psychoanalytic psychotherapy. Some have proposed that the number of sessions and the use of the couch distinguished psychotherapy from psychoanalysis (Migone, 2000). In its transportation from Germany to the United States, classical psychoanalysis also morphed from a focus on the id and biology to one on the ego and, later, interpersonal relations, distancing itself from its biological roots. From a sociocultural perspective, while there may have been theoretical reasons for these changes, in essence, the new context and the changing culture molded and transformed psychoanalysis into new variants of psychotherapy. For example, Freud's disagreement with Jung may have stemmed from cultural and contextual differences. As Cushman (1992) questioned, "Could it be that the cultural differences between Freud's vibrant, passionate, conflicted, dangerous, diverse Vienna and Jung's more stable, homogeneous Zurich were reflected in their two theories" (p. 37)?

Immediately after World War II, the treatment needs of a large number of veterans and the lack of trained personnel opened the door to a significant change in the psychotherapeutic format: from individual to group. Again, the changing social context molded the practice of psychotherapy, paving the way for what has become an important theoretical approach (Brabender & Fallon, 2009). Group psychotherapy gave way to other modalities, such as family, couples, and network therapy. The cybernetic revolution prompted practitioners dissatisfied with individual therapy to conceptualize problems in broader systems, resulting in family and couples therapy. Family therapy emerged in the 1950s, challenging the absence of context in individual psychotherapy and proposing profound technical and philosophical alternatives to treatment (Beels, 2002; Broderick & Schrader, 1981). The development of family approaches occurred during the postwar period, a time when the nuclear family was idealized. During the war, women had become part of the workforce, but with the men returning home, women were now expected to leave their jobs and go back to working at home. Perhaps it was no coincidence that family therapy emerged at a time when social adjustments and economic processes were affecting the interior of the family vis-à-vis the idealized nuclear model of the family.

Some adaptations to psychotherapy were framed as new or distinct theoretical positions. Within psychoanalysis, there are many examples of cultural adaptations framed as theoretical advances, such as Freud's moving away from an id-based psychology in Europe to an ego psychology in the

United States. In Europe, at the turn of the 19th century, the self had been conceptualized as a structure to contain violent aggressive instincts, while in the United States the self was envisioned as "ambitious, energetic, seeker of spiritual and practical improvement" (Cushman, 1992, p. 35). The new focus on ego was more attuned to the U.S. cultural context, valuing individualism, optimism, and a worldview that sees the future with hope.

Harry Stack Sullivan was one of the first theoreticians to present a more socially informed view of personality that emphasized interpersonal processes in context. His approach was pragmatic and reflected an awareness of ethnicity and political processes (Cushman, 1992). His notion of the self was derived from the interpersonal context, including social interactions and broader social processes such as cultural mores and beliefs. Thus, Sullivan's theoretical proposal essentially represents a cultural adaptation of a drive-based psychoanalytic theory to the social interaction values of the United States in the 1920s and 1930s. Indeed, ego psychology in the United States, object relations theory in England, and later Lacanian psychoanalysis are all examples of the changes in the theoretical content of psychoanalytic psychotherapy toward the interpersonal realm, responding to changing cultural contexts. Alfred Adler joined Sullivan in this new focus on the social and interpersonal process in what Cushman (1995) called an "Americanization of psychoanalysis."

Perhaps one of the best examples of the cultural adaptation of psychoanalysis is Carl Rogers's client-centered psychotherapy. Rogers essentially maintained the key curative element of psychoanalysis (i.e., the transference relationship) but recast it in a way that was culturally aligned with the predominant middle- and upper-middle-class values in the United States, such as the therapist's assuming a position of unconditional positive regard. The focus of the treatment was in the present as opposed to the past, and the overall goal of the treatment was for the client (not *patient*) to achieve personal growth and development. Thus, supporting self-actualization goes hand in hand with the cultural value of independence, and the focus on the here and now is more attuned with the U.S. ethos to deemphasize the past. Addressing a client rather than a patient distanced psychotherapy from the medical model. So, in a sense, this shift may be a reflection of the "distrust of the expert" phenomenon in U.S. culture (Meadow, 1964, cited in Tseng, 1999). The genius of Rogers was to formulate a treatment modality in terms that were closely aligned to the cultural values of independence, autonomy, growth, present-orientation, and optimism.

At present, psychotherapy is framed as evidence-based. EBTs (formerly termed *empirically supported treatments* and *empirically validated treatments* [EVTs]) are tested for efficacy mainly through randomized clinical trials. While the push for evidence started (in the mid-1990s) with stringent criteria tied to specific manuals and specific criteria for worthy evidence, the field has evolved. Currently, evidence-based psychological practice is informed by the best available research, clinical expertise, and individual preferences (APA Presidential Task Force on Evidence-Based Practice, 2006).

Psychotherapy's Potential as a Vehicle for Oppression

Psychotherapy is a Western cultural phenomenon, originating in Europe and the United States. Indeed,

> the idea of sitting in a room with a healer, confiding in the healer, responding to questions, and following the implicit or explicit ritualistic expectations of the psychotherapeutic protocol . . . would be an absurdity in 99% of the societies past or present. (Wampold, 2001, p. 79)

Yet, as a healing practice, psychotherapy has areas in common not only with medicine but also with spiritual healing rituals that have been part of all cultures.

One of the risks of transporting a Western cultural product from one cultural group to another is the imposition of Western values, norms, and beliefs on others, particularly subordinated groups. As early as 1959, Paul Meehl cautioned the field on the role of religious values and views of morality in psychotherapy. He used the term "crypto-missionaries" (p. 257) to describe psychotherapists who promoted religious and moral values. At that time, Meehl was referring to research findings that patient improvement was highly associated with changes in moral values of the patient similar to those of the patient's therapist (Rosenthal, 1955). These findings challenged the prevailing view that therapy was not about proselytizing or converting patients to the therapist's view of morality.

A multicultural critique of psychotherapy is that it may promote assimilation. As Gone (2009) pointed out, the specific danger of EBTs is that they are imbued with Western cultural norms, values, and particular views of what constitutes the person. In the therapy process, therapists socialize clients to particular life experiences and worldviews. Gone noted, "by virtue of their own cultural assumptions and expectations, these interventions may well purchase amelioration of symptoms or improvement in functioning at the expense of tacit Western cultural assimilation" (p. 760). The risk of disseminating EBTs without sound evidence of their external validity may result in the imposition of treatment models developed and tested in one group and exported to another. The *presumptive truth fallacy* may be at work here. Ford and Urban (1998) noted that "presumptive truth evolves into misplaced belief when people become fervently committed to their model; it ceases to be provisional and becomes ... dogma" (p. 35). When people insist that their models and beliefs should be adopted, the *imperialist fallacy* comes into effect. Thus, a cultural variant of the imperialist fallacy may be underway with the global dissemination of EBTs, particularly to ethnocultural communities within the United States and to Third World countries (Bernal & Scharrón-del-Río, 2001).

In the more extreme conceptualizations, cultural imperialism is intentional and self-serving. For others, it may be an unintentional consequence of thoughtless guided action. Either way, the results are highly problematic. In the recent book *Crazy Like Us: The Globalization of the American Psyche*, Ethan Watters (2010) called attention to how Western "advances" in mental health may be creating more distress than they are relieving. In Watters's words,

> Offering the latest Western mental health theories in an attempt to ameliorate the psychological stress caused by globalization is not a solution; *it is part of the problem.* By undermining both local beliefs about healing and culturally created conceptions of the self, we are speeding along the disorienting changes that are at the very heart of much of the world's mental distress. It is the psychiatric equivalent of handing out blankets to sick natives without considering the pathogens that hide deep in the fabric. (p. 253)

Clearly, psychotherapy can be used in the service of assimilation (Gone, 2004), enculturation (Ramirez, 1991), and acculturation (Comas-Díaz, 2006) to the extent that ethnic minority groups are treated and the so-called remedy is used to knowingly or unknowingly inculcate values, beliefs, and norms of the dominant culture with the result of devaluing, dismissing, replacing, or even eliminating the culture and language of origin.

Despite the risks of promoting assimilation, EBTs can be used in the service of empowerment, decolonization, and liberation. Cultural adaptations can be systematic, rigorous, and based on scientific findings regarding health and well-being of ECGs (see Chapter 2, this volume). The cultural adaptations of treatment and interventions addressed in this book are centered on constructs that entail altering treatments so that these are aligned with the values, beliefs, and assumptions of the ECG in question. Thus, notions such as interdependence, spirituality, relational views of self or the person, and particular worldviews are woven into the treatment. How to perform such cultural adaptations in a systematic way that documents the changes made to treatment, treatment provider, and treatment context is the basis for this book. We believe cultural adaptations can be used to support the culture and language of origin and the development and maintenance of cultural values, both of which are empowerment strategies.

CULTURAL ADAPTATIONS

In general, *cultural adaptations* are changes made to psychotherapy processes and/or content with the intention of increasing the congruence between the client's ethnocultural worldview and EBTs. There are two core motivating factors for engaging in cultural adaptation of treatments: to protect the scientific integrity of evidence-based research and dissemination by promoting the ecological validity of treatment studies (Bernal, Bonilla, & Bellido, 1995) and to reduce health disparities by making EBTs broadly available to ECGs.

More specifically, cultural adaptation has been defined as "the systematic modification of an EBT or intervention protocol to consider language, culture, and context in such a way that it is compatible with the client's cultural patterns, meanings, and values" (Bernal et al., 2009, p. 362). This definition further specifies the need for changes to be conducted in a systematic manner that is itself meticulously documented so that it might be observable and replicable. This transparency in the process of cultural adaptation can lead to tests of effectiveness, thus informing both treatment and research advances.

The definitions of cultural adaptation reach beyond the intervention protocol and can also include "the approach to service delivery, in the nature of the therapeutic relationship or in the components of the treatment" (Whaley & Davis, 2007, pp. 570–571) to incorporate cultural aspects—attitudes, beliefs, and behaviors—of ECGs of interest. This definition draws from the work of Miranda, Nakamura, and Bernal (2003), who noted that standard psychotherapies needed to be modified to account for cultural beliefs of the population being treated, as well as from Muñoz and Mendelson (2005), who advocated for changes based on knowledge specific to the cultural groups in order to increase positive outcomes using methods that are both acceptable and accessible given the cultural values of particular ECGs.

Cultural Adaptations and EBTs

Institutional definitions of general competence increasingly include the ability to work with culturally, linguistically, and ethnically diverse clients (American Psychological Association, [APA] 2003, 2010). In addition, there has been a call to consider cultural, racial, ethnic, and contextual issues specifically in EBTs (U.S. Department of Health and Human Services, 2002) and a formal policy on evidence-based practice in psychology specifically stating that "*evidence-based practice in psychology* (EBPP) is the integration of the best available research with clinical expertise in the context of patient characteristics, culture, and preferences" (APA Presidential Task Force on

Evidence-Based Practice, 2006, p. 273). Yet these aspirations are difficult to put into practice.

As of the mid-1990s, there were no known efficacy trials conducted with ethnic minorities (Task Force on Promotion and Dissemination of Psychological Procedures, 1995). Over a decade later, despite an NIH-mandated policy on the inclusion of ethnic minorities in research (NIH, 1994), there is still a stark underrepresentation of ethnic minorities in NIH-funded clinical trials (Mak, Law, Alvidrez, & Pérez-Stable, 2007). Moreover, of the studies that have been conducted, most offer little guidance or practical information on how to adapt EBTs.

Both cultural adaptation models and EBT recommendations reflect the empirical foundations of the science of psychology. These two areas within the field of applied psychology have been developing simultaneously, with some notable similarities. For example, the most often-cited cultural adaptation framework (Bernal et al., 1995) was published the same year as the original EVT report (Chambless, 1996; Task Force on Promotion and Dissemination of Psychological Procedures, 1995). Yet, as the two areas have evolved, critics have implied that they are in conflict. For example, Elliott and Mihalic (2004) suggested that cultural adaptations are unnecessary in light of the empirical approach to treatment. Also, Kazdin (2000) argued that tailoring treatments to particular populations is not feasible given the number of treatments, disorders, developmental stages, and a host of other factors that would generate a matrix impossible to study. Conversely, others have questioned whether EBTs are valid for ethnic minorities (Bernal & Scharrón-del-Río, 2001), and some have cautioned that EBTs may interfere with clinicians' ability to provide culturally responsive treatments to ethnic minorities (Gone, 2008).

These arguments are not new. Intervention researchers have been adapting interventions even before the term *cultural adaptation* emerged. The work of Costantino, Malgady, and Rogler (1986) showcased *cuento* therapy as a treatment designed specifically for Puerto Rican children, based on social learning principles. In Florida, José Szapocznick first studied Cuban values to later develop treatments for Cubans and other ethnic minority families, basing adaptations on empirical findings and an ecological developmental theory (Coatsworth, Pantin, & Szapocznik, 2002; Santisteban et al., 2003; Szapocznik et al., 1989). Important steps were well underway to sensitize treatments to a variety of ECGs.

The phenomenon of cultural adaptations transcends national borders. Mental health professionals outside the United States have expressed strong interest in culturally adapted interventions. For example, therapists in Japan have translated and published a culturally adapted manual for acceptance and commitment therapy (Tanaka-Matsumi, 2008), and the government of

Norway implemented a countrywide dissemination of parent management training–Oregon model and multisystemic therapy to target youth behavior problems (Ogden, Amlund Hagen, Askeland, & Christensen, 2009). Western methods of psychotherapy are being adapted across the globe (e.g., Stevens & Gielen, 2007), and implementers abroad also face challenges in targeting heterogeneous populations (e.g., Rey & Sainz, 2007).

Fidelity and Fit

Perhaps the strongest point of contention in considering cultural adaptations to EBTs is the tension between fidelity to the EBT protocol and fit with the preferences, culture, and context of the client. On one side of the debate are those that favor remaining true to the treatment protocol and its components. A primary concern from this perspective is the risk of diluting the content of treatments that have demonstrated efficacy. On the other end of the debate is the position that questions the use of structured treatments in the form of manual-based therapies because these do not consider the singularity of clients and each therapy is essentially unique. Perhaps less extreme is the perspective that treatments need to be developed for particular cultural groups. These debates have not engaged different types of cultural adaptations, although it is likely that advocates for as-is interventions (or adhering strictly to fidelity) might accept minor modifications to interventions, such as literal language translations and changes in ethnicity of models in intervention materials. These are considered surface changes, whereas deeper structural changes would address core values, beliefs, and norms (Resnicow, Soler, Braithwaite, Ahluwalia, & Butler, 2000).

CONCLUSION

When viewed from a historical perspective, cultural adaptations have been integral to the development of psychotherapy. Many of the modifications historically framed as theoretical were, in part, adaptations in response to social, historical, political, and demographic changes. Cultural adaptations emerged as part of a multicultural movement that called attention to the consideration of culture, language, and context in providing psychotherapy and, later, EBTs to ECGs. Cultural adaptation of EBTs is a middle-ground position in the debate of whether or not to adapt (Bernal et al., 2009). We believe that it may not be necessary to reinvent the wheel and that building on treatments that have demonstrated efficacy is a sensible starting point from which to provide effective interventions to ECGs. A number of scholars, many of them represented in this volume, have shown that EBTs can be culturally adapted, and for the most part, these adaptations yield positive outcomes. In a recent meta-analysis of 65 studies (with 8,620 patients), culturally adapted treatments were moderately more effective than traditional nonadapted treatments (effect size $d = .46$), and the most effective treatments were those that had the highest number of adaptations (T. B. Smith et al., 2011). In another meta-analysis directly comparing adapted versus unadapted treatments, the culturally adapted psychotherapy was found to be more effective than the unadapted ones (effect size $d = .32$; Benish et al., 2011).

Generally, a conceptual framework that in one way or another applies the principle of ecological validity guides this process of adaptation, namely, using procedures to increase the congruence between the client's ethnocultural experience and the properties of the psychotherapy as assumed by the therapist. In this process, it is critical to document all adaptations, citing how many and what kinds are made, as well as the reasons for them. Finally, an evaluation of the process of cultural adaptation, as well as the impact of the changes made, serves to further refine the treatment with the aim of improving client outcomes.

OVERVIEW OF THE BOOK

The chapters in this book provide conceptual and methodological tools for cultural adaptation that are indispensable for clinicians and researchers alike. Overall, this edited volume presents a unifying theoretical foundation that asserts that adaptation of evidence-based interventions is a productive and empirically viable approach to delivering interventions to ethnic minorities and culturally diverse groups. While other approaches (i.e., nonadaptation, culturally grounded interventions, and new interventions designed for particular cultural groups) may also be valid, this book focuses solely on adaptations of evidence-based interventions.

I. Foundations

The book opens with important foundational information regarding historical and current developments in cultural adaptations as well as ethical considerations. In Chapter 1, Bernal and Domenech Rodríguez place cultural adaptations in their proper historical context, documenting a rather long history of adaptations in psychotherapy. In Chapter 2, Domenech Rodríguez and Bernal review the conceptual frameworks and the specific methodologies for the adaptation of EBTs for use with diverse populations. Known models of cultural adaptations are presented in detail. In Chapter 3, Trimble, Scharrón-del-Río, and Hill propose the need to balance the researcher's consideration of strong science with the benefits for the communities in question. Individuals who intervene with ECGs must make ethical decisions guided by strong considerations of the particular sociohistorical and cultural contexts of these individuals and families. The chapter includes suggestions for applying culturally respectful views when evaluating risk and benefits, informed consent, and confidentiality and disclosure policies and engaging community participants based on principled cultural sensitivity.

II. Applications and Advancing Frameworks

The six chapters in this section document applications of cultural adaptation frameworks to specific ECGs as well as recommendations for advancing frameworks based on lessons learned. In Chapter 4, Nicolas and Schwartz provide background information on mental health and service utilization of ethnocultural youth as well as EBTs to set the stage for their own work with Haitian American adolescents diagnosed with depression. The authors present their work of culturally adapting an evidence-based intervention, the Adolescent Coping With Depression Course, using the ecological validity framework (EVF; Bernal et al., 1995).

Sáez-Santiago, Bernal, Reyes-Rodríguez, and Bonilla-Silva (Chapter 5) present their work on the development and cultural adaptation of psychoeducational workshops for Puerto Rican parents, known in Spanish as *Taller de Educación Psicológica para Padres y Madres*. These workshops were based in part on a reality management approach to cognitive behavior therapy (CBT; Muñoz, Ghosh Ipen, Rao, Le, & Dwyer, 2000). The intervention was designed for parents who have an adolescent suffering from depression. The authors review the parent intervention for this population, discuss how they selected the intervention, and describe in detail the development and adaptation processes using the EVF (Bernal et al., 1995).

In Chapter 6, Barrera, Toobert, Strycker, and Osuna present the Mediterranean Lifestyle Project, an intervention adapted using Barrera and Castro's (2006) heuristic model and implemented with Latinas diagnosed with Type 2 diabetes. Pilot data results suggest that the adaptation, ¡*Viva Bien!*, was effective in recruiting and retaining Latinas and showed strong outcomes. The authors close with recommendations to clinicians and program developers.

Lau, in Chapter 7, presents lessons learned on a journey to attempt to culturally adapt a parenting intervention with Chinese immigrant families using her own selective and directed treatment adaptation framework (Lau, 2006). She found important blind alleys in her program of research that led to recommended changes to her cultural adaptation model. Lau began with a series of quantitative studies to inform the necessary adaptations and learned that the answers needed were not discoverable through the methods her research team employed. Shifting gears to qualitative, community-based methods of inquiry, they prepared to culturally adapt the Incredible Years program for Chinese immigrant parents. The team incorporated lessons learned in the implementation in the overall evaluation.

Wallis, Amaro, and Cortés (Chapter 8) present the theoretical rationale and the procedures used in the cultural adaptation of a trauma intervention for Latinas using three cultural adaptation models. How and why changes were made are carefully described. The adaptations made are used to inform practice. In their approach, both emic and etic perspectives are employed, thus maintaining fidelity to the core trauma concepts while incorporating cultural notions to respond to cultural-specific needs of the population. The authors discuss the strengths and weaknesses of their work with Latina victims of trauma.

Finally, in Chapter 9, Hwang introduces a combined top-down theory-based approach (psychotherapy adaptation and modification framework) and a bottom-up formative approach (formative method for adapting psychotherapy) to culturally adapting psychotherapy. Hwang provides examples of how he has applied this integrative approach to culturally adapt a CBT treatment for depression in a Chinese American population.

III. New Frontiers

This section highlights work on the cutting edge of the field, including chapters on early stages of cultural adaptation research and practice with ECGs that have been woefully understudied. In Chapter 10, Gray discusses the absence of culturally informed EBTs with American Indians, key considerations in using and evaluating evidence-based approaches, and examples of cultural adaptations from the field within the Indian Country. She presents her own emerging cultural adaptation model for use with Native clients. As indigenous values of the family, clan, and tribe are central to the experience of American Indians, cultural adaptation centers on incorporating such values into the treatment itself. Particular techniques are offered as examples that use positive therapeutic strategies, including gift offerings and approaches to grief work.

The focus of Chapter 11, by Brown, Conner, and McMurray, is the use of interpersonal psychotherapy (IPT) with older African Americans experiencing depression. Most studies examining cultural adaptations have focused on CBT treatments. Brown and colleagues venture into another treatment modality. While evidence from IPT treatment trials seemed to suggest that this therapeutic model held promise, they found that it was not as effective in treating depression for African Americans as it has been for White

Americans. From this finding, the authors make recommendations for cultural adaptation of IPT that could potentially increase its effectiveness for older African Americans.

Maríñez-Lora and Atkins wrap up this part in Chapter 12 with a fresh perspective on cultural adaptations. They shift the focus of adaptations to the work clinicians already do to make EBTs more accessible and relevant for their culturally diverse patients. Informed by their consultation work, Maríñez-Lora and her colleagues developed a two-step training model to prompt clinicians to think first, whether cultural adaptations are truly needed, and if so, which ones. The areas of cultural adaptation that clinicians are prompted to consider in understanding adaptation needs are the dimensions of cultural adaptation put forth by Bernal et al. (1995). Case examples illustrate the application of Maríñez-Lora et al.'s model.

IV. The Future of Cultural Adaptations

The book closes with practical considerations in the research and application of cultural adaptations to existing interventions. In the closing chapter, Domenech Rodríguez and Bernal close with an integrative set of guidelines and recommendations culled from existing models and based on content and process issues. In addition, general principles and guiding questions for cultural adaptations of EBTs are presented, and we offer our comments on the future of culturally adapted EBTs and practice.

Can the consideration of culture and treatments based on sound evidence be reconciled? We believe the answer is yes. Yet there are many unexplored questions about the cultural adaptation of psychotherapy. Why and when are adaptations needed? Are adaptations needed for each and every cultural and language group? For whom are adaptations most appropriate? How does one go about making cultural adaptations? The chapters in this volume answer many of these questions, based on the best available evidence. All the contributors to this book approach cultural adaptation using a scientific lens, with the aim of making EBTs more accessible, relevant, and indeed helpful to diverse ECGs. Each chapter offers examples of how cultural adaptation serves as a methodological or conceptual resource from which to attune EBTs to the culture, context, and preferences of specific client groups.

REFERENCES

American Psychological Association. (2003). Guidelines on multicultural education, training, research, practice, and organizational change for psychologists. *American Psychologist, 58,* 377–402. doi:10.1037/0003-066X.58.5.377

American Psychological Association. (2010). *Ethical principles of psychologists and code of conduct: 2010 amendments.* Retrieved from http://www.apa.org/ethics/code/index.aspx

APA Presidential Task Force on Evidence-Based Practice. (2006). Evidence-based practice in psychology. *American Psychologist, 61*, 271–285. doi:10.1037/0003-066X.61.4.271

Bandura, A. (1989). *Principles of behavior modification.* Oxford, England: Holt, Rinehart & Winston.

Barrera, M., Jr., & Castro, F. G. (2006). A heuristic framework for the cultural adaptation of interventions. *Clinical Psychology: Science and Practice, 13*, 311–316.

Beels, C. C. (2002). Notes for a cultural history of family therapy. *Family Process, 41*, 67–82. doi:10.1111/j.1545-5300.2002.40102000067.x

Benish, S. G., Quintana, S., & Wampold, B. (2011). Culturally adapted psychotherapy and the legitimacy of myth: A direct comparison meta-analysis. *Journal of Counseling Psychology, 58*, 279–289. doi:10.1037/a0023626

Bernal, G., Bonilla, J., & Bellido, C. (1995). Ecological validity and cultural sensitivity for outcome research: Issues for cultural adaptation and development of psychosocial treatments with Hispanics. *Journal of Abnormal Child Psychology, 23*, 67–82. doi:10.1007/BF01447045

Bernal, G., Jiménez-Chafey, M. I., & Domenech Rodríguez, M. M. (2009). Cultural adaptation of treatments: A resource for considering culture in evidence-based practice. *Professional Psychology: Research and Practice, 40*, 361–368. doi:10.1037/a0016401

Bernal, G., & Scharrón-del-Río, M. R. (2001). Are empirically supported treatments valid for ethnic minorities? Toward an alternative approach for treatment research. *Cultural Diversity and Ethnic Minority Psychology, 7*, 328–342. doi:10.1037/1099-9809.7.4.328

Betancourt, H., & Lopez, R. S. (1993). The study of cultue, ethnicity, and race in American psychology. *American Psychologist, 48*, 629–637. doi:10.1037/0003-066X.48.6.629

Brabender, V., & Fallon, A. (2009). Theoretical history of group development in its application to psychotherapy groups. In V. Brabender & A. Fallon (Eds.), *Group development in practice: Guidance for clinicians and researchers on stages and dynamics of change* (pp. 27–62). Washington, DC: American Psychological Association. doi:10.1037/11858-003

Broderick, C. G., & Schrader, S. S. (1981). The history of professional marriage and family therapy. In A. S. Gurman & D. P. Kniskern (Eds.), *Handbook of family therapy* (pp. 5–35). New York, NY: Brunner/Mazel.

Chambless, D. L. (1996). In defense of dissemination of empirically supported psychological interventions. *Clinical Psychology: Science and Practice, 3*, 230–235. doi:10.1111/j.1468-2850.1996.tb00074.x

Coatsworth, J. D., Pantin, H., & Szapocznik, J. (2002). Familias Unidas: A family-centered ecodevelopmental intervention to reduce risk for problem behavior among Hispanic adolescents. *Clinical Child and Family Psychology Review, 5,* 113–132. doi:10.1023/A:1015420503275

Comas-Díaz, L. (2006). Latino healing: the integration of ethnic psychology into psychotherapy. *Psychotherapy: Theory, Research, Practice, Training, 43,* 436–453.

Costantino, G., Malgady, R. G., & Rogler, L. H. (1986). Cuento therapy: A culturally sensitive modality for Puerto Rican children. *Journal of Consulting and Clinical Psychology, 54,* 639–645. doi:10.1037/0022-006X.54.5.639

Cushman, P. (1992). Psychotherapy to 1992: A historically situated interpretation. In D. K. Freedheim, H. J. Freudenberger, J. W. Kessler, S. B. Messer, D. R. Peterson, H. H. Strupp, & P. L. Wachtel (Eds.), *History of psychotherapy: A century of change* (pp. 21–64). Washington, DC: American Psychological Association. doi:10.1037/10110-001

Cushman, P. (1995). *Constructing the self, constructing America: A cultural history of psychotherapy.* Reading, MA: Addison-Wesley.

Elliott, D. S., & Mihalic, S. (2004). Issues in disseminating and replicating effective prevention programs. *Prevention Science, 5,* 47–52. doi:10.1023/B:PREV.0000013981.28071.52

Ford, D. H., & Urban, H. B. (1998). *Contemporary models of psychotherapy: A comparative analysis* (2nd ed.). Hoboken, NJ: Wiley.

Freedheim, D. K. (1995). Historical perspectives on psychotherapy. In H. E. Adler & R. W. Rieber (Eds.), *Aspects of the history of psychology in America 1892–1992* (pp. 123–132). New York, NY: New York Academy of Sciences and American Psychological Association.

Garfield, S. L. (1992). Major issues in psychotherapy research. In D. K. Freidheim, H. J. Freudenberger, J. W. Kessler, S. B. Messer, D. R. Peterson, H. H. Strupp, & P. L. Wachtel (Eds.), *History of psychotherapy: A century of change* (pp. 335–359). Washington, DC: American Psychological Association. doi:10.1037/10110-009

Gone, J. P. (2004). Mental health services for Native Americans in the 21st century United States. *Professional Psychology: Research and Practice, 35,* 10–18. doi:10.1037/0735-7028.35.1.10

Gone, J. P. (2008). "So I can be like a Whiteman": The cultural psychology of space and place in American Indian mental health. *Culture & Psychology, 14,* 369–399. doi:10.1177/1354067X08092639

Gone, J. P. (2009). A community-based treatment for Native American historical trauma: Prospects for evidence-based practice. *Journal of Consulting and Clinical Psychology, 77,* 751–762. doi:10.1037/a0015390

Kazdin, A. E. (2000). Developing a research agenda for child and adolescent psychotherapy. *Archives of General Psychiatry, 57,* 829–835. doi:10.1001/archpsyc.57.9.829

Lau, A. S. (2006). Making the case for selective and directed cultural adaptations of evidence-based treatments: Examples from parenting training. *Clinical Psychology: Science and Practice, 13,* 295–310.

Mak, W. W. S., Law, R. W., Alvidrez, J., & Pérez-Stable, E. J. (2007). Gender and ethnic diversity in NIMH-funded clinical trials: Review of a decade of published research. *Administration and Policy in Mental Health and Mental Health Services Research, 34,* 497–503. doi:10.1007/s10488-007-0133-z

McGoldrick, M., Giordano, J., & Pearce, J. K. (1982). *Ethnicity and family therapy.* New York, NY: Guilford Press.

Meadow, A. (1964). Client-centered therapy and the American ethos. *International Journal of Social Psychiatry, 10,* 246–259.

Meehl, P. E. (1959). Some technical and axiological problems in the therapeutic handling of religious and valuational material. *Journal of Counseling Psychology, 6,* 255–259. doi:10.1037/h0049181

Migone, P. (2000). A psychoanalysis on the chair and a psychotherapy on the couch: Implications of Gill's redefinition of the differences between psychoanalysis and psychotherapy. In D. K. Silverman & D. L. Wolitzky (Eds.), *Changing conceptions of psychoanalysis: The legacy of Merton M. Gill* (pp. 219–235). Mahwah, NJ: Analytic Press.

Miranda, J., Nakamura, R., & Bernal, G. (2003). Including ethnic minorities in mental health intervention research: A practical approach to a long-standing problem. *Culture, Medicine and Psychiatry, 27,* 467–486. doi:10.1023/B:MEDI.0000005484.26741.79

Muñoz, R. F., Ghosh Ipen, C., Rao, S., Le, H.-N., & Dwyer, E. V. (2000). *Manual for group cognitive-behavioral therapy of major depression: A reality management approach (instructor's manual).* Retrieved from http://medschool.ucsf.edu/latino/pdf/CBTDEN/overview.pdf

Muñoz, R. F., & Mendelson, T. (2005). Toward evidence-based interventions for diverse populations: The San Francisco General Hospital prevention and treatment manuals. *Journal of Consulting and Clinical Psychology, 73,* 790–799. doi:10.1037/0022-006X.73.5.790

National Institutes of Health. (1994). *NIH guidelines for the inclusion of women and minorities as subjects in clinical research.* Retrieved from http://grants.nih.gov/grants/guide/notice-files/not94-100.html

Ogden, T., Amlund Hagen, K., Askeland, E., & Christensen, B. (2009).Implementing and evaluating evidence-based treatments of conduct problems in children and youth in Norway. *Research on Social Work Practice, 19,* 582–591. doi:10.1177/1049731509335530

Pedersen, P. (1988). *A handbook for developing multicultural awareness.* Alexandria, VA: American Association for Counseling.

Pedersen, P. (1989). Developing multicultural ethical guidelines for psychology. *International Journal of Psychology, 24,* 643–652.

Pedersen, P. (1990). The multicultural perspective as a fourth force in counseling. *Journal of Mental Health Counseling, 12,* 93–95.

Pedersen, P. B. (1997). Recent trends in cultural theories. *Applied & Preventive Psychology, 6,* 221–231. doi:10.1016/S0962-1849(97)80011-X

Ponterotto, J. G., & Casas, J. M. (1991). *Handbook of racial/ethnic minority counseling research*. Springfield, IL: Charles C Thomas.

Ramirez, M., III. (1991). *Psychotherapy and counseling with minorities: A cognitive approach to individual and cultural differences*. Elmsford, NY: Pergamon Press.

Resnicow, K., Soler, R., Braithwaite, R. L., Ahluwalia, J. S., & Butler, J. (2000). Cultural sensitivity in substance use prevention. *Journal of Community Psychology, 28*, 271–290.

Rey, G. N., & Sainz, M. T. (2007). Tailoring an intervention model to help indigenous families cope with excessive drinking in central Mexico. *Salud Mental, 30(6)*, 32–42.

Rosenthal, D. (1955). Changes in some moral values following psychotherapy. *Journal of Consulting Psychology, 19*, 431–436. doi:10.1037/h0045777

Santisteban, D. A., Coatsworth, J. D., Perez-Vidal, A., Kurtines, W. M., Schwartz, S. J., LaPerriere, A., & Szapocznik, J. (2003). Efficacy of brief strategic family therapy in modifying Hispanic adolescent behavior problems and substance use. *Journal of Family Psychology, 17*, 121–133. doi:10.1037/0893-3200.17.1.121

Smith, L. (2005). Psychotherapy classism and the poor: Conspicuous by their absence. *American Psychologist, 60*, 687–696. doi:10.1037/0003-066X.60.7.687

Smith, T. B., Domenech Rodríguez, M., & Bernal, G. (2011). Culture. *Journal of Clinical Psychology, 67*, 166–175. doi:10.1002/jclp.20757

Stevens, M. J., & Gielen, U. P. (Eds.). (2007). *Toward a global psychology: Theory, research, intervention, and pedagogy*. Mahwah, NJ: Erlbaum.

Strupp, H. H. (1989). The outcome problem in psychotherapy: Contemporary perspectives. In J. H. Harvey & M. M. Parks (Eds.), *Psychotherapy research and behavior change* (Vol. 1, pp. 43–57). Washington, DC: American Psychological Association.

Strupp, H. H., & Howard, K. I. (1992). A brief history of psychotherapy research. In D. K. Freedheim, H. J. Freudenberger, J. W. Kessler, S. B. Messer, D. R. Peterson, H. H. Strupp, & P. L. Wachtel (Eds.), *History of psychotherapy: A century of change* (pp. 309–334). Washington, DC: American Psychological Association. doi:10.1037/10110-008

Sue, D. W., Bingham, R. P., Porche-Burke, L., & Vasquez, M. (1999). The diversification of psychology: A multicultural revolution. *American Psychologist, 54*, 1061–1069. doi:10.1037/0003-066X.54.12.1061

Szapocznik, J., Rio, A., Murray, E., Cohen, R., Scopetta, M., Rivas-Vazquez, A., . . . Kurtines, W. (1989). Structural family versus psychodynamic child therapy for problematic Hispanic boys. *Journal of Consulting and Clinical Psychology, 57*, 571–578. doi:10.1037/0022-006X.57.5.571

Tanaka-Matsumi, J. (2008). Functional approaches to evidence-based practice in multicultural counseling and therapy. In U. P. Gielen, J. G. Draguns, & J. M. Fish (Eds.), *Principles of multicultural counseling and therapy* (pp. 169–198). New York, NY: Routledge/Taylor & Francis.

Task Force on Promotion and Dissemination of Psychological Procedures. (1995). Training in and dissemination of empirically-validated treatments: Report and recommendations. *Clinical Psychologist, 48*, 2–23.

Triandis, H. (2007). Culture and psychology: A history of the study of their relationship. In S. Kitayama & D. Cohen (Eds.), *Handbook of cultural psychology* (pp. 59–76). New York, NY: Guilford Press.

Tseng, W.-S. (1999). Culture and psychotherapy: Review and practical guidelines. *Transcultural Psychiatry, 36*, 131–179. doi:10.1177/136346159903600201

U.S. Department of Health and Human Services. (2002). *Mental health, culture, race, and ethnicity—A supplement to* Mental Health: A Report of the Surgeon General. Rockville, MD: Department of Health and Human Services, Public Health Services, Office of the Surgeon General.

Wampold, B. E. (2001). Contextualizing psychotherapy as a healing practice: Culture, history, and methods. *Applied & Preventive Psychology, 10*, 69–86.

Watters, E. (2010). *Crazy like us: The globalization of the American psyche*. New York, NY: Free Press.

Whaley, A. L., & Davis, K. E. (2007). Cultural competence and evidence-based practice in mental health services: A complementary perspective. *American Psycholowgist, 62*, 563–574. doi:10.1037/0003-066X.62.6.563

Wolpe, J. (1958). *Psychotherapy by reciprocal inhibition*. Stanford, CA: Stanford University Press.

2

FRAMEWORKS, MODELS, AND GUIDELINES FOR CULTURAL ADAPTATION

MELANIE M. DOMENECH RODRÍGUEZ AND GUILLERMO BERNAL

Treatment development and outcomes research has been primarily situated in a positivist paradigm emphasizing systematic observation and scientific discovery. Contemporary efforts to transport treatments from one cultural group to another are situated in a pragmatist tradition. Pragmatists believe in both subjective and objective perspectives and use inductive and deductive logic to inform their efforts (Onwuegbuzie, 2002). Whereas positivists privilege randomized controlled trials as the gold standard for testing the utility of interventions, pragmatists use qualitative and quantitative methods, attempting integration either within or across studies (Onwuegbuzie, 2002). This approach has also been called problem-focused methodological pluralism (Dawson, Fischer, & Stein, 2006).

Within a pragmatist paradigm, cultural adaptation models have been developed primarily to work in concert with cognitive–behavioral or behavioral approaches to interventions. These interventions themselves were born of positivist approaches and are typically manualized. Cultural adaptations have been put forth as models, frameworks, or guidelines. In general, models tend to provide a design, perhaps even a visual representation, of a system to be replicated. Frameworks, in contrast, typically provide a conceptual structure, provide a frame of reference, or describe an approach. Finally, guidelines are specific, albeit aspirational, recommendations for professional behaviors. Guidelines are not prescriptive, and as such they do not represent required actions (American Psychological Association [APA], 2008). Cultural adaptation models, frameworks, and guidelines offer perspectives that vary considerably in scope, breadth, and depth. Our objective in this chapter is to briefly summarize existing models, frameworks, and guidelines for cultural adaptation of psychological interventions.

BROAD FRAMEWORKS

Models were found through searches in psychological databases and references in published works. Although we have attempted to be exhaustive in our search, it would be presumptuous to assume we have covered the literature exhaustively. In the birth of a new area of inquiry, scholars from a multitude of specialties make contributions across broad domains. As a critical mass of evidence gathers, a specialization emerges and then begins to find a common language and identifiable outlets. The specific models, frameworks, and guidelines presented in this section were selected because they specifically address cultural adaptation of evidence-based treatments. They are presented in their order of publication.

The Multidimensional Model for Understanding Culturally Responsive Psychotherapies

This cultural adaptation framework posits that all psychotherapies can be situated along two dimensions: culture and structure (Koss-Chioino & Vargas, 1992). These two dimensions loosely attach to therapist characteristics and the therapy modality, respectively. Within the culture dimension there are two categories of content and context. *Cultural content* "refers to the specific meanings through which social phenomena are constructed, deconstructed, and reconstructed, including patterns of individual behavior, interpersonal interactions, emotions, and so on" (Koss-Chioino & Vargas, 1992, p. 14). *Cultural context* refers to the interpersonal interactions between the client and the therapist and how each other's expectations play out in psychotherapy. Koss-Chioino and Vargas (1992) specified two categories along the structure dimension: process and form. *Process* refers to "the gradual steps or changes that produce a particular result in psychotherapy" (Koss-Chioino & Vargas, 1992, p. 16), whereas *form* indicates the "manner or style of carrying out psychotherapy according to guidelines or recognized standards, encompassing both method and modality" (Koss-Chioino & Vargas, 1992, p. 17).

The multidimensional model was developed under the guiding assumption that cultural responsiveness is essential to "good enough" psychotherapy and is intended to provide a framework that can help clarify where particular therapeutic approaches lie. This framework then guides the choices that psychotherapists make regarding the tools and procedures of their psychotherapy modality. Koss-Chioino and Vargas (1992) provided an example from play therapy, in which attending to the ethnicity of dolls that children played with indicated cultural responsiveness to form and attending to the different use of toys in the play therapy indicated cultural responsiveness to cultural content.

Koss-Chioino and Vargas (1992) advocated that therapists develop their own adaptations to interventions according to the population they work with and the presenting concern. They called for great care in implementing interventions, given the relative nature of "normality" across content (specific issue) and context (interaction). Koss-Chioino and Vargas warned that skills in one context can be understood differently in another context. For example, assertiveness can be understood as aggression, depending on context.

Ecological Validity Framework

The ecological validity framework (EVF) is based on the ecological systems theory, which privileges ecological validity (Bronfenbrenner, 1977, 1989). *Ecological validity* essentially refers to the congruence between the client's experiences of his or her ethnocultural and linguistic context and the cultural properties embedded in a treatment or the properties of that treatment assumed by the clinician. If the criteria of ecological validity are met, then one can assume that the treatment is aligned with the culture, language, and worldview of the client. This framework lists eight broad areas for consideration in culturally adapting an intervention: language, persons, metaphors, content, concepts, goals, methods, and context (Bernal, Bonilla, & Bellido, 1995; Bernal & Sáez-Santiago, 2006). Congruence between client and treatment along these dimensions is considered essential in order to achieve engagement and positive outcomes.

Language applies to both oral and written communication as well as to specific jargon (e.g., regionalisms, adolescent slang). The persons dimension refers to the client–therapist dyad and includes structural considerations, such as ethnic match, as well as interactional considerations such as client expectations of the therapist. Metaphors are prescribed to be culturally relevant in both verbal (e.g., folk sayings) and visual (e.g., objects) forms, within the intervention itself (metaphors to put cultural content into intervention) as well as outside (e.g., relevant artwork in the therapy office). Therapists and treatment developers who attend to values, customs, and traditions of the client are making adaptations on the content dimension. The EVF calls for situating treatment goals in the context of those values, customs, and traditions. Treatment goals are achieved via methods that are adapted to work well within the client's cultural context. Finally, the context dimension recommends attention to social and political contexts of clients and how these can inform therapy engagement, content, and outcomes.

The eight dimensions cover therapist, client, and the treatment characteristics. In addition, the EVF emphasizes the consideration of developmental, technical, and theoretical issues. For applications of this model, see Matos, Bauermeister, and Bernal (2009); Rosselló and Bernal (2005); and, in this volume, Chapters 4, 5, 8, and 12.

Cultural Accommodation Model

Leong's cultural accommodation model (CAM; Leong & Lee, 2006) is an update of his integrative framework for cross-cultural psychotherapy (Leong, 1996). The framework is based on Kluckhorn and Murray's (1948) tripartite model of personality, which posits, in the simplest terms, that all people are like all others, like some others, and like none other. These three dimensions of universal, group-specific, and individual characteristics map onto biological, social, and psychological variables that explain human behavior. These dimensions are considered to interact in a complex and dynamic way in the cross-cultural encounter.

The CAM prescribes a three-step process. In the first step, "cultural gaps" are identified. These gaps are believed to limit the cultural validity of the theory or interventions. In the second step, relevant literature is examined to inform the content that will fill the cultural gap (e.g., acculturation, collectivism). Finally, the third step calls for testing the new theory or intervention to check for improved validity over the unaccommodated approach. The first two steps are understood to occur at the level of the therapist; thus, psychotherapists make their own adaptations because of the client's ethnic origin, the presenting concern, and cultural gaps identified in the literature. The final step is intended for researchers to undertake in making contributions to psychotherapy practice.

A central purpose of the CAM is to identify what is missing from psychotherapy theories and models in the way of specific cultural variables that are posited to be necessary for a treatment to be valid and have improved effectiveness. Leong and Lee (2006) recommended a careful evaluation of cultural validity rather than development of new theories for each ethnocultural group. In this sense, *cultural accommodation* refers to the changes that are made in psychotherapeutic interventions to increase their cultural validity.

Cultural Sensitivity Framework

In their cultural sensitivity framework (CSF), Resnicow, Soler, Braithwaite, Ahluwalia, and Butler (2002) offered a broad framework for cultural adaptation. They used the term *cultural sensitivity* to refer to "the extent to which ethnic/cultural characteristics, experiences, norms, values, behavioral patterns, and beliefs of a target population as well as relevant historical, environmental, and social forces are incorporated in the *design, delivery, and evaluation* [emphasis added] of targeted health promotion materials and programs" (Resnicow et al., 2002, p. 272). Resnicow et al. referred to the characteristics of intervention materials, a definition that is consistent with the definition of cultural adaptation offered in this volume. They offered two dimensions for cultural adaptation: surface and deep adaptations. *Surface* adaptations are targeted when intervention materials are made to "look like" and "sound like" the population of interest. This can involve visual materials as well as intervention content or messages. Surface adaptations also include a consideration of the locations that are deemed most important for the ethnocultural group of interest. *Deep* adaptations, on the other hand, include a consideration of predictors for the problem of interest and include consideration of important contextual influences on behavior (e.g., socio-historical, psychological, environmental, and cultural processes).

Unlike the previous two frameworks, the CSF requires a higher engagement in research. It was developed to address implementation of substance use prevention and intervention programs with ethnocultural groups. To inform cultural adaptations, Resnicow et al. (2002) suggested a combination of qualitative and quantitative approaches and the use of existing databases as well as new data collection. Indeed, the rationale for engaging in cultural adaptation of interventions to target substance use is based on data that document different prevalence rates, patterns, risk factors, and predictors of substance use across groups.

Cultural Adaptation Process Model

Domenech-Rodríguez and Wieling (2004) developed the cultural adaptation process model (CAPM) for use in research and practice contexts. It includes three phases: (a) setting the stage, (b) initial adaptations, and (c) adaptation iterations. In setting the stage, four interrelated and parallel steps occur: (a) establishing collaboration between treatment developer and cultural adaptation specialist, (b) examining the fit of the intervention with relevant literature, (c) meeting with key community leaders to examine interest and need for intervention, and (d) assessing community needs and gathering information that will inform adaptations to the intervention. In the second stage, the CAPM outlines two foci: measures and intervention. In the measurement area, the cultural adaptation specialist selects the measures and reviews them for appropriateness of use with the group participating in the intervention. Changes are made as needed. In the intervention area there are two central activities: a priori tailoring of the intervention and postimplementation tailoring. A priori tailoring is conducted with a combination of data gathered in the first phase and the use of the EVF (Bernal et al., 1995). Finally, the third phase calls for continued adaptation to the culturally adapted intervention and measures as well as the exploration for adaptation or evolution of the original intervention, based on Sue's notion that "ethnic research is good science" (Sue & Sue, 2003, p. 198) and can contribute to interventions aimed at the majority ethnocultural group. For an application of the CAPM, see Baumann, Domenech Rodríguez, and Parra-Cardona (2011).

The CAPM was based on the work on diffusion of innovations (Rogers, 1995, 2002). Important roles derived from this work are change agents (i.e., treatment developers) and opinion leaders (i.e., cultural adaptation specialist; Baumann et al., 2011). Important concepts borrowed from Rogers are "reinvention" and "technology." In reinventing, a specific ethnocultural group may adopt a novel intervention ("technology") in a way that is different than was originally intended with positive outcomes. At its core, this framework places much emphasis on gathering knowledge and building collaborative relationship with local communities.

Hybrid Prevention Program Model

The hybrid prevention program model (HPPM) is based on the premise that there is a need to examine the match between the validation group and the current implementation group of an intervention (Castro, Barrera, & Martinez, 2004). Castro et al. (2004) identified group characteristics, program delivery staff, and administration and/or community factors as the three areas in which match must be examined. In addition, they specifically recommended attending to three dimensions in making cultural adaptations: (a) cognitive information processing (understanding the content of the intervention), (b) affective motivational characteristics (relevance of content to the particular ethnocultural group's values and traditional practices), and (c) environmental characteristics (understanding of and fit with local community) of the ethnocultural group receiving the intervention. Castro et al. specified that adaptations may be made to the program content, whether by changing or adding modules to an existing intervention or the program delivery or by changing the persons delivering the intervention (e.g., therapists vs. health educators), the manner in which the intervention is delivered (e.g., community vs. Internet), and/or the location of the delivery (e.g., church vs. mental health agency).

Castro et al. (2004) posited that cultural adaptations are intended to generate a "culturally equivalent" version of an intervention. They presented their work in the context of interventions to prevent substance use initiation and/or abuse. Their model is centered on achieving a balance between fidelity and fit. An intervention with a high degree of *fidelity* maintains a rigorous adherence to the delivery of intervention components that are believed to be the predictors of desired change. An intervention that provides a good *fit* is responsive (and thus acceptable) to the specific needs of the group that is participating in the intervention. The HPPM is informed by Backer's (2002) program adaptation guidelines and Resnicow et al.'s (2000) CSF. Castro et al. stressed the importance of conducting systematic adaptations and rigorous scientific testing of the adapted vis-à-vis the nonadapted intervention.

Selective and Directed Treatment Adaptation Framework

Lau (2006) proposed a framework that distinguishes between engagement and outcomes and is focused on adaptations that could target either or both. Evidence-based treatments (EBTs) may not generalize to ethnocultural groups, either because of challenges in engaging participants in treatment or because of aspects of the treatment that do not lead to positive outcomes. The selective part of the framework addresses the basic question of whether or not to adapt, suggesting that adaptations be undertaken only where there is evidence of a lack of congruence between an EBT and particular ethnocultural groups. Directed adaptations address the question "what to adapt?" Adaptations are made to content or procedures only when there is evidence that modifications are needed to increase engagement or positively impact outcomes. Within directed adaptations, Lau distinguished between efforts aimed at enhancing engagement or at contextualizing content. The former are intended to improve the link between an ethnocultural group and an intervention, and the latter are engaged to ensure appropriateness of the context of the treatment to the particular ethnocultural group.

According to Lau (2006), the selective and directed treatment adaptation framework (SDTAF) is to be guided by evidence at all times. In this sense, this framework is very conservative, as it supports cultural adaptations only when evidence suggests that delivering a standard treatment would meet with a high probability of failure. The evidence that feeds the decision-making process is found at multiple levels. Lau provided examples of risk factors that are unique to ethnocultural groups (e.g., discrimination) or that function differently across cultural groups (e.g., criticism from family members in Latino vs. White American samples of persons with schizophrenia). Lau also provided examples of distinct symptom presentation (e.g., symptom expression of posttraumatic stress disorder in Southeast Asian refugees) that would warrant cultural adaptation. Evidence can also be found in data on engagement and perceptions of treatment (relevance, acceptability). The application of this framework (Chapter 7, this volume) led to significant changes in the conceptualization of the cultural adaptation framework.

Heuristic Framework

The heuristic framework was generated to complement Lau's (2006) SDTAF and is built with a broader intervention context in mind (Barrera & Castro, 2006). The heuristic framework is guided by a central question: Which features of an EBT warrant cultural adaptation? The question is answered by evaluating equivalence in engagement and similarity in intervention effects on mediating variables and outcomes (predicted by moderators). In particular, Barrera and Castro (2006) recommended that scholars engaging in cultural adaptations follow four steps: gather information, make preliminary adaptations to the intervention, test the preliminary adaptations, and refine adaptations.

The first step in the four-step process is quite broad, including gathering information from published sources and gathering new information through quantitative surveys, qualitative studies, and collaboration with "relevant stakeholders" such as program developers, agency staff, and community members. An earlier model, the HPPM (Castro el al., 2004), is located within this step, as Barrera and Castro (2006) suggested that it can be useful for understanding the intervention fit with a particular population. The knowledge gained in the first step is used to make changes to an existing evidence-based intervention in Step 2. Barrera and Castro suggested that more information can be gathered for stakeholders once materials are available for review, such that Step 2 can have within it several iterations of cultural adaptation. In the third step, case studies or pilot studies reveal the success of the culturally adapted treatment through engagement, satisfaction, and outcomes. In the last step, refinements are made that allow for a more robust test of the culturally adapted treatment.

Despite their data-driven approach, Barrera and Castro (2006) stressed the importance of clinicians' judgment in determining when cultural adaptations are needed. They also underscored the importance of psychotherapists' cultural competence in the delivery of interventions, noting that therapeutic processes are not easily manualized and can undermine the effect of a cultural adaptation. For an application of this model, see Barrera, Toobert, Strycker, and Osuna (Chapter 6, this volume).

Culturally Specific Prevention

Whitbeck (2006) developed a culturally specific prevention (CSP) framework for cultural adaptations based on his work in American Indian communities. It includes six assumptions: (a) prevention efforts must be undertaken by a specific ethnocultural group, (b) the group has all the knowledge necessary to prevent problems and promote positive outcomes, (c) local knowledge must be at par with social science knowledge, (d) there are culturally specific risk and protective factors that must be considered in the treatment, (e) there must be community ownership of the treatment, and (f) ethnocultural groups have a desire for cultural knowledge.

Cultural adaptations are conducted across five stages. During the first stage, existing research models for children and adolescents are identified to help inform available resources for understanding the prevention target. During Stage 2, existing research pertaining to ethnic minorities is reviewed, with a specific focus on risk and protective factors that can inform treatment targets. Stage 3 entails engaging in cultural translation of key risk and protective factors; for example, monitoring may operate differently across distinct ethnocultural groups. In Stage 4, unique cultural risk and protective factors are identified and measured. In Stage 5, researchers undertake culturally specific intervention trials and assessments.

The CSP model is developed within a research paradigm and includes significant steps prior, during, and after the cultural adaptation. Whitbeck (2006) called for the treatment target to be identified by the local community prior to adaptation. He included the recommendation that formal/ceremonial steps be taken to create a working alliance with the local community. Whitbeck recommended working with various groups after a problem is defined to further define the problem and develop and/or adapt measures to evaluate its extent and specific associated mechanisms. Prevention components are designed in consultation with important community stakeholders, such as older people, service providers, youths, and parents. Whitbeck recommended seeking active participation of community stakeholders (via observation and evaluation) once a preventive intervention is in its pilot phase.

Integrated Top-Down and Bottom-Up Approach to Adapting Psychotherapy

Introduced by Hwang in its integrated form in this volume (see Chapter 9, this volume), the integrated top-down and bottom-up approach to adapting psychotherapy is built on two separate models of cultural adaptation: the psychotherapy adaptation and modification framework (PAMF; Hwang, 2006) and the formative method for adapting psychotherapy (FMAP; Hwang, 2009). The PAMF is characterized by a top-down approach and has six domains: (a) dynamic issues and cultural complexities, (b) orientation, (c) cultural beliefs, (d) client–therapist relationship, (e) cultural differences in expression and communication, and (f) cultural issues of salience. Each domain includes specific recommendations for undertaking the adaptation in the form of therapeutic principles. These principles target therapist self-awareness (e.g., therapist awareness of own culture and identity), knowledge (e.g., know the concept of dynamic sizing), and skills (e.g., provide clients with an orientation to therapy) that are characteristic of cultural competence models.

In contrast, the FMAP is a bottom-up approach to cultural adaptation that covers five phases and is intended to stimulate collaboration with persons potentially receiving treatment. The five phases are (a) generating knowledge and collaborating with stakeholders, (b) integrating information with theory and empirical and clinical knowledge, (c) reviewing the initial culturally adapted clinical intervention with stakeholders and revising the culturally adapted intervention, (d) testing the culturally adapted intervention, and (e) finalizing the culturally adapted intervention. The FMAP is more consistent with the cultural adaptation models presented in this chapter. Hwang (2009) presented how each phase was used to inform specific interventions of an EBT for Chinese Americans with depression.

Adaptation for International Transport

On the basis of at least a decade and a half of work in culturally adapting the Strengthening Families Program (SFP) to cultural groups within and outside the United States, Kumpfer, Pinyuchon, Teixiera de Melo, and Whiteside (2008) published guidelines for cultural adaptation. In total, 17 countries have implemented the SFP. The cultural adaptation guidelines are built on the principle that "fidelity *includes* [emphasis added] cultural adaptation but not modification of program components, timings, or overall structure" (Kumpfer et al., 2008, p. 230). Kumpfer et al. recommended the following prior to implementation: (a) gather needs assessment data on etiological precursors; (b) carefully select the best EBT to culturally adapt and transport; (c) implement original intervention with only minor modifications (e.g., translation); (d) carefully select staff and provide training/supervision to assure quality implementation; (e) implement program with fidelity and quality, including constant monitoring of both fidelity and participant evaluations; (f) make cultural adaptations continuously with pilot groups, based on their feedback but also on new developments in the field; (g) revise program materials to improve engagement of families; (h) evaluate empowerment to improve outcomes, with attention to cultural appropriateness of instruments and procedures used; and (i) disseminate the results of the effectiveness of the culturally adapted version. This last step is intended to feed the knowledge in the field on the effectiveness of culturally adapted EBTs.

SPECIFIC APPLICATIONS

Broad cultural adaptation models help guide adaptations without regard to specific presenting concern. Specific applications exemplify the application of global considerations to what Barrera and Castro (2006) called "small theory," or specific theoretical mechanisms that are understood to ameliorate the presenting concern. In these studies, the adaptations reported can be found in the broader models. For example, Hinton et al. (2004) developed a cognitive behavior therapy (CBT) treatment protocol for Vietnamese refugees that used specific knowledge regarding symptom presentation of posttraumatic stress disorder to inform specific interventions, with excellent results on therapeutic outcomes. Huey and Pan (2006) compared a culturally adapted versus nonadapted intervention for Asian Americans with phobia and found superior treatment effects with the culturally adapted version. Unfortunately, the cultural adaptations were not documented in their research report. Coard, Wallace, Stevenson, and Brotman (2004) built a convincing argument for augmenting a parenting intervention for African American families by including strategies on racial socialization, a ubiquitous parenting practice among African American parents. Similarly, López, Kopelowicz, and Cañive (2002) made recommendations for culturally adapting treatments for patients with schizophrenia who are Latino on the basis of their findings that stress the difference in the role of criticism and warmth in Latino families and White American families. These efforts highlight the importance of maintaining a depth of knowledge regarding a particular population of interest.

Some authors have developed very specific models of cultural adaptation. In England, Rathod, Kingdon, Phiri, and Gobbi (2010) worked with patients with psychosis. Based on this population, they recommended four areas for consideration in culturally adapting CBT for (a) preengagement and engagement, (b) assessment and case formulation, (c) delusions and hallucinations, and (d) treatment barriers. These recommendations were based on an exploratory study of the views of both patients and therapists about the utility of CBT for patients with psychosis. Participants were primarily members of ethnocultural minorities (Afro Caribbean, Black African/Black British, and South Asian Muslims) from mental health centers in Hampshire and West London. CBT and mental health practitioners working with these communities conducted focus groups and semistructured interviews with patients with schizophrenia from the lay ethnic minority communities.

Similarly, Interián and Díaz-Martínez (2007) proposed a cultural adaptation model for the treatment of depression with Latinos who are recent immigrants. They covered seven dimensions for adaptation. The dimension of ethnocultural assessment is implemented first, as it can be used to inform the need and type of adaptations on the remaining dimensions. With the second dimension, interpersonal style and values, Interián and Díaz-Martínez suggested particular attention to values of *personalismo* (emphasis on close personal relations), *simpatía* (agreeableness), *familismo* (emphasis on family), *formalism* (formality), *respeto* (respect), and *fatalism* (fatalism) and how these values inform expectations of therapy and client–therapist relationships. The expectation of *desahogo* (venting) is a dimension for consideration as a particular client expectation of treatment that might inform how clients engage in the therapy process. As with broader frameworks, *dichos* or *refranes* (sayings or idioms) are used as culturally relevant metaphors for treatment goals and strategies. The last three dimensions cover considerations specifically tied to implementing CBT with depressed Latino clients, namely, cognitive techniques, behavioral techniques, and problem complexity in the context of the CBT case conceptualization approach.

Other scholars have undertaken cultural adaptation efforts by following broader theoretical models. For example, Podorefsky, McDonald-Dowdell, and Beardslee (2001) described the adaptation of a psychoeducational preventive intervention to improve resilience in children in families whose parents had a mood disorder. The objective was to make the necessary changes for work with a high-risk urban sample. Podorefsky et al. used an ecological framework (Bronfenbrenner, 1989; Cooper & Denner, 1998), emphasizing process elements such as community engagement with caregivers and family members. Examples of these elements are conducting needs assessments of key stakeholders (e.g., community leaders, clergy, teachers, clinicians) and providing workshops to families on parenting and child development. Collaborations with care providers led to better recruitment and retention of families and the engagement of families provided the language and terminology employed in the intervention. A key principle that guided the adaptation was flexibility (i.e., persons who carry out the intervention must remain flexible to accommodate the needs and characteristics of their clients). This notion was extended to the recruitment of staff interested and sensitive to language and ethnocultural issues. In addition, reconceptualizing depression and resiliency based on life experiences relevant to the participants served to give meaning to the intervention. Podorefsky et al. also posited that timing and support for the intervention, focus on daily experiences, and emphasis on strengths and resources were important areas for consideration.

Other complementary models have been developed for work with specific populations that may or may not be ethnocultural in nature. Wingood and DiClemente's (2008) ADAPT-ITT model was developed for use in adapting HIV prevention programs for research and implementation. The model has eight steps: (a) assessment, (b) decision, (c) administration, (d) production, (e) topical experts, (f) integration, (g) training, and (h) testing. In each of these steps are concepts and procedures of great importance to cultural adaptations. For example, Wingood and DiClemente recommended the use of a theater testing methodology during the administration phase that elicits participant feedback about the intervention as well as input from important stakeholders. As with pilot studies recommended across cultural adaptation models, within the ADAPT-ITT framework feedback is systematically collected, analyzed, and incorporated into an adapted intervention. Wingood and DiClemente suggested developing an "adaptation plan" during the production phase. In the fifth phase, consultation with content experts is sought to inform either the first adaptation or the next adaptation following the initial adaptation and feedback process to ensure that changes are worthwhile. The integration of the knowledge provided by experts occurs in Phase 6. In testing, the third draft of the adapted EBT is pilot tested with 20 participants who belong to the group that the adaptation has been undertaken to fit. As in Whitbeck's (2006) model, key stakeholders are asked to observe the implementation. All provide feedback on how the adapted version was received. The ADAPT-ITT model lends itself naturally to use as a cultural adaptation model, and, indeed, Latham et al. (2010) used the model to adapt an evidence-based intervention for HIV prevention in African American adolescent girls. Wingood and DiClemente attended to both gender and ethnicity in examining adaptations using the ADAPT-ITT model.

RECOMMENDATIONS

Renowned scholars have provided support and recommendations for cultural adaptation. Many of these are notably tied to cultural competence. These recommendations are likely to be needed before the work with clients begins and typically are intended to prepare the psychotherapist to work competently with ethnocultural groups (Hays & Iwamasa, 2006). In addition to providing a depth of literature in cultural competence, some have offered specific recommendations of relevance to cultural adaptations. The work of Patricia Arredondo, Lillian Comas-Díaz, Pamela Hays, Ricardo Muñoz, Stanley Sue, and José Szapocznik is highlighted here as being of particular importance.

Patricia Arredondo is the lead author and champion of the "Guidelines on Multicultural Education, Training, Research, Practice, and Organizational Change for Psychologists" (APA, 2003). These guidelines, and the many years of research findings that were amassed to support them, specify important components of treatment that suggest cultural adaptations would be considered ethical and competent practice of psychology. Of the six guidelines, three pertain to cultural adaptations of psychotherapy. The most relevant perhaps is Guideline 5, which calls on psychologists "to apply culturally appropriate skills in clinical and other applied psychological practices" (p. 390). The first guideline encourages psychologists "to recognize that, as cultural beings, they may hold attitudes and beliefs that can detrimentally influence their perceptions of and interactions with individuals who are ethnically and racially different from themselves" (p. 382). Guideline 2 encourages psychologists "to recognize the importance of multicultural sensitivity/responsiveness, knowledge, and understanding about ethnically and racially different individuals" (p. 385). In an observation very much relevant to the cultural adaptation discussion, Arredondo and her task force specified that psychologists need not develop entirely new skills to apply Guideline 5; rather, psychologist need to have the awareness and knowledge to recognize when there is a need for "culture-centered adaptations" to interventions and practices that will render treatment more effective.

Lillian Comas-Díaz (2006) explicitly expressed a need for culturally adapting psychotherapies and suggested three important dimensions in doing so: contextualism, interconnectedness, and magical realism. Comas-Díaz referred to existing research on field dependence and independence to highlight the importance of considering how the client situates him- or herself within the context. The therapist should also consider how the client conceptualizes his or her interactions with people, places, and things present in his or her context, keeping in mind that "presence" of persons is not limited to those who are living. Finally, Comas-Díaz warned against pathologizing the infusion of magical belief and fantasy into discussions, as research suggests that the interaction of the real and surreal could be indicative of normal functioning or even resilience among some ethnocultural groups. She specifically recommended using *cuentos* (stories) and *dichos* (sayings), increasing knowledge and interventions in the spiritual realm, and providing in-depth information regarding *sanación* (healing) and *espiritus*, *santos*, and *orishas* (spirits, saints, and Yoruba deities). These concepts speak to healing beliefs, values, and rituals that shape clients' understanding about illness and achieving better health.

With regard to CBT, Hays (2009) presented 10 recommendations for "culturally responsive" treatment:

1. Evaluate the individual and family needs, focusing on behaviors that are culturally respectful.
2. Identify resources (interpersonal and environmental) related to cultural strengths.
3. Clarify the nature of the problem (environmental, individual) and attend to cultural influences.
4. Focus on environmental challenges by supporting the client in minimizing stressors and maximizing personal strengths,

support, and more positive relations with the social and physical context.

5. Acknowledge and support the client's report of discrimination and other experiences of oppression.
6. Support collaboration vis-à-vis conflict attending to differences between the client and therapist.
7. Question the utility of "dysfunctional thoughts" or "irrational beliefs" in cognitive restructuring.
8. Avoid challenging cultural beliefs.
9. Develop a list of cultural strengths and supports to replace thoughts and beliefs considered unhelpful.
10. Provide regular homework, giving emphasis to the client's goals and cultural congruence.

These recommendations could well be followed within cultural adaptation models to help inform adaptations to psychotherapy process and intervention content.

The work of Ricardo Muñoz spans 3 decades of commitment to implementing treatments with ethnocultural groups in San Francisco. Muñoz and his research team reported that their development of culturally appropriate interventions began with theory selection (social learning theory) that was understood to be relevant to socioeconomically disadvantaged ethnocultural groups. Once the theory was selected, therapeutic approaches based on the theory were identified (i.e., CBT). Finally, efforts were always concluded with evaluation of outcomes (Muñoz & Mendelson, 2005). Within that structure, Muñoz and colleagues cited important elements that were present in their efforts to culturally adapt interventions, specifically, (a) participation of ethnocultural within-group members in the intervention development process; (b) acknowledgment and integration of relevant cultural values into interventions; (c) openness to incorporating religion and spirituality in treatment procedures; (d) direct encouragement to discuss acculturation and negotiation of cultural differences; and (e) acknowledgment of the existence and impact of racism, prejudice, and discrimination in the lives of clients. Although they are not tied to a particular model of adaptation, Muñoz and colleagues have generated robust evidence of good outcomes for these culturally adapted interventions (Muñoz & Mendelson, 2005).

Stanley Sue's work stands out as a beacon that has illuminated the path for many ethnic minority scholars and investigators. Sue devoted his career to the understanding of ethnic and cross-cultural influence on behavior, focusing on mental health and personality with ethnocultural groups in general and with Asian Americans in particular (Sue & Morishima, 1982). His work on cultural competence (e.g., Sue, 2003), ethnic match between therapist and client (e.g., Zane et al., 2005), and culturally responsive mental health services (e.g., Sue, Fujino, Hu, Takeuchi, & Zane, 1991) paved the way for much of the current thinking on culturally adapted treatments.

José Szapocznik and his research team have made enormous contributions to understanding the role of culture in psychotherapy. Working from a theoretical approach in structural systems family therapy, Szapocznik and his colleagues worked to clarify the context in which Cuban American families operated and how specific immigration histories and acculturation challenges could be understood to generate or exacerbate parent–adolescent conflicts (Szapocznik & Kurtines, 1993). Szapocznik generated important concepts, such as detouring and reframing, that became central to bicultural effectiveness training, which espoused a culturally informed goal of establishing "crossed alliances" that would allow parents and adolescents room to connect. Szapocznik's work was built on Bronfenbrenner's (1979) ecological systems theory, which is also the base of Bernal et al.'s (1995) EVF.

In addition to those authors who have published models, many scholars have made outstanding contributions to the literature informing cultural adaptations of EBTs. These scholars include Teresa LaFromboise (1988); Gerardo Marín (e.g., Marín & Marín, 1991); Gordon N. Hall (2011); Paul Pedersen (1990); the research team of Rogler, Costantino, and Malgady (e.g., Rogler, Malgady, Costantino, & Blumenthal, 1987); and Nolan Zane, who leads the Asian American Center on Health Disparities (Sue & Zane, 2011). More recently, Esteban Cardemil (e.g., Cardemil, 2010) and Martin La Roche (e.g., La Roche & Lustig, 2010) have made important conceptual contributions to the field.

CONCLUSION

Prescriptive recommendations for cultural adaptations published since the mid-1990s appear to have been developed in relative isolation; that is, interventions researchers seem to have identified a need for cultural adaptation and developed a model that they later published without knowledge that other models existed. It is critical to note that the dates of publication for these models are close. Of the 12 cultural adaptation models listed in the chapter, seven were published between 2004 and 2006. This suggests that authors were working in parallel to help define their needs in attempting to reach ethnocultural groups.

It becomes powerful to note the similarities across frameworks and what these similarities may represent in terms of concurrent validity. Most authors call for a systematic and rigorous process informed by a conceptual framework. Many of the frameworks focus on ecological validity, with common roots in Bronfenbrenner's ecological systems theory. Framework authors seek to be informed by the expertise of stakeholders, whether these are communities, agencies, or individuals, with some frameworks having common roots in Rogers' diffusion of innovation theory. Many also seek to be informed by existing research findings on important variables of interest (e.g., acculturative stress, discrimination, immigration, spirituality, cultural values). Frameworks consider engagement and preengagement issues and are explicitly or implicitly concerned with modifying the process and content of treatments to support increased engagement, acceptability, and/or relevance of treatments. There is also a focus on improved outcomes for the population receiving the treatment. Across frameworks, we find consideration of treatment provider and/or therapist characteristics central to the success of the intervention or therapy. Framework authors recommend and use multiple/flexible methods of observation to gather information regarding cultural adaptations. Finally, across models we find authors addressing fidelity and fit.

In addition to attending to the collective wisdom of experts who have been implementing treatments with ethnocultural populations and heeding the similarities in these perspectives, it is important to note that the concept of cultural adaptations is not specific to the field of psychology. The relevance of moving across cultures in a respectful manner, while attempting to understand others and be understood by others, is as old as recorded history. The idea of cultural adaptations in interventions, although more modern, is also not unique to psychology. Communications and media experts have spent considerable time and effort trying to understand how to transmit messages in transnational and transcultural contexts for pure entertainment and for economic gain (e.g., Moran & Keane, 2009a, 2009b). The contrast between the purposes of making money from sales and promoting mental health is stark, but the actions implied in transporting technologies (e.g., the show *Friends* or CBT for depression) across cultural and national borders are quite similar.

Scholars across disciplines could benefit from examining the lessons learned across professional applications, a point similarly stressed by Backer (2002). Ultimately, we share a common ground in the desire to influence thoughts, feelings, and/or behaviors. Influencing another person, group, or community takes (a) understanding and being understood and (b) building a sense of a collective "we" from which to influence and be influenced.

However, the question concerning influence is an ethical one. Who benefits from the influence or change? In whose interest is the adaptation? In a poignant example, Watters (2010) documented the shift in attitudes and behaviors as a result of mega-marketing in Japan. Prior to 1990, Japanese culture did not regard depression as a serious public health issue and seemed almost immune to the market penetration of antidepressants. Yet processes were set in motion by a careful and well-orchestrated (U.S.-led) marketing campaign to change attitudes and beliefs about depression. The campaign was highly effective in influencing a cultural shift that resulted in a widespread market penetration of SSRIs. The irony of this account is that scientific information from scholars involved in the study of how culture influences the experiences of depression was used to first change attitudes and later sell the product.

Cultural imperialism and some aspects of globalization are the epitome of one-way communication in which an entity simply seeks to assimilate and influence "the other" with little regard to the question of who benefits from the influence. Cultural adaptation is an approach that makes explicit the understanding of others and prescribes being influenced by others so that we may learn how to be understood and how to influence as well, in the service of creating a "we." The broader the "we," the stronger the science and practice of psychology.

REFERENCES

American Psychological Association. (2003). Guidelines on multicultural education, training, research, practice, and organizational change for psychologists. *American Psychologist, 58,* 377–402. doi:10.1037/0003-066X.58.5.377

American Psychological Association. (2008). *Report of the APA Task Force on the Implementation of the Multicultural Guidelines.* Washington, DC: Author.

Backer, T. E. (2002). *Finding the balance: Program fidelity and adaptation in substance abuse prevention: A state of the art review.* Washington, DC: U.S. Department of Health and Human Services.

Barrera, M., Jr., & Castro, F. G. (2006). A heuristic framework for the cultural adaptation of interventions. *Clinical Psychology: Science and Practice, 13,* 311–316. doi:10.1111/j.1468-2850.2006.00043.x

Baumann, A., Domenech Rodríguez, M., & Parra-Cardona, J. R. (2011). Community-based applied research with Latino immigrant families: Informing practice and research according to ethical and social justice principles. *Family Process, 52,* 132–148. doi:10.1111/j.1545-5300.2011.01351.x

Bernal, G., Bonilla, J., & Bellido, C. (1995). Ecological validity and cultural sensitivity for outcome research: Issues for the cultural adaptation and development of psychosocial treatments with Hispanics. *Journal of Abnormal Child Psychology, 23,* 67–82. doi:10.1007/BF01447045

Bernal, G., & Sáez-Santiago, E. (2006). Culturally centered psychosocial interventions. *Journal of Community Psychology, 34,* 121–132. doi:10.1002/jcop.20096

Bronfenbrenner, U. (1977). Toward an experimental ecology of human development. *American Psychologist, 32,* 513–531. doi:10.1037/0003-066X.32.7.513

Bronfenbrenner, U. (1979). *The ecology of human development: Experiments by nature and design.* Cambridge, MA: Harvard University Press.

Bronfenbrenner, U. (1989). Ecological systems theory. *Annals of Child Development,* *6,* 187–249.

Cardemil, E. V. (2010). Cultural adaptations to empirically supported treatments: A research agenda. *Scientific Review of Mental Health Practice, 7,* 8–21.

Castro, F. G., Barrera, M., Jr., & Martinez, C. R., Jr. (2004). The cultural adaptation of prevention interventions: Resolving tensions between fidelity and fit. *Prevention Science, 5,* 41–45.

Coard, S. I., Wallace, S. A., Stevenson, H. C., & Brotman, L. M. (2004). Towards culturally relevant preventive interventions: The consideration of racial socialization in parent training with African American families. *Journal of Child and Family Studies, 13,* 277–293. doi:10.1023/B:JCFS.0000022035.07171.f8

Comas-Díaz, L. (2006). Latino healing: The integration of ethnic psychology into psychotherapy. *Psychotherapy: Theory, Research, Practice, Training, 43,* 436–453. doi:10.1037/0033-3204.43.4.436

Cooper, C. R., & Denner, J. (1998). Theories linking culture and psychology: Universal and community-specific processes. *Annual Review of Psychology, 49,* 559–584. doi:10.1146/annurev.psych.49.1.559

Dawson, T. L., Fischer, K. W., & Stein, Z. (2006). Reconsidering qualitative and quantitative research approaches: A cognitive developmental perspective. *New Ideas in Psychology, 24,* 229–239. doi:10.1016/j.newideapsych.2006.10.001

Domenech-Rodríguez, M., & Wieling, E. (2004). Developing culturally appropriate, evidence-based treatments for interventions with ethnic minority populations. In M. Rastogi & E. Wieling (Eds.), *Voices of color: First-person accounts of ethnic minority therapists* (pp. 313–333). Thousand Oaks, CA: Sage.

Hall, G. C. N. (2001). Psychotherapy research with ethnic minorities: Empirical, ethical, and conceptual issues. *Journal of Consulting and Clinical Psychology, 69,* 502–510. doi:10.1037/0022-006X.69.3.502

Hays, P. A. (2009). Integrating evidence-based practice, cognitive–behavior therapy, and multicultural therapy: Ten steps for culturally competent practice. *Professional Psychology: Research and Practice, 40,* 354–360. doi:10.1037/a0016250

Hays, P. A., & Iwamasa, G. Y. (Eds.). (2006). *Culturally responsive cognitive–behavioral therapy: Assessment, practice, and supervision.* Washington, DC: American Psychological Association.

Hinton, D. E., Pham, T., Tran, M., Safren, S. A., Otto, M. W., & Pollack, M. H. (2004). CBT for Vietnamese refugees with treatment-resistant PTSD and panic attacks: A pilot study. *Journal of Traumatic Stress, 17,* 429–433. doi:10.1023/B:JOTS.0000048956.03529.fa

Huey, S. J., & Pan, D. (2006). Culture-responsive one-session treatment for phobic Asian Americans: *Psychotherapy: Theory, Research, Practice, Training, 43,* 549–554. doi:10.1037/0033-3204.43.4.549

Hwang, W. (2006). The psychotherapy adaptation and modification framework: Application to Asian Americans. *American Psychologist, 61,* 702–715. doi:10.1037/0003-066X.61.7.702

Hwang, W. (2009). The Formative Method for Adapting Psychotherapy (FMAP): A community-based developmental approach to culturally adapting therapy. *Professional Psychology: Research and Practice, 40,* 369–377.

Interián, A., & Díaz-Martínez, A. M. (2007). Considerations for culturally competent cognitive-behavioral therapy for depression with Hispanic patients. *Cognitive and Behavioral Practice, 14,* 84–97.

Kluckhohn, C., & Murray, H. A. (1948). *Personality in nature, society, and culture.* New York, NY: Knopf.

Koss-Chioino, J. D., & Vargas, L. A. (1992). Through the cultural looking glass: A model for understanding culturally responsive psychotherapies. In L. A. Vargas & J. D. Koss-Chioino (Eds.), *Working with culture* (pp. 1–22). San Francisco, CA: Jossey-Bass.

Kumpfer, K. L., Pinyuchon, M., Teixeira de Melo, A., & Whiteside, H. O. (2008). Cultural adaptation process for international dissemination of the Strengthening Families Program. *Evaluation & the Health Professions, 31,* 226–239. doi:10.1177/0163278708315926

LaFromboise, T. D. (1988). American Indian mental health policy. *American Psychologist, 43,* 388–397. doi:10.1037/0003-066X.43.5.388

La Roche, M. J., & Lustig, K. (2010). Cultural adaptations: Unpacking the meaning of culture. *Scientific Review of Mental Health Practice, 7,* 26–30.

Latham, T. P., Sales, J. M., Boyce, L. S., Renfro, T. L., Wingood, G. M., DiClemente, R. J., & Rose, E. (2010). Application of ADAPT-ITT: Adapting an evidence-based HIV prevention intervention for incarcerated African American adolescent females. *Health Promotion Practice, 11,* 53S–60S. doi:10.1177/1524839910361433

Lau, A. S. (2006). Making the case for selective and directed cultural adaptations of evidence-based treatments: Examples from parenting training. *Clinical Psychology: Science and Practice, 13,* 295–310. doi:10.1111/j.1468-2850.2006.00042.x

Leong, F. T. L. (1996). Toward an integrative model for cross-cultural counseling and psychotherapy. *Applied and Preventive Psychology, 5,* 189–209. doi:10.1016/S0962-1849(96)80012-6

Leong, F. T. L., & Lee, S. H. (2006). A cultural accommodation model of psychotherapy: Illustrated with the case of Asian Americans. *Psychotherapy: Theory, Research, Practice, Training, 43,* 410–423. doi:10.1037/0033-3204.43.4.410

López, S. R., Kopelowicz, A., & Cañive, J. M. (2002). Strategies for developing culturally congruent family interventions for schizophrenia: The case of Hispanics. In H. P. Lefley & D. L. Johnson (Eds.), *Family interventions in mental illness: International perspectives* (pp. 61–90). Westport, CT: Praeger.

Marín, G., & Marín, B. V. (1991). *Research with Hispanic populations.* Newbury Park, CA: Sage.

Matos, M., Bauermeister, J. J., & Bernal, G. (2009). Parent–Child Interaction Therapy for Puerto Rican preschool children with ADHD and behavior problems: A pilot efficacy study. *Family Process, 48,* 232–252. doi:10.1111/j.1545-5300.2009.01279.x

Moran, A., & Keane, M. (2009a). *Cultural adaptation.* New York, NY: Routledge.

Moran, A., & Keane, M. (2009b). Introduction: The global flow of creative ideas. *Continuum, 23,* 107–114. doi:10.1080/10304310802710579

Muñoz, R. F., & Mendelson, T. (2005). Toward evidence-based interventions for diverse populations: The San Francisco General Hospital prevention and treatment manuals. *Journal of Consulting and Clinical Psychology, 73,* 790–799. doi:10.1037/0022-006X.73.5.790

Onwuegbuzie, A. J. (2002). Positivists, post-positivists, post-structuralists, and post-modernists: Why can't we all get along? Towards a framework for unifying research paradigms. *Education, 122,* 518–530.

Pedersen, P. (1990). The multicultural perspective as a fourth force in counseling. *Journal of Mental Health Counseling, 12*(1), 93–95.

Podorefsky, D. L., McDonald-Dowdell, M., & Beardslee, W. R. (2001). Adaptation of preventive interventions for a low-income, culturally diverse community. *Journal of the American Academy of Child & Adolescent Psychiatry, 40,* 879–886. doi:10.1097/00004583-200108000-00008

Rathod, S., Kingdon, D., Phiri, P., & Gobbi, M. (2010). Developing culturally sensitive cognitive behaviour therapy for psychosis for ethnic minority patients by exploration and incorporation of service users' and health professionals' views and opinions. *Behavioural and Cognitive Psychotherapy, 38,* 511–533. doi:10.1017/S1352465810000378

Resnicow, K., Soler, R., Braithwaite, R. L., Ahluwalia, J. S., & Butler, J. (2002). Cultural sensitivity in substance use prevention: Bridging the gap between research and practice in community-based substance abuse prevention. *Journal of Community Psychology, 28,* 271–290.

Rogers, E. M. (1995). *Diffusion of innovations* (4th ed.). New York, NY: Free Press.

Rogers, E. M. (2002). Diffusion of preventive innovations. *Addictive Behaviors, 27,* 989–993. doi:10.1016/S0306-4603(02)00300-3

Rogler, L. H., Malgady, R. G., Costantino, G., & Blumenthal, R. (1987). What do culturally sensitive mental health services mean? The case of Hispanics. *American Psychologist, 42,* 565–570. doi:10.1037/0003-066X.42.6.565

Rosselló, J., & Bernal, G. (2005). New developments in adapting cognitive–behavioral and interpersonal treatments for depressed Puerto Rican adolescents. In E. Hibbs & P. S. Jensen (Eds.), *Psychosocial treatments for child and adolescent disorders* (2nd ed., pp. 187–217). Washington, DC: American Psychological Association.

Sue, S. (2003). In defense of cultural competency in psychotherapy and treatment. *American Psychologist, 58,* 964–970. doi:10.1037/0003-066X.58.11.964

Sue, S., Fujino, D. D., Hu, L., Takeuchi, D. T., & Zane, N. (1991). Community mental health services for ethnic minority groups: A test of the cultural responsiveness hypothesis. *Journal of Consulting and Clinical Psychology, 59,* 533–540. doi:10.1037/0022-006X.59.4.533

Sue, S., & Morishima, J. K. (1982). *The mental health of Asian Americans.* San Francisco, CA: Jossey-Bass.

Sue, S., & Sue, L. (2003). Ethnic research is good science. In G. Bernal, J. E. Trimble, A. K. Burlew, & F. T. L. Leong (Eds.), *Handbook of racial and ethnic minority psychology* (pp. 198–207). Thousand Oaks, CA: Sage.

Sue, S., & Zane, N. (2011). Asian American Center on Disparities Research. In J. C. Norcross, G. R. VandenBos, & D. K. Freedheim (Eds.), *History of psychotherapy: Continuity and change* (2nd ed., pp. 421–427). Washington, DC: American Psychological Association.

Szapocznik, J., & Kurtines, W. (1993). Family psychology and cultural diversity: Opportunities for theory, research, and application. *American Psychologist, 48,* 400–407. doi:10.1037/0003-066X.48.4.400

Watters, E. (2010). *Crazy like us: The globalization of the American psyche.* New York, NY: Free Press.

Whitbeck, L. B. (2006). Some guiding assumptions and a theoretical model for developing culturally specific preventions with Native American people. *Journal of Community Psychology, 34,* 183–192. doi:10.1002/jcop.20094

Wingood, G. M., & DiClemente, R. J. (2008). The ADAPT-ITT model: A novel method of adapting evidence-based HIV interventions. *Journal of Acquired Immune Deficiency Syndromes, 47*(Suppl. 1), S40–S46. doi:10.1097/QAI.0b013e3181605df1

Zane, N., Sue, S., Chang, J., Huang, L., Huang, J., Lowe, S., . . . Lee, E. (2005). Beyond ethnic match: Effects of client–therapist cognitive match in problem perception, coping orientation, and therapy goals on treatment outcomes. *Journal of Community Psychology, 33,* 569–585. doi:10.1002/jcop.20067

3

ETHICAL CONSIDERATIONS IN THE APPLICATION OF CULTURAL ADAPTATION MODELS WITH ETHNOCULTURAL POPULATIONS

JOSEPH E. TRIMBLE, MARÍA R. SCHARRÓN-DEL-RÍO, AND JILL S. HILL

The goal of reaching culturally diverse groups through psychotherapy interventions is consistent with the multicultural guidelines set forth by the American Psychological Association (APA; 2003). However, the mechanics associated with providing culturally appropriate, relevant, and competent services and conducting research into these processes opens many areas of discussion within the realm of ethics (Sue et al., 1998; Trimble & Fisher, 2005). At the forefront of these discussions are questions about what is most ecologically valid (e.g., adapting an intervention, creating a new intervention for a specific cultural group) and scientifically sound (e.g., empirically supported; Trickett & Espino, 2004). However, equally important are ethical considerations about beliefs and values of the members of the *ethnocultural groups*—communities sharing similarities stemming from their ethnic, racial, and/or cultural background that have been marginalized and oppressed by dominant or colonial populations—being targeted for interventions.

To ethically deliver relevant interventions, we must balance the considerations to achieve both strong science and optimal benefits to the persons and/or community being served. Therefore, before embarking on a research or clinical endeavor, we must ask ourselves questions such as, How does the cultural group understand the phenomenon in question (e.g., child noncompliance)?

What are seen as appropriate points of intervention? and, What are cultur-ally sanctioned ways to intervene? We must also consider the appropriateness of structural matters (e.g., who delivers an intervention, where, and in what format) and their cultural congruence for the ethical practice of adapting exist-ing interventions. Accordingly, the major goal of this chapter is to encourage ethical decision making in intervention research that reflects the unique his-torical and sociocultural realities of ethnocultural communities. We advocate that researchers and clinicians working with these communities must apply a culturally resonant perspective to the evaluation of research risk and benefits, develop and implement culturally respectful informed consent procedures, construct culturally appropriate confidentiality and disclosure policies, and engage in community and participant consultation with a standard of *principled cultural sensitivity*—a multidimentional construct that can be easily overlooked.

The distinguished Venezuelan community psychologist Maritza Montero (2009) wrote that communities effect change through political action, "insisting and persisting in producing transformations that radically modify their quality of life, and their relation to society to which they belong and to their environment" (p. 151). Her poignant observations point to the need for field-based and intervention researchers to consider the fact that their presence and potential influence in ethnocultural communities may actually empower and transform the communities in ways that may not only seem unanticipated but also contradictory to the researchers' goals and inten-tions. Moreover, clinical interventions may be modified and transformed by ethnocultural community members to accommodate deeply rooted local life-ways and thoughtways that are seemingly impermeable to change, including the community's particular worldview and epistemology. These systems of belief impact the community members' perception of their reality and are embedded profoundly in its legends, folklore, and folk healing.

Some of the epistemological differences have often been viewed as pathological or dismissively labeled as *magical* by Western science. What is often referred to as *magical thinking* is characteristic of the way many indig-enous populations account for the events that occur in their daily lives. These thought processes and behaviors are derived from the belief in fundamental interconnectedness and reciprocal influence between humankind and the universe, such that, for example, it is possible to heal or harm a person through the casting of certain stones (Frazer, 1996; Kiev, 1964; Moodley & West, 2005; Rosengren, Johnson, & Harris, 2000; Serban, 1982; Trimble, 2010; Zusne & Jones, 1989).

In the psychiatric literature, such beliefs have been characterized as delusional, dysfunctional, irrational, and wishful thinking. For example, Castro-Blanco (2005) criticized Martínez-Taboas's (2005b) treatment of a client presenting psychogenic seizures. Martínez-Taboas (2005b) framed the client's treatment, within her *espiritismo* beliefs, to integrate "her cultural religious beliefs with some current psychotherapeutic techniques" (p.18). Castro-Blanco critiqued Martínez-Taboas's departure from cognitive therapy by not challenging the "dysfunctional nature of [the client's espiritismo and spirit possession] beliefs" (p. 15). Instead, Castro-Blanco advocated a "more conventional approach to treatment," including challenging the "utility of the belief[s] in spiritual possession" and replacing them with more "adaptive, functional ones" (p. 15). Castro-Blanco's assessment of the "functionality" and "utility" of cultural beliefs, as well as his belief that they need to be exchanged for, is deeply rooted in an ethnocentrism that hides behind advocacy for a "more conventional approach to treatment" (p. 15). At its best, this is a difference of opinion between providers with varying levels of understanding of what constitutes competent intervention. At its worst, it is an ethnocentric stance that evidences the lingering pathologization of ethnocultural beliefs and traditions, which reinforces the long-standing oppression that ethnocultural communities and people have historically endured, and results in continued to mental and health disparities.

The epistemological differences between Western worldviews of science and ethnocultural communities, and the privilege that Western science has been historically afforded, have important implications regarding efficacious ecological validity (e.g., adapting an intervention, creating a new intervention for a specific cultural group; Trickett & Espino, 2004; Trickett, Kelly, & Vincent, 1985; Trickett & Mitchell, 1993). Culturally appropriate, relevant, and competent services and research within ethnocultural communities require developing awareness about interpersonal and epistemological power relationships (i.e., relations, dynamics, and privilege). This chapter emphasizes the deep-seated principle that ethical intervention researchers and clinicians refrain from imposing their worldview onto the community and instead privilege the community's knowledge and epistemology over their own.

Community acceptance and the establishment of collaborative relations and research partnerships, therefore, begin with the acknowledgement that there are cultural differences and that they must be respected and tempered with active solidarity, goodness, kindness, and justice as guiding moral principles for ethical decision making. We discuss these areas using the multicultural competencies model (Sue et al., 1998) as a way to structure how to approach ethics in cultural adaptation research.

To engage in culturally adapting interventions, ethical researchers must be culturally sensitive and particularly attuned to the manner in which clinical interventions are introduced and conducted in ethnocultural communities. Cultural sensitivity has to do with the person, and adaptation has to do with the cultural resonance of the intervention (Bernal & Domenech Rodríguez,

2009; Bernal, Jiménez-Chafey, & Domenech Rodríguez, 2009; Trimble, 2003; Trimble & Mohatt, 2005).

In the past 3 decades, a number of publications have emerged on ethnocultural groups with bibliographies on African Americans, Latinos, Asian Americans, and American Indians. There has been an overwhelming increase in research with American Indians and Alaska Native populations. For example, 1,363 citations were listed between 1930 and 1981 (Kelso & Attneave, 1981), whereas 2,328 psychological and behavioral articles on Indians and Alaska Natives were published from 1967 to 1994 (Trimble & Bagwell, 1995). More recently, a review of citations appearing in PsycINFO for all major ethnic minority groups outlined in the U.S. Census documented about 2,300 articles using "ethnic minority" as the search term during and before the 1960s, as compared with about 15,000 documented since that time to 2008. The rapid growth of interest and levels of research activity must be tempered by an awareness of the ethical implications of efforts involving groups with whom most investigators often have little familiarity (Bernal, Trimble, Burlew, & Leong, 2002).

The increase of ethnic minority research has stirred the unsettling and sometimes passionately angry voices of many ethnocultural community people worldwide about the problems some outside researchers create for their villages, reservations, neighborhoods, and communities. Indeed, considerable documented abuse by outside researchers has contributed to the growing community and tribal discontent (American Indian Law Center, 1999; Beauvais & Trimble, 1992; Trimble, 2009; Trimble & Fisher, 2005; Trimble, Scharrón-del Río, & Bernal, 2010). The apparent rapid growth of concern within communities about the presence of "outside" researchers has led some to be intolerant and unforgiving of past research efforts. As a result, the presence of itinerant and transient researchers is no longer welcomed or acceptable in a majority of communities. The so-called safari-scholar approach to field-based research (Trimble et al., 2010) is being replaced by the ethnocultural communities' demand for research conducted under their communities' direction and control, including granting approval for publications. Therefore, researchers should be prepared to collaborate with communities, share results that have practical value, and accept the conditions imposed by the community in gaining access to information and respondents (Fisher et al., 2002; Trimble & Fisher, 2005).

To illustrate the breadth of community concerns and problems with researchers, the American Indian Law Center (1999) compiled a list of 15 major complaints expressed by Indian and Native tribal groups. Some of these grievances include having been persuaded to participate in research in which they did not fully understand the nature of the risk to their health and safety; lack of respect for basic human dignity of the individual participants or their religious and cultural beliefs; publishing of sensitive religious and cultural information, in some cases destroying its efficacy by publication; failure or refusal to follow through on promised benefits, to share preliminary results with the community, or give the community an opportunity to participate in the formulation and recommendations or of a final report.

Other ethnocultural communities have experienced many of these research and moral transgressions. For example, the infamous Tuskegee Syphilis Experiment conducted by the U.S. Public Service from 1932 to 1972 in Macon County, Georgia, involved the monitoring (while withholding treatment) of 399 African American males diagnosed with the disease (Jones, 1993; Reverby, 2009). The outcry about the study launched a major U.S government investigation that led to significant changes in the protection research participants at all levels. Such indignities reproduce the history of oppression and exploitation of and discrimination toward ethnic minorities and fuel the mistrust of outside researchers and interventionists.

GUIDELINES FOR SENSITIVE COMMUNITY-BASED PARTICIPATION

The list of concerns mirrors those expressed by numerous communities, including the First Nations populations in Canada, Aboriginal populations in Australia, Maori communities in Aotearoa (New Zealand), and from countries encompassing the vast Amazon region of South America. As a result, the voices of Canada's First Nations people guided the publication of "a set of principles to assist in developing ethical codes for the conduct of research internal to the Aboriginal community or with external partners" (Castellano, 2004, p. 98). These principles name Canada's Aboriginal People as the true owners of the information they provide for researchers, thus obliging researchers to consider in their research plans the Aboriginal People's struggles for self-determination. Similarly, according to a document written in collaboration with Aboriginal and Torres Strait Island representatives and released by Australia's National Health and Medical Research Council (2003), "the construction of ethical relationships between Aboriginal and Torres Strait Islander Peoples on the one hand and the research community on the other must take into account the principles and values of Aboriginal and Torres Strait Islander cultures" (p. 3).

These research guidelines, coupled with the accumulation of complaints from other ethnocultural communities, resonated with beliefs and values of many community-based researchers and thus have generated a number of relevant guidelines and principles. A number of conscientious scholars have expanded the normative professional research ethical standards to include guidelines and practices that emphasize the importance of establishing firm collaborative relationships with community leaders (Fisher et al., 2002; Jason, Keys, Suarez-Balcazar, & Davis, 2004; Mohatt, 1989; Mohatt & Thomas, 2006). According to Trickett and Espino (2004),

> It is time to place the collaboration concept in the center of inquiry and work out its importance for community research and intervention. Although some would see it as merely a tool or strategy to getting the "'real" work of behavioral science done, our strong preference is to view the research relationship in community research and intervention as a critical part of the "'real" work itself (p. 62).

Other authors have written about ethics that are centered on solidarity, relationships, conversation, engagement, and sovereignty (Ellis, 2007; Glesne, 2007; Grande, 2007; Montero, 2003). It is not merely a methodological exercise, a series of steps to carry out, nor a side-by-side aseptic sharing of the work. Rather, it is a sense of interconnection, respect, and commitment that must be communicated and experienced by the community as genuine and sincere. For this to happen, an epistemological shift is needed. Without establishing and working through community partnerships, research ventures are doomed to failure at every stage of the process. Yet there is evidence that a culturally adapted intervention initiated from the "ground up" can be successful; the outcome of the venture is dependent on the quality and depth of the relationships between researchers and communities (Bernal & Domenech Rodríguez, 2009; Bernal et al., 2009; Domenech Rodríguez & Wieling, 2004; Mohatt & Thomas, 2006; Trimble & Mohatt, 2005). Researchers also must be aware of scientific, social, and political factors governing definitions of race, ethnicity, and culture, understand within-group differences, and be skilled in constructing culturally valid assessment instruments.

The researchers' perspective and orientation also add new challenges to conducting research with ethnocultural populations. The process of research is an intervention in itself, one that can contribute to the reparation of past oppressions and exploitations. To truly engage in a paradigmatic shift, it is not enough to "learn" a new, step-by-step methodology, the underlying assumptions from which researchers formulate questions, justify their research, conceptualize issues, view the communities themselves and their participation in the process, analyze the results, and decide on further dissemination and action need to be examined and challenged. Many would argue that the epistemological shift has occurred, opening the door for participatory action research and community-based endeavors. However, the pervasive pathologization and discriminatory discourse and policies within the mental health fields is often perpetuated by the academic and medical language and rituals, as well as by the institutions that sanction research. Solidarity and engagement are the antithesis of *hacer por hacer*, doing for the sake of doing. The needed epistemological shift entails challenging personal, methodological, and academic assumptions that permeate the research endeavor.

The rigors of scientific inquiry and methods often are foreign to the residents of ethnocultural communities, who frequently view researchers as socially and culturally marginal to their communities. Researchers often know this all too well (Powdermaker, 1966). Thus,

> no matter how skilled he is in the native tongue, how nimble in handling strange social relationships, how artistic in performing social and religious rituals, and how attached he is to local beliefs, goals, and values, [the researcher] rarely deludes himself to thinking that many community members really regard him as one of them. (Freilich, 1970, p. 2)

COMMUNITY RESIDENTS ARE NOT "SUBJECTS"

Approaching a community setting as though it were a sterile laboratory in which respondents are handled as "subjects" to be manipulated according to strict scientific principles is not likely to be embraced by the ethnocultural community. In fact, it may completely undermine the research endeavor, as it might well lead respondents to tell researchers what they believe the researchers want to hear and nothing more (Trimble & Mohatt, 2006). The social and behavioral sciences' overemphasis on variable control at all levels contradicts the fact that people live in contexts that intensely influence actions, thoughts, and feelings. Laboratory-based methodologies, typically foreign to ethnocultural communities, and the corresponding findings might be different from those obtained by research activities that embody a collaborative process between the researchers (as participant observers) and the community members.

Glesne (2007) wrote about four scenarios of resistance to qualitative research in oppressed communities and proposes alternative ethics that should guide any inquiry that are rooted in the ethic of solidarity, community and hospitality. These alternatives include the research purpose based in "solidarity" with the community, data collection through the process of accompanying and sharing, data collection viewed as collective process of coconstruction, and data interpretation that includes awareness of the multiple ways of understanding the world and seeking other perspectives different from our own.

The following paragraphs provide information that can enhance community participation, knowledge, and the application of principles framed in the context of cultural competence and the psychosocial science of community-based interventions. The points described are not intended as regulations, policies, or absolute prescriptions for research ethics practices and community-based partnership research. Rather, the purpose is to assist stakeholders in the responsible conduct of research—investigators, funding agencies, institutional review boards (IRBs), research participants, and ethnocultural communities—in identifying crucial ethical crossroads and in developing culturally sensitive and adaptive decision-making strategies.

ETHICAL RESEARCH AND MULTICULTURAL COMPETENCIES

An ethical researcher is a multiculturally competent researcher (Trimble, 2003; Trimble et al., 2010) who has worked on developing awareness, knowledge, and skills relating to the emerging principles of culturally adapted interventions (Sue et al., 1998). Ethics requires self-reflection and an ability to recognize and share with others personal values, errors of judgment, and lessons learned along the path toward the respectful and responsible conduct of research. No matter how the topic is expressed, researchers should seriously consider framing their field-based research around the formation and maintenance of responsible relationships. One will soon discover that community members will put the researcher through a sequence of tests to assess their level of commitment to working closely with them and to learn about their cultural ways. In effect, a relational methodology means that one takes the time to nurture relationships not merely for the sake of expediting the research and gaining acceptance and trust but because one should care about the welfare and dignity of all people (Trimble & Mohatt, 2005).

Awareness

To become multiculturally competent, we must be committed to self-awareness by actively examining our personal biases, beliefs, values, and worldview and how they influence our perceptions and interactions with others. In addition, we must also practice other-awareness by being open to learning about other people's beliefs and worldviews. When engaging in research with ethnic minority populations, it is particularly important to consider the beliefs and values of the members of the communities for whom we hope to adapt our interventions. How does the community understand the phenomenon that we seek to influence? How do they explain its origin? What are the communities' traditional solutions, interventions, or responses to the issue? We must be mindful of the possibility that ethnocultural communities have evolved culturally specific forms of treatment and interventions as they relate to what Western psychiatry defines as emotional and psychological disorders.

For decades, psychologists were not at all interested in cultural explanations or explorations of human affect, behavior, and cognition. The sociologist–anthropologist William Fielding Ogburn, one of Margaret Mead's professors, constantly pointed out that one should "never look for a psychological explanation unless every effort to find a *cultural* one has been exhausted" (Mead, 1959, p. 16). We agree with Ogburn's position that there is an urgent need to identify and study cultural correlates that are vital to understanding the sum of the conscious and unconscious events that make up an individual's life in ethnocultural community settings.

It is imperative that when addressing the questions that started this section, we consider how the differences in worldviews, assumptions, values, and beliefs between our own culture, Western methodologies, and the community's culture reproduce historical power structures. From the perspective of historically oppressed and marginalized communities, Western-based research, methodologies, and interventions have not benefited them but rather have served to further oppress and assimilate them into the dominant culture (L. T. Smith, 1999). For well-intentioned contemporary researchers, this is a tragic history that cannot simply be dismissed. Instead, this is a history that needs to be addressed often, in a process-oriented manner, to reestablish trust.

It is not our intention to create a false dichotomy between the Western worldview of scientific methodologies and the values, beliefs, and traditions of ethnocultural communities. Rather, our intent is to emphasize the historical context of the detrimental application of the Western worldview of science within ethnocultural communities and the harmful consequences that still reverberate today. For many ethnocultural communities, the Western worldview of science has been experienced as oppressive, never liberating. For example, *familismo* has been labeled as enmeshment, the belief in the spiritual world has been described as psychotic process, and the achievement gap has been deemed as proof to support White supremacy (Droge, 2005; Jorgensen, 1995; Martínez Taboas, 2005a, 2005b; Rogler, 2008; Welch, 2002).

The need for contemporary researchers to truly grasp the meaning of this historical context cannot be overstated. For many ethnocultural communities, in the Western worldview of science, certain approaches to research served as colonizing and assimilative forces (L. T. Smith, 1999). These trends continue today within the view of Western psychology through the institutionalization and widespread exportation of various discipline-specific technologies, including diagnostic nosologies, assessment instruments, and psychotherapeutic approaches. Traditionally, these technologies have not been used to foster or advocate for self-determination within ethnocultural communities. However, we do not believe that this

trend is irreversible. Therefore, it is imperative for contemporary researchers to communicate to ethnocultural community members that rather than
continuing to take, re-present, and oppress, Western methods benefit communities in need when used in culturally congruent ways to advocate for and
foster self-determination.

As researchers, we must remain mindful that our roles within ethnocultural communities will differ across various contexts. In addition, the
historical context of the Western worldview of science as applied within
ethnocultural communities is the baggage we bring as researchers whenever we endeavor to work with unique ethnic and cultural contexts (L. T.
Smith, 1999). Community members usually are well aware that whenever
ethnocultural explanations of the world departed from the evidence produced by the application of the scientific method devoid of the appropriate
context, they were typically dismissed or devalued as magical thinking. As
researchers, we need to initiate a dialogue with community members about
these demeaning and oppressive relations and genuinely listen to and value
the perspectives of community members in order to reestablish the shat-
tered bonds of trust.

Earlier, we mentioned that the Western worldview of psychology and
psychiatry often labels as magical the things it cannot explain or understand
(Subbotsky, 2010; Trimble, 2010). These events are also often referred to
as *supernatural*, as if they are above the laws of nature. There is an inherent
hubris connected to this terminology, one that resides in the spirit of positivist science itself: Nature is to be tamed, controlled, exploited, and its secrets
revealed. Because science has studied nature, we assume that we know its laws
and that which does not adhere to those laws (as derived through positivist
and decontextualizing research methods) is not natural. If it is something
that we want to condemn, perhaps we deem it as unnatural (i.e., homosexu-
ality). If it is something that is powerful, then we label it as supernatural.
The hubris comes from the belief that we control the limits of nature, that
what we have explained is nature itself, and that because we know nature,
whatever science cannot observe, measure, and understand is outside of the
natural world. Therefore, it does not exist.

Pathologizing a different worldview as magical thinking denotes Eurocentric bias. Echoing the voices of many ethnic minority, indigenous, feminist, and
community researchers, Denzin and Giardina (2007) advocated for a "sacred,
existential epistemology [that] places humans in a noncompetitive, nonhierar-
chical relationship to the earth, to nature, to the larger world" (p. 29). Battiste
(2007) described this indigenous epistemology as one "derived from the immediate ecology, their experiences, perceptions, thoughts, and memory, including experiences shared with others and from the spiritual world discovered in
dreams, visions, and signs interpreted with the guidance of healers or elders"

(pp. 115–116). In this worldview, there is an inherent respect to the world and all its inhabitants and events: What we do not understand still exists and impacts our lives and world.

Magical Thinking and Realism

One of the major sources of resistance to psychosocial intervention with ethnocultural communities is an epistemological clash, particularly around the deeply rooted and enduring presence of folk wisdom, healing traditions, and ancestral knowledge. Often hidden from outsiders, sacred and ancient knowledge is the source of explanations of various events ranging from the occurrence of natural phenomena to the cause and treatment of physical and psychological conditions. Countless stories compiled by missionaries, traders, wandering travelers, and more recently, folklorists and ethnographers attest to the profound and mysterious influences of folk beliefs and the unexplainable effects they have on the traditional ethnocultural communities (Frazer, 1996; Katz, Biesele, & St. Denis, 1997; Kiev, 1964; Sullivan, 2000; Torrey, 1986; Trimble, 2010; Witko, 2006; Zusne & Jones, 1989).

Outsiders invariably frame explanations of these traditions in the realm of sorcery, witchcraft, spiritualism, shamanism, magic, superstition, ghosts, illusions, spirituality, and delusions. Cynics and critics most often relegate these "magical" phenomena to "hooey," "hogwash," fallacy, psychiatric conditions, and nonsense. Steeped in cultural imperialism and Eurocentric bias, these pejorative terms and pathologizing explanations are incapable of accurately portraying the experiences of the communities. As Christians (2007) stated, "when rooted in a positivist worldview, explanations of social life are considered incompatible with the renderings offered by the participants themselves" (p. 61).

Regardless of the credibility of the explanations and attributions, the presence of the folk and ancestral traditions and beliefs must be acknowledged because they exist and persist, to some extent, in all cultures. For example, prayer, wearing talismans, superstitious behavior and thoughts, and believing that one can affect outcomes through spells and incantations are widespread and, in fact, commonplace in most cultural groups (e.g., Frazer, 1996; Kiev, 1964; Nicholson, 1987; Torrey, 1986). Most important, these practices and belief systems are resistant to change because they are deeply rooted in the ebb and flow of daily life. Communities, sensing the delegitimization of their knowledge and traditions, often resist interventions, recognizing them as instances of cognitive imperialism (Battiste, 1986, 2007).

Descriptions of nonempirically based sources of causal and correlational explanations often are cast in the realm of magical thinking and are exemplified in the literary genre of magical realism. More often than not, communities' worldviews and practices are pathologized and infantilized, thus reproducing the colonizing ideology that continues to oppress them. From a Western worldview of science, some psychiatrists and psychologists claim that the presence of magical thinking in childhood can continue into adulthood, creating untoward psychological problems such as obsessive–compulsive behavior, depression, psychoses, and bipolar disorders (George & Neufeld, 1987; Serban, 1982).

Across all cultures, rituals, ceremonies, mannerisms, songs, daily routines, and an assortment of related activities give people the feeling that they're not completely helpless and at the whim and mercy of the uncontrollable. The essence of living in a particular culture or community becomes an everyday reality and therefore is not magical or bizarre. What we define and perceive as reality emerges as a complex "web of relationships" that links ecological context, language (vocabulary, linguistic categories, and rules), and human and nonhuman relationships within a particular community; therefore, its contents, meanings, and customs can only be understood within this web (Battiste, 2007, p. 117). Thus, for outsiders steeped in Eurocentric-biased epistemology, what is perceived to be exotic, mysterious, and beyond their knowledge, is genuine for the insiders; what is perceived as magical is commonplace. In essence, the extraordinary is ordinary, and that puzzle often bewilders the researcher and outsider.

Depending on the depth and nature of the relationship outside researchers establish with ethnocultural communities, in time, one comes to realization that what the Western worldview considers to be magical thinking and realism dominate the local worldview. Depending on the researchers' moral principles and value orientations—built on the fundamental ethical principle of "do no harm," or better yet, solidarity—and their willingness to suspend judgments, in time trustworthiness, respect, reverence, rapport, benevolence, and integrity will promote and advance collaborative relations and partnerships with ethnocultural communities (Trimble & Mohatt, 2005). In turn, knowledge, rituals, ceremonies, and belief systems associated with the deep cultural lifeways and thoughtways may be revealed in bits and pieces. From an ethical standpoint of solidarity and community, it is unethical to challenge the legitimacy, validity, value, and influence of what is real for community members. From a methodological perspective, undoubtedly it would be foolhardy and likely lead to the researchers' dismissal and removal. At first, suspicions about the outsiders' willingness to be open minded will quietly surface and as the suspicions intensify the outsiders will be shunned, ignored, spurned, and rebuffed and eventually asked to leave.

Points of Intervention, Points of Contention

As delineated above, communities' suspicions toward outside researchers are fueled by researchers' assumptions and value judgments that undermine the communities' sovereignty and right to self-determination. Within mental health research, self-determination entails recognizing a community's right to have control over how psychological health and maladjustment are defined, assessed, and addressed within their own contexts (Hill, 2005; Trimble et al., 2010). An ethical and multiculturally competent researcher will engage the community in conversation about what the community views as relevant issues within itself that warrant intervention and will respect the community's priorities. Researchers must also assess what are culturally sanctioned points of intervention: Gender role rules, traditional decision-making processes, among other values, may influence the community's views of who is responsible to enact change and who should participate in the intervention process. One will often discover that certain community members and their extended families may not agree on these elements; polling community members helps sort out the discrepancies and points of contention and disagreement. The researchers must also be mindful of intracultural diversity within the communities. Other structural matters, such as who delivers the intervention, where it takes place, and what format is used are also culturally sensitive issues in need of attention.

Knowledge

Culturally competent researchers actively pursue accurate knowledge about the communities with whom they seek to collaborate. Moreover, it is necessary to understand the history of oppressions lived by the community, including the history of exploitation and abuse that nondominant communities have experienced at the hands of individuals steeped in the Western world view of science (L. T. Smith, 1999). What has been the community's experience with researchers in the past? This knowledge is of utmost importance to understand the power differences between the researcher and the community.

Battiste and Henderson (2000) juxtaposed what they called the orthodox context of knowledge, Eurocentrism, with indigenous knowledge. According to these authors, Eurocentric thought is based on four broad assumptions regarding the natural world: (a) the natural world exists independent of any beliefs about it, (b) perceptions may provide an accurate impression of the natural world, (c) linguistic concepts may describe the natural world, and (d) certain rules of inference are reliable means for arriving at new truths about the natural world (p. 23).

Battiste and Henderson (2000) further stated that the perceived rela-tionship between humans and the natural world constitutes the primary differ-ence between indigenous and Eurocentric thought; that is, indigenous thought does not view humanity as separate from the natural world, in contrast to the Eurocentric perspective. These four assumptions about the natural world lead to Eurocentric assumptions, that

> the human mind uses reason to discover that some things are "by nature" right for human beings and that others are created by artificial conven-tion. As the categories imposed by reason are arbitrary, the question is, what impels the mind to analyze the world in one way rather than in another? The generally accepted answer is desire. (p. 27)

Shaky assumptions and desires, therefore, form the foundation for the Eurocentric worldview, as well as all its disciplinary derivatives, especially science. As Foucault (1980) suggested, the underpinnings of scientific state-ments (and procedures) within the modern context are political. L. T. Smith (1999) placed this notion within an indigenous context:

> From an indigenous perspective Western research is more than just research that is located in a positivist tradition. It is research which brings to bear, on any study of indigenous peoples, a cultural orientation, a set of values, a different conceptualization of such things as time, space and subjectivity, different and competing theories of knowledge, highly specialized forms of language, and structures of power. (p. 42)

The differences between Eurocentric and indigenous thought, while abstract by nature, are essential to acknowledge and substantively under-stand when considering contextually and culturally appropriate research skills. Indigenous thought, frequently dismissed as superstitious or magical, affords legitimized space to life forces that are simply unknowable within a Eurocentric system. Other researchers have considered these key differences between Western and indigenous ontological and epistemological founda-tions and the methodologies derived from them, concluding that traditional (Western) methodologies are incapable of fostering social change or further-ing the cause of social justice (Strega, 2005).

Indigenous scholars (Eason & Robbins, 2011; L. T. Smith, 1999) and researchers (Gone & Kirmayer, 2010; Hill, Pace, & Robbins, 2010; Trimble et al., 2010) have engaged in a "discourse of struggle," in which they have identified significant sites of struggle within the academy, communities, local and national government, professional organizations, ethical codes, diagnos-tic criteria and nosology, curricula, and countless other areas. This discourse has served as a road map for those who bridge multiple worlds, live in the margins, or otherwise find themselves needing tools to clear the brush in the overgrown forest of Western values, standards, and intellectual practices.

Skills

Research skills, in the traditional Western sense, are filtered through the lens of Eurocentrism. Researchers trained in Western academic institutions rarely emerge from those institutions with knowledge or skills deemed locally valuable by nondominant groups. Such researchers and the methods they use are tainted by Eurocentric prejudice (Battiste & Henderson, 2000) that ultimately produce and reproduce forms of knowledge that validate and further legitimate Western hegemony, invariably, negating, denying, or silencing local, sacred ethnocultural knowledge, epistemologies, and ontologies.

To conduct their activities ethically, researchers and interventionists must address the historical and present oppressions experienced by the ethnocultural communities, as well as the shortcomings and biases of their own personal and academic experiences. Researchers also must recognize that steadfast ethical principles and codes of conduct that have endured for centuries abound in ethnocultural communities. Consequently, it would behoove the intervention researcher to learn what these principles are and to include them into their research endeavors and relationship with the communities. Tuck and Fine (2007) talked about four quadrants that are crucial to any ethical conversation with indigenous and nondominant communities—preparedness, listening, reflection, and reparation:

> Preparedness involves an intimate epistemological shift, thoughtfulness, and anticipation; listening; humility; and respect. Reflection, an attention that circles back and forward. Reparation requires coming clean, coming out, investing in infrastructure, honoring sovereignty, *un*forgetting. *Un*forgetting can happen within an epistemological frame that rejects individualism, and so doing, occupation. (p. 155)

We have addressed preparedness and reflection throughout this chapter by acknowledging the need for a continuous process of increasing self-awareness and other-awareness. Part of this never-ending process is increasing our knowledge based on the history of oppressions, the communities' struggles, and epistemology. Deconstructing skills are necessary throughout this process; one could argue that thoughtfulness, listening, humility, and communicating respect are skills as well. Perhaps the most controversial yet cardinal point brought up by Tuck and Fine (2007) is reparation. To engage in reparation (and in conversations about it), humility is vital. We have to become aware of, and counter, the hubris that permeates the paradigm that still structures most of academic training. Personal, professional, and cultural humility is essential to honor sovereignty and self-determination in nondominant communities.

The ethical quandaries around cultural adaptations are situated in the midst of these conversations. Western positivist science principles have produced both the body of empirical research in mental health and the criteria that determine what is efficacious, effective, and evidence-based among clinical interventions (Bernal & Scharrón-del Río, 2001). Moreover, most of the interventions that are considered empirically supported or evidence based are built on studies using mostly White, American, middle-class samples. The underrepresentation of ethnic minorities within this body of research is stark (Bernal et al., 2002, 2009; Myers, Echemendia, & Trimble, 1991), and the validity of delivering these interventions within ethnic minority communities divides researchers and clinicians. Some advocate for creating new treatments; others believe in delivering treatments as they are; a third option is to culturally adapt or "attune" existing treatments (Falicov, 2009).

When culturally adapting interventions—and doing research with nondominant groups—the ethical researcher needs to approach the community from a stance that privileges the community's sovereignty and self-determination. Researchers must be prepared to embrace methodological pluralism and integrate the communities in every aspect of the process (Trimble et al., 2010). Research studies and interventions must directly benefit the community in positive ways and respect the community's priorities as well as extend their knowledge of what might be efficacious ways to promote healing and community development and stability.

Because each group, context, and circumstances will be different, there is no fixed step-by-step method of integrating Western science and indigenous methodologies. This is a site of struggle: There is no single model for the integration of Western science and indigenous methodologies (Hill, 2005; Hill et al., 2010). Grande (2007) eloquently described the challenges of this integration when talking about indigenous (Red) epistemology and pedagogy:

> Red pedagogy is not a method or technique to be memorized, implemented, applied, or prescribed. Rather, it is a space of engagement. It is the luminal and intellectual borderlands where indigenous and nonindigenous scholars encounter one another, working to remember, redefine, and reverse the devastation of the original colonialist encounter. Therefore, Red pedagogy is not something one does, but rather a process to engage; it is based on the presumption that ideas are neither borne in isolation nor are they inert. (pp. 134–135)

As researchers and clinicians, we may find ourselves negotiating the crossroads of how to meet the obligations of two or more cultures (Anzaldúa, 1999); thus, we need to develop cognitive and epistemological flexibility. In addition, we may become painfully aware of how academic validation is still primarily located within the Western positivist paradigm: Quantitative methodology is still privileged, and scholarly pursuits (including publications and tenure) are evaluated against the criteria of "rigorous science" (Trimble et al., 2010). Conducting ethical and culturally competent intervention research with ethnocultural populations can entail a level of involvement that may be personally and professionally demanding.

Various authors have offered directions that can guide us in this process. From a community psychology perspective, D'Augelli (2003) stated that it is quite a challenge to develop culturally sensitive methodology; he called for an integration of qualitative and quantitative methodologies to achieve strong cultural analysis, as well as the "integration of ideographic and nomothetic perspectives." He went on to say that

> the challenge is one faced by any cultural analyst: The systematic deconstruction of embedded meanings must be followed by a reconstruction of some kind. There are, unfortunately, no scripts for the reconstruction process except for the requirement of the use of multiple sources of data gathered in diverse ways as well as methods to determine the correspondence of interpreted meanings by different observers. (p. 348)

Martín-Baró (1998) advocated for a psychology anchored in liberating practices that is, above all, committed to the well-being of the oppressed. Ellis (2007) talked about relational ethics, in which maintaining and nurturing the conversation, engagement, and bond with the community is privileged. Glesne (2007) urged us to rethink research as solidarity, promoting an ethic of community and sharing that entails "communal decision making rather than negotiating individual to individual" (p. 174).

L. T. Smith (1999) offered a number of questions that need to be addressed from the onset when conducting research in a cross-cultural context. These include, For whom is this study worthy and relevant? Who says so? Who benefits? What knowledge will the community gain from this study? What knowledge will the researcher gain? What are some possible negative outcomes (including individual, collective, and cultural levels)? How can negative outcomes be eliminated or effectively addressed? and, To whom is the researcher accountable?

To seriously and systemically consider these questions might require recreating how academia develops and views its community partnerships, how it views itself within the community, and how the community perceives academia (Martín-Baró, 1998; G. H. Smith, 2003; L. T. Smith, 1999). Such established institutional bodies and traditions, including IRBs, informed consent guidelines, and definitions and standards of scholarship and productivity, would have to be rethought. Our elders in our fields—senior and established researchers and faculty—would have to take the lead in promoting these changes.

CONCLUSION

The ethical researcher and interventionist balances considerations to achieve both strong science and optimal benefit to the persons, community, or both, being served. Cultural adaptation is similar to a process of translation from one language to another: Although there will probably be some analogous concepts and processes between languages (cultures), there will be others that exist in only one of them. Under the assumption of universality, the dominant culture tends to impose its terms and concepts onto the nondominant one. Ethical intervention researchers will resist such practices and, instead, privilege the ethnocultural communities' knowledge, practices, and worldview. What to do if there is no translation possible? Ethical and multiculturally competent researchers and interventionists must start from the communities' perceptions of the problem and its solutions, engaging the communities in solidarity and respecting their sovereignty and right to self-determination.

REFERENCES

American Indian Law Center. (1999). *Model tribal research code, with materials for tribal regulation for research and checklist for Indian health boards* (3rd ed.). Albuquerque, NM: American Indian Law Center.

American Psychological Association. (2003). Guidelines on multicultural education, training, research, practice, and organizational change for psychologists. *American Psychologist, 58,* 377–402. doi:10.1037/0003-066X.58.5.377

Anzaldúa, G. (1999). *Borderlands/la frontera: The new mestiza* (2nd ed.). San Francisco, CA: Aunt Lute Books.

Battiste, M. (1986). Micmac literacy and cognitive assimilation. In J. Barman, Y. Hébert, & D. McCaskill (Eds.), *Indian education in Canada: The legacy* (pp. 23–45). Vancouver, British Columbia, Canada: University of British Columbia Press.

Battiste, M. (2007). Research ethics for protecting indigenous knowledge and heritage: Institutional and researcher responsibilities. In N. K. Denzin & M. D. Giardina (Eds.), *Ethical futures in qualitative research: Decolonizing the politics of knowledge* (pp. 111–132). Walnut Creek, CA: Left Coast Press.

Battiste, M., & Henderson, J. Y. (2000). *Protecting indigenous knowledge: A global challenge.* Saskatoon, Saskatchewan, Canada: Purich Press.

Beauvais, F., & Trimble, J. E. (1992). The role of the researcher in evaluating American Indian alcohol and other drug abuse prevention programs. In M. Orlandi (Ed.), *Cultural competence for evaluators working with ethnic minority communities: A guide for alcohol and other drug abuse prevention practitioners* (pp. 173–201). Rockville, MD: Office for Substance Abuse Prevention, U.S. Department of Health and Human Services.

Bernal, G., & Domenech Rodríguez, M. (2009). Advances in Latino family research: Cultural adaptations of evidence-based interventions. *Family Process, 48*, 169–178. doi:10.1111/j.1545-5300.2009.01275.x

Bernal, G., Jiménez-Chafey, M. I., & Domenech Rodríguez, M. (2009). Cultural adaptation of treatments: A resource for considering culture in evidence-based practice. *Professional Psychology: Research and Practice, 40*, 361–368. doi:10.1037/a0016401

Bernal, G., Trimble, J., Burlew, K., & Leong, F. (Eds.). (2002). *Handbook of racial and ethnic minority psychology.* Thousand Oaks, CA: Sage.

Bernal, G., & Scharrón-del Río, M. R. (2001). Are empirically supported treatments (EST) valid for ethnic minorities? *Cultural Diversity & Ethnic Minority Psychology, 7*, 328–342. doi:10.1037/1099-9809.7.4.328

Castellano, M. B. (2004). Ethics of aboriginal research. *Journal of Aboriginal Health, 1*, 98–114.

Castro-Blanco, D. R. (2005). Cultural sensitivity in conventional psychotherapy: A comment on Martínez-Taboas (2005). *Psychotherapy: Theory, Research, & Practice, 42*, 14–16. doi:10.1037/0033-3204.42.1.14

Christians, C. G. (2007). Neutral science and the ethics of resistance. In N. K. Denzin & M. D. Giardina (Eds.), *Ethical futures in qualitative research: Decolonizing the politics of knowledge* (pp. 47–66). Walnut Creek, CA: Left Coast Press.

D'Augelli, A. R. (2003). Coming out in community psychology: Personal narrative and disciplinary change. *American Journal of Community Psychology, 31*, 343–354. doi:10.1023/A:1023923123720

Denzin, N. K., & Giardina, M. D. (Eds.) (2007). *Ethical futures in qualitative research: Decolonizing the politics of knowledge.* Walnut Creek, CA: Left Coast Press.

Domenech-Rodríguez, M., & Wieling, E. (2004). Developing culturally appropriate evidence based treatments for interventions with ethnic minority populations. In M. Rastogi & E. Wieling (Eds.), *Voices of color: First person accounts of ethnic minority therapists* (pp. 313–333). Thousand Oaks, CA: Sage.

Droge, D. (2005). Race science, academic freedom, and the limits of scientific self-correction. *Free Speech Yearbook, 42*, 30–40.

Eason, A., & Robbins, R. R. (2011). *Walking in beauty.* Manuscript in preparation, University of Oklahoma.

Ellis, C. (2007). "I just want to tell my story": Mentoring students about relational ethics in writing about intimate others. In N. K. Denzin & M. D. Giardina (Eds.), *Ethical futures in qualitative research: Decolonizing the politics of knowledge* (pp. 209–227). Walnut Creek, CA: Left Coast Press.

Falicov, C. J. (2009). Commentary: On the wisdom and challenges of culturally attuned treatments for Latinos. *Family Process, 48*, 292–309. doi:10.1111/j.1545-5300.2009.01282.x

Fisher, C. B., Hoagwood, K., Boyce, C., Duster, T., Frank, D. A., Grisso, T., . . . Zayas, L. H. (2002). Research ethics for mental health science involving ethnic minority children and youths. *American Psychologist, 57,* 1024–1040. doi:10.1037/0003-066X.57.12.1024

Foucault, M. (1980). *Power and knowledge.* New York, NY: Pantheon Books.

Freilich, M. (Ed.). (1970). *Marginal natives: Anthropologist at work.* New York, NY: Harper & Row.

Frazer, J. G. (1996). *The Golden Bough: A study in magic and religion* (3rd ed.). London, England: Macmillan.

George, L., & Neufeld, R. W. J. (1987). Magical ideation and schizophrenia. *Journal of Consulting and Clinical Psychology, 55,* 778–779. doi:10.1037/0022-006X.55.5.778

Glesne, C. (2007). Research as solidarity. In N. K. Denzin & M. D. Giardina (Eds.), *Ethical futures in qualitative research: Decolonizing the politics of knowledge* (pp. 169–178). Walnut Creek, CA: Left Coast Press.

Grande, S. (2007). Red pedagogy: Indigenizing inquiry or, the un-methodology. In N. K. Denzin & M. D. Giardina (Eds.), *Ethical futures in qualitative research: Decolonizing the politics of knowledge* (pp. 133–143). Walnut Creek, CA: Left Coast Press.

Gone, J. P., & Kirmayer, L. J. (2010). On the wisdom of considering context and culture in psychopathology. In T. Millon, R. Krueger, & E. Simonsen (Eds.), *Contemporary directions in psychopathology: Toward the DSM–V, ICD–11, and beyond* (2nd ed., pp. 72–96). New York, NY: Guilford Press.

Hill, J. S. (2005). *Decolonizing personality assessment: An examination of the Minnesota Multiphasic Personality Inventory—2.* Unpublished doctoral dissertation, University of Oklahoma, Norman.

Hill, J. S., Pace, T. M., & Robbins, R. R. (2010). Decolonizing personality assessment and honoring indigenous voices: A critical examination of the MMPI–2. *Cultural Diversity and Ethnic Minority Psychology, 16,* 16–25. doi:10.1037/a0016110

Jason, L., Keys, C., Suarez-Balcazar, Y., & Davis, M. M. (Eds.) (2004). *Participatory community research: Theories and methods in action.* Washington, DC: American Psychological Association.

Jones, J. H. (1993). *Bad blood: The Tuskegee syphilis experiment* (rev. ed.). New York, NY: Free Press.

Jorgensen, C. (1995). The African American critique of White supremacist science. *Journal of Negro Education, 64,* 232–242. doi:10.2307/2967205. Retrieved from http://eric.ed.gov

Katz, R., Biesele, M., & St. Denis, V. (1997). *Healing makes our hearts happy.* Rochester, VT: Inner Traditions.

Kelso, D., & Attneave, C. (Eds.). (1981). *Bibliography of North American Indian mental health.* Westport, CT: Greenwood.

Kiev, A. (1964). *Magic, faith. and healing.* New York, NY: Free Press.

Martín-Baró, I. (1998). *Psicología de la liberación* [*Liberation psychology*]. Madrid, Spain: Editorial Trotta.

Martínez-Taboas, A. (2005a). The plural world of culturally sensitive psychotherapy: A response to Castro-Blanco's (2005) comments. *Psychotherapy, 42*, 17–19. doi:10.1037/0033-3204.42.1.17

Martínez-Taboas, A. (2005b). Psychogenic seizures in an *espiritismo* context: The role of culturally sensitive psychotherapy. *Psychotherapy: Theory, Research, Practice, Training, 42*, 6–13. doi:10.1037/0033-3204.42.1.6

Mead, M. (1959). *An anthropologist at work: Writings of Ruth Benedict.* Boston, MA: Houghlin-Mifflin.

Mohatt, G. V. (1989). The community as informant or collaborator? *American Indian and Alaska Native Mental Health Research, 2*, 64–70. doi:10.5820/aian.0203.1989.64

Mohatt, G. V., & Thomas, L. R. (2006). "I wonder, why would you do it that way?" Ethical dilemmas in doing participatory research with Alaska Native communities. In J. E. Trimble & C. B. Fisher (Eds.), *Handbook of ethical and responsible research with ethnocultural populations and communities* (pp. 93–116). Thousand Oaks, CA: Sage. doi:10.4135/9781412986168.n6

Montero, M. (2009). Community action and research as citizenship construction. *American Journal of Community Psychology, 43*, 149–161. doi:10.1007/s10464-008-9224-6

Montero, M. (2003). *Teoría y práctica de la psicología comunitaria. La tensión entre comunidad y sociedad [Theory and practice in community psychology: Tensions between community and society].* Buenos Aires, Brazil: Editorial Paidós.

Moodley, R., & West, W. (2005). *Integrating traditional healing practices into counseling and psychotherapy.* Thousand Oaks, CA: Sage.

Myers, H. F., Echemendia, R. J., & Trimble, J. E. (1991). The need for training ethnic minority psychologists. In H. F. Myers, P. Wohlford, L. P. Guzman, R. J. Echemendia, & V. Montenegro (Eds.), *Ethnic minority perspectives on clinical training and services in psychology* (pp. 3–11). Washington, DC: American Psychological Association. doi:10.1037/10102-001

National Health and Medical Research Council. (2003). *Values and ethics: Guidelines for ethical conduct in Aboriginal and Torres Strait Islander health research.* Canberra, Australian Capital Territory, Australia: Author.

Nicholson, S. (Ed.). (1987). *Shaminism.* Wheaton, IL: Theosophical Publishing House.

Powdermaker, H. (1966). *Stranger and friend: The way of the anthropologist.* New York, NY: Norton.

Reverby, S. (2009). *The infamous syphilis study and its legacy: Examining Tuskegee.* Chapel Hill: University of North Carolina Press.

Rogler, L. H. (2008). *Barrio professors.* Walnut Creek, CA: Left Coast Press.

Rosengren, K., Johnson, C., & Harris, P. (Eds.). (2000). *Imaging the impossible: Magical, scientific, and religious thinking in children.* New York, NY: Cambridge University Press.

Serban, G. (1982). *The tyranny of magical thinking.* New York, NY: Dutton.

Smith, G. H. (2003, December). *Kaupapa Maori theory: Theorizing indigenous trans-formation of education and schooling.* Paper presented at the Kaupapa Maori Symposium at the New Zealand Association for Research in Education/Australian Association for Research in Education Joint Conference, Auckland, NZ. Retrieved from http://www.aare.edu.au/03pap/pih03342.pdf

Smith, L. T. (1999). Decolonizing methodologies: Research and indigenous peoples. London, England: Zed Books.

Strega, S. (2005). The view from the poststructural margins: Epistemology and methodology reconsidered. In L. Brown & S. Strega (Eds.), *Research as resistance: Critical, Indigenous, and anti-oppressive approaches* (pp. 199–235). Toronto, Ontario, Canada: Canadian Scholars' Press.

Subbotsky, E. (2010). *Magic and the mind: Mechanisms, functions, and development of magical thinking and behavior.* New York, NY: Oxford University Press.

Sue, D. W., Carter, R. T., Casas, J. M., Fouad, N. A., Ivey, A. E., Jensen, M., . . . Vazquez-Nutall, E. (1998). *Multicultural counseling competencies: Individual and organizational development.* Thousand Oaks, CA: Sage.

Sullivan, L. E. (Ed.). (2000). *Native religions and cultures of North American.* New York, NY: Continuum International.

Torrey, E. F. (1986). *Witchdoctors and psychiatrists: The common roots of psychotherapy and its future.* New York, NY: Harper & Row.

Trickett, E. J., & Espino, S. L. (2004). Collaboration and social inquiry: Multiple meanings of a construct and its role in creating useful and valid knowledge. *American Journal of Community Psychology, 34,* 1–69. doi:10.1023/B:AJCP.0000040146.32749.7d

Trickett, E. J., Kelly, J. G., & Vincent, T. A. (1985). The spirit of ecological inquiry in community research. In E. Susskind & D. Klein (Eds.), *Community research: Methods, paradigms, and applications* (pp. 331–406). New York, NY: Praeger.

Trickett, E. J., & Mitchell, R. E. (1993). An ecological metaphor for research and intervention in community psychology. In M. S. Gibbs, J. R. Lachenmeyer, & J. Sigal (Eds.), *Community psychology: Theoretical and empirical approaches* (2nd ed., pp. 13–28). New York, NY: Wiley.

Trimble, J. (2003). Cultural competence and cultural sensitivity. In M. Prinstein & M. Patterson (Eds.), *The portable mentor: Expert guide to a successful career in psychology* (pp. 13–32). New York, NY: Kluwer Academic/Plenum.

Trimble, J. E. (2009). No itinerant researchers tolerated: Principled and ethical perspectives and research with North American Indian communities [Commentary]. *Ethos, 36,* 379–382.

Trimble, J. E. (2010). Bear spends time in our dreams now: Magical thinking and spiritual considerations in counselling theory and practice. *Counselling Psychology Quarterly, 23,* 241–253. doi:10.1080/09515070.2010.505735

Trimble, J. E., & Bagwell, W. M. (Eds.). (1995). *North American Indians and Alaska Natives: Abstracts of the psychological and behavioral literature, 1967–1994.* Washington, DC: American Psychological Association.

Trimble, J. E., & Fisher, C. B. (Eds.). (2005). *Handbook of ethical considerations in conducting research with ethnocultural populations and communities.* Thousand Oaks, CA: Sage.

Trimble, J. E. & Mohatt, G. V. (2005). Coda: The virtuous and responsible researcher in another culture. In J. E. Trimble & C. B. Fisher, (Eds.), *The handbook of ethical research with ethnocultural populations and communities* (pp. 325–334). Thousand Oaks, CA: Sage.

Trimble, J. E., Scharrón-del Río, M. R., & Bernal, G. (2010). The itinerant researcher: Ethical and methodological issues in conducting cross-cultural mental health research. In D. C. Jack & A. Ali (Eds.), *Silencing the self across cultures: Depression and gender in the social world* (pp. 73–98). New York, NY: Oxford University Press.

Tuck, E., & Fine, M. (2007). Inner angles: A range of ethical responses to/with indigenous/decolonizing theories. In N. K. Denzin & M. D. Giardina (Eds.), *Ethical futures in qualitative research: Decolonizing the politics of knowledge* (pp. 145–168). Walnut Creek, CA: Left Coast Press.

Welch, K. (2002). *The Bell Curve* and the politics of negrophobia. *Race and intelligence: Separating science from myth* (pp. 177–198). Mahwah, NJ: Erlbaum. Retrieved from http://apa.org/psycinfo/

Witko, T. (Ed.). (2006). *Mental health care for urban Indians: Clinical insights from Native practitioners.* Washington, DC: American Psychological Association. doi:10.1037/11422-000

Zusne, L., & Jones, W. H. (1989). *Anomalistic psychology: A study of magical thinking* (2nd ed.). Hillsdale, NJ: Erlbaum.

II

APPLICATIONS AND ADVANCING FRAMEWORKS

4

CULTURE FIRST: LESSONS LEARNED ABOUT THE IMPORTANCE OF THE CULTURAL ADAPTATION OF COGNITIVE BEHAVIOR TREATMENT INTERVENTIONS FOR BLACK CARIBBEAN YOUTH

GUERDA NICOLAS AND BILLIE SCHWARTZ

It is estimated that approximately 20% of the children in the United States, or 13.7 million, have a diagnosable mental disorder and that about two thirds of these children do not receive any mental health care (Center for Mental Health Services, 2005), which ultimately affects their development and functioning (U.S. Department of Health and Human Services [USD-HHS], Public Health Service, Office of the Surgeon General, 2000). Current census data estimate that by the year 2050 ethnocultural minorities will make up more than 50% of the U.S. population (U.S. Census Bureau, 2001, 2010). This demographic shift calls for mental health interventions that integrate the cultural values and strengths of individuals, including children and adolescents, the most ethnically diverse segment of the society (Weisz, Sandler, Durlak, & Anton, 2005). Many researchers are successfully responding to this need by developing evidence-based mental health treatments for children and adolescents. Although evidence-based treatments (EBTs) have gained popularity in the field for their overall effectiveness, some researchers have begun to question their utility and validity for ethnically diverse populations, highlighting the need to ensure that existing treatments are culturally appropriate for diverse populations (Bernal, Trimble, Burlew, & Leong, 2003; Miranda, 2000).

These inquiries have led to the development of strategies for culturally adapting EBTs for different ethnic and cultural populations (Bernal Rosselló, & Martínez 1997; Miranda, 2000). In this chapter, we provide an overview of the mental health and service utilization of ethnically diverse youth, along with a review of literature on EBTs. We also demonstrate evidence that this measure needed to be culturally adapted to work effectively with Haitian American youth. The chapter concludes with a summary of the methods used and lessons learned in the process of culturally adapting an evidence-based group treatment for Haitian American adolescents diagnosed with depression.

AN OVERVIEW OF THE MENTAL HEALTH AND SERVICE UTILIZATION OF ETHNOCULTURAL AND IMMIGRANT YOUTHS

Ethnocultural adolescents experience psychological problems such as depression, low self-esteem, anxiety, and loneliness (Chiu & Ring, 1998; James, 1997; National Alliance on Mental Illness, 2003). Among immigrants, Pumariega, Rothe, and Pumariega (2005) noted that the main mental health problems reported are depression and anxiety disorders, particularly post-traumatic stress disorders. Other mental health risk factors for ethnocultural and immigrant adolescents include poverty, lack of education, subsequent unemployment, low self-esteem, and poor physical health (Fenta, Hyman, & Noh, 2004). In addition to these documented risk factors for mental health issues among immigrants, many other barriers prevent their access to services, including lack of health insurance; limited access to mental health services in some insurance plans; absence of appropriately trained providers on insurance panels; lack of care appropriate for children and adolescents; geographic inaccessibility; fear of stigma; and differences in language, cultural attitudes, and beliefs between service providers and recipients.

In addition to the risk factors identified in the preceding paragraph, research has shown that insensitivity toward cultural experiences (Hall, 2001) and stigma (USDHHS, 1999) are most likely the strongest causes for the underutilization of mental health services by ethnically diverse populations. The lack of integration of culture in treatment delivery for ethnically diverse and immigrant populations decreases the retention rate for mental health treatment (S. Sue, 1998). Mental health providers and researchers have a professional and social responsibility to address the underutilization of mental health services and reduce dropout rates among ethnically diverse and immigrant populations. Further, they also have a responsibility to better understand the impact of underutilization among ethnic youth. In general, ethnocultural and immigrant adolescents have less access to adequate mental and physical health care, are receiving a poorer quality of mental health services, and in fact are disadvantaged by having fewer and less qualified culturally relevant and skilled clinicians to aid them in their emotional struggles (Davis & Stevenson, 2006; President's New Freedom Commission on Mental Health, 2003).

AN OVERVIEW OF EVIDENCE-BASED TREATMENT

In this section, we summarize some of the gaps in mental health interventions, methods for addressing these gaps, and a rationale for implementing an EBT to address these gaps.

Trends and Gaps in Mental Health Interventions

In 1994, S. Sue, Zane, and Young noted the importance of psychotherapy research with communities of color in advancing the field of psychology and psychotherapy. Despite such recommendations and the many benefits cited by researchers (Bernal, Bonilla, & Bellido, 1995), most treatment research with adults and children did not permit generalization to ethnocultural populations. In 2003, the "Guidelines on Multicultural Education, Training, Research, Practice, and Organizational Change for Psychologists" urged professionals to incorporate culture into all aspects of practice (American Psychological Association [APA], 2003). There are several reasons for incorporating cultural factors in the development of interventions, including cultural relevance and importance from the clinician's perspective (Bernal & Scharrón-Del-Río, 2001; Smith, Domenech-Rodríguez, & Bernal, 2011), service utilization (Gonzalez et al., 2010), and treatment preference (Constantino, Malgady, & Rogler, 1994). Taken together, these findings suggest that ethnically diverse populations respond differently to psychotherapy interventions than do their White American counterparts (Huey & Polo, 2008) and therefore require cultural adaptation both necessary and sufficient for clinical use.

A recent review of the clinical trials mental health literature documented the lack of integration of culture in mental health research (USDHHS, 2001) and the lack of availability of efficacious treatments for ethnocultural populations (Gray-Little & Kaplan, 2000; Huey & Polo, 2008; Miranda, Azocar, Organista, Muñoz, & Lieberman, 1996; Tharp, 1991). Hence, a growing trend in psychological research has been a focus on the cultural adaptation of treatment and measurements for use with ethnically diverse populations, particularly for treatment efficacy and ethnic minority youth (Huey & Polo, 2008). Other barriers and stigma include language because the vast majority of instruments designed to assess mental health outcomes in the United States have been developed for English speakers (Bullinger et al., 1998). In short, from the perspective of the conventional scientific model, we know very little, if anything, about the efficacy of treatments for ethnically diverse individuals (Bernal & Scharrón-Del-Río, 2001). However, the growing development of methods and strategies for integrating culture into mental health treatment for ethnically diverse populations is coming through EBTs, which seek to promote the use of efficacious interventions for youths (Cortés et al., 2007; Huey & Polo, 2008).

Addressing Gaps in Mental Health Treatment: The Rise of Evidence-Based Practice in Psychology

The lack of efficacious mental health treatment for children and adolescents led to increasing advocacy among researchers and clinicians to develop and implement treatments leading to positive outcomes among youth (Flynn, 2005). Researchers responded to this challenge and began designing and evaluating evidence-based interventions known as evidence-based practice in psychology (EBPP) specifically for youths. *EBPP* is defined as therapies and techniques proven to be effective through research (Rishel, 2007).

A significant limitation of EBPP is its applicability for different ethnocultural and immigrant groups (Sue, Arrendondo, & McDavis, 1992). Essentially, the majority of EBTs do not take into account multicultural concepts in the development, implementation, and evaluation of interventions, nor do they include ethnocultural groups in the study protocol (Bernal & Scharrón-Del-Río, 2001; Mays & Albee, 1992; Miranda, Nakamura, & Bernal, 2003). When EBTs do include ethnocultural groups in research and clinical trials, there are only small sample sizes or participants who are grouped together into a single "minority" group, which does not take into account the diversity between and within different ethnic and immigrant populations (Weisz et al., 2005).

In the face of these issues, the APA Presidential Task Force on Evidence Based Practice (2006) attempted to stress the importance of culture within the definition of EBPP. The task force highlighted that future EBTs need to address culture by requiring that researchers and practitioners take into account diverse patient characteristics (e.g., gender, culture, ethnicity, race, religious beliefs, sexual orientation) because these characteristics influence personality, values, worldviews, relationships, psychopathology and attitudes toward treatment. Hence, the task force recognized that culture influences not only the nature and expression of psychopathology but also patients' understanding of psychological and physical health and illness. Although the APA task force report stresses the importance of culture, it provides no clear method to evaluate the appropriateness of an EBT or EBPP for a particular group (e.g., ethnocultural; immigrant; lesbian, gay, bisexual, and transgendered). Models, guidelines, and strategies developed by many researchers for integrating culture in EBPPs and EBTs with various ethnocultural populations are useful in evaluating existing practices and treatments (Bernal et al., 1995; Rosselló & Bernal, 1996; Smith et al, 2011; Weisz et al., 2005).

The ecological validity and culturally sensitive framework (EVF) developed by Bernal and colleagues (1995) focuses on eight culturally sensitive elements: language, person, metaphors, concepts, goals, methods, and context (see Chapters 2, 5, 8, and 12, this volume, for more details on this framework). EVF has been successfully used to culturally adapt cognitive behavior therapies (CBTs) for depressed Puerto Rican adolescents (Bernal et al., 1995; Bernal & Sáez-Santiago, 2006). The results of these studies indicated that adapting CBT interventions for Puerto Rican adolescents was effective in reducing depression symptoms. Based on these studies, it would follow that adapting depression treatments to meet the specific needs of special populations is not only valuable but also necessary for both epidemiological accuracy and clinical effectiveness.

In the next section, we describe the process and outcome of using the EVF to culturally adapt the Adolescent Coping With Depression Course (ACDC) with Haitian adolescents. The process included developing a partnership with the community, training the selected focus group leaders, conducting focus group sessions with Haitian adolescents, and integrating focus group data in the final treatment manual. In addition, we sought to develop strategies on how best to deliver the treatment and to understand cultural factors that are likely to engage and retain Haitian American youths in mental health treatment.

Rationale for Use of Cognitive–Behavioral Therapy With Haitian American Adolescents

The effectiveness of cognitive–behavioral models for youths has been reported in a number of studies (Brent et al., 1997; Curry, 2001; Lewinsohn, Clarke, Hops, & Andrews, 1990; Stark et al., 1996; Weiss, 2004). Specifically, reviews of psychotherapy for the treatment of adolescent depressive disorders provide empirical support for the benefits of CBT over other forms of treatment (Brent et al., 1997; Clarke, Hawkins, Murphy, & Sheeber, 1995; Reinecke, Ryan, & DuBois, 1998). Brent and Poling (1997) developed and tested a CBT manual for depressed youth and found that the adolescents in the individual CBT conditions demonstrated marked improvement from pre- to posttreatment as demonstrated by reported lower rates of major depression disorder compared with individual nondirective supportive therapy (17.1%

vs. 42.4%) and a higher rate of remission than systemic behavior family therapy (37.9%) or nondirective supportive therapy (39.4%). CBT interventions with depressed youth have been replicated in a number of studies (Clarke, Rohde, Lewinsohn, Hops, & Seeley, 1999; March et al., 2004) with similar results. Although there is evidence for the efficacy of CBT with adolescents, there is no known study focused on Haitian youths.

The Treatment: The Adolescent Coping With Depression Course

The ACDC is a psychoeducational, cognitive–behavioral intervention for adolescent with depression. The current version consists of twelve 2-hour sessions conducted over an 8-week period. The intervention is designed for use with groups of five to 10 adolescents, and the sessions are divided into three major themes: how thoughts (Sessions 1–4), daily activities (Sessions 5–8), and interactions with other people (Sessions 9–12) influence mood. An important feature of this intervention is that it is nonstigmatizing because the treatment is presented and conducted as a class, not as therapy. During treatment sessions a group leader teaches the adolescents skills for controlling their depression. Some of the topics covered in the class are relaxation, pleasant events, negative thoughts, social skills, communication, and problem solving. At the start of the program, each client is provided with a student workbook consisting of homework assignments, quizzes, and other documents that reinforce the materials learned from the class. The class times consist of individual and group activities around the different topics.

A variety of studies have demonstrated the efficacy of the ACDC with adolescents (Clarke et al., 1999; Rohde, Lewinsohn, & Seeley, 1994). The initial study (Clarke et al., 1995) was conducted with 21 adolescents, 14 of whom met research diagnostic criteria for either major depression or intermittent depression at intake. From intake to posttreatment, the mean depression scores of the treated clinically depressed adolescents dropped significantly from 15.0 to 4.1 on the Beck Depression Inventory (Clarke et al., 1995). Furthermore, these same adolescents did not meet criteria for any affective disorders at the end of treatment. In the second outcome study (Lewinsohn, Clarke, Hops, Andrews, & Williams, 1990), a total of 59 clinically depressed adolescents were randomly assigned to one of three conditions: (a) a cognitive–behavioral, psychoeducational group for adolescents ($n = 21$); (b) an identical group for adolescents, plus a separate group for parents ($n = 19$); and (c) a waiting-list control group ($n = 19$). Overall, multivariate analyses demonstrated significant pre- to posttreatment changes in all dependent variables across treatment conditions. The course has been adapted for depressed Puerto Rican adolescents and tested against a control group (Rosselló & Bernal, 1999). A moderate effect size (0.43) was obtained for the group receiving the adapted ACDC course, suggesting that the average treated participant exhibited fewer depressive symptoms than those not treated.

Methods Used to Culturally Adapt the Adolescent Coping With Depression Course

As previously mentioned, the EVF was used to culturally adapt the ACDC because it highlights researchers' need to assess multiple components, including the language, metaphors, context, concepts, goals, methods, and contexts of an intervention for a particular cultural group. For our cultural adaptation, Bernal and colleagues' (1995) method was used through an integration of participatory action research methods (Nicolas, Arntz, Hirsch, & Schmiedigen, 2009), including a focus on community partnership, the use of advisory board members, and the use of community stakeholders (Domenech-Rodríguez & Wieling, 2004).

Community Partnership

Community partnerships are essential to long-lasting and valuable intervention projects. As such, we took the necessary steps and subsequent time to develop relationships with several community agencies and schools in the area before beginning the intervention. Through the use of this bottom-up approach, the combined collaboration of researchers, agency directions, school principals, and teachers helped to produce multiple prevention and intervention programs based on community needs. Community partners and academic researchers alike worked together in all phases of project development—from design to implementation to evaluation.

Selection and Training of Focus Group Leaders

Focus group leaders were trained graduate mental health counseling students with prior experience working with adolescents with mental health needs. They were trained on a variety of topics through lectures, group discussions, and exercises during two 6-hour sessions focusing on enhancing the group leaders' awareness about diversity and cross-cultural research. During these meetings, the group leaders were provided the opportunity to discuss their experiences, assumptions, and fears regarding working with immigrant and culturally diverse adolescents as well as to reflect on and share their own diverse identity in small- and large-group discussions. Further trainings focused on the ACDC treatment manual as well as a summary of the culture, values, immigration history, role of family and religion, and migration history of Haitians. Subsequent to these trainings, group leaders were given homework to read related to diversity, culturally sensitive research, Haitian culture, and focus group methodology.

Focus Group Methodology

The standard method of focus groups (Krueger, 1994) includes the use of two group facilitators, a leader for the discussion, and a facilitator (a note taker) to document the process and content of the group sessions. In total, there were four focus group meetings that covered topics such as introduction to a scientific project, cultural conceptions of depression, appropriate treatments for depression, and manual review following the EVF categories. Agendas and topic guides about each of the focus group sessions were developed prior to the meetings, and summary analyses were developed after each session.

Focus Group Advisory Board

Maintaining best efforts to include community partners throughout the process, the researchers compiled an advisory board. Several stakeholders in the community were invited to be members of the advisory board, and the group consisted of a teacher, a director of a community agency, a pastor from a Christian church, and a parent. The board members met quarterly with the lead investigator to provide feedback about the research plan. In addition, the advisory board helped to have a better perspective on the influence of cultural factors such as immigration and acculturation on the results, which were then reported back to the research team.

Focus Group Participants

To create a project that was grounded in the perspectives of the community, we first reached out to targeted community partners, such as certain school personnel. These recruits were asked to identify potential people for the focus groups. The research team then contacted and interviewed each participant to see if he or she met the criteria (e.g., Haitian American or Haitian immigrant, ages 13–18, fluent in English) prior to final selections.

On meeting days, each adolescent and his or her guardian were provided a packet that contained a description of the project as well as the process of the focus group meeting for the day. The key documents, such as the consent form and demographic information, were translated into French and Creole to be culturally sensitive to the language needs of the clients and their parents. In addition to obtaining written consent or assent, we required additional consent regarding the use of video- and audiotaping. In summary, a total of 16 Haitian American adolescents (ages 14–17) participated in the focus group meetings. The adolescents were then divided into two mixed-gender groups of eight. Each focus group lasted approximately 90 minutes. After each session, transportation vouchers (if needed) and a catered meal were provided as compensation for participating in the study.

Data Collected From the Focus Group Meetings

After parental consent and participant assent were obtained, participants attended the group sessions and discussed a review of inclusion and exclusion criteria. All participants were administered a demographic questionnaire to obtain information on ethnicity, gender, age, level of education, marital status, proficiency in English, years in the United States, nativity, literacy, experience seeking mental health services, and religious affiliation. The meeting concluded with a discussion of the day's proceedings and follow-up questions. This sequence of proceedings has been shown to be effective with focus group participants (Morgan, Krueger, & King 1998).

As previously mentioned, each session focused on different topics: In Sessions 1 and 2, participants were asked to talk about how depression symptoms might manifest among Haitian adolescents, including perceptions of precipitating factors of depression and how these symptoms should be treated. For example, in the first group meeting, the participants were asked to discuss the concept of *gaz*, a symptom often used by Haitians to discuss their mood (Nicolas et al., 2007). Given the cultural difference and relevance of this term, participants were asked to discuss their knowledge regarding this concept, any observations of individuals experiencing it, and their thoughts on adolescents' experience of such a symptom. In Session 2, participants were asked about their perception of Haitian adolescents' experience of depression with respect to symptoms manifestations and etiology.

In preparation for the third group meeting, participants were given materials on the EVF and the ACDC treatment manual to take home to review. All participants were asked to write questions or comments regarding difficulties comprehending the material and the fit of the content to their experiences. In addition, participants were asked to examine the parts of the ACDC program including sessions, homework assignments, and examples for relevance and continuity. The facilitators requested that the participants create their own wording and examples for any items they had difficulties with and also that they keep a record of any items they changed for discussion at the next meeting. A research assistant contacted each participant to remind him or her of the meeting, the homework assignment of reviewing the materials, and the importance of bringing his or her notes to the next session.

Sessions 3 and 4 were focused on an evaluation of the intervention, ethnic minority youths' perceptions of barriers to mental health treatment, challenges that mental health professionals face working with ethnic minority youths, and best strategies to use to ensure treatment adherence and reduce dropouts. Two sessions were scheduled to allow for a comprehensive review of all course material as well as for in-group processing of the manual changes. Each of the adolescents came to the following session with his or her reviewed treatment manual and suggestions. During Session 3, the first four areas of the EVF (language, person, metaphors, and content) were discussed, and the last four areas (concepts, goals, methods, and context) were discussed during Session 4. During these sessions, participants took turns sharing their perspectives about the convergence and divergence of the ACDC manual with Haitian culture and Haitian adolescents. Observation notes were obtained from the focus groups, and all materials were transcribed. At the end of the focus group meetings, all materials were returned to the researchers, and a summary table with each of the elements was created, including specific comments and recommendations from each of the participants. Also, areas in which there was at least 50% agreement among all of the participants were revised in the adapted ACDC manual. Participants' notes and reflections on the treatment were reviewed during the fourth group meeting.

Data Analysis

All of the focus group sessions were taped and professionally transcribed, which enabled the inflection and tone of the speakers to be highlighted when necessary. The qualitative methods described by Miles and Huberman (1994) were used on the materials obtained from the focus group meetings and carefully reviewed, validated, and inspected through independent reviewing of the documents by two doctoral students. The reviewers arrived at consensual themes of the materials through an open reading of the materials. The creation of the consensual themes allowed for the next phase of the coding process, which entailed creating a coding protocol, coding of the materials by independent reviewers, discussion meetings between reviewers to arrive at and confirm existing codes, discussion of new codes, and revision of the coding protocol if necessary. Glaser's (1994, 1995) grounded theory approach and Emerson, Fretz, and Shaw's (1995) framework for coding, themes detection, and discordant instances were used to capture the themes in the data from each focus group. A grounded theory framework was useful because "data collection, analysis, and theory stand in close relationship to each other. . . . One begins with an area of study and what is relevant to that area is allowed to emerge" (Strauss & Corbin, 1998, p. 12). The data were subsequently transcribed using HyperResearch, a computer-assisted program for analyzing qualitative data (Dupuis, 1994).

Feedback Regarding the Treatment

An analysis of the qualitative data indicated that the participants agreed that the most difficult domains in the treatment were language, content, concepts, and metaphors. Specifically, the majority of the participants reported significant difficulty understanding the meaning of certain words, some of the concepts, and metaphors used throughout the manual. The participants provided alternatives for describing some of the content in a way that most urban adolescents might understand.

With regard to the language domain, the researchers followed Bernal and colleagues' (1995) criteria to evaluate the adolescents' comments regarding the treatment: Is the vocabulary of the treatment manual clear and understandable? Do Haitian American adolescents understand the language, idioms, and words used? According to the EVF, the language of a treatment should be culturally appropriate and syntonic with one's culture. Adolescents reported having difficulty understanding the language used in the treatment manual, which could be based on adolescent cultural understanding and/or ethnocultural differences. A 15-year-old girl stated, "There were many words that they used that I did not understand at all, and I am taking AP [advanced placement] classes." In the same group, a 17-year-old boy said, "I don't think that they created this treatment for adolescents because we do not use words as 'critical situations,' 'assertive imagery,' or some of the other words that they use. We just don't talk like that." A 14-year-old girl punctuated her concern by showing the book to the group: "Look at my book, I have many words circled because they just did not make any sense to me." A 15-year-old boy in her group also reported comprehension problems: "I should not have to need a dictionary in order for me to be in this treatment." What is clear from their many comments about the language used in the treatment manual was that the words used were not reflective of their background and/or experiences. Thus, the language used in the treatment manual did not meet cultural sensitivity criteria for these adolescents.

The content of the treatment manual was the second most agreed-on domain by the adolescents. The content domain of the model called for an evaluation of the treatment with respect to Bernal et al.'s (1995) criteria: (a) Does the treatment manual use case examples that reflect common values and other issues presented by Haitians (e.g., *lakou* [family], respect, spirituality, and gender roles)? (b) Does the adolescent feel understood by the therapist? (c) Does the adolescent feel that the therapist respects his or her cultural values? In this paragraph and the paragraphs that follow, one of the comments provided by the participants from the two groups is given. In one group, a boy (age 15 and in Group B) said, "I did not see anything at all in the book that came close to Haitian culture." A girl (age 16 and in Group A) said, "Actually I don't think that there was anything in the manual that looked like the culture of many of my friends either, and they are not Haitians." Another girl (age 15 and in Group B) said, "When I was reading the different sections, I felt like someone was just talking down to me, like I did not know anything at all. We are young, not stupid."

The participants reported seeing not only an absence of their culture represented in the treatment manual but also an absence of the culture of many other individuals, which left them wondering about the treatment's intended population. What is also surprising is that the participants felt insulted by this omission or what they perceived to be a "talk down" approach of the treatment manual. Thus, an integration of the cultural knowledge as well as the strengths of the adolescents is needed in the implementation of this treatment.

The domain that received the third most attention and discussion by the two groups was concepts. Specifically, the EVF calls for more sensitivity of treatment concepts using the following criteria: Are treatment concepts framed within acceptable cultural values? Does the patient understand the problem and the reason for the treatment? Is the patient in agreement with the definition of the problem and the specific treatment? Following are some of the comments regarding this area of questioning. One boy (age 16 and in Group A) stated, "Can someone please tell me what is 'activating event!' I had to read that at least 10 times before it made any sense [laughter]." One 16-year-old girl from Group B said, "The one that I had a very hard time with was 'negative thoughts baseline.' To be honest, I still do not get it. Why do they make it so hard?" Additionally, another 16-year-old girl from Group B commented, "You know you are right [referring to a previous comment], even something like 'emotions' is described in a difficult way. Now I know what emotions are and what this means, but I found it difficult to know what they were talking or asking me to do for that section."

As with the other two domains (language and content), many of the adolescents expressed difficulties with understanding or making meaning of some of the key concepts used throughout the treatment manual. Many of the participants noted difficulties comprehending the concepts even after several attempts at reading the materials. The last domain that was discussed extensively by the groups was metaphors. This discussion elicited the most laughter and playfulness among the adolescents in both groups. According to the EVF, this domain is evaluated using the following criteria: Are sayings or *dichos* common to Haitians or adolescence part of the treatment manual? Are symbols associated with Haitians part of the treatment? Some of the sample comments about the metaphors that were displayed throughout the treatment manual came from people like this 14-year-old boy from Group B: "OK . . . who is Calvin and Hobbes? I have heard of Garfield, but Calvin and Hobbes?" Another girl (age 15 and in Group B) said, "There are some things that they say to do that I could never do with Haitian adults . . . things like make eye contact, use the person's name . . . these are things that I can only do if they were my friends." In addition, one girl (age 16 and in Group A) commented, "I agree with you [pointing to another group member], I did not find the cartoons funny or helpful to understand feelings because they were not familiar to me. It would be best to use quotes and pictures of things that we know."

Although we did not expect that the symbols and concepts used in the treatment manual would be reflective of Haitian culture, we felt that some of the metaphors might be understood by the general population. It was clear from their comments that there are significant generational and cultural gaps with the metaphors used in the treatment manual.

A surprising area of concern for the adolescents was around the theoretical conceptualization of the onset of depression. The ACDC treatment is based on an integrative model developed by Lewinsohn et al. (1985) that dictates that depression is initiated by the occurrence of an event that evokes a depressive mood, which leads to a disruption of the individual's daily cognitive, behavioral, and/or emotional response patterns. This is followed by less reinforcement, leading to an increase in negative self-evaluations and dysphoric and/or depressed mood, further leading to changes in behavior, cognition, emotion, and interpersonal relationships, which are related to depression. The youths questioned where Haitian cultural beliefs regarding the onset of illness would fit in this theoretical model of depression. For example, one of the female participants (age 15) noted, "Every time someone gets sick or something bad happens my family always say that it must be because of voodoo, someone did something bad to the person. . . . I think that is how my family would talk about mental illness." Specifically, they discussed the cultural beliefs of supernatural forces (Desrosiers & St Fleurose, 2002; Kemp, 2002), often induced spiritually by an offended *lwa*, (a spiritual god), a common belief among many Haitians as one of the key origins of illnesses, which are often treated by spiritual healers and traditional remedies such as massage, herbal or leaf teas, and religious ceremonies. Such a belief system is contradictory to the theoretical premise of the ACDC treatment and has many implications for clients with respect to treatment adherence and treatment compliance.

Collectively, the feedback provided by the adolescents regarding the treatment manual provides the reader with an idea of the importance of culture in design, implementation, and evaluation of mental health treatment for immigrant and ethnically diverse populations. The ACDC treatment manual was refined after suggestions from the focus group participants. The manual was subsequently presented to the advisory board in a group meeting lasting 1.5 hours. Advisory board members reviewed the process, results, and the final treatment manual. Advisory board members recommended that the refined treatment protocol be evaluated by another group of adolescents to determine its readiness for use with a clinical sample of adolescents. We are currently in the process of completing this second round of focus group meetings following the same criteria and method described previously for the first round.

Lessons Learned

First, the method of using community members as informants in evaluating the utility and validity of treatment for a particular group was very fruitful. The participants in the project were able to thoroughly review the treatment manual and provided a critical review and analysis of the treatment. Second, the EVF provided a clear structure for the adolescents to evaluate the treatment as well as for the researchers to organize the feedback received from the participants. The elements of the model were easy to explain to the participants, and they in turn had little difficulty comprehending the definition of the concepts of the EVF. Third, focus group findings suggest it was necessary for us to culturally adapt the treatment prior to implementing it with a clinical sample of depressed Haitian adolescents because there were many areas (e.g., theory, language, metaphors) that did not reflect the cultural values and beliefs of our intended group. In total, ensuring that a treatment is culturally relevant, valid, and sensitive to a particular culture is a necessary first step to implementing an intervention with a target population.

CONCLUSION

Although existing research findings support the efficacy of CBT interventions for adolescents with internalizing disorders such as depression, there exists a gap on the utility and effectiveness of these interventions with ethnic and immigrant adolescents in this country. In general, ethnocultural groups have less access to adequate mental and physical health care, are receiving poorer quality of mental health services, and in fact are disadvantaged by having fewer qualified, culturally relevant, and skilled clinicians and age-appropriate treatment manuals to aid them in their emotional struggles (Davis & Stevenson, 2006; President's New Freedom Commission on Mental Health, 2003). Research has shown that insensitivity toward cultural experiences is most likely the strongest cause for the underutilization of mental health services by ethnic and diverse populations (Hall, 2001; D. W. Sue, Bingham, Porché-Burke, & Vasquez, 1999). The lack of integration of culture in treatment delivery for ethnic minority and immigrant populations decreases the retention rate for mental health treatment (S. Sue, 2003). Mental health providers and researchers have the social responsibility to address the underutilization of mental health services and reduce dropout rates among ethnic minority and immigrant populations.

In this chapter, we provided a summary of the method used to culturally adapt a group CBT for use with Haitian American adolescents. Specifically, we highlighted the importance of developing a partnership with the community of the population of interest, the centrality of providing culturally sensitive training to the researchers involved in the project prior to implementing it in the community, and the importance of using a culturally sensitive framework (i.e., Bernal et al.'s, 1995, model) to evaluate the sensitivity of the EBT of interest (Bernal, Jiménez-Chafey, & Domenech-Rodríguez, 2009). The information obtained through the adaptation of the ACDC intervention has contributed significantly to our knowledge of what works and how it works for depressed adolescents. More important, the process summarized in this chapter highlights the need to ensure that EBTs are culturally appropriate for different ethnocultural groups.

Although it can be argued that mental health treatments should be developed with different culture and diversity perspectives infused into them, it is crucial that current EBTs are evaluated and adapted for use with different ethnocultural groups. Otherwise, the disparities in mental health service delivery and access will continue. It has been argued that lack of attention to culture in treatment is unethical treatment. It is no longer acceptable for researchers to develop interventions that are not culturally relevant to different ethnocultural groups given the evidence demonstrating the importance of cultures in the mental health field. In fact, many in the field would argue that the lack of integration of culture into EBPPs would generally be considered incompetent practice. As such, culture must be put first in designing, implementing, and evaluating mental health interventions.

REFERENCES

American Psychological Association. (2003). Guidelines on multicultural education, training, research, practice, and organization change for psychologists. *American Psychologist, 58*, 377–402. doi:10.1037/0003-066X.58.5.377

American Psychological Association, Task Force on Evidence-Based Practice. (2006). Report of the 2005 Presidential Task Force on Evidence-Based Practice. *American Psychologist, 61*, 271–285.

Bernal, G., Bonilla, J., & Bellido, C. (1995). Ecological validity and cultural sensitivity for outcome research: Issues for the cultural adaptation and development of psychosocial treatments with Hispanics. *Journal of Abnormal Child Psychology, 23*, 67–82. doi:10.1007/BF01447045

Bernal, G., Jiménez-Chafey, M., & Domenech-Rodríguez, M. (2009). Cultural adaptation of treatments: A resource for considering culture in evidence-based practice. *Professional Psychology: Research and Practice, 40*, 361–368. doi:10.1037/a0016401

Bernal, G., Rosselló, J., & Martínez, A. (1997). The Children's Depression Inventory: Psychometric properties in 2 Puerto Rican samples. *Revista de Psicología Contemporanea, 4*, 12–23.

Bernal, G., & Sáez-Santiago, E. (2006). Culturally centered psychosocial interventions. *Journal of Community Psychology, 34,* 121–132. doi:10.1002/jcop.20096

Bernal, G., & Scharrón-Del-Río, M. R. (2001). Are empirically supported treatments valid for ethnic minorities? Toward an alternative approach for treatment research. *Cultural Diversity and Ethnic Minority Psychology, 7,* 328–342. doi:10.1037/1099-9809.7.4.328

Bernal, G., Trimble, J. E., Burlew, K. A., & Leong, F. (2003). *Handbook of racial and ethnic minority psychology.* Thousand Oaks, CA: Sage.

Brent, D. A., Holder, D., Kolko, D., Birmaher, B., Baugher, M., Roth, C., . . . Johnson, B. A. (1997). A clinical psychotherapy trial for adolescent depression comparing cognitive, family, and supportive therapy. *Archives of General Psychiatry, 54,* 877–885. doi:10.1001/archpsyc.1997.01830210125017

Brent, D., & Poling, K. (1997). *Cognitive therapy treatment manual for depressed and suicidal youth.* Pittsburg, PA: Star Center.

Bullinger, M, J., Alonso, G., Apolone, A., Leplege, M., Sullivan, S., Wood-Dauphinee, B., . . . Ware, J. E. (1998). Translating health status questionnaires and evaluating their quality: The IQOLA Project approach. *Journal of Clinical Epidemiology, 51,* 913–923. doi:10.1016/S0895-4356(98)00082-1

Center for Mental Health Services. (2005). *Mental health statistics.* Retrieved from http://www.mentalhealth.samhsa.gov/cmhs

Chiu, Y. W., & Ring, J. M. (1998). Chinese and Vietnamese immigrant adolescents under pressure: Identifying stressors and interventions. *Professional Psychology: Research and Practice, 29,* 444–449. doi:10.1037/0735-7028.29.5.444

Clarke, G. N., Hawkins, W., Murphy, M., & Sheeber, L. B. (1995). Targeted prevention of unipolar depressive disorder in an at-risk sample of high school adolescents: A randomized trial of group cognitive intervention. *Journal of the American Academy of Child & Adolescent Psychiatry, 34,* 312–321. doi:10.1097/00004583-199503000-00016

Clarke, G. N., Rohde, P., Lewinsohn, P. M., Hops, H., & Seeley, J. R. (1999). Cognitive-behavioral treatment of adolescent depression: Efficacy of acute group treatment and booster sessions. *Journal of the American Academy of Child & Adolescent Psychiatry, 38,* 272–279. doi:10.1097/00004583-199903000-00014

Cortés, D. E., Gerena, M., Canino, G., Aguilar-Gaxiola, S., Febo, V., Magaña, C., . . . Eisen, S. V. (2007). Translation and cultural adaptation of a mental health outcome measure: The basis-R(c). *Culture, Medicine, and Psychiatry, 31,* 25–49. doi:10.1007/s11013-006-9043-x

Costantino, G., Malgady, R. G., & Rogler, L. H. (1994). Storytelling through pictures: Culturally sensitive psychotherapy for Hispanic children and adolescents. *Journal of Clinical Child Psychology, 23,* 13–20. doi:10.1207/s15374424jccp2301_3

Curry, J. F. (2001). Specific psychotherapies for childhood and adolescent depression. *Biological Psychiatry, 49,* 1091–1100. doi:10.1016/S0006-3223(01) 01130-1

Davis, G. Y., & Stevenson, H. C. (2006). Racial socialization experiences and symptoms of depression among Black youth. *Journal of Child and Family Studies, 15,* 293–307. doi:10.1007/s10826-006-9039-8

Desrosiers, A., & St Fleurose, S. (2002). Treating Haitian patients: Key cultural aspects. *American Journal of Psychotherapy,, 56,* 508–521.

Domenech-Rodríguez, M., & Wieling, E. (2004). Developing culturally appropriate evidence-based treatments for interventions with ethnic minority populations. In M. Rastogi & E. Wieling (Eds.), *Voices of color: First-person accounts of ethnic minority therapists* (pp. 313–333). Thousand Oaks, CA: Sage.

Dupuis, P. R. (1994). *HyperResearch* (Version 1.56). Randolph, MA: Research Ware.

Emerson, R., Fretz, R. I., & Shaw, L. L. (1995). *Writing ethnographic fieldnotes.* Chicago, IL: The University of Chicago Press.

Fenta, H., Hyman, I., & Noh, S. (2004). Determinants of depression among Ethiopian immigrants and refugees in Toronto. *Journal of Nervous and Mental Disease, 192,* 363–372. doi:10.1097/01.nmd.0000126729.08179.07

Flynn, L. M. (2005). Family perspectives on evidence-based practice. *Child and Adolescent Psychiatric Clinics of North America, 14,* 217–224. doi:10.1016/j.chc.2004.04.003

Glaser, B. G. (1994). *More grounded theory methodology: A reader.* Mill Valley, CA: Sociology Press.

Glaser, B. G. (1995). *Grounded theory 1984–1994 (Vol. 1).* Mill Valley, CA: Sociology Press.

González, H. M., Vega, W. A., Williams, D. R., Wassim Tarraf, W., West, B. T., & Neighbors, H. W. (2010). Depression care in the United States: Too little for too few. *Archives of General Psychiatry, 67,* 37–46. doi:10.1001/archgenpsychiatry.2009.168

Gray-Little, B., & Kaplan, D. (2000). Race and ethnicity in psychotherapy research. In C. R. Snyder & R. E. Ingram (Eds.), *Handbook of psychological change: Psychotherapy processes & practices for the 21st century* (pp. 591–613). Hoboken, NJ: Wiley.

Hall, G. C. N. (2001). Psychotherapy research with ethnic minorities: Empirical, ethical, and conceptual issues. *Journal of Consulting and Clinical Psychology, 69,* 502–510. doi:10.1037/0022-006X.69.3.502

Huey, S. J. J., & Polo, A. J. (2008). Evidence-based psychosocial treatments for ethnic minority youth. *Journal of Clinical Child and Adolescent Psychology, 37,* 262–301. doi:10.1080/15374410701820174

James, D. C. (1997). Coping with a new society: The unique psychosocial problems of immigrant youth. *The Journal of School Health, 67(3),* 98–102. doi:10.1111/j.1746-1561.1997.tb03422.x

Kemp, C. (2002). *Haitian immigrants and refugees.* Retrieved from http://www.fachc.org/pdf/mig_haitians.pdf

Krueger, R. A. (1994). *Focus groups: A practical guide for applied research* (2nd ed.). Thousand Oaks, CA: Sage.

Lewinsohn, P. M., Clarke, G. N., Hops, H., & Andrews, J. (1990). *Cognitive-behavioral group treatment of depression in adolescents: A replication.* Unpublished manuscript, Oregon Research Institute.

Lewinsohn, P. M., Clarke, G. N., Hops, H., Andrews, J., & Williams, J. (1990). *Cognitive-behavioral treatment for depressed adolescents.* Unpublished manuscript, Oregon Research Institute.

Lewinsohn, P. M., Hoberman, H M., Teri, L., & Hautzinger, M. (1985). An integrative theory of unipolar depression. In S. Reiss & R. R. Bootzin (Eds.), *Theoretical issues in behavioral therapy* (pp. 313–359). New York, NY: Academic Press.

March, J., Silva, S., Petrycki, S., Curry, J., Wells, K., Fairbank, J., . . . Severe, J. (2004). Fluoxetine, cognitive-behavioral therapy, and their combination for adolescents with depression: Treatment for Adolescents with Depression Study (TADS) randomized controlled trial. *JAMA, 292,* 807–820. doi:10.1001/jama.292.7.807

Mays, V. M., & Albee, G. W. (1992). Psychotherapy and ethnic minorities. In D. K. Freedheim & H. J. Freudenberger (Eds.), *History of psychotherapy: A century of change* (pp. 552–570). Washington, DC: American Psychological Association. doi:10.1037/10110-015

Miles, M. B., & Huberman, A. M. (1994). *Qualitative data analysis: An expanded sourcebook* (2nd ed.). Thousand Oaks, CA: Sage.

Miranda, J. (2000). *Mental health outcomes for Latinos: Current knowledge base for improving mental health services.* Washington, DC: Georgetown University Medical Center.

Miranda, J., Azocar, F., Organista, K. C., Muñoz, R. F., & Lieberman, A. (1996). Recruiting and retaining low-income Latinos in psychotherapy research. *Journal of Consulting and Clinical Psychology, 64,* 868–874. doi:10.1037/0022-006X.64.5.868

Miranda, J., Nakamura, R., & Bernal, G. (2003). Including ethnic minorities in mental health intervention research: A practical approach to a long-standing problem. *Culture, Medicine and Psychiatry, 27,* 467–486. doi:10.1023/B:MEDI.0000005484.26741.79

Morgan, D. L., Krueger, R. A., & King, J. A. (1998). *The focus group kit* (Vols. 1–6). Thousand Oaks, CA: Sage.

National Alliance on Mental Illness. (2003). *Latino community mental health facts.* Retrieved from http://www.nami.org/Template.cfm?Section=Fact_Sheets1&Template=/ContentManagement/ContentDisplay.cfm&ContentID=88869

Nicolas, G., Arntz, D. L., Hirsch, B., & Schmiedigen, A. (2009). Cultural adaption of a group treatment for Haitian American adolescents. *Professional Psychology: Research and Practice, 40,* 378–384. doi:10.1037/a0016307

Nicolas, G., DeSilva, A., Subrebost, K., Breland-Noble, A., Gonzalez-Eastep, D., Prater, K., & Manning, N. (2007). Expression of depression by Haitian women in the U.S.: Clinical observations. *American Journal of Psychotherapy, 61,* 83–98.

President's New Commission on Mental Health. (2003). *Report*. Retrieved from http://govinfo.library.unt.edu/mentalhealthcommission/press/july03press.htm

Pumariega, A. J., Rothe, E., & Pumariega, J. B. (2005). Mental health of immigrants and refugees. *Community Mental Health Journal, 41*, 581–597. doi:10.1007/s10597-005-6363-1

Reinecke, M. A., Ryan, N., & DuBois, D. (1998). Cognitive behavioral therapy of depression and depressive symptoms during adolescence: A review and meta-analysis. *Journal of the American Academy of Child & Adolescent Psychiatry, 37*, 26–34. doi:10.1097/00004583-199801000-00013

Rishel, C. W. (2007). Evidence-based prevention practice in mental health: What is it and how do we get there? *American Journal of Orthopsychiatry, 77*, 153–164. doi:10.1037/0002-9432.77.1.153

Rohde, P., Lewinsohn, P. M., & Seeley, J. R. (1994). Are adolescents changed by an episode of major depression? *Journal of the American Academy of Child & Adolescent Psychiatry, 33*, 1289–1298. doi:10.1097/00004583-199411000-00010

Rosselló, J., & Bernal, G. (1996). Adaptation of cognitive-behavioral and inter-personal treatments for depressed Puerto Rican adolescents. In E. Hibbs & P. S. Jensen (Eds.), *Psychosocial treatments for child and adolescent disorders* (pp. 157–185). Washington, DC: American Psychological Association.

Rosselló, J., & Bernal, G. (1999). The efficacy of cognitive–behavioral and interpersonal treatments for depression in Puerto Rican adolescents. *Journal of Consulting and Clinical Psychology, 67*, 734–745.

Smith, T. B., Domenech-Rodríguez, M., & Bernal, G. (2011). Culture. *Journal of Clinical Psychology, 67*, 166–175. doi:10.1002/jclp.20757

Stark, K. D., Napolitano, S., Swearer, S., Schmidt, K., Jaramillo, D., & Hoyle, J. (1996). Issues in the treatment of childhood depression. *Applied & Preventive Psychology: Current Scientific Perspectives, 5*, 59–84.

Strauss, A., & Corbin, J. (1998). *Basics of qualitative research: Techniques and procedures for developing grounded theory* (2nd ed.). Thousand Oaks, CA: Sage.

Sue, D. W., Arredondo, P., & McDavis, R. J. (1992). Multicultural counseling competencies and standards: A call to the profession. *Journal of Multicultural Counseling and Development, 20(2)*, 64–88. doi:10.1002/j.2161-1912.1992.tb00563.x

Sue, D. W., Bingham, R. P., Porché-Burke, L., & Vasquez, M. (1999). The diversification of psychology: A multicultural revolution. *American Psychologist, 54*, 1061–1069. doi:10.1037/0003-066X.54.12.1061

Sue, S. (1998). In search of cultural competence in psychotherapy and counseling. *American Psychologist, 53*, 440–448. doi:10.1037/0003-066X.53.4.440

Sue, S. (2003). In defense of cultural competency in psychotherapy and treatment. *American Psychologist, 58*, 964–970. doi:10.1037/0003-066X.58.11.964

Sue, S., Zane, N., & Young, K. (1994). Research in psychotherapy with culturally diverse populations. In A. E. Bergin & S. L. Garfield (Eds.), *Handbook of psychotherapy and behavior change* (4th ed., pp. 783–820). New York, NY: Wiley.

Tharp, R. G. (1991). Cultural diversity and treatment of children. *Journal of Consulting and Clinical Psychology, 59*, 799–812. doi:10.1037/0022-006X.59.6.799

U.S. Census Bureau. (2001). *Projections of the total resident population by 5-year age groups, race, and Hispanic origin with special age categories: Middle series, 2050 to 2070.* Retrieved from http://www.census.gov/population/projections/nation/summary/np-t4-g.txt

U.S. Census Bureau. (2010). *Current population reports, Series P25-1104, population projections of the United States, by age, sex, race, and hispanic origin: 1993 to 2050.* Retrieved from http://www.census.gov/population/www/pop-profile/natproj.html

U.S. Department of Health and Human Services, Public Health Service, Office of the Surgeon General. (1999). Mental health: A report of the Surgeon General—Executive summary. Rockville, MD: Author.

U.S. Department of Health and Human Services, Public Health Service, Office of the Surgeon General. (2000). Report of the Surgeon General's conference on children's mental health: A national action agenda. Washington, DC: Author.

U.S. Department of Health and Human Services, Public Health Service, Office of the Surgeon General. (2001). Mental health: Culture, race, and ethnicity–A supplement to mental health: A report of the Surgeon General. Rockville, MD: Author.

Weiss, D. J. (2004). Computerized adaptive testing for effective and efficient measurement in counseling and education. *Measurement and Evaluation in Counseling and Development, 37*, 70–84.

Weisz, J. R., Sandler, I. N., Durlak, J. A., & Anton, B. S. (2005). Promoting and protecting youth mental health through evidence-based prevention and treatment. *American Psychologist, 60*, 628–648. doi:10.1037/0003-066X.60.6.628

5

DEVELOPMENT AND CULTURAL ADAPTATION OF THE *TALLER DE EDUCACIÓN PSICOLÓGICA PARA PADRES Y MADRES* (TEPSI): PSYCHOEDUCATION FOR PARENTS OF LATINO/A ADOLESCENTS WITH DEPRESSION

EMILY SÁEZ-SANTIAGO, GUILLERMO BERNAL,
MAE LYNN REYES-RODRÍGUEZ, AND KAREN BONILLA-SILVA

During the past few decades a great number of research studies have consistently evidenced the influence of parents and family factors in adolescent depression. The family literature on adolescent depression shows that parental cognitions, parental pathology, parenting behaviors of warmth and emotional availability, individual coping with the family environment, and family conflict are factors that have been strongly related to depression in youth (Sander & McCarty, 2005). Despite the strong support for family factors on depression, there is a notable absence of family interventions in the research literature on treatment of adolescent depression, with a few exceptions (Braswell, 1991; Kovacs & Sherrill, 2001). In this chapter, we describe both the development and cultural adaptation process of a psychoeducational intervention for parents with a depressed adolescent, the *Taller de Educación Psicológica para Padres y Madres* (TEPSI; Psychological Education Workshop for Mothers and Fathers). The TEPSI was designed to optimize the impact of individual cognitive behavior therapy (CBT) on a group of Latino/a adolescents with major depression in Puerto Rico.

PARENT INVOLVEMENT IN INTERVENTIONS
FOR DEPRESSED ADOLESCENTS

A small number of psychosocial treatment studies for adolescent depression have included a parent intervention component (Brent et al., 1997; Lewinsohn, Clarke, Hops, & Andrews, 1990; Lewinsohn, Clarke, Seeley, & Rhode, 1994). These parenting intervention components have varied in form and intensity. Asarnow, Scott, and Mintz (2002) included one multi-family meeting in which a videotape demonstrating the use of CBT skills was presented to the families of adolescents participating in group CBT. This family meeting was intended to educate parents and encourage them to support learning that occurred in the adolescent group sessions. Of the parents participating, 94% rated the intervention as helpful, but 40% reported that more family sessions would have been more helpful. In contrast, Stark, Brookman, and Frazier (1990) included a monthly family meeting to teach parents how to encourage their child to use the CBT skills taught in therapy. Lewinsohn, Clarke, Rhode, Hops, and Seeley (1996) had a more intense parenting component wherein parents participated in nine sessions that covered the skills that were taught to the teenagers (communication and problem solving). Two of these nine sessions were joint parent–adolescent sessions.

At least two studies have tested the impact of the parenting intervention by comparing outcomes with and without the parent component. In one study, 59 adolescents with depression were randomly assigned to one of three conditions: (a) group CBT, (b) group CBT plus parent, and (c) waiting list (Clarke, Hops, Lewinsohn, & Andrews, 1992). Both active treatments resulted in significant adolescent improvement. The adolescent plus parent condition showed improvements in child outcomes as measured by the Child Behavior Checklist. One of the characteristics associated with treatment response was parent involvement in treatment. In a second study, 96 adolescents were randomly assigned to the three treatment conditions with similar results (Lewinsohn et al., 1996). In addition, recovery rates were superior in the two treatment conditions when compared with the waiting-list group.

Brent and colleagues (1997) provided a family psychoeducation intervention to all treatment conditions: (a) CBT, (b) systemic behavior family therapy, and (c) nondirective support treatment. This family psychoeducation intervention included information about the affective illness and ways in which the family could help the depressed adolescent. Parental involvement helped parents comprehend the seriousness of their adolescent's condition and reduced the attrition rate (only 10% dropped out).

More recently, the Treatment for Adolescents With Depression Study (TADS) compared CBT, selective serotonin reuptake inhibitor medication, and combined medication and CBT. The CBT included two parent psychoeducation sessions and at least five parent–teen conjoint sessions following optional modules (K. C. Wells & Albano, 2005). The two psychoeducational sessions were given to the parents at Weeks 3 and 5 of treatment; at least one parent–child conjoint session (up to three) was conducted during Weeks 7 to 12; from one to three conjoint sessions were performed during Weeks 13 to 18; and finally, one to three conjoint sessions were conducted during the end of treatment (maintenance phase). The purpose of the parent psychoeducational sessions was to teach parents about the nature of depression and about the skills that their child learned as part of the CBT. The optional parent–child conjoint sessions were focused on specific parent–adolescent concerns. Results showed that the treatment combining medication and CBT was significantly more effective than the medication alone, CBT alone, or a pill placebo (March, 2004). TADS faced several challenges with the parent component, such as parent engagement, parent psychopathology, parents who were divorced, and parents from a variety of family constellations and cultural backgrounds (K. C. Wells & Albano, 2005), which, as the TADS researchers suggested, need further attention when implementing a parent intervention.

Of the studies that included parent interventions, only two controlled treatment outcome studies included and evaluated the parent intervention as part of their experimental design (Lewinsohn et al., 1990, 1994). Results from these studies demonstrated the efficacy of CBT but failed to establish strong support for the parent intervention. However, a limitation of these studies is that they did not evaluate other domains of treatment beyond the adolescents' symptoms. Sander and McCarty (2005) agreed that "ruling out parent involvement as unnecessary is premature" (p. 26). These investigators recommended further research focusing on parent and adolescent variables that mediate and moderate the outcome of treatment for depression.

There are many reasons to include parents in the treatment of depressed youth. As Kovacs and Sherrill (2001) noted, having the cooperation of parents in treatment can ensure adherence and retention. Parents can play a psychological and educational role in the management of their child's depression and serve as resources to help minimize the impact of depression on the parent–child relationship. Parents can sometimes misinterpret their adolescent's depressive symptoms and conduct as misbehavior and manipulation. If they have a better understanding of their child's condition, they can be more accepting of their adolescent and collaborate actively in treatment. Involving parents can help address treatment resistance, accelerate treatment effects, and maintain therapeutic changes (Kovacs & Sherrill, 2001). Several investigators have recommended this avenue of research (Kazdin & Weisz, 1998; Sanford et al., 1995). On the basis of a review of the empirical and clinical focus of child and adolescent psychotherapy research, Kazdin, Bass, Ayers, and Rodgers (1990) established several priorities for treatment research. They noted the scant attention to parental influences that may moderate outcome, and they recommended that research be conducted to ascertain whether parent involvement is critical in clinical work.

PARENT INVOLVEMENT IN INTERVENTION FOR DEPRESSED YOUTHS IN PUERTO RICO

Because of the cultural characteristics of the Latino/a population, the family and family variables can be of particular importance in the treatment of depression in adolescence. Familism (*familismo*) has been identified as a strong cultural value among Latinos/as (Bernal, Cumba-Avilés, & Sáez-Santiago, 2006; Bernal & Sáez-Santiago, 2005; Sáez-Santiago & Bernal, 2003). *Familismo* refers to the strong value placed on the establishment and maintenance of close-knit relationships with family members, including not only the immediate family but also extended family members. For many Latinos/as the ideal standard is to be both physically and emotionally close to family members, particularly to parents (Falicov, 1998).

Studies conducted with Puerto Rican adolescent samples have documented the strong relationship between parental and family variables to adolescent depression (Martínez & Rosselló, 1995; Sáez & Rosselló, 1998). Results from a clinical trial for the treatment of depression in Puerto Rican adolescents revealed that 40% of the adolescents participating considered their most frequent problem as originating within the family (Padilla, Dávila, & Rosselló, 2002), and 70% believed that their most frequent interpersonal problem was with one or both parents (Rosselló & Rivera, 1999). Additionally, Sáez and Rosselló (2001, 2005) found that family negative criticism had the strongest direct relationship to symptoms of depression, indicating that negative criticism may play an important role in the treatment of adolescents with depression.

Although findings from family studies conducted with Puerto Rican adolescents reinforced the impact of family, particularly of parents, in the adolescents' depression, no treatment research studies on Puerto Rican—or other Latino/a—adolescents with depression have been conducted until now. In this chapter, we describe the development, cultural adaptation, and implementation process of the TEPSI to optimize an individual CBT intervention for adolescents with depression in Puerto Rico. In the sections that follow, we first describe the TEPSI and later describe the development, cultural adaptation, and implementation of the intervention. We conclude with a brief evaluation of the parents' acceptance and the feasibility of implementing the TEPSI as part of depression treatment in Latino/a adolescents.

TALLER DE EDUCACIÓN PSICOLÓGICA
PARA PADRES Y MADRES

The TEPSI was designed to teach parents signs and symptoms of depression in adolescents, to support their adolescents' coping with depressed mood states, and to provide parents with the necessary tools to identify family patterns that can contribute to their child's depression. The intervention consists of eight 2-hour sessions delivered in a group format. Each session includes didactic material, in-session practice exercises, and personal and/or family projects to be completed between sessions. The eight sessions are divided into one introductory session and two modules: cognitive and interpersonal. Some scholars have proposed an integration of cognitive and interpersonal therapy, particularly with regard to Latino/a adults (Aguilar-Gaxiola, Muñoz, & Guzman, 2001; Perez, 1999), because of the interpersonal nature of depression (Joiner & Coyne, 1999) as well as the cultural value placed on interpersonal relationships. Based on our previous experiences with Latino/a adults with depression, the integration of both components represents a cultural consideration in that interpersonal relationships and, in particular, family relationships are at its core (Bernal & Reyes, 2008).

The TEPSI Content

The introductory session, titled "Understanding Your Child's Depression," focused on a discussion of symptoms, myths, and causes of depression in adolescents. This session also presented information about the impact of depression on the family and the family's impact on depression. General effective coping strategies for parents to deal with their child's depression were also presented. This session included an explanation of the basics of the CBT theory about depression and a description of the TEPSI.

In Session 2, "Thoughts and Your Child's Mood," the following topics were discussed: (a) relationship between the child's thoughts and mood, (b) the cycle of depression (relationship among feelings, thoughts, interactions, and actions), (c) identification of the child's positive and negative thoughts, and (d) identification of harmful thought categories. Session 3, "Reducing Negative Thoughts to Improve Your Child's Mood," was devoted to teaching strategies to challenge negative thoughts, which include (a) identifying harmful thoughts, (b) examining the evidence, (c) conducting experiments, (d) finding constructive alternative thoughts, (e) setting up time to worry and time free from worry, (f) stopping thoughts, (g) balancing thoughts, and (h) mindfulness exercises. Session 4, "Increasing Your Child's Positive Thoughts," concluded the cognitive module with a discussion of strategies to increase positive thoughts and manage internal and external reality. The main goals of the cognitive module were to (a) provide parents with a better understanding about the CBT vision of depression, (b) create awareness about dysfunctional cognitive styles in the family environment, and (c) promote and reinforce new and positive cognitive styles in the family.

The interpersonal module began with Session 5, "Interpersonal Relationships and Your Mood," which presented information about the interpersonal nature of depression, specific family interactional patterns, the importance of breaking the cycle of depression by changing interpersonal dynamics, and the establishment of a healthy social support network. Session 6, "Interpersonal Problems, Mood, Thoughts and Behaviors," focused on the identification of interpersonal factors that could contribute to the child's depression: (a) loss or grief, (b) change of roles or transition, (c) disagreements in roles or disputes, and (d) deficiencies in interpersonal skills. Session 7, "Improving your Interpersonal Relationships and Dealing With Your Mood," introduced the topic of communication, explaining the different styles of communication (passive, assertive, and aggressive). The importance of being assertive and avoiding negative criticism when expressing feelings was highlighted. In this session, parents were also taught to be active listeners and to identify family patterns of communication. The closing session was Session 8, "Additional Tools to Improve Interpersonal Relationships and Your Mood," which provided hints for overcoming obstacles in solving interpersonal problems, such as identifying fears, low energy, negative thoughts, and habits. Also discussed in this session was the importance of examining rules of interpersonal relationships, balancing one's own needs and the needs of others, and setting limits.

Every session ended with a review and closing comments. The main goals of the interpersonal module were to (a) identify interpersonal and communication family patterns background, (b) reinforce healthy patterns and promote changes in unhealthy patterns in the family interaction, and (c) endorse an interpersonal family interaction that integrate boundaries and autonomies considering the stage of life of each family member. Table 5.1 summarizes the approach, content, and specific exercises for each session.

The TEPSI Development Process

In this section, we describe the process of developing the TEPSI. This process is described separately from the adaptation processes for illustrative purposes, although both were performed concurrently. *Development* in this context refers to (a) selecting an intervention model to be used, (b) changing the focus of the model intervention from therapeutic to psychoeducational, (c) evaluating the feasibility and acceptance of this intervention among targeted parents, and (d) testing the intervention.

Selecting the Intervention

The idea for including a parental intervention to treat adolescent's depression came from the findings of two previous clinical trials (Rosselló & Bernal, 1999; Rosselló, Bernal, & Rivera-Medina, 2008) in which we observed that many of the adolescents seen in CBT or interpersonal psychotherapy were presenting with family difficulties that required additional attention. With this in mind, the research team began a process to identify and select the most pertinent family intervention to be added to the adolescent's individual CBT (which was found to be the most efficacious treatment condition in our clinical trials). After considering a number of alternatives, the team settled on a 16-session CBT manual developed by Muñoz and collaborators for the treatment of depression in Latinos/as (Muñoz, Ghosh-Ippen, Valdes-Dwyer, Rao, & Le, 2000) that consists of four modules covering cognitive, behavioral, interpersonal, and health issues.

The protocol, *Manual de Terapia Cognitiva Conductual de la Depresión: Aprendiendo a manejar su modalidad personal.Cuaderno para Participantes* (Muñoz et al., 2000), was selected as the basis for our parental intervention for a number of reasons. First, this 16-session manual is a revised version of a highly effective 12-session protocol tested in a variety of contexts (Miranda, 2000; Muñoz et al., 1995; K. B. Wells et al., 2000) and settings, including Puerto Rico (Rosselló & Bernal, 1999). Second, the manual was used in a pilot study conducted in a primary care clinic to treat depression in Puerto Rican adults (Reyes-Rodríguez, 2002). Reyes-Rodríguez (2002) culturally adapted the manual-based intervention using the ecological validity framework developed by Bernal, Bonilla, and Bellido (1995). The CBT manual was adapted to ensure the cultural and contextual relevance for the Puerto Rican population. Findings from this pilot study showed that the 16-CBT sessions were effective for the treatment of depression in adult women living in Puerto Rico. Third, we were interested in an intervention for parents that was parallel to that for the adolescents. Finally, Guillermo Bernal had a history of personal collaboration with the developers of the manual.

Shifting the Intervention Focus to Psychoeducation

The original intervention was therapeutic and aimed at adults with depression. The research team worked to tailor the intervention to be psycho-educational and focus on the participant's adolescent child as the target of the intervention. A team of doctoral-level clinical psychologists were in charge of this task. To have a psychological education intervention, all sessions consisted of instructive material related to depression symptoms in adolescence. To achieve this educational focus, many of the practice exercises, both in sessions and at home, focused on the child. Some activities that illustrate these

TABLE 5.1

Summary of Taller de Educación Psicológica Para Padres y Madres (TEPSI) Sessions

Session	Approach	Content	Exercises and homework
1	Cognitive	■ Depression definition ■ Symptoms of depression ■ Myths about depression ■ Depression causes ■ Family and depression ■ Development life stages ■ Effective coping skills	■ Mood monitor
2	Cognitive	■ What are thoughts? ■ Categories of thoughts (+, −) ■ Identifying thought pattern ■ Cycle of depression	■ Mood monitor
3	Cognitive	■ Different ways to debate dysfunctional thoughts ■ Examine the evidence ■ Make an experiment ■ Constructive alternative for the thought pattern	■ Time to worry and time free of worry ■ Stop the negative thought ■ Exercise to improve concentration and mindfulness ■ Mood monitor

#	Type	Content	Activities
4	Cognitive	■ How to increase positive thoughts ■ Positive observation ■ Identify positive thoughts in the adolescent ■ Internal and external realities	■ Mental journey: past, present ■ Observation exercise ■ Mood monitor
5	Interpersonal	■ Depression and relationships ■ Family patterns ■ Social support	■ Family tree ■ Mood monitor
6	Interpersonal	■ How to strengthen the social support ■ Identify an interpersonal area: 　■ Loss or grief 　■ Transition 　■ Disputes ■ Improve relations with others ■ Problem-solving skills	■ Discussion of family patterns using the genogram ■ Mood monitor
7	Interpersonal	■ Improving the relationship ■ Communication skills ■ Ways of communication (passive, aggressive, assertive)	■ Communication exercise (speaking and listening) ■ Mood monitor
8	Interpersonal	■ Tools to improve the relationship ■ Identify the family patterns ■ An overview of the workshop ■ Closing	■ TEPSI feedback from participants

changes were (a) a personal project in which parents identified and monitored their child's mood state and thoughts; (b) having the parents identify the interpersonal problem(s) their child presents and how to help their child to overcome those interpersonal difficulties; and (c) having the parents identify their child's social support network, among other practice exercises. The team of clinicians also conducted all the modifications related to the TEPSI development and the additional cultural adaptation, described in detail later. All aspects of the manual were reworded to center the exercises on the adolescents and not on the participating parents.

Exploring Feasibility

Focus groups were conducted with the parents of the depressed adolescents who participated in our previous clinical trial (Rosselló & Bernal, 1999; Rosselló et al., 2008). The objectives of these focus groups were to (a) receive the parents' feedback of their experiences while having their child in treatment for depression, (b) evaluate the need for a parental intervention in the adolescent's treatment for depression, and (c) explore the feasibility of a parental psychoeducational intervention or a treatment for parents. A total of 10 mothers and one father participated in two separate 1.5-hour focus groups conducted by Emily Sáez-Santiago and Guillermo Bernal. Focus groups were audio recorded, notes were taken by an observer research assistant, and content analyses of the notes were conducted. All parents who participated reported that having a son or daughter with depression meant facing serious challenges for the family. All groups were conducted in Spanish, and the quotes reported in this chapter were translated into English by Emily Sáez-Santiago, Guillermo Bernal, Mae Lynn Reyes-Rodríguez, and Karen Bonilla-Silva. All parents reported a need for "support" and "tools" to deal with their son or daughter at the time of his or her depression. Some parents noted feeling "excluded" while their child was receiving individual psychotherapy.

All the parents participated in an initial and a closing meeting with the therapist in the clinical trial, yet they reported not having enough information about the therapeutic process of their son or daughter (e.g., treatment modality, topics discussed in therapy). Consequently, most parents recommended having several meetings during treatment to discuss "general information about the process." All parents agreed that a parental psychoeducational intervention would be helpful in handling the challenges they faced because of their child's depression. In contrast, only one mother recommended a therapeutic intervention for the parents. All parents pointed out that they would participate in a parental psychoeducational intervention if this intervention were provided when their son or daughter received treatment. The already adapted psychoeducational sessions were briefly described to the parents to obtain their feedback. All parents agreed that all session topics were highly informative for a parent of an adolescent with depression. Focus group parents appeared interested in and committed to participating in a psychoeducational intervention.

Intervention Pilot Test

After the focus groups, we conducted a small pilot study with four parents (three mothers and one father) of adolescents with depression to test the first version of the TEPSI manual. Information gathered during this pilot was used to refine the protocol. Major modifications included the addition of family exercises to explore familial interpersonal patterns (e.g., genogram, family life cycle) and to devote more time to skill development during sessions. Other modifications are described in the TEPSI Cultural Adaptation Process section.

Intervention Test

The final step of the development process of the TEPSI was a randomized clinical trial (RCT) in which 121 depressed adolescents were randomly assigned to one of two conditions: CBT or CBT plus the TEPSI. The full development and adaptation process is illustrated in Figure 5.1. Sixty parents participated in nine different TEPSI groups over a period of 5 years. Groups met weekly for an 8-week per iod. Group size varied from five to nine members. Of the 60 TEPSI participants, 55 were women and five were men. Two sessions from each of the nine TEPSI groups ($n = 18$, 25% of the sessions) were randomly selected to be transcribed. However, because of technical or audio problems, only 10 of the selected sessions could be transcribed. Content analyses of these transcripts were conducted, and relevant information is presented in the TEPSI Cultural Adaptation Process and Observations About Acceptability and Engagement sections of this chapter.

The TEPSI Cultural Adaptation Process

The cultural adaptations described in this section occurred throughout the development and implementation process (from focus groups to the RCT). The adaptation process included selecting the cultural framework to guide the process, making the necessary modifications using the framework as a guide, and testing and making new modifications with the target population. The TEPSI was refined and culturally adapted using the ecological validity model, which outlines eight dimensions for modification: language, persons, metaphors, content, concepts, goals, methods, and context (Bernal et al., 1995; see also Chapter 2, this volume). These eight dimensions are

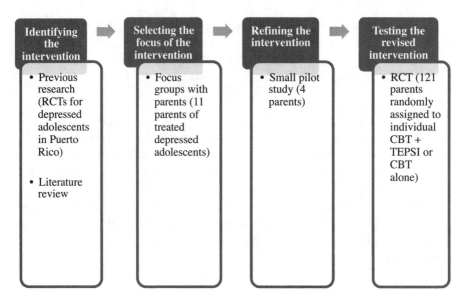

Figure 5.1. Development and adaptation process of the *Taller de Educación Psicológica Para Padres y Madres* (TEPSI). RCT = randomized clinical trial; CBT = cognitive behavioral treatment.

considered relevant in any given intervention in relation to the corresponding culturally sensitive elements necessary for cultural adaptation.

Language

The first dimension considers the language of the intervention, placing particular attention on participants' understanding of the language, idioms, and words used in the intervention. Although the original manual was in Spanish, language was adapted to use more appropriate wording syntonic with the Puerto Rican culture and idioms. For example, originally the term *psychoeducation* was translated to *psicoeducativo*, but this term did not seem to make much sense to most families. Then the term was changed to *taller de educación psicológica* (workshop of psychological education), which focused more on the experience of learning through participation, and it was a preferred terminology to parents. Thus, we named our intervention *Taller de Educación Psicológica para Padres y Madres*. In addition, we maintained the translation used in the Puerto Rican CBT adaptation. For example, in a mindfulness exercise called *ejercicio de la naranja* (the orange exercise), the name of the exercise was changed to *ejercicio de la china*, which is the term used by Puerto Ricans to refer to an orange. Another language modification was related to its use when delivering the intervention. The original manual included formal language (e.g., *usted* or the formal *you*); however, the TEPSI facilitators used a more informal and personal wording (i.e., *tú*, the informal *you*), known as *tuteo*. The use of tuteo helped to develop a personal and close relationship between the group members, including with the facilitators. It was also useful in the establishment of a comfortable and relaxing atmosphere.

Persons

The second dimension refers to ethnic and racial similarities and differences between the provider and client. The TEPSI facilitators were two female Puerto Rican doctoral-level clinical psychologists within age range of the TEPSI participants. Having an ethnic, nationality, and gender match between the facilitators and the majority of the TEPSI participants promoted a comfortable and understanding ambiance. This was not a deliberate cultural adaptation but rather the result of carrying out the implementation in Puerto Rico.

Metaphors and Content

Two additional dimensions were those of metaphors and content. Metaphors are those symbols and concepts shared by the population in question. Bernal and colleagues (1995) asked, are sayings or *dichos* common to the ethnic group part of the intervention? Content refers to how to handle cultural information about values, customs, and traditions within the intervention. One way to approach this question is to ask participants directly in focus groups or guided interviews. Do participants feel understood by the facilitators? Do participants feel that the facilitators respect their cultural values? The TEPSI included metaphors and content pertinent to Puerto Rican parents. Integrated metaphors reflect symbols and concepts shared by participants.

One major modification was the addition of a new first session designed to include information about the nature of depression in adolescents, such as symptoms, causes, myths, realities, and impact on family. This session was added in response to the needs identified by the parents in the focus groups, which had not been incorporated into the original intervention. The inclusion of information about how the adolescent's depression affects the family systems was a great asset. By discussing this topic, parents had an opportunity to voice their own worries, and interventionists had an opportunity to address them directly in the group. Some of the other parents' worries were related to the presence of depressive moods in themselves and other family members. One mother stated, "It is contagious; you get depressed too just by seeing them depressed." Another remarked, "His younger brother is being affected too." Similarly, "A part of her depression comes from the fact that her father suffers from major depression . . . depression is something that is contagious and depletes your energy." One mother simply said, "Depression is contagious." Other mothers' concerns were related to the difficulty of having a child with depression, including statements such as "You can't fall asleep thinking about what's happening in his room" and "It's difficult to deal with a depressed son; it hurts a lot to see your son in that situation" (as the mother cried). Other participants were able to discuss openly how depression in one of their family members affected the entire family system: "No one [in the family] can go to work or sleep feeling relaxed. Everybody is tense; everybody is tense because of what is happening to him" (referring to the child's depression).

In the first session, many of the parents, more frequently the mother, asked about the cause of depression in their son or daughter. They were particularly interested in knowing if they—as parents—were somehow responsible for their child's depression. Feelings of guilt were frequent in mothers who believed they had done something wrong in rearing their child. One mother in the RCT expressed this guilt openly: "One feels guilty because you feel you are not providing adequate discipline" (to the child). The facilitators had the opportunity to clarify misconceptions about the cause of depression, discussing some cultural myths associated with depression in adolescent children, such as "depression in adolescents occurs because of lack of discipline" and explaining the multifactor nature of the condition.

After the small pilot study was conducted to refine the TEPSI, some additional content modifications were made. Although the intervention was well received and had a positive impact in the pilot families, it became clear that the TEPSI should include more material related to family processes. It was evident that parents were very concerned about their role in their child's depression onset, development, and recovery. Consequently, we included material on a developmental perspective by adding information on family life stages in Session 1. The purpose was to connect the adolescent depression with the conflicts and problems that might arise when a family has adolescents growing up. This discussion was guided by a table that shows the stages of family life and the challenges for the family at each period of development (Sorensen & Bernal, 1987). The aim was to help reduce feelings of guilt associated with the onset of depression in a parent's child. Also, information about family patterns transmitted across generations was presented in Session 5 (the first session of the interpersonal module). Parents were asked to complete a family genogram as a personal or family project. This exercise was discussed during Session 6, emphasizing relationship patterns passed on from generation to generation.

In addition to presenting information about family patterns, the preparation of the genogram provided the opportunity to reflect on maladaptive patterns that parents wanted to interrupt or reinforce and maintain in their current family. An example of this provided by a participant was, "If you got hit by accident, then your parents hit you to stop you from crying. I don't want to raise my children the same way. I have never hit my own kids." Another mother commented on her own process of reflection when preparing the family tree:

> It was helpful to see the patterns of women rearing their children alone, being strong and strict. . . . All of us [women in the family] are similar. That's incredible. I don't know if that's learned or genetic, but it is pretty clear; grandmothers helping their daughters raise their children.

This process of reflection was not exclusive to the parents. A mother reported the following commentary made by her son while preparing the family tree:

> Mom, if everybody in the family has stayed together, why are you the only one that has gotten divorced? We're the only ones that are alone [in reference to not having the father living with them]. . . . In the family history the women have put up with a lot, but you have broken the cycle.

Concepts and Goals

Concepts refer to the constructs used within a theoretical psychosocial model. Important questions here include, Are intervention concepts framed within cultural values? Are the concepts consonant with culture and context? Do participants feel understood by the therapists? Are the participants in agreement with the definition of the problem and the specific intervention? *Goals* refer to the congruence between group facilitator and participant as to the goals of the intervention. In many cases it is desirable to frame goals within the values, customs, and traditions of the group in question. The concepts and goals of the TEPSI were consonant with Puerto Rican culture and context. For example, the concept of assertiveness, which was taught as part of the adolescents' CBT, was discussed with the parents. The discussion of children's assertiveness was linked to the value of respect for others, a strong cultural value for Latinos/as (Bernal & Sáez-Santiago, 2005). In this discussion parents were taught that the adolescents' assertiveness is not an attempt to disrespect them. This is very important because respect for parents is a central value for Latinos/as, and we did not want to create the impression that children's assertiveness could challenge this value.

Methods

This dimension takes into consideration the incorporation of cultural knowledge into intervention procedures. It implies that methods and procedures used by group facilitators respond to and are compatible with the participants' culture. As was mentioned earlier, the results from the focus groups with parents of adolescents who had depression indicated that most would want to participate in a supplemental intervention while their children were individually treated but were not interested in a "therapeutic" intervention. Because the manual by Muñoz et al. (2000) is for the treatment of depression in adult Latinos/as, the focus of the intervention to be delivered was modified from a therapeutic to a psychoeducational one.

Context

Finally, several contextual issues were considered to increase the parents' acceptance of and attendance to the intervention. Context, the last dimension of the framework, is the consideration of such processes as acculturative stress, phases of migration, developmental stages, availability of social supports, and the person's relationship to the country or culture of origin. Taking these contextual elements into consideration, we made some adjustments in regard to day and time for the meetings. First of all, the TEPSI was conducted on a Saturday because many parents had commitments during weekdays. Second, the TEPSI was carried out concurrently with the adolescents' therapy session. Thus, the parents had to come only once per week to our center. Third, the transportation expenses of some of the parents who reported serious financial problems were covered by the research project.

OBSERVATIONS ABOUT ACCEPTABILITY AND ENGAGEMENT

In general, the TEPSI was successfully delivered to the nine groups. It was feasible within the treatment for the adolescents' depression. Group attendance was high, with a 70% group attendance across all nine groups. The highest group attendance was 80%, and the lowest was 54%. At the individual level, 67% of parents attended at least six of the eight sessions. Participant attendance is very important given the sequential nature of group material.

Overall, the TEPSI was well received by the parents. At the end of the TEPSI, at the closing session, most parents expressed satisfaction with the intervention and with the benefits of participation. Parents reported that the TEPSI contributed to reducing their child's depression symptoms and improving family interactions. These parents' reception supports the notion that the TEPSI is sensitive to the participants' needs and characteristics.

The following quotes illustrate the parents' acceptance of the TEPSI, which in general they described as supportive and informative. A father commented on how comforting it was to realize that other parents were also dealing with depression in their children:

> I believe that all of us have learned it: We are not the only ones in this
> world that have this problem [a child with depression]. There are a lot of

us in the same situation. There are others [parents] out there, and I try, from the few things that I have learned, to deliver the message. That's one of the most important things that I have learned here. We all are in the same boat.

This father was so grateful that he stated he would teach other parents how to deal with their child's depression. He also mentioned that the strategies discussed were very useful and that he would continue using the manual provided as part of the TEPSI:

I believe that if I had taken this program before my daughter was born, maybe I wouldn't be here. I feel that this is a program where we have learned to deal with the child rearing . . . and this is a guide. . . . I recommend we not throw out this [the manual], that we continue using it, reading it, so it can be part of our natural language.

One mother said that the TEPSI helped her realize that she and her husband had to make changes in their child-rearing practices to support their son's therapeutic process:

My husband and I are happy because we have seen a change in him [son], and we have also had to change. If we have to make adjustments, we make them . . . the workshop [the TEPSI] has been excellent. I have changed a lot of things because I was doing them out of ignorance. I have changed a lot of the techniques I used because they've worked. You think you're doing things right and you say, why do I have to go [to the TEPSI]?—the one who has to go is my son; but the truth is that it was good. My son is calmer, following the rules more. He knows that if he doesn't, there will be consequences. He's doing OK.

This statement also demonstrates the impact of the TEPSI on a parent who did not attend the intervention, in this case the father. In many cases, the participant parent commented often on how some information would be beneficial for other family members (his or her partner, the child's father or mother, the grandmother) who did not participate in the TEPSI. The participant parent was asked to share the information with the family member, and some of them reported in session how the family member had responded to new information.

From our experience throughout all the TEPSI groups, there is no doubt that in many cases family environment plays a critical role in the development, maintenance, and remission of depression symptoms in adolescents (Bernal et al., 2006). Thus, it is necessary to have family members involved in some way in the adolescent's treatment. This is particularly true for Latino/a families, who are characterized by values of *familismo* and *personalismo*. The TEPSI is an alternative to educate the parents of depressed adolescents about the nature of depression and how to deal with their child depression.

Limitations in the implementation phase were the scarce male presence and assistance to the groups. Even though the group was open to both parents or to the custodial parent and his or her partner, most groups were mainly composed of mothers. Only five men participated across the nine groups. Some of the female group participants shared their belief that it would have been beneficial if their male partner had attended the meetings with them. According to some mothers, fathers did not come to sessions for several reasons, such as they were working, taking care of another child or other children at home, or not feeling summoned to participate. The lack of participation of one parent affects the proper implementation of family changes, activities, or tasks learned and agreed on in the group.

Given the influential cultural expectation of mothers as the principal child caretaker, specific strategies need to be used in future groups to openly acknowledge the need and importance of male attendance and participation. Specifically, we recommend using a personal approach through phone calls, personalized letters, one-to-one contact, or a combination of these to invite fathers or male partners to attend and participate in group meetings. Another strategy is to have personalized manuals—for each father and mother—and always make room arrangements for both parents.

CONCLUSION

A psychoeducational intervention for parents of Latino/a adolescents with depression was culturally developed and adapted using an ecological validity model (Bernal et al., 1995) and following several research phases that are essential for an intervention development and evaluation. The TEPSI was successfully implemented as part of the treatment for adolescents receiving individual CBT. This intervention is one of the treatment conditions that is being evaluated as part of an RCT. Results from this RCT will be published upon completion of the study. However, preliminary qualitative data show that the TEPSI was well received by the parents. Many parents who participated in the TEPSI reported benefits for themselves and their children (e.g., decreasing symptoms of depression in their child, improved family interactions and communication). Although the majority of the parents who have participated in the TEPSI groups have been Puerto Rican (with a few Dominican parents), we believe that this intervention, with some modifications, could be implemented with other Latinos/as as well as with other ethnocultural groups. In addition, we believe that the research process presented in this chapter could be useful when developing or adapting any psychosocial intervention for any ethnocultural groups as well.

REFERENCES

Aguilar-Gaxiola, S. A., Muñoz, R. F., & Guzman, J. (2001). *Integrating cognitive-behavior therapy techniques and interpersonal therapy goals: Enhancing the treatment of depression in Hispanics.* Unpublished manuscript, Department of Psychology, California State University, Fresno.

Asarnow, J. R., Scott, C. V., & Mintz, J. (2002).A combined cognitive-behavioral family education intervention for depression in children: A treatment development study, *Cognitive Therapy and Research, 26,* 221–229. doi: 10.1023/A:1014573803928

Bernal, G., Bonilla, J., & Bellido, C. (1995). Ecological validity and cultural sensitivity for outcome research: Issues for the cultural adaptation and development of psychosocial treatments with Hispanics. *Journal of Abnormal Child Psychology, 23,* 67–82. doi:10.1007/BF01447045

Bernal, G., Cumba-Avilés, E., & Sáez-Santiago, E. (2006). Cultural and relational processes in depressed Latino adolescents. In S. R. H. Beach, M. Z. Wamboldt, N. Kaslow, R. E. Heyman, M. B. First, L. G. Underwood, & D. Reiss (Eds.), *Relational process and DSM–V. Neuroscience, assessment, prevention, and intervention* (pp. 211–224). Washington, DC: American Psychiatric Publishing.

Bernal, G., & Reyes, M. (2008). Psychosocial treatments for depression with adult Latinos. In Aguilar-Gaxiola, S. Gullota, & T. Magaña (Eds.), *Depression in Latinos: Assessments, treatments, and prevention* (pp. 189–204). New York, NY: Springer-Verlag.

Bernal, G., & Sáez-Santiago, E. (2005). Toward culturally centered and evidenced-based treatments for depressed adolescents. In W. Pinsoff & J. Lebow (Eds.), *Family psychology: The art of the science* (pp.471–489). New York, NY: Oxford University Press

Braswell, L. (1991). Involving parents in cognitive–behavioral therapy with children and adolescents. In P. C. Kendall (Ed.), *Child and adolescent therapy* (pp. 316–351). New York, NY: Guilford Press.

Brent, D. A., Holder, D., Kolko, D., Brimaher, B., Baugher, M., Roth, C., . . . Johnson, B. A. (1997). A clinical psychotherapy trial for adolescent depression comparing cognitive, family, and supportive treatments. *Archives of General Psychiatry, 54,* 877–885. doi:10.1001/archpsyc.1997.01830210125017

Clarke, G. N., Hops, H., Lewinsohn, P. M., & Andrews, J. (1992). Cognitive–behavioral group treatment of adolescent depression: Prediction of outcome. *Behavior Therapy, 23,* 341–354. doi:10.1016/S0005-7894(05)80162-5

Falicov, C. J. (1998). *Latino families in therapy: A guide to multicultural practice.* New York, NY: Guilford Press.

Joiner, T., & Coyne, J. C. (Eds.). (1999). *The interactional nature of depression: Advances in interpersonal approaches.* Washington, DC: American Psychological Association. doi:10.1037/10311-000

Kazdin, A. E., Bass, D., Ayers, W. A., & Rodgers, A. (1990). Empirical and clinical focus of child and adolescent psychotherapy research. *Journal of Consulting and Clinical Psychology, 58,* 729–740. doi:10.1037/0022-006X.58.6.729

Kazdin, A. E., & Weisz, J. R. (1998). Identifying and developing empirically supported child and adolescent treatments. *Journal of Consulting and Clinical Psychology, 66,* 19–36. doi:10.1037/0022-006X.66.1.19

Kovacs, M., & Sherrill, J. T. (2001). The psychotherapy management of major depressive and dysthymic disorders in childhood and adolescence: Issues and prospects. In I. M. Goodyear (Ed.), *The depressed child and adolescent: Developmental and clinical perspectives* (2nd ed., pp. 325–352). Cambridge, England: Cambridge University Press. doi:10.1017/CBO9780511543821.013

Lewinsohn, P. M., Clarke, G. N., Hops, H., & Andrews, J. (1990). Cognitive–behavioral group treatment of depression in adolescents. *Behavior Therapy, 21,* 385–401. doi:10.1016/S0005-7894(05)80353-3

Lewinsohn, P. M., Clarke, G. N., Rhode, P., Hops, H., & Seeley, J. R. (1996). A course in coping: A cognitive–behavioral approach to the treatment of depression. In E. D. Hibbs & P. S. Jensen (Eds.), *Psychosocial treatments for child and adolescent disorders: Empirically based strategies for clinical practice* (pp. 109–135). Washington, DC: American Psychological Association. doi:10.1037/10196-005

Lewinsohn, P. M., Clarke, G. N., Seeley, J. R., & Rhode, P. (1994). Major depression in community adolescents: Age at onset, episode duration, and time to recurrence. *Journal of the American Academy of Child & Adolescent Psychiatry, 33,* 809–818. doi:10.1097/00004583-199407000-00006

March, J. (2004). Fluoxetine, cognitive–behavioral therapy, and their combination for adolescents with depression: Treatment for Adolescents With Depression Study (TADS) randomized controlled trial. *JAMA, 292,* 807–820. doi:10.1001/jama.292.21.2578-c

Martínez, A., & Rosselló, J. (1995). Depresión y funcionamiento familiar en niños/as y adolescentes puertorriqueños/as [Depression and family functioning in Puerto Rican children and adolescents]. *Revista Puertorriqueña de Psicología, 10,* 215–245.

Miranda, J. (2000). *Mental health outcomes for Latinos: Current knowledge base for improving mental health services.* Washington, DC: Georgetown University Medical Center.

Muñoz, R. F., Ghosh-Ippen, C., Valdes-Dwyer, E., Rao, S., & Le, H. (2000). *Manual de terapia de grupo para el tratamiento cognitivo-conductual de la depresión: Aprendiendo a manejar su realidad personal. Cuaderno para participantes* [Manual for group cognitive-behavioral therapy of major depression: A reality management approach. Participant manual]. University of California, San Francisco.

Muñoz, R. F., Yin, Y., Bernal, G., Pérez-Stable, E. J., Sorensen, J. D., Hargraves, W. H., . . . Miller, L. S. (1995). Prevention of clinical depression with primary care patients: A randomized controlled trial. *American Journal of Community Psychology, 23,* 199–222. doi:10.1007/BF02506936

Padilla, L., Dávila, E., & Rosselló, J. (2002). Problemas presentados por un grupo de adolescentes puertorriqueños/as con depresión y por sus padres [Presented prob-

lems of a group of Puerto Rican adolescents with depression and their parents].
Pedagogía, 36, 80–91.

Perez, J. E. (1999). Integration of cognitive–behavioral and interpersonal therapies
for Latinos: An argument for technical eclecticism. *Journal of Contemporary
Psychotherapy*, 29, 169–183. doi:10.1023/A:1021912900366

Reyes-Rodríguez, M. (2002, November). *Treatment for depression with adult primary
care patients in Puerto Rico: Preliminary findings of a pilot study*. Oral presentation
at Robert Wood Johnson Medical School, University of Medicine & Dentistry
of New Jersey, Princeton.

Rosselló, J., & Bernal, G. (1999). The efficacy of cognitive–behavioral and interpersonal treatments for depression in Puerto Rican adolescents. *Journal of Consulting and Clinical Psychology*, 67, 734–745. doi:10.1037/0022-006X.67.5.734

Rosselló, J., Bernal, G., & Rivera-Medina, C. (2008). Randomized trial of CBT and
IPT in individual and group format for depression in Puerto Rican adolescents.
Cultural Diversity and Ethnic Minority Psychology, 14, 234–245. doi:10.1037/1099-
9809.14.3.234

Rosselló, J., & Rivera, Z. (1999). Problemas interpersonales presentados por adolescentes puertorriqueños/as con depresión [Presented interpersonal problems of
Puerto Rican adolescents with depression]. *Revista Puertorriqueña de Psicología*,
12, 55–76.

Sáez-Santiago, E., & Bernal, G. (2003). Depression in ethnic minorities: Latinos
and Latinas, African Americans, Asian Americans, and Native Americans. In
G. Bernal, J. E. Trimble, A. K. Burlew, & F. T. L. Leong (Eds.), *Handbook of
racial ethnic minority psychology* (pp.401–428). Thousand Oaks, CA: Sage.

Sáez, E., & Rosselló, J. (1998). Percepción sobre los conflictos maritales de los padres,
ajuste familiar y sintomatología depresiva en adolescentes puertorriqueños [Per-
ception of parental marital conflicts, family adjustment, and depressive symp-
tomatology in Puerto Rican adolescents]. *Interamerican Journal of Psychology*,
31, 279–291.

Sáez-Santiago, E. & Rosselló, J. (2001). Relación entre el ambiente familiar, los síntomas depresivos y los problemas de conducta en adolescentes puertorriqueños/
as [Relationship among family environment, depressive symptoms, and behavior problems in Puerto Rican adolescents]. *Interamerican Journal of Psychology*,
35,113–125.

Sáez Santiago, E. & Rosselló, J. (2005). Contexto familiar, síntomas depresivos y del
trastorno de conducta en un grupo de adolescentes puertorriqueños/as [Family
context, symptoms of depression, and conduct disorder in a group of Puerto
Rican adolescents]. *Revista Puertorriqueña de Psicología*, 16, 1–25.

Sander, J. B., & McCarty, C. A. (2005). Youth depression in the family context:
Familial risk factors and models of treatment. *Clinical Child and Family Psychology
Review*, 8, 203–219. doi:10.1007/s10567-005-6666-3

Sanford, M., Szatmari, P., Spinner, M., Monroe-Blum, H., Jamieson, E., Walsh,
C., & Jones, D. (1995). Predicting the one-year course of adolescent major

depression. *Journal of the American Academy of Child & Adolescent Psychiatry, 34,* 1618–1628. doi:10.1097/00004583-199512000-00012

Sorensen, J. L., & Bernal, G. (1987). *A family like yours: Breaking the patterns of drug abuse.* New York, NY: Harper & Row.

Stark, K. D., Brookman, C. S., & Frazier, R. (1990). A comprehensive school-based treatment program for depressed children. *School Psychology Quarterly, 5,* 1990, 111–140.

Wells, K. B., Sherbourne, C., Schoenbaum, M., Duan, N., Meredith, L., Unuetzer, J., . . . Rubenstein, L. V. (2000). Impact of disseminating quality improvement programs for depression in managed primary care: A randomized controlled trial. *JAMA, 283,* 212–220. doi:10.1001/jama.283.2.212

Wells, K. C., & Albano, A. M. (2005). Parent involvement in CBT treatment of adolescent depression: Experiences in the Treatment for Adolescents With Depression study (TADS). *Cognitive and Behavioral Practice, 12,* 209–220. doi:10.1016/S1077-7229(05)80026-4

6

HEALTH PSYCHOLOGY IN PRACTICE: ADAPTATION OF AN INTERVENTION FOR LATINAS WITH TYPE 2 DIABETES

MANUEL BARRERA JR., DEBORAH J. TOOBERT, LISA A. STRYCKER, AND DIEGO OSUNA

The national discussion on health disparities draws needed attention to the ways in which racial and ethnic subgroups differ in the prevalence of diseases and in access to health care for those disorders. Because of its elevated prevalence in African American, Native American, and Latino communities, Type 2 diabetes is a disorder that shows large health disparities. Its progression carries the risk of serious health consequences, such as blindness, heart disease, kidney failure, and amputations. Type 2 diabetes was once called adult-onset diabetes (or non-insulin-dependent diabetes) to distinguish it from Type 1 (or juvenile-onset, insulin-dependent) diabetes. Some 90% to 95% of individuals who are diagnosed with diabetes have Type 2 diabetes (U.S. Department of Health and Human Services, National Institutes of Health, National Institute of Diabetes and Digestive and Kidney Diseases, 2008). Because of the rise in obesity and other lifestyle risk factors, the prevalence of diabetes is expected

The work reported here was supported by Grant R01 HL077120 from the National Heart, Lung, and Blood Institute. We acknowledge the invaluable contributions of the assessment and intervention staffs of the ¡Viva Bien! project, including Cristy Geno Rasmussen, Alyssa Doty, Fabio Almeida, Sara Hoerlein, Carmen Martin, Angela Casola, Eve Halterman, and Breanne A. Griffin. We are deeply indebted to the 280 dedicated and committed women who participated in the study. We are also indebted to our esteemed colleague, Diego Osuna, who passed away just prior to the completion of this chapter.

to grow to epidemic proportions in the years to come and to affect younger segments of the U.S. population (Narayan, Boyle, Thompson, Sorensen, & Williamson, 2003). In addition to the influences of genetics and biological processes, the critical importance of behavior in the self-management and prevention of Type 2 diabetes has made it a prominent health psychology topic (Gonder-Frederick, Cox, & Ritterband, 2002).

For Latinos, Type 2 diabetes has special significance. Not only is the prevalence of diabetes among Latinos nearly twice as high as for White Americans (Centers for Disease Control and Prevention, National Center for Health Statistics, 2007) but also there are barriers to effective health services for Latinos with diabetes. As a result, in part, of a relative lack of health insurance, Latinos do not always have ready access to health professionals who can formally diagnose and treat diabetes. And for those with insurance, there is a scarcity of bilingual and culturally appropriate resources.

In this chapter, we describe the considerations for and process of adapting an evidence-based behavioral intervention for Latinas who are diagnosed with Type 2 diabetes. We provide a brief review of the efficacy of lifestyle interventions for Type 2 diabetes; describe the original evidence-based treatment, the Mediterranean Lifestyle Program (MLP), that was the source of the cultural adaptation; present the conceptual framework, process, and methods used in adapting the intervention; and put forth recommendations to clinicians and program developers.

PSYCHOSOCIAL INTERVENTIONS FOR TYPE 2 DIABETES

Because Type 2 diabetes is a chronic illness influenced by many lifestyle behaviors, psychosocial interventions often focus on diabetes self-management (Norris, Lau, Smith, Schmid, & Engelgau, 2002). Self-management involves the daily practice of eating a healthful diet, being physically active, self-monitoring blood glucose, taking medication, solving problems, and reducing complications secondary to diabetes (Toobert, Strycker, Glasgow, Barrera, & Angell, 2005). Several interventions have been successful in improving self-management behaviors, at least in the short term (Brown, Garcia, Kouzekanani, & Hanis, 2002; Norris et al., 2002; Toobert et al., 2005). Such interventions can improve glycemic control and body weight (Irwin et al., 2000; Norris et al., 2002). Improved glycemic control is also related to increased contact time in the intervention, suggesting a dosage effect (Brown et al., 2005; Norris et al., 2002). That finding raises the possibility that intense contact with treatment staff and other participants might lead to greater beneficial outcomes than do less intense interventions.

Without continued contact, self-management interventions have only a short-term impact (less than 6 months) on diabetes-related outcomes (Norris et al., 2002). Newman, Steed, and Mulligan (2004) pointed out that an enduring issue for diabetes self-management interventions is the maintenance of behavior changes that were achieved through treatment. Expectation of long-term effects from short-term diabetes self-management interventions might be unreasonable in the same way that withdrawing diabetes medications after 6 months might be contraindicated.

Behavioral-risk-factor trials typically address weight loss alone (Gonder-Frederick et al., 2002), diet alone (Swinburn, Metcalf, & Ley, 2001), physical activity alone (Hurley & Roth, 2000), and diet combined with physical activity (Wing & Anglin, 1996). Interventions targeting multiple risk factors in addition to diet and physical activity are sorely lacking.

There have been several efforts to deliver behavioral diabetes interventions to Latinos. A review found 11 published intervention studies directed specifically at Latino adults with Type 2 diabetes (Whittemore, 2007). Most of the interventions were diabetes education programs that offered 2- to 2.5-hour weekly classes over a 4- to 6-week period. Notable exceptions were programs developed by Sharon A. Brown and her colleagues that combined diabetes education with support groups extending over 12 months (Brown et al., 2002, 2005). Culturally relevant intervention strategies illustrated across the various studies were the use of Spanish in meetings and materials, employment of bilingual and bicultural staff, inclusion of family members in some intervention activities, use of ethnic foods and music, provision of classes at accessible community venues, and use of support groups or other opportunities for social engagement. The results of these interventions were promising but also showed that there is much more work to be done. Only three studies found improvements in healthful dietary behaviors, two studies found improvements in exercise behaviors, and none found improvements in blood lipids and body mass. Also, intervention effects were never assessed for more than 16 months and often for far less time. Overall, there is still a need for randomized trials of interventions that (a) are comprehensive in addressing the several important elements of diabetes self-management (e.g., diet, exercise, stress management); (b) have sustained effects over long time periods; and (c) include practices that will attract, engage, and successfully treat Latinos and others who have a high prevalence of diabetes.

SELECTING A SOURCE PROGRAM FOR ADAPTATION: THE MEDITERRANEAN LIFESTYLE PROGRAM

The MLP is an evidence-based multicomponent intervention for women with diabetes. The intervention aimed to decrease dietary fat intake and increase physical activity, stress management practices, supportive resources, and problem-solving skills for a predominantly White American sample of 279 postmenopausal women with Type 2 diabetes in Lane County, Oregon (Toobert et al., 2005). Because postmenopausal women with diabetes are at particularly high risk for heart disease, the MLP had the specialized goal of reducing the risk for heart disease as well as improving diabetes self-management. The program was modeled after intervention procedures shown to be effective in reducing heart disease risk with middle-age men (Ornish et al., 1990) and with women (Toobert, Glasgow, & Radcliffe, 2000). After an intense 6-month intervention period, the MLP also extended intervention activities over 2 years in hopes of improving the maintenance of beneficial effects. The MLP is unique among diabetes lifestyle interventions in that providing an intense multicomponent intervention that is intended to make sizable sustained changes in a number of outcomes, including those that have special relevance for heart disease.

Intervention Components

The MLP began with a 2.5-day nonresidential retreat during which women were taught all program components. Retreats were followed by 6 months of weekly meetings consisting of 1 hour each of physical activity, stress management, a Mediterranean diet potluck, and support groups. Participants received manuals that detailed each aspect of the MLP and videotapes to guide stress management and exercise. An exercise physiologist, stress management leader, and support group leaders were present at every program meeting.

Dietary Practices

A registered dietitian taught participants the Mediterranean alpha-linolenic acid–rich diet (de Lorgeril et al., 1994). The diet recommended more whole-grain bread; more root vegetables, green vegetables, and legumes; more fish and poultry; less red meat; daily fruit; and avoidance of butter and cream, to be replaced by olive or canola oil products.

Physical Activity

Participants were advised to build up to 1 hour of moderate aerobic activity per day (e.g., walking), at least 3 days per week. At the retreat and weekly meetings, participants could choose between 1-hour aerobic sessions led by an exercise physiologist or an outdoor walk led by trained exercise assistants. The exercise physiologist held a doctorate and was a university instructor of physical education. Resistance training also was included. The complete physical activity program was as follows: (a) moderate aerobic activity 30 minutes most days per week; (b) 10 strength-training exercises performed two times per week, building up to three sets of 10 to 15 repetitions; and (c) formal warm-up and cool-down routines.

Stress Management

Participants were instructed in yoga, progressive deep relaxation, meditation, and directed or receptive imagery (Ornish et al., 1990; Toobert, Strycker, & Glasgow, 1998). Stress management leaders were certified yoga instructors. Participants were asked to practice the techniques for at least 1 hour per day.

Support Groups

One professional with at least master's level training in counseling psychology and one peer leader led each support group. Professional and peer leaders received extensive training in the supportive-expressive group therapy model used with the chronically and terminally ill (Spiegel & Classen, 2000). All leaders were supervised weekly by a clinical psychologist who was a research project staff member.

Intervention Outcomes

The MLP was evaluated in a clinical trial that randomly assigned 279 women to either the MLP or a usual care (UC) condition. All participants were recruited from primary care practices in which they received their medical care for diabetes. Participants in the UC condition continued with their regular medical care and did not receive any of the MLP intervention activities. UC typically followed standards of care recommended by the American Diabetes Association and was directed at diabetes control, management of complications associated with diabetes, and monitoring of other health factors, such as cholesterol and hypertension. Participants were assessed on a battery of measures at baseline, after 6 months, and then annually from 12 through 84 months. The short- and long-term effects of the MLP intervention through the first 2 years of data collection have been reported in several publications (Toobert et al., 2005, 2007). The intervention reduced the consumption of total fat and saturated fat and increased fiber, fruit, and vegetable servings. Compared with the UC participants, the MLP participants increased physical activity outcomes at the 6-, 12-, and 24-month follow-ups and significantly increased the time engaged in stress management activities at both the 6- and 12-month follow-ups. The MLP improved perceptions of social support and social ecological resources at the 6-, 12-, and 24-month follow-ups. Also, there were significant decreases in body mass index and glycated hemoglobin in the MLP women compared with the UC women at 6 months.

Participation and attendance rates indicated that despite the time commitment, women with Type 2 diabetes and their providers viewed the MLP as attractive and feasible. Results demonstrated that the MLP was efficacious, producing several significant improvements across a variety of behavioral, physical, and psychosocial measures. Furthermore, the MLP demonstrated effects on diet, exercise, and body mass (many of them maintained over follow-up assessments) that were not found consistently in interventions used with Latinos (Whittemore, 2007).

METHODS FOR ADAPTING AN EFFECTIVE INTERVENTION

The motivations for considering an adaptation of the MLP for Latinas were obvious. There was good evidence that the MLP was effective in improving a number of outcomes central to the health of women with diabetes. Also, the high prevalence of diabetes among Latinas pointed to the necessity for effective interventions to improve the self-management of diabetes and to prevent disease complications. Although it was apparent that Latinas had a need for a diabetes intervention, it was not apparent whether the MLP was appropriate for them; whether the MLP would benefit from adaptations to increase its appeal and effectiveness; and if it were to be adapted, how those changes should be made.

The process of determining whether a cultural adaptation is justified and how the adaptation should be conducted is neither straightforward nor well understood, but inroads have been made. Thoughtful analyses describe conditions that justify cultural adaptations (see the review of models in Chapter 2, this volume). An early version of Barrera and Castro's (2006) heuristic model was developed to guide adaptations of the MLP. The model specifies four stages of adaptation: (a) information gathering, (b) preliminary adaptation design, (c) preliminary adaptation tests, and (d) adaptation refinement. These stages combine quantitative and qualitative data to inform decisions about the justification for conducting a cultural adaptation and for developing the adaptation itself.

Information Gathering

The purpose of the first stage, information gathering, is to clarify the need for a cultural adaptation and to become better informed about the form and content of needed adaptations by searching literature for relevant data, and conducting qualitative research with potential participants using a structured focus group format. In the literature search on Latinas, data on several topics were relevant: (a) the prevalence of diabetes and its complications,

(b) the prevalence of risk factors, and (c) the relation of risk factors to diabetes indicators. Studies that showed ethnic group differences in the prevalence of diabetes and its risk factors would support the need for an intervention directed at Latinas (Resnicow, Baranowski, Ahluwalia, & Braithwaite, 1999). Research showing ethnic differences in the magnitude of relations between risk factors and outcomes, or the presence of unique risk factors, might suggest different underlying mechanisms and the need for intervention methods that might be uniquely suited for Latinas.

The literature revealed a substantial need to provide diabetes interventions to Latinas. Latinos living in the United States have high rates of diabetes and associated complications; diabetes prevalence is twice as high and more severe in Latinos compared with White Americans (Mokdad et al., 2000). Furthermore, Latinas differ from others on the prevalence of key diabetes risk factors. They were more likely to report no leisure-time physical activity than African American and White American women (Crespo, Keteyian, Heath, & Sempos, 1996) and were more likely to be obese than White American women (Ogden et al., 2006). With one important exception, the literature provided little evidence to suggest that Latinas differ from other groups in the relations between risk factors and diabetes-relevant characteristics.

The exception was a study showing that even after controlling for obesity indicators such as body mass and waist-to-hip ratios, Mexican Americans had greater impairment on underlying diabetes disease processes (e.g., greater insulin resistance, lower insulin sensitivity) than White Americans (Black, 2002). Those findings suggest the possibility of unique biological factors that contribute to diabetes mechanisms for those of Mexican heritage and perhaps other Latino subgroups. On the other hand, the Diabetes Prevention Project, a multisite national study of more than 3,000 participants, was an impressive demonstration of how an intervention to change diet and exercise behaviors of adults could prevent the incidence of Type 2 diabetes (Diabetes Prevention Program Research Group, 2002). Furthermore, the intervention was as effective for Latinos as it was for participants of other races and ethnicities. Overall, the literature review suggested that interventions directed at nutrition, physical activity, and other risk factors could be as effective in managing diabetes for Latinos as for White Americans.

In the information-gathering stage, we conducted focus groups with Latinas to assess the perceived need for an intervention and to answer key feasibility questions (Osuna et al., 2011). Four focus groups were held, two conducted in English and two in Spanish. Focus group leaders described the original MLP and then used an outline of specific questions to guide the discussions. The three central questions were: (a) What do you like about the program that we just described? (b) What do you not like about it? and (c) What would make it difficult for you to participate in a program like that?

When time permitted, focus group leaders asked follow-up questions to elicit reactions to the core features of the MLP, such as the retreat and the 4-hour weekly meetings. The focus group interviews were audiotaped, transcribed, and analyzed for major themes and trends.

A focus group participant articulated a general need for Latinas to have access to an organized, group-format program like ¡Viva Bien!, which she referred to as a "support group":

> I believe in a support group because sometimes one feels very lonely . . . and especially Latinos are very much badly affected. . . . They don't know how good it is to have a support group. I need this group class to support people because we don't have enough people or groups to support us. We are alone. I never thought I would ever have diabetes.

Although we invited participants to criticize the core components of the program (nutrition, exercise, stress management, and support) and the meeting structure, no strong objections were voiced. One suggested addition was some form of family involvement and an element of prevention:

> Hispanic people are always thinking about the family. . . . I think that in the group, there could be something that could attract the family members. For example, on one occasion, have a meeting with all the family members so that you explain to them what is happening. . . . Give them a presentation so they know about diabetes before they have it, because it goes in the family. Then do a prevention sort of thing so they will know what to do not to get it in the future. And so that they start cooking, maybe not every day, but progressively, to help them avoid an illness.

Overall, from the focus group discussions we learned that participants (a) were aware that lifestyle has a significant impact on health, (b) expressed a desire to learn more about healthful lifestyles, (c) were motivated to improve health because of desires to prolong an active life with family members (e.g., play with one's grandchildren) and to improve the lifestyle habits of family members, (d) perceived a scarcity and subsequent need for such programs designed for them, and (e) were amenable to an intensive program format like the one used in the MLP.

Preliminary Adaptation Design

The literature review and focus group components of the information-gathering stage did not suggest that any drastic changes should be made to the MLP before piloting it with Latinas. As a result, we maintained the core aspects of the MLP. In the next stage, preliminary adaptation design, the professional team of intervention developers prepared the intervention for pilot testing. The MLP was renamed ¡Viva Bien! for its application exclusively with Latina women. A key departure from the recruitment strategy used in the MLP was the decision to implement ¡Viva Bien! in a large health maintenance organization and a community health center. That decision created the possibility of testing the effectiveness of the program within organizations that might realistically adopt the intervention if it proved cost-effective.

The ¡Viva Bien! research team included all of the primary investigators who had developed and evaluated the MLP as well as a new set of investigators who were familiar with Latinas served by health care systems. Investigators included those of Mexican, Central American, and South American heritages whose professional backgrounds were in medicine, nutrition, psychology, public health, and social work. The team used information from the first stage and its own knowledge of Latina and health care system cultures to develop initial recruitment and intervention procedures. In the absence of evidence suggesting a need for fundamental changes to the original evidence-based treatment, we determined that surface structure (Resnicow et al., 1999) changes in the recruitment and intervention procedures were warranted. *Surface structure* "involves matching intervention materials and messages to observable 'superficial' (though nonetheless important) characteristics of a target population" (Resnicow et al., 1999, p. 11). Our decision was consistent with Lau's (2006) admonition to alter just those core aspects of evidence-based treatments identified as being in need of adaptation by qualitative or quantitative data.

Informed Consent

Research team members who worked within the host health care system were keenly aware of the long and complex informed consent documents typically used in their studies. Adapted informed consent procedures were developed in English and Spanish to encourage participation by Latina women with a range of literacy skills and education. All recruitment materials reflected a fifth-grade reading level. The institutional review board approved an abbreviated user-friendly informed consent form that combined the consent and Health Insurance Portability and Accountability Act forms into one document; information about the program was printed as a separate brochure. The changes resulted in a streamlined consent form that was engaging and much less legalistic than forms typically used by health organizations.

Intervention Content and Procedures

The ¡Viva Bien! intervention sessions at the retreat and weekly meetings were structured so that information was conveyed in Spanish and English concurrently. For most sessions at the retreat, visual information was provided in slide presentations on separate screens for Spanish and English, and further information was given by either bilingual speakers or English speakers with Spanish translators.

Diet

The ¡Viva Bien! diet component was adapted from the alpha-linolenic acid-rich Mediterranean diet (de Lorgeril et al., 1994) by the project's Latina dietitian. Latin American recipes were altered to conform to the ¡Viva Bien! diet principles by lowering fat and calories while maintaining flavor with traditional ingredients and spices. Because Latinas represent a diverse group, there is no typical "Latino diet." Thus, recipes from specific Latin American countries were modified using common staples.

Physical Activity and Stress Management

The ¡Viva Bien! activity and stress management activities were modified slightly to include cultural elements. For example, physical activity and stress management classes were led in both English and Spanish, with Latin (e.g., salsa) style steps and music, and take-home physical activity and stress management CDs were created in both English and Spanish.

The research team considered making adaptations to the stress management intervention component before the preliminary adaptation test. Because yoga and meditation are practices whose origins lie in part in Asian cultures and some may perceive a religious component in these practices, some staff members were concerned that these activities might be incongruent with Latina participants' cultural and religious experiences and practices. Without research evidence supporting these concerns, and because the focus group participants did not raise similar concerns, we decided to preserve the stress management procedures.

Social Support

In mediation analyses of the MLP, we found evidence that improvements in problem solving (Glasgow, Toobert, Barrera, & Strycker, 2004) and social support resources (Barrera, Strycker, MacKinnon, & Toobert, 2008) partially accounted for intervention effects. As a result, we modified the social support group component used in the MLP for ¡Viva Bien! not so much because of cultural considerations but more to explicitly teach problem solving and to mobilize social support among family members and friends. To accommodate language preferences, women were offered groups conducted primarily in English or primarily in Spanish.

Summary

Planning the preliminary adaptation design identified intervention components (e.g., stress management) that caused us to consider making significant changes to the original MLP. However, without convincing data, we resisted changes. What did change from the MLP to ¡Viva Bien! was a shift in recruitment from individual practitioner offices to large health organizations, the introduction of clear and engaging informed consent procedures, inclusion of Spanish and English in written and verbal communication, modification of the diet component to include familiar Latin American foods, and changes to the support groups to emphasize behavior change activities.

Preliminary Adaptation Test (Pilot Study)

The third stage, the preliminary adaptation test, was a 3-month pilot study with 12 participants. It was conducted as an initial assessment of cultural adaptation procedures in preparation for the full 2-year lifestyle-change program planned for the main study of nearly 300 Latina women. The pilot study was designed to test recruitment procedures (including modified informed consent procedures and materials), pre- and posttest assessment measures, and the first 3 months of the 2-year intervention. Its primary value was the opportunity to collect (a) reactions from staff and participants on the engagement and intervention procedures and (b) suggestions about elements to add or change to increase cultural fit. The pilot study design also allowed for crude tests of pre- to postintervention change on a variety of measures and for satisfaction ratings. The statistical significance of pre- to posttreatment change on specific measures was not the primary interest; rather, we wanted to know whether the data generally indicated that participants implemented the program and demonstrated expected changes on outcome and mediating variables.

Demographic, physiologic, behavioral, and psychosocial measures were collected at baseline and immediately following the abbreviated intervention at 3 months. Ongoing feedback from intervention staff and participants about all aspects of the program was recorded in the minutes of staff meetings and weekly social support group supervision sessions. Support group sessions were audiotaped and reviewed by a Latino clinical psychologist coinvestigator. Attendance was taken at all program meetings, and a one-item satisfaction survey was administered on all days of the retreat and at the final weekly meeting.

Adaptations From the Pilot Study

Feedback from staff and participants during the pilot study led to several valuable additions to the original intervention procedures.

Additional Family Involvement

During support group sessions, we learned that women wanted their family members to be better informed about the ¡Viva Bien! intervention to more fully support their lifestyle changes throughout the intervention. Subsequently, we added a "Family Night" so that family members could observe participants during program activities, join them in the potluck dinner, and exchange questions and answers. Educating families about participants' lifestyle changes and soliciting their support was not trivial because families can be major sources of resistance to change or major sources of encouragement. Families were also invited to a final celebratory meeting at the end of the 3-month program. The involvement of Latino families in the intervention is consistent with *familismo*, one of the most fundamental cultural values for Latinos and one that is not specific to a particular Latino nationality (Sabogal, Marin, Otero-Sabogal, Marin, & Perez-Stable, 1987).

Additional Behavioral Modeling

During the adaptation planning, we did not anticipate how much participants would value behavioral modeling by the project's Latina dietitian. The adaptation of the Mediterranean diet used foods and preparation methods that were familiar to participants as well as some that were not (e.g., certain types of seafood, grilling vegetables). The dietitian allayed participants' fears about preparing new foods by conducting 30- to 40-minute demonstrations, often involving some of the participants, showing all of the preparation steps from uncut raw foods to the completed meals. These interactive teaching methods were instrumental in transforming goals for dietary change into actions that were so critical for diabetes self-management.

Additional Physician Presentations for Addressing Embarrassment (Vergüenza)

During support group meetings, some participants identified sensitive issues that they were reluctant to discuss with their personal health care providers. They voiced interest in hearing presentations on those topics by the bilingual, bicultural physician member of the research project. The presentation format (with premeeting collection of questions) gave participants the desired information without the embarrassment of personally discussing sensitive matters with health care providers or the embarrassment of not speaking English fluently. The participants also repeatedly expressed a desire to learn more about diabetes causes, treatments, and complications. Therefore, diabetes group education sessions were initiated and conducted by the study physician.

Analyses of Pre- to Posttreatment Change

Together with verbal feedback from participants and staff, the quantitative data were useful in evaluating participant engagement and effectiveness of the adapted program. There was a consistent pattern of improvement, with 70 of the 76 outcomes tested indicating improvement from baseline to 3 months. The binomial probability of returning 70/76 positive results is quite low, $p < .00001$. It was encouraging to observe significant pre-to-post change on primary outcomes and mediators: grams of saturated fat, body mass index, social support for diet and exercise, and problem solving.

Two important process measures were attendance and satisfaction. Attendance at the retreat was 92% the first 2 days and 100% the 3rd day. Weekly meeting attendance averaged 89% over the 3 months, ranging from 67% to 100% per meeting. Regarding program satisfaction, all (100%) of the women said they liked each day of the retreat "a lot"; 91% said they liked the weekly meetings "a lot."

Of the first three stages of adaptation development, the stage containing the uncontrolled pilot study was by far the most informative. Although support group meetings were not intended to be primary vehicles for delivering information about adaptations, they proved to be particularly helpful in gauging what Latina participants liked, what they perceived as barriers, and what additional resources they needed. Additions to social support groups, and added contact with the dietitian and physician resulted directly from that feedback. In general, pre-to-post data showed that participants were making changes in the desired directions.

Adaptation Refinement and Controlled Evaluation

Changes indicated by pilot study experiences were incorporated into an intervention refinement that was evaluated with 280 Latinas who were recruited through a health maintenance organization and community health center (Barrera, Toobert, Strycker, Osuna, King, & Glasgow, 2011). Latinas with Type 2 diabetes who completed baseline assessment were randomly assigned to either a 2-year version of the ¡Viva Bien! intervention ($n = 142$) or UC ($n = 138$) through their health plan. On average, participants were 57 years old and had been diagnosed with diabetes approximately 10 years prior. About 15% indicated a preference for Spanish (although nearly twice that percentage participated in the Spanish language support groups). The 2-year duration of ¡Viva Bien! was divided into four 6-month periods. Four-hour meetings were held weekly for the first 6-month period, twice each month for the second period, monthly for the next period, and every other month for the final period. Participants received an extensive battery of measures similar to those used in the MLP at pretreatment, 6 months, 12 months and 24 months.

Main findings from ¡Viva Bien! have been published (see Barrera, Toobert, Strycker, Osuna, King, & Glasgow, 2011). The ¡Viva Bien! condition improved considerably more than UC at the 6-, 12-, and 24-month assessments of problem solving (respective effect sizes of 0.50, 0.50, and 0.75) and perceived support (respective effect sizes of 1.00, 0.85, and 0.75). A significant intervention effect was found for participants' reduction of saturated fat consumption at the 6-, 12-, and 24-month assessments (respective effect sizes of 1.00, 0.33, and 0.33). All of those effects compared very favorably with those found in the MLP. However, unlike in the MLP trial, there were no significant intervention effects for increased physical activity or reductions in glycated hemoglobin, areas in need of future adaptation efforts. Further analyses indicated that the adapted intervention's effects on putative mediators and outcomes were comparable for women who varied across levels of acculturation (Barrera, Toobert, Strycker, & Osuna, 2011).

On the basis of their reports of profound improvements, we have no doubt that ¡Viva Bien! was a life-changing experience for some participants:

> Well, you know, I hated the exercise and I hate walking, and now, unbelievable. I walk in the morning and I walk at night. And, uh, I just . . . love it. . . . I don't care how fat or what I look like, I don't care. But knowing that this exercise makes my blood come down [blood sugar reductions] . . .

A similar sentiment was expressed by another participant:

> It's like I didn't even want to do the 2 years. . . . I didn't even want to make that commitment. . . . And when I finally came out, it's like, this program is doing good, and I'm really eating more than I ever used to eat. You know, I thought to lose weight, you don't eat. Now I'm eating, and I'm losing weight, and I'm feeling better, and I'm able to walk now, which I didn't do.

Participants discussed the motivation they experienced by observing others make lifestyle changes:

> You know, I see other people willing to do it. I see women far older than me that are in far worse condition than me. They're sitting there trying to do this stuff. . . . So, by seeing other people making the effort to do it, it's like, you know, you have no excuse not to do it.

Still others expressed appreciation for opportunities to share successes and failures:

> You're able to open your feelings, which a lot of us do not open our feelings. I've always, all my life, kept hold in, private, very private. And I've really come out of my shell and am able to talk about things . . . right now feels like we're family, you know. More than family.

The sample included Latinas of various nationalities who were bilingual, monolingual Spanish speaking, and monolingual English speaking. This heterogeneity was both a strength and a challenge. For some, heterogeneity accentuated the solidarity they felt with other women who despite differences were united in some cultural communalities and in their efforts to improve their health. For others, the inability to communicate with all participants was a source of regret and a factor that, at times, fractured the larger group into language-based subgroups.

Practitioners and researchers are often skeptical that 4-hour weekly intervention sessions that extend over many months are feasible and appealing. In contrast, ¡Viva Bien! participants routinely expressed disappointment at the end of each 6-month period when the frequency of meetings was reduced.

Recommendations to Clinicians and Intervention Developers

Multiple Components

Comprehensive treatment of Type 2 diabetes requires intervention strategies for addressing multiple risk behaviors. ¡Viva Bien! emphasized nutrition, physical activity, smoking cessation, stress management, and social support. Those emphases supplemented general diabetes education through the health care system that included blood glucose monitoring, foot exams, and other self-care regimens. The multifaceted nature of Type 2 diabetes calls for a multifaceted approach to its daily self-management.

Personalized

Within a comprehensive intervention, there should be opportunities for personalizing the specific aspects that deserve special emphasis for each patient. In ¡Viva Bien! all participants experienced the four main components at each group session. Bilingual materials and activities allowed participants to select best fit options. In support group sessions, women engaged in collaborative goal setting, assessment of patient-specific barriers, and problem solving to address those barriers.

Long-Term

Type 2 diabetes is a chronic illness that typically requires the modification of well-established behaviors. There is, no doubt, considerable variation in the lengths of intervention durations that are optimal for making lifestyle changes. Clinicians should seek to create programs or to leverage accessible community resources to permit patients to engage in long-term programmatic efforts (e.g., Ackermann, Finch, Brizendine, Zhou, & Marrero, 2008).

Social Support

Evidence from the MLP indicated that the mobilization of support from families and friends was a partial explanation of how the intervention affected changes in healthful eating and physical activity (Barrera et al., 2008). That evidence is consistent with reports from ¡Viva Bien! participants who described how friends and family members can be positive or negative influences on their attempts to change their lifestyles. Clinicians can create group or individual support structures that can serve two functions: (a) assisting patients in marshaling support from members of their natural support network and (b) providing support to patients directly to encourage them in their behavior change efforts.

Accommodating Engagement Features and Fidelity of Content

The key conflict in conducting cultural adaptations of interventions is the clashing values of fidelity to evidence-based procedures and sensitivity to cultural fit (Castro, Barrera, & Martínez, 2004). We feel that even in the early stages of cultural adaptation, there are roles for both change inspired by cultural sensitivity and consistency inspired by fidelity. Specifically, we urge intervention developers to consider cultural fit to increase engagement (activities to draw participants into an intervention and to keep them actively involved) and to emphasize fidelity when considering treatment content (the things participants learn and do to achieve desired changes). This suggestion is based on the hypothesis that cultural features promote participation by making interventions attractive, welcoming, and accessible; the core content of an intervention makes it effective in changing behavior. The core content should be altered only after there are persuasive data to suggest cultural group differences in responses to the source intervention.

Pilot With Feedback Mechanisms

Although focus groups conducted prior to our adaptation had some value in gauging people's reactions to hypothetical situations, there was still greater value in the reactions of those who were actively involved in the pilot. The importance of mechanisms for collecting reactions from staff and participants during the pilot cannot be overemphasized. We were fortunate to have weekly social support sessions (that were audiotaped) and weekly supervision meetings (that were documented by minutes) that provided iterative feedback to guide program modifications. We advise other investigators adapting interventions to build in regular meetings between staff and participants during the preliminary adaptation test stage.

CONCLUSION

In this chapter, we illustrated the process that was used to transform an evidence-based diabetes intervention (the MLP) into ¡Viva Bien!, an intervention for Latinas with diabetes. The adaptation was motivated by the high prevalence of Type 2 diabetes among Latinas and the need for effective interventions that could assist them in managing diabetes and reducing the risk of heart disease and other related disorders. Barrera and Castro's (2006) adaptation development stages of information gathering, preliminary adaptation design, preliminary adaptation tests, and adaptation refinement proved to be valuable in sequencing the steps that resulted in the intervention that was evaluated in a randomized controlled trial. We combined quantitative and qualitative data to justify conducting the cultural adaptation and to inform decisions about the content of the adaptation itself. Prior to the intervention trial, there was little evidence to support changes to the fundamental mechanisms underlying the intervention and its influence on the health outcomes. We heeded Lau's (2006) admonitions for making just those initial adaptations that appeared to be warranted by qualitative or quantitative data. Evidence from the formal intervention trial showed that ¡Viva Bien! was as effective as the MLP in many respects, but the need for future adaptations to the physical activity intervention was indicated.

REFERENCES

Ackermann, R. T., Finch, E. A., Brizendine, E., Zhou, H., & Marrero, D. G. (2008). Translating the Diabetes Prevention Program into the community: The DEPLOY study. *American Journal of Preventive Medicine, 35,* 357–363. doi:10.1016/j.amepre.2008.06.035

Barrera, M., Jr., & Castro, F. G. (2006). A heuristic framework for the cultural adaptation of interventions. *Clinical Psychology: Science and Practice, 13,* 311–316. doi:10.1111/j.1468-2850.2006.00043.x

Barrera, M., Jr., Strycker, L. A., MacKinnon, D. P., & Toobert, D. J. (2008). Social-ecological resources as mediators of two-year diet and physical activity outcomes in Type 2 diabetes patients. *Health Psychology, 27*(2 Suppl.), S118–S125. doi:10.1037/0278-6133.27.2(Suppl.).S118

Barrera, M., Jr., Toobert, D. J., Strycker, L. A., & Osuna, D. (2011). Effects of acculturation on a culturally-adapted diabetes intervention for Latinas. *Health Psychology.* Advance online publication. doi: 10.1037/a0025205

Barrera, M., Jr., Toobert, D. J., Strycker, L. A., Osuna, D., King, D. K., & Glasgow, R. E. (2011). Multiple behavior change interventions for women with Type 2 diabetes. *Diabetes Spectrum, 24,* 75–80. doi:10.2337/diaspect.24.2.75

Black, S. A. (2002). Diabetes, diversity, and disparity: What do we do with the evidence? *American Journal of Public Health, 92,* 543–548. doi:10.2105/AJPH.92.4.543

Brown, S. A., Blozis, S. A., Kouzekanani, K., Garcia, A. A., Winchell, M., & Hanis, C. L. (2005). Dosage effects of diabetes self-management education for Mexican Americans: The Starr County Border Health Initiative. *Diabetes Care, 28,* 527–532. doi:10.2337/diacare.28.3.527

Brown, S. A., Garcia, A. A., Kouzekanani, K., & Hanis, C. L. (2002). Culturally competent diabetes self-management education for Mexican Americans: Starr County Border Health Initiative. *Diabetes Care, 25,* 259–268. doi:10.2337/diacare.25.2.259

Castro, F. G., Barrera, M., Jr., & Martínez, C. R., Jr. (2004). The cultural adaptation of prevention interventions: Resolving tensions between fidelity and fit. *Prevention Science, 5,* 41–45. doi:10.1023/B:PREV.0000013980.12412.cd

Centers for Disease Control and Prevention, National Center for Health Statistics. (2007). Health, United States, 2007 with chartbook on trends in the health of Americans. Retrieved from http://www.cdc.gov/nchs/data/hus/hus07.pdf

Crespo, C. J., Keteyian, S. J., Heath, G. W., & Sempos, C. T. (1996). Leisure time physical activity among U.S. adults. *Archives of Internal Medicine, 156,* 93–98. doi:10.1001/archinte.1996.00440010113015

de Lorgeril, M., Renaud, S., Mamelle, N., Salen, P., Martin, J. L., Monjaud, I., . . . Delaye, J. (1994). Mediterranean alpha-linolenic acid-rich diet in secondary prevention of coronary heart disease. *The Lancet, 343,* 1454–1459. doi:10.1016/S0140-6736(94)92580-1

Diabetes Prevention Program Research Group. (2002). Reduction in the incidence of Type 2 diabetes with lifestyle intervention or metformin. *The New England Journal of Medicine, 346,* 393–403. doi:10.1056/NEJMoa012512

Glasgow, R. E., Toobert, D., Barrera, M., Jr., & Strycker, L. (2004). Assessment of problem-solving: A key to successful long-term diabetes self-management. *Journal of Behavioral Medicine, 27,* 477–490. doi:10.1023/B:JOBM.0000047611.81027.71

Gonder-Frederick, L. A., Cox, D. J., & Ritterband, L. M. (2002). Diabetes and behavioral medicine: The second decade. *Journal of Consulting and Clinical Psychology, 70,* 611–625. doi:10.1037/0022-006X.70.3.611

Hurley, B. F., & Roth, S. M. (2000). Strength training in the elderly: Effects on risk factors for age-related diseases. *Sports Medicine, 30,* 249–268. doi:10.2165/00007256-200030040-00002

Irwin, M. L., Mayer-Davis, E. J., Addy, C. L., Pate, R. R., Durstine, J. L., Stolarczyk, L. M., & Ainsworth, B. E. (2000). Moderate-intensity physical activity and fasting insulin levels in women: The Cross-Cultural Activity Participation Study. *Diabetes Care, 23,* 449–454. doi:10.2337/diacare.23.4.449

Lau, A. S. (2006). Making the case for selective and directed cultural adaptations of evidence-based treatments: Examples from parent training. *Clinical Psychology: Science and Practice, 13,* 295–310. doi:10.1111/j.1468-2850.2006.00042.x

Mokdad, A. H., Ford, E. S., Bowman, B. A., Nelson, D. E., Engelgau, M. M., Vinicor, F., & Marks, J. S. (2000). Diabetes trends in the U.S.: 1990–1998. *Diabetes Care, 23*, 1278–1283. doi:10.2337/diacare.23.9.1278

Narayan, K. M. V., Boyle, J. P., Thompson, T. J., Sorensen, S. W., & Williamson, D. F. (2003). Lifetime risk for diabetes mellitus in the United States. *JAMA, 290*, 1884–1890. doi:10.1001/jama.290.14.1884

Newman, S., Steed, L., & Mulligan, K. (2004). Self-management interventions for chronic illness. *The Lancet, 364*, 1523–1537. doi:10.1016/S0140-6736 (04)17277-2

Norris, S. L., Lau, J., Smith, S. J., Schmid, C. H., & Engelgau, M. M. (2002). Self-management education for adults with Type 2 diabetes: A meta-analysis of the effect on glycemic control. *Diabetes Care, 25*, 1159–1171. doi:10.2337/diacare.25.7.1159

Ogden, C. L., Carroll, M. D., Curtin, L. R., McDowell, M. A., Tabak, C. J., & Flegal, K. M. (2006). Prevalence of overweight and obesity in the United States, 1999-2004. *JAMA, 295*, 1549–1555. doi:10.1001/jama.295.13.1549

Ornish, D., Brown, S. E., Scherwitz, L. W., Billings, J. H., Armstrong, W. T., Ports, T. A., . . . Gould, K. L. (1990). Can lifestyle changes reverse coronary heart disease? The Lifestyle Heart Trial. *The Lancet, 336*, 129–133. doi:10.1016/0140-6736(90)91656-U

Osuna, D., Barrera, M., Jr., Strycker, L. A., Toobert, D. J., Almeida, F., Rasmussen, C. G., . . . Glasgow, R. E. (2011). Methods for the cultural adaptation of a diabetes lifestyle intervention for Latinas: An illustrative project. *Health Promotion Practice, 12*, 341–348. doi:10.1177/1524839909343279

Resnicow, K., Baranowski, T., Ahluwalia, J. S., & Braithwaite, R. L. (1999). Cultural sensitivity in public health: Defined and demystified. *Ethnicity & Disease, 9*, 10–21.

Sabogal, E., Marin, G., Otero-Sabogal, R., Marin, B. V., & Perez-Stable, E. J. (1987). Hispanic familism: What changes and what doesn't? *Hispanic Journal of Behavioral Sciences, 9*, 397–412. doi:10.1177/07399863870094003

Spiegel, D., & Classen, C. (2000). *Group therapy for cancer patients: A research-based handbook of psychosocial care*. New York, NY: Basic Books.

Swinburn, B. A., Metcalf, P. A., & Ley, S. J. (2001). Long-term (5-year) effects of a reduced-fat diet intervention in individuals with glucose intolerance. *Diabetes Care, 24*, 619–624. doi:10.2337/diacare.24.4.619

Toobert, D. J., Glasgow, R. E., & Radcliffe, J. L. (2000). Physiologic and related behavioral outcomes from the Women's Lifestyle Heart Trial. *Annals of Behavioral Medicine, 22*, 1–16. doi:10.1007/BF02895162

Toobert, D. J., Glasgow, R. E., Strycker, L. A., Barrera, M., Jr., Ritzwoller, D. P., & Weidner, G. (2007). Long-term effects of the Mediterranean Lifestyle Program: A randomized clinical trial for postmenopausal women with Type 2 diabetes. *The International Journal of Behavioral Nutrition and Physical Activity, 4*, 1–12. doi:10.1186/1479-5868-4-1

Toobert, D. J., Strycker, L. A., & Glasgow, R. E. (1998). Lifestyle change in women with coronary heart disease: What do we know? *Journal of Women's Health, 7,* 685–699. doi:10.1089/jwh.1998.7.685

Toobert, D. J., Strycker, L. A., Glasgow, R. E., Barrera, M., & Angell, K. (2005). Effects of the Mediterranean Lifestyle Program on multiple risk behaviors and psychosocial outcomes among women at risk for heart disease. *Annals of Behavioral Medicine, 29,* 128–137. doi:10.1207/s15324796abm2902_7

U.S. Department of Health and Human Services, National Institutes of Health, National Institute of Diabetes and Digestive and Kidney Diseases. (2008). *National diabetes statistics, 2007* (NIH Publication No. 08-3892). Retrieved from http://www.diabetes.niddk.nih.gov/dm/pubs/statistics/

Whittemore, R. (2007). Culturally competent interventions for Hispanic adults with Type 2 diabetes: A systematic review. *Journal of Transcultural Nursing, 18,* 157–166. doi:10.1177/1043659606298615

Wing, R. R., & Anglin, K. (1996). Effectiveness of a behavioral weight control program for blacks and whites with NIDDM. *Diabetes Care, 19,* 409–413. doi:10.2337/diacare.19.5.409

7

REFLECTIONS ON ADAPTING PARENT TRAINING FOR CHINESE IMMIGRANTS: BLIND ALLEYS, THOROUGHFARES, AND TEST DRIVES

ANNA S. LAU

Being raised in a context outside the White American middle-class experience can lead an interventionist to approach parent training (PT) dissemination with some trepidation about the fit of standard practice with the sensibilities of immigrant families. How would my own immigrant Chinese parents have responded to this guidance in childrearing? How would specific PT practices be viewed, and how could they be encouraged in families who may be wary of or wholly unaccustomed to these strategies?

I have previously argued that cultural adaptations should be guided by data that inform the design of specific content or process adaptations (Lau, 2006). This would safeguard against less defensible, improvised drifts away from fidelity that may be inert or even detrimental to treatment outcomes. For example, displacing skills training to include discussion of cultural values decreased the efficacy of the Strengthening Families Program adapted for Asian American and Latino families (Kumpfer, Alvarado, Smith, & Bellamy, 2002). Accordingly, we conducted a series of studies to inform adaptations

This study was supported by a grant from the National Institute of Mental Health (K01 MH66864) and additional funding from the University of California, Los Angeles, Asian American Studies Center.

that would be relevant and responsive to the needs of Chinese Americans. This chapter includes reflections on the research pursuits that proved fruitful and those that did not.

At the outset, our approach to adaptation was top-down, to be driven empirically by research findings in the aggregate rather than by clinical observation. Many clinical scientists have been socialized to mistrust such observations, valuing only data from conventional research methods, which may not shed light on rich clinical phenomena (Miller, 1998). This can be contrasted with a bottom-up approach, where adaptation starts with observations made during implementation. Adopting the former strategy had much to do with our initial readiness to exploit survey research methods, focus groups, and semistructured interviews for gathering information from families and community clinicians. In practice-ready contexts, deployment-focused models of adaptation may be more quickly pursued in a bottom-up approach.

Cultural adaptations were envisioned as falling into two categories: those designed to *enhance engagement* of ethnic minorities in evidence-based treatments and those meant to *contextualize intervention content* to ensure the fit with the needs of the target group (Lau, 2006; see also Chapter 2, this volume). A set of Phase 1 studies was designed to inform these two types of adaptations to be worked out in Phase 2 and tested in Phase 3. In hindsight, the utility of much of the data that could be generated by these Phase 1 studies may have been overestimated. In contrast, the lessons learned in the intervention deployment in Phase 3 have been highly instructive. We did not fully appreciate the feedback loop from deployment to adaptation design and the vital importance of practice-based evidence in informing evidence-based practice.

In this chapter, we discuss the path traversed to our revised hypotheses about promising strategies for optimizing PT for immigrant Chinese families. This path had some blind alleys and detours, but thankfully some thorough-fares, too.

PHASE 1A: DATA COLLECTION EFFORTS FOR ENHANCING ENGAGEMENT

Social Validity Survey

Previous efforts to produce cultural adaptations of PT have been fueled by concerns about the acceptability of PT strategies for ethnocultural groups (e.g., McCabe, Yeh, Garland, Lau, & Chavez, 2005). Since there is wide variation in parenting practices across cultures, there may likewise be wide variation in receptivity to prescribed changes in parent–child interactions (Kazdin, 1997). Forehand and Kotchick (1996) outlined central cultural values, sociocultural experiences, and common parenting practices among the four major ethnocultural groups that may require reconciliation with PT approaches. Mistrust may arise if PT is seen as promoting conformity to a White American standard unshared by ethnocultural groups. Understanding the acceptability of PT interventions across groups may direct our attention to techniques that require adaptation.

Social validity studies ask potential consumers to rate specific PT techniques along dimensions of acceptability (i.e., is the treatment palatable, feasible, or helpful?). Research on the acceptability of PT across immigrant groups is sparse in general. We collected data on the perceived acceptability of common PT strategies among immigrant Chinese parents, examining cultural correlates of treatment attitudes (Ho, McCabe, Yeh, & Lau, 2011). We presented parents with an externalizing behavior problem vignette and described six PT strategies (praise, differential reinforcement, tangible rewards, effective commands, time out, and response cost). Parents rated statements pertaining to acceptability (e.g., "I would be willing to use this method"), barriers (e.g., "This method would be difficult to do"), and anticipated support for this method from others (e.g., "My spouse would help me with this method").

We found that parents rated praise, effective commands, and tangible rewards as more acceptable than time out, response cost, and differential attention. These findings were at odds with clinical descriptions of Chinese parents disliking praise and rewards given their cultural belief that children should simply be expected to obey and comply (Ho et al., 1999; Lieh-Mak et al., 1984). PT acceptability ratings were positively associated with indices of acculturation, parenting stress, and authoritative parenting, but negatively associated with cultural values concerning the use of shaming as a child socialization practice and a history of child protective services involvement. Our findings supported the concern that less acculturated immigrant parents who endorse traditional values regarding hierarchy and control in the parent–child relationship may be more difficult to engage in PT. Thus, the data confirmed impressions from the clinical literature that there is some cultural distance between PT strategies and values concerning parent-centered control among Chinese parents.

The findings were limited in practical utility in informing how to better engage Chinese parents in the intervention. We could not infer how to adapt teaching "time out and ignore" simply on the basis of lower acceptability ratings. Furthermore, we had to be circumspect about our interpretations given the analogue design of the study. Ultimately, surveys of treatment acceptability among non–treatment-seeking samples may not be a reliable indicator of the social validity of interventions when offered in treatment settings. Among parents who have received PT, perceptions of the acceptability, relevance, effectiveness, and demandingness of procedures are associated with treatment persistence and outcomes (Kazdin, 2000; Kazdin, Holland, & Crowley, 1997). In contrast, ratings of treatment acceptability among parents not yet in treatment fail to predict the initiation of care across ethnic groups (Bennett, Power, Rostain, & Carr, 1996; Krain, Kendall, & Power, 2005). Reactions to descriptions of PT procedures may not predict engagement when quality care is received within a therapeutic relationship. On the other hand, attitudes toward techniques tend to become more favorable following initiation of PT (Hobbs, Walle, & Caldwell, 1984).

Our data did not provide guidance on how to tailor PT to be more engaging for the Chinese American families who are most likely to be skeptical—those who are less acculturated and who have had involvement with child protective services. Thus, the data were interesting but not instrumental in the adaptation process—the first blind alley. In hindsight, by relying on survey methods, we missed an opportunity to engage in open-ended discussions with Chinese American parents about what they liked, what they would engage in, and why. Qualitative data may have been instrumental in learning how pretreatment attitudes could be affected through effective engagement processes during PT. Toward this end, we did enter into conversations with therapists working with Chinese immigrant families in community settings.

Focus Groups With Community Clinicians

We conducted three focus groups with 24 bicultural, bilingual Asian American (70.8% Chinese American) psychologists, social workers, and marriage and family counselors with experience treating immigrant parents and their children in community clinics. None of the therapists reported training in a specific evidence-based PT intervention, although most were providing individual or group parent counseling. We began each group with an orientation to the basic skills taught in a typical evidence-based PT program. We introduced and showed videotapes to illustrate child-directed play, praise, tangible rewards, differential reinforcement, and response cost. We then facilitated discussion about the cultural relevance and acceptability of each strategy and likely barriers to engagement or effectiveness when delivered to Chinese immigrants. Presented next are clinician impressions about the cultural relevance of PT practices that emerged using steps outlined in Krueger's (1994) practical framework analysis approach. Raw transcript data were indexed and charted from transcribed text into tables, and criteria for theme extraction were based on frequency, extensiveness, and specificity following Krueger and Casey (2000).

Play

In many PT programs, child-directed play is introduced first as a means toward strengthening the parent–child relationship in families where child compliance and positive parenting are in low supply. The effective application of positive discipline is thought to be accomplished best when the child is invested in a responsive relationship with the parent. This type of play requires the parent to increase attention to the child's prosocial behavior, follow the child's lead (rather than directing the play), and use descriptive commenting and praise. Focus group clinicians' comments about play skills fell into three related categories of concern: (a) lack of familiarity, (b) credibility of the goal, and (c) need for experiential learning.

Several therapists remarked on the incongruence between the concept of child-directed play and the nature of parent–child interactions in East Asian cultures. One therapist explained, "Play generally isn't something that Asian parents and their kids do, it's not hierarchical. . . . There's a proper position of the parent and the child so that following the child doesn't fit." This commentary is consistent with the common description of Confucian family structure, in which parental authority and child obedience organize interactions. Another therapist elaborated, "Culturally, this kind of play is almost nonexistent. It's not seen as something that's beneficial. The Chinese culture is more achievement oriented. So everything has to have educational value." In PT, parents may be asked to refrain from play that places academic demands on children (e.g., counting or adding objects). A third therapist anticipated parent objections:

> They will say, "Well when I was a kid no one played with me. I just had to do my work. Therefore, I expect my child to work." So, I think just in terms of cultural factors, the idea of play is foreign and maybe not acceptable.

Yet many clinicians saw play as integral to the success of repairing parent–child relations that have gone awry in clinic-referred families where child behavior problems and ineffective discipline have taken root. Many emphasized the importance of experiential learning in place of didactic instruction on playing: "They need to experience it, they just have to try it and feel it . . . We played two sessions and they were so loud, they used to be really quiet. I was surprised . . . it's better than just talking about it."

Another therapist was more circumspect about engaging his clients in learning the skills involved in child-directed play. He anticipated reluctance and a steep learning curve:

> Asian parents would say "I don't have the time" and also that they probably would tell the kid what to do instead of follow the child's lead. I think it would take us maybe 5 months to get the concept into their mind and to get them to carry it out.

Although therapists reported or anticipated problems in teaching child-directed play, there was optimism among the clinicians who had incorporated play into their work with Chinese immigrant families. These therapists tended to adopt an enactment strategy to engage parents in developing this skill. There was a shared impression that immigrant parents who did not initially see the value of play would be compelled to change their interactions with their child once they engaged in this self-reinforcing activity. Thus, behavior change may precede changes in attitudes or values. Although some therapists indicated that it would be important to address parents' misgivings about play (e.g., children would have less respect for parents), at least one therapist felt that too much time focused on cultural barriers would by itself be unproductive.

Praise

Focus group participants described cultural beliefs about motivations that contraindicate praise: "They believe the more you praise them, the more you'll spoil them," and "Everyone says they won't try hard if you praise them." This is consistent with research indicating that East Asians tend to hold a self-improving orientation in which criticism of performance motivates task persistence, whereas White Americans hold a self-enhancing orientation to maintain self-esteem (Heine et al., 2001):

> Praising—that's not in the formula. They don't praise for what is an expectation—to do well in school, to do your chores. . . . And if you're doing a good job you should know it. When you are not doing it right, that's when they start telling you. And they bring it up over and over. The parent has to remind you about the bad thing that you did wrong rather than discipline you for that behavior and move on.

As a result, some clinicians reported difficulties trying to teach praise as a culturally unfamiliar practice:

> Praise comes from a very Western stance of nurturing as a parent, and for an Asian parent it can be very foreign. Their role as parent is not about nurturing emotional development . . . So it's really it's very difficult to engage in.

Praise was also thought to misalign the desired hierarchy in the Chinese parent–child relationship: "I think that [parents] have their status threatened. They feel that respect is commanded . . . if they praise their kid too much, the kid will think they are better than them."

A number of seasoned clinicians offered suggestions for countering these concerns to engage parents in using praise. Again, therapists discussed therapy process and experiential learning. They described the parallel process of praising their parent clients:

> I just sit back and say "How do you feel about how I praise you?" And most of them have very positive feedback, "Oh teacher, I really feel a little bit more confident." "What do you think your child would feel if you try doing that? Do you think your child would have overblown self-esteem because of too much praising?"

Another therapist remarked on the importance of using acceptable translations of the concept, which can drive treatment attitudes:

> In Chinese, praise is sort of like sugar-coating something. I change the word to encouragement, to reflect how it's good to reinforce their behaviors. So I don't use the word "praise" (biao yan kan). Instead, I say "li kan" (encouraging).

Other therapists stressed the importance of psychoeducation about the special family context of the immigrant parent raising a child in a new culture:

> I go back to the need for bicultural parenting and their understanding that they are not raising a child that will be socially appropriate in China, but a child that is going to be socially appropriate in America, and that requires different skills.

This therapist captured the notion that therapy can be a vehicle for adaptation of immigrants into the host "American" culture (Bernal & Domenech Rodríguez, 2009). Such adaptation can be promoted in a supportive, affirming manner without requiring a loss or condemnation of the person's culture of origin, and even with a celebration of that culture. In contrast, behavior change can be promoted through PT in a culture-disconfirming manner, communicating that traditional parenting practices are inferior or deficient. Introducing the goal of bicultural competence is one avenue toward engaging parents in a culture-affirming manner.

Therapists illustrated the bicultural context of children in immigrant families by highlighting how children must bridge across both home and school cultures. Since school adjustment is a major concern of Chinese American parents, they may be encouraged to try praise to align with American school culture. One therapist shared her approach:

> I say, "All of this worked back in China, and it was great. It worked on you, you turned out fine. But here your children have a lot of different influences. They're getting different cultural feedback from teachers and friends and other people. So, you're not necessarily doing things wrong, but it's different here because of what your kids are experiencing."

Likewise, another therapist attempted to build empathy for the bicultural child: "When the kid enters school, the teachers always praise them. And now they come home and they expect you to say something. And when you don't do it and always criticize, how does he feel?"

Moreover, Chinese parents' lack of personal experience being praised presents difficulties even when they are willing to try. "They just can't say it out loud. It's like they don't know how to say it in words. I try to have them practice in class, you know, it's really hard for them." Another therapist observed that learning to use praise is a long and slow process for immigrant parents:

> It's not one session you talk about praise, and then they will learn how to praise. They need to learn how to see the positive side of the kid. Usually it's towards almost the end of the treatment they will start getting just a little more positive.

So even when Chinese immigrant parents can be convinced that praise is a helpful strategy, they may need additional support in learning it.

Tangible Rewards

In all three focus groups, there was consensus about Chinese American parents' attitudes toward tangible rewards for increasing desired behaviors in children. Chinese American parents reportedly felt that concrete reinforcers were acceptable, but they had difficulty implementing the systems effectively: "They were open to trying it out. But they had issues following through with it." Several therapists reported problems with execution: "They just don't do it. . . . So each time I go to the home visit I reintroduce the whole strategy all over." Another stated,

> You tell them how to do it. We give them the sticker sheet and all that, and walk them through it, step by step. They always miss something. And then they give up so easily. They say, "Oh it doesn't work."

Other therapists reported that their clients don't adhere to the plan:

> Once they get home, the rewards start to change. They don't give the kid the rewards according to what was put on the paper. Because they feel the kid is now getting the advantage. They start changing it at home, it starts to drift into something else. They demand more for the rewards.

The therapists did not locate these difficulties as uniquely cultural; they instead emphasized the importance of best practices in setting up and monitoring tangible reward systems with Chinese American families. In establishing the system,

Chinese parents will say, "Do well. Be good." I say that's not concrete enough. When they say "be good" that means a lot of things. So, we practice in the class. I say, "Okay, tell me what do you mean by 'be good'?"

The therapists cited the importance of close monitoring and accountability:

Consistency has really been difficult for most parents. So I have them bring in their behavior charts every session to make sure that they've been consistent. And then I also ask the children, "Has your mom been giving you the stickers when you did this or that this week?" Sometimes they'll say as they come in, "My mom didn't give me stickers this week and I did all the dishes!" So that really helps to point it out because if you're not consistent then they don't need to be consistent.

These comments suggest that clinicians may not necessarily encounter a cultural impasse regarding the appropriateness of rewards; rather, sometimes the challenges concerned getting the parents to adhere to a consistent reinforcement schedule. It may be productive to proceed under the assumption that parents have genuine difficulty implementing a novel strategy and to address possible "resistance" when parents explicitly raise concerns or objections.

Differential Reinforcement (Ignoring Misbehavior)

Therapists discussed common cultural barriers to Chinese American parents' acceptance of the differential reinforcement of other behavior, in which bothersome behaviors (e.g., protesting) are ignored and attention is restored when appropriate behavior (e.g., compliance) begins. Ignoring annoying misbehavior and tantrums is difficult for parents across groups. Common concerns were raised: "They have a really hard time because 'the neighbors will complain, we live in an apartment, it's so embarrassing.'" In addition, our informants located Chinese parents' concerns in cultural ideals about the appropriate role of parents. "They are very cultured to reprimand and criticize and yell and direct . . . When you talk about ignoring the kid, they think you are giving the child more power." A central concern about ignoring misbehavior centered on threats to face:

Ignoring is very hard for Chinese parents because usually they will do whatever it takes to stop the misbehavior, especially in public, because they think it's really shameful. To just stand by and wait for the behavior to stop is unacceptable. . . . They cannot tolerate what they see as doing nothing.

The impulse to do something to quell misbehavior feels urgent—not only for correcting the child but also because of those who may be watching and judging the parent.

One therapist described an instance of how she used therapeutic process to leverage these concerns about shame and embarrassment to motivate parents:

> One kid would tantrum from my clinic all the way home. He would cry and scream and the mom would be so embarrassed. At the next session she would say "You asked me to ignore his tantrum, but as we walked people were looking at us and I feel so embarrassed." And that's when I took the opportunity to validate her feeling, provide support, and help her understand that, yes, at the time you may feel embarrassed, but I ask her, "So, do you want him to change? Do you want him to continue to tantrum every time he wants something? If you set your firm limits 'No, you're not gonna get it' and ignore him, he may tantrum one time, two times, but then likely his behavior will change. But, if he doesn't change, that means a lot more embarrassment in the future."

While some therapists reported avoiding the concept of ignoring misbehavior because of cultural concerns, others reported that Chinese parents often arrive at the clinic at a critical teachable moment when their level of distress is high. One therapist explained,

> They have to yell a lot, they feel like they're so exhausted, so stressed because they have to keep doing that. So I try to motivate them, "Okay, try something new. You don't have to keep doing that." I try to convince them, "You'll use less energy later because it works." So I think when they are so desperate and so exhausted, they'll come to a point that they'll try something different.

One therapist described how she explains to distressed parents that ignoring can be a form of self-care, telling them, "Ignoring is a good place to take a break."

Time Out

As in our discussion of ignoring, many practical concerns were raised about implementing time out in close living quarters with neighbors all around, and harried days where it is hard to take the time for time out. "They will not do time out. It's too inconvenient. It's just easier to yell or spank right away and then it's done. Time out takes too much time and effort, and it's hard to do." In addition, specific cultural barriers to time out were detailed:

> I think that Western culture emphasizes that the reason for time out is that the child will be able to calm down and think over what's going on. Time out is sort of a social deprivation. But, at the same time, the Chinese do not think of it that way. I think the Chinese culture focuses on more immediate correction. Right back to the reprimand; not "You're on your own to think about it" But "I'll tell you what to think."

In this view, parental control and hierarchy trump using time out as a way to help children cultivate self-regulation. Some therapists described Chinese parents' more punitive orientation as a barrier to effective use of time out:

> It is important to educate the parents about what you really want to accomplish through time out, to encourage it to be practiced right, instead of them using time out as a punishment. . . . They say, "You kneel down there on the floor in front of the altar." Sometimes they put uncooked rice on the floor, so it is borderline abuse. So really they don't understand what time out is trying to accomplish.

These examples suggest that some Chinese parents may be inclined to use punitive responses to misbehavior and require a very clear explanation of the rationale of negative reinforcement.

Other therapists described Chinese immigrant families who felt that time out was too aversive and threatening to the parent–child relationship:

> They think it's too cruel to leave your kids somewhere all locked up by themselves and a lot of times the parents cry, too. They have a hard time with their kids not liking them if they put them in time out. So, I try not to do time out because they'll say "Oh sure, I'll use it," but then they won't follow through.

Another therapist reported, "Some Chinese parents see this as worse than hitting because it is social deprivation." From these examples, it is difficult to predict responses to an intervention strategy in a given cultural group because of the large intragroup variability. The same range of responses to time out was reported by McCabe et al. (2005) in their work with Mexican American parents, with some viewing time out as too aversive to children and some viewing it as not punitive enough. These observations highlight the challenge of ensuring that an intervention is flexible enough to accommodate variability within any particular cultural group.

Response Cost

Therapists reported that Chinese parents are generally very open to using loss of privileges as a consequence for child misbehavior. They reported few cultural barriers to acceptability, but many shared examples of common barriers to teaching effective use of response cost. For example, Chinese American parents with a more punitive orientation required extra guidance in using realistic and enforceable consequences, "so I also have to teach them is that you don't give them consequences until you cool down. Don't tell him you're grounded for the whole week if you're not ready to follow through with it that whole week." Therapists described the need to teach and reteach this strategy a number of times.

They need constant reminding. Just because this week they did it beautifully, the next week you still have to remind them, reinforce them for
their own behavior as parents. And their own commitment to change,
you constantly have to reinforce that too. Because otherwise, even
though they did it once last week, they may say "Well, I don't need to do
that. Forget it, that's hard."

Thus, the challenge in teaching response cost was not as much about
overcoming misgivings as about providing sufficiently sustained training
and reinforcement of an acceptable technique that requires practice and
reinforcement.

Results and Implications for Adaptation

Many by-products emerged from the conduct of these focus groups.
First, mutual interest in PT was kindled, and good things came of it. None
of our participants had previously been trained in an evidence-based PT
intervention, but the majority had been providing treatment informed by
social learning principles. Among some participants, attendance at the group
catalyzed interest in receiving training, and facilitating these conversations
led to community–university partnerships that were instrumental in building
capacity for implementation. Three of the focus group participants ultimately
became involved in the later phases of our research as clinicians, administra-
tors, and consultants.

Second, it was instructive to hear from clinicians in practice, to adopt
a learning role, and to receive feedback that not only described problems but
also provided solutions. Table 7.1 summarizes some observations about specific cultural barriers to engagement in PT among Chinese parents, as well as
the specific strategies for addressing these barriers.

PHASE 2A: A ROAD MAP FOR ENGAGEMENT

Gathering perspectives on PT from parents and clinicians working with
this population yielded interesting areas of convergence and divergence in terms
of implications for cultural adaptation. For example, discussions with therapists
who had varying levels of success implementing PT indicated that Chinese
immigrant parents do not use praise and thus may be likely to reject instruction
in this skill. Yet, parent survey data suggested high absolute levels of acceptability of this strategy. One possible interpretation is that parents who are most
likely to have misgivings about praise are the ones who have typically ended up
in treatment contexts for PT (e.g., less acculturated parents mandated to treatment). Immigrant Chinese parents may want to use praise but have not had
the experiences that let them learn how. It may be unfair to attribute failure

TABLE 7.1
Summary of Therapist Feedback

Technique	Barriers	Solutions

Praise	■ Beliefs about praise reducing effort, humility
	■ Praise is foreign hence difficult
		■ Experiential learning
		  ■ Praise in the therapeutic relationship
		  ■ Behavior change precedes attitude change

Child-directed play	■ Challenges parent–child hierarchy ■ No experience, play does not come naturally	■ Psychoeducation on bicultural parenting ■ Ample modeling and supported rehearsal
Differential reinforcement	■ Ignoring misbehavior threatens face ■ Prefer punishment	■ Behavior problems at clinic entry represent a teachable moment ■ Framing as instrumental for reducing future "shameful" behavior ■ Ignore/time out in the context of self-care ■ Make purpose clear
Time-out	■ Seen as inconvenient, difficult ■ Prefer punishment, ad hoc punitive measures added ■ Separation seen as cruel by some	
Response cost	■ Generally acceptable ■ Difficult to set enforceable consequences when angry	■ Hold parents accountable for consistency ■ Thorough teaching of concepts, emphasize feasibility and sustainability ■ Monitor use throughout treatment
Tangible rewards	■ Generally acceptable ■ Difficult to follow through, parents withhold agreed-upon rewards	

to praise as culturally rooted resistance when real skills deficits need to be addressed through additional supportive instruction. One must also consider that the focus group clinicians had varying levels of experience and did not have training in an evidence-based protocol. Their frustration was apparent at times, and their statements suggested that they may not have been supported with sufficient training and supervision in PT.

Taking together the data from parents and clinicians suggested distinctive directions for PT adaptation. First, cultural barriers to engagement are likely to be significant, especially for parents with low levels of acculturation who are not voluntarily seeking PT. Some barriers may be located within culturally rooted misgivings about prescribed PT strategies, whereas other barriers may be attributed to immigrant parents' difficulties in initiating foreign practices. As such, culturally competent PT must flexibly address parental concerns about cultural incongruence of techniques through effective therapeutic process. This is accomplished in a culturally affirming manner driven by respectful listening and discussion to reveal points of concern that motivate change toward shared and valued goals. However, motivational enhancements to address cultural concerns may not be sufficient without highly supportive instruction in novel techniques. Modeling, enactment, rehearsal, and monitoring of parental use of PT techniques is essential precisely because of potential cultural misgivings and the strangeness of the techniques. Thus, engagement must involve (a) anticipating but not assuming cultural misgivings about PT, (b) building in therapeutic process elements to reveal points of cultural concern and to responsively motivate change toward valued goals, and (c) supporting progress in behavior change.

As an optimal starting point, we selected a PT model with evidence of engagement and efficacy for immigrant parents. The Incredible Years (IY) program utilizes videotape modeling and group discussion to teach effective parenting skills in a collaborative rather than didactic manner (Webster-Stratton, 2011). Given the potential for low acceptability of some fundamental PT strategies, such as praise and ignore, the intervention builds in methods to address attitudinal barriers to engagement. As each technique is introduced, the group collectively generates a list of benefits and barriers. Thus, the leader actively elicits and explores cultural barriers to using the technique but also motivates uptake by drawing parallels between the benefits of the technique and parents' stated goals. In each session, videos of parent–child interactions are viewed, and the group leader facilitates a discussion in which the parents construct the key principles underlying effective parenting. Treatment manuals orient leaders toward common attitudinal barriers to each skill (e.g., concerns that praise will "spoil" children) and provide guidance on using group process to address these concerns. Group processes leverage experiential learning, such as praising and rewarding parents in session as they are instructed to do with their children. In addition, IY emphasizes enactment and rehearsal, with role-plays, homework assignments, and close monitoring and feedback on parent performance.

In these ways, the IY model has built-in strategies for enhancing engagement of culturally diverse parents in ways that were described as necessary by our focus group participants. Our material preparation, training, and ongoing supervision emphasized methods to capitalize on the manualized therapeutic processes outlined in the IY program to enhance engagement. In our translated manuals, we highlighted common misgivings about each technique that were listed (e.g., praise will lead to poorer effort) and the relevant discussion points to address each concern. In supervision, we role-played culturally responsive strategies for engaging Chinese parents (e.g., how to initiate and support role-plays), discussed culturally sensitive communication styles (e.g., how to address reticent or mistrustful Chinese parents), and shared ways of explaining concepts that included reference to cultural idioms (e.g., *li kan* instead of *biao yan kan*) and references (e.g., in discussing communication we present the Chinese character for "listen," which includes radicals for "heart" and "ear").

PHASE 1B: DATA COLLECTION FOR CONTEXTUALIZING TREATMENT CONTENT

The second thrust of the adaptation was premised on the identification of culturally relevant risk factors for ineffective discipline in immigrant Chinese families. If the target problem emerges within a distinctive sociocultural context, adaptations should address culturally specific risk processes (Lau, 2006). PT has often been augmented to address ancillary stressors (e.g., marital conflict) that interfere with the uptake of effective parenting skills (Miller & Prinz, 1990). We conducted a survey to examine correlates of punitive discipline among Chinese immigrant parents to identify instrumental treatment goals to target in an augmented PT program for high-risk families (Lau, 2010).

For immigrant families, stress associated with immigration, acculturation, and minority status may interfere with effective parenting. Parents may be subject to acculturative stress stemming from discrimination, communication barriers, discomfort with new cultural norms, lack of social support, or downward social mobility (Liebkind, 1996; Williams & Berry, 1991). These strains may erode effective parenting when coping resources are overwhelmed. Within the immigrant family system, adjustment difficulties can arise as children acculturate more rapidly than their parents, resulting in estrangement (Portes & Rumbaut, 2001). These acculturation gaps have been associated with increased conflict, low cohesion, and parental aggression in Asian American families (Farver, Narang, & Bhadha, 2002; Lee, Choe, Kim, & Ngo, 2000; Park, 2001; Ying, Lee, Tsai, Lee, & Tsang, 2001). Another potential source of stress concerns academic performance. In Chinese families, schooling is considered the primary responsibility of parents, and a child's success in school indicates parenting competence (Chao & Tseng, 2002). Chinese immigrants often migrate to invest in their children's schooling, sacrificing the security of extended family, community, and homeland (Fuligni & Yoshikawa, 2004). A child's poor performance in school may be risky given both the cultural traditions valuing achievement and the lofty investment of immigration made for educational opportunity.

In our survey of Chinese immigrant families, we examined cultural values related to parental control, contextual stressors related to acculturation, parent–child acculturation conflicts, and problems in children's schooling as predictors of physical discipline (Lau, 2010). Our findings indicated that children's problems in school were directly associated with increased risk of physical discipline. Parental acculturative stress contributed to risk indirectly through increased child school problems and acculturation conflicts. In addition, parent–child acculturation conflicts were related to risk of physical discipline when parents held traditional values about firm parental control. Immigrant Chinese parents who strongly valued hierarchy and control may respond more punitively to an acculturated child's bid for autonomy.

PHASE 2B: AUGMENTING PARENT TRAINING TO REDUCE RISK

This survey provided the data to guide the design of an augmented IY protocol to reduce ineffective discipline among immigrant Chinese. We augmented the IY Basic Parenting program by including three supplemental modules to target the strains we found to be most proximal to use of physical discipline in immigrant Chinese families. Content and materials for these sessions were extracted from IY Advanced program and the IY School-Aged program for Supporting Your Child's Education. The resultant protocol included 14 sessions, nine of which covered the basic skills of goal setting, child-directed play, praise, tangible rewards, effective commands, ignoring misbehavior, time out, and logical consequences. The augmented content covered the skill domains introduced to address the identified risk factors.

First, cognitive restructuring was introduced to help parents to control upsetting thoughts about children's bids for autonomy and school-related problems that concerned the use of punitive discipline. Cognitive restructuring activities were focused specifically on maladaptive cognitions triggered by child misbehavior or school-related problems. Parents were taught to identify their upsetting thoughts about child noncompliance that lead to ineffective parenting. Common examples are blaming attributions that lead to overly punitive discipline or helpless thoughts that lead to inconsistent discipline. Parents were taught to replace upsetting thoughts with nonblaming, self-efficacious thoughts that mobilized effective behavior management strategies. For example, when a child leaves a mess and does not comply with a request to tidy up, parents are taught to identify their blaming thoughts ("He is lazy and spoiled, he shows me no respect") or helpless ("No matter what I do, he never listens") and replace them with calming and empowering thoughts ("He's still young, it's my job to help him follow directions").

Second, training in psychoeducation and communication skills was added to help reframe and resolve recurrent conflicts in immigrant families. This content was introduced to support bicultural parenting skills in immigrant families. Training focused on active listening and communication skills to be used in structured, routine family meetings. Parents were taught problem-solving steps to elicit the child's perspective on the problem, communicate their own concerns effectively, collaborate in generating a variety of solutions, evaluate the options, make a plan, and monitor the results. This technique may run counter to cultural expectations for parental authority and is introduced as an important adaptation for the bicultural family. We emphasized that parents guide and evaluate the appropriateness of solutions generated, and thus parental authority is not incompatible with open discussion and problem solving.

Third, to prevent punitive responses to school problems, strategies were introduced for increasing positive parental involvement in children's schooling. Although Chinese American parents are deeply invested in their children's achievement and provide significant instrumental support in the form of resources (e.g., study materials, computers, tutors) or relief from other obligations (e.g., household chores), they are less likely to monitor homework, assist with school problems, or guide study habits than are White American parents (Asakawa, 2001). First, parents were encouraged to show interest in their child's learning to further build the parent–child relationship. Next, they were taught strategies for structuring a homework routine, with attention to limiting screen time. Parents were instructed on how to support study skills and coach persistence in the face of academic difficulties. Finally, parents were taught how to communicate effectively with teachers to proactively address challenges their children encounter in school.

PHASE 3: DEPLOYMENT-FOCUSED RESEARCH—THE TEST DRIVE

We conducted a waiting-list controlled pilot trial to evaluate the feasibility and effects of the augmented IY program (Lau, Fung, Ho, Liu, & Gudino, 2011). Fifty-two Cantonese or Mandarin-speaking Chinese immigrant parents were referred to treatment for concerns about ineffective parental discipline or child behavior problems. Referral sources included schools, community mental health clinics, and child protective services. Participants were assigned to groups of six to nine parents on the basis of their area of residence and preferred language (Cantonese or Mandarin). Six groups were randomized to receive either immediate ($n = 31$) or delayed ($n = 21$) treatment. At baseline, 40.8% of children had elevated internalizing problems, 38.8% had elevated externalizing problems, and 48.1% had either elevated internalizing or externalizing problems. Intent-to-treat analyses indicated a significant group by time interaction in predicting positive involvement ($\eta^2 = .17, p < .01$) and negative discipline ($\eta^2 = .12, p < .05$) on the Alabama Parenting Questionnaire (Shelton, Frick, & Wootton, 1996) and total behavior problems ($\eta^2 = .17, p < .01$) on the Child Behavior Checklist (Achenbach & Rescorla, 2001). Engagement was high, with 79.1% of parents attending at least 10 out of 14 sessions.

Trained observers viewed 36% of sessions and completed the IY Parent Group Leader Process Rating to rate elements of collaborative teaching, enactment support, and group process skills. The data suggested that the group leaders adhered well to manualized therapy process with mean ratings of 4.31 to 4.79 out of 5 across the therapy process elements. As another measure of fidelity, therapists completed detailed session checklists to ensure that the requisite intervention content was delivered. On average, 79.6% of videotaped vignettes were shown and discussed, 74.5% of assigned role-plays were completed, and 82.0% of homework guidance and monitoring items were completed. These data suggested that therapy process was responsive and adherent, but problems with fidelity arose with insufficient time to deliver the interventions in the time allotted. This provided some indirect evidence that PT with immigrant parents might require adaptations in pacing and length of the intervention.

The therapists in our pilot trial duly noted their concerns about pacing and dosage of the adapted intervention. Following the completion of the groups, we convened a meeting of the six master's level Chinese American therapists involved in the pilot trial to gather their impressions of the implementation. Three group leaders were staff clinicians at our community partner agency. Three additional group leaders were doctoral students in clinical psychology who colead groups with agency staff. Group leaders were asked what contributed to success of the program, what barriers to implementation were perceived, and what led to improved outcomes for this population. First, they shared their impressions about the therapy content that was most valuable for the immigrant Chinese families served. Group leaders nominated the sessions covering child-directed play, praise, ignoring misbehavior, and controlling upsetting thoughts as the intervention components that were critical to improving outcomes for the families they treated. They noted that "these are brand new skills for our families." For example, one leader remarked, "Culturally we are produced to be didactic. Everything, play, or whatever, has to have an educational purpose behind it." This made child-directed play particularly novel and difficult to learn.

Praise was not a new concept to Chinese parents, but the techniques were difficult to implement. One leader noted, "Parents know in theory that praise is helpful, but when they actually praised, the words, the statements that they used, were not necessarily praise. It was always weighted with criticism." Group leaders remarked that these lessons required ample rehearsal for making and sustaining gains. One leader described parents' backsliding:

> We found out towards the end of the group the parents forgot all the beginning basic skills, like praising, spending time, those skills. Forgot! Initially, when we introduced to them they were able to do it right, with homework. And then, towards the end, it was all gone.

Compounding the problem, the group leaders noted that the basic skills are prerequisite for later lessons (e.g., family problem-solving) where immigrant parents "are still trying to get hold of the foundation skills, so they are not yet ready for the more advanced skills."

Second, group leaders commented on the therapeutic process elements that led to change. They reported that the intervention seemed effective to the extent that parents were supported in practicing new strategies in role-play and home activities. For example, leaders felt it was necessary to make home assignments as customized as possible. "We came up with specifically what they should do for their homework, not just a general assignment." This specificity in home assignments made the application of the strategy as concrete as possible and engaged each parent in a clear social contract for the week. Group leaders believed that many of the basic skills were difficult for traditional Chinese parents to carry out and remarked that "monolingual first-generation parents need more guidance, more support and hands-on practice." Unfortunately, they also felt it was difficult to provide enough facilitated practice in the course of treatment. In one group leader's words, "It seems like we do not have sufficient time to kind of walk them through the practice enough on those particular skills to be reinforced because we have to move on to the next topic." Despite her belief that rehearsal was a key mechanism of change, another group leader admitted with honesty, "If we are pressed for time and setting priorities—get through the curriculum or the role-play practice—the role-play is often left off."

Thus, our findings suggested that PT that attends responsively to cultural barriers to engagement can indeed yield strong treatment effects in improving parenting and child behavior problems in high-risk immigrant Chinese families. However, our implementation experience also indicated that slowing the pacing of skill lessons and increasing the dosage of behavioral rehearsal might be an important adaptation in achieving meaningful and enduring changes in parenting in immigrant families.

This need for additional learning support was suggested in previous trials of PT with Chinese communities. Ho et al. (1999) encountered difficulty in teaching Hong Kong parents to praise their children and had to bolster their instruction with the use of feedback on videotaped behavior samples as well as live coaching. Ho et al. (1999) reported that some parents refused to praise, but those who tried initially used praise in a "mechanistic and unemotional manner," limiting its effectiveness. Likewise, Crisante and Ng (2003) reported that Chinese Australian parents required substantial practice of the unfamiliar behaviors of both giving and receiving praise in role-plays so that they better understood the intention to evoke positive affect. PT with Chinese parents is successful to the extent that rehearsal is buttressed. The fact that child-directed play, praise, ignoring misbehavior, and time out are culturally distal has dual implications. First, we need to bridge attitudinal barriers that limit motivation. Second, we need to ensure ample opportunity to enact, rehearse, and become facile in using unfamiliar practices.

LESSONS AND TESTS TO COME

Over the course of this work, our thoughts about the likely best strategies for adapting parent training for immigrant Chinese families have evolved. A prevailing concern has been identifying ways to ensure parental engagement in the face of common cultural misgivings about specific PT techniques. Initially, the plan was to include specific manualized directives for framing each strategy in a culturally congruent manner to promote acceptability. This approach revealed itself to be overly prescriptive, lacking the flexibility to address the heterogeneity in parent attitudes toward PT skills among Chinese families (e.g., time out viewed as alternately cruel or not punitive enough). Instead, our data suggested that the cultivation of the therapeutic relationship and dynamic group process is integral to promoting engagement. A working alliance may be achieved most effectively by assuming a hypothesis testing approach informed by cultural knowledge rather than by making assumptions about treatment attitudes based on membership in a given ethnocultural group (Lopez, 1997). Eliciting an exchange of diverse viewpoints on PT strategies can serve to motivate their uptake when their benefits can be aligned with parents' own goals. This process is marshaled in collaborative approaches to PT that build in close attention to attitudinal barriers. Cultural competence has evolved from "the making of assumptions about individuals on the basis of their background to the implementation of the principles of patient-centered care, including exploration, empathy, and responsiveness to patients' needs, values, and preferences" (Betancourt, 2004, p. 953). Cultural adaptations of evidence-based treatments may provide a handy road map to leverage these therapeutic process elements within a given intervention model.

The second guiding principle governing our adaptation was to ensure that therapeutic content attends to culturally relevant stressors that may undermine behavior change in PT. Augmentation was intended to contextualize the intervention with components to address the distinctive context of parenting in immigrant Chinese families. Presuming that contextual stress can interfere with the uptake of positive parenting practices, augmentations were designed to lower known correlates of ineffective discipline among Chinese immigrant families, school-related problems, and familial acculturative stress. For example, after we introduce the skill of ignoring misbehavior, we introduce the augmented session on controlling upsetting thoughts.

We anticipated that Chinese parents would encounter difficulty in ignoring behaviors that were construed as disrespectful, and this would provide a good juncture for cognitive restructuring. Thus, parents were asked to describe the thoughts that interfered with their ability to ignore misbehaviors (e.g., child refuses to eat the dinner prepared equals "What an ungrateful and selfish son!") and are able to help the parent construct a calming replacement thought (e.g., "Kids are so picky at this age, but I can't give in"). This calming skill can make way for parents to use basic strategies such as differential reinforcement, praise, and appropriate consequences.

The last of the three avenues for adapting PT emerged from our implementation as well as clinician focus groups and involves optimizing enactment of core PT strategies when cultural factors (e.g., learning history, experience, attitudes) make it difficult for immigrant parents to become facile with the skills. This involves providing treatment with sufficient intensity for immigrant parents to ensure adequate orientation, enactment, rehearsal, consolidation, and generalization of PT skills. The often-cited concerns about cultural differences in parenting practices and values across groups can certainly affect attitudes toward PT strategies, but they may also make mastery of these new behaviors more challenging.

The conclusions from our pilot work reflect the broader tension in the debate over the balance between adaptation and fidelity. At this point, we are not able to conclude whether our treatment effects were enhanced by the inclusion of culturally tailored content to reduce contextual stress in immigrant Chinese families. Nor have we determined whether increasing the standard dose of enactment and rehearsal of core PT skills will enhance treatment effects. Our next step is to investigate whether these two alternative approaches to cultural adaptation (cultural augmentation vs. intensification of treatment dose) yield improvements in outcomes among immigrant families. Posing this question will help us understand the extent to which it is advantageous to do more of the same (increasing the dose of high fidelity PT) or to tailor skills training for salient group-specific presenting problems (contextualizing content).

REFERENCES

Achenbach, T. E., & Rescorla, L. (2001). *Manual for the ASEBA school-age forms and profiles*. Unpublished manuscript, Department of Psychiatry, University of Vermont, Burlington, VT.

Asakawa, K. (2001). Family socialization practices and their effects on the internalization of educational values for Asian and White American adolescents. *Applied Developmental Science, 5*, 184–194. doi:10.1207/S1532480XADS0503_6

Bennett, D. S., Power, T. J., Rostain, A. L., & Carr, D. E. (1996). Parent accept-ability and feasibility of ADHD interventions: Assessment, correlates, and predictive validity. *Journal of Pediatric Psychology, 21*, 643–657. doi:10.1093/jpepsy/21.5.643

Bernal, G., & Domenech Rodríguez, M. M. (2009). Advances in Latino family research: Cultural adaptations of evidence-based interventions. *Family Process, 48*, 169–178. doi:10.1111/j.1545-5300.2009.01275.x

Betancourt, J. R. (2004). Cultural competence—Marginal or mainstream movement? *The New England Journal of Medicine, 351*, 953–955. doi:10.1056/NEJMp048033

Chao, R. K., & Tseng, V. (2002). Parenting of Asians. In M. H. Bornstein (Ed.), *Handbook of parenting: Vol 4. Social conditions and applied parenting.* Mahwah, NJ: Erlbaum.

Crisante, L., & Ng, S. (2003). Implementation and process issues in using Group Tri-ple P with Chinese parents: Preliminary findings. *AeJAMH (Australian e-Journal for the Advancement of Mental Health), 2*, 1–10.

Farver, J. A. M., Narang, S. K., & Bhadha, B. R. (2002). East meets West: Ethnic identity, acculturation, and conflict in Asian Indian families. *Journal of Family Psychology, 16*, 338–350. doi:10.1037/0893-3200.16.3.338

Forehand, R., & Kotchick, B. A. (1996). Cultural diversity: A wake-up call for parent training. *Behavior Therapy, 27*, 187–206. doi:10.1016/S0005-7894(96)80014-1

Fuligni, A. J., & Yoshikawa, H. (2004). Investments in children among immigrant families. In A. Kalil & T. DeLeire (Eds.), *Family investments in children's potential: Resources and parenting behaviors that promote success* (pp. 139–162). Mahwah, NJ: Erlbaum.

Heine, S. J., Kitayama, S., Takada, T., Ide, E., Leung, C., & Matsumoto, H. (2001). Divergent consequences of success and failure in Japan and North America: An investigation of self-improving motivations and malleable selves. *Journal of Personality and Social Psychology, 81*, 599–615. doi:10.1037/0022-3514.81.4.599

Ho, J., McCabe, K. M., Yeh, M., & Lau, A. S. (in press). Perceptions of the acceptability of Parent Training among immigrant Chinese parents. *Behavior Therapy.* Retrieved from http://www.sciencedirect.com/science/article/pii/S0005789411001419?v=s5

Ho, T.-P., Chow, V., Fung, C., Leung, K., Chiu, K.-Y., YU, G., . . . Lieh-Mak, F. (1999). Parent management training in a Chinese population: Application and outcome. *Journal of the American Academy of Child & Adolescent Psychiatry. 38*, 1165–1172. doi:10.1097/00004583-199909000-00022

Hobbs, S. A., Walle, D. L., & Caldwell, S. (1984). Maternal evaluation of social reinforcement and time-out: Effects of brief parent training. *Journal of Consult-ing and Clinical Psychology, 52*, 135–136. doi:10.1037/0022-006X.52.1.135

Kazdin, A. E. (1997). Parent management training: Evidence, outcomes, and issues. *Journal of the American Academy of Child & Adolescent Psychiatry, 36*, 1349–1356. doi:10.1097/00004583-199710000-00016

Kazdin, A. E. (2000). Perceived barriers to treatment participation and treatment acceptability among antisocial children and their families. *Journal of Child and Family Studies, 9*, 157–174. doi:10.1023/A:1009414904228

Kazdin, A. E., Holland, L., & Crowley, M. (1997). Family experience of barriers to treatment and premature termination from child therapy. *Journal of Consulting and Clinical Psychology, 65*, 453–463. doi:10.1037/0022-006X.65.3.453

Krain, A. L., Kendall, P. C., & Power, T. J. (2005). The role of treatment acceptability in the initiation of treatment for ADHD. *Journal of Attention Disorders, 9*, 425–434. doi:10.1177/1087054705279996

Krueger, R. A. (1994). *Focus groups: A practical guide for applied research* (2nd ed.). Thousand Oaks, CA: Sage.

Krueger, R. A., & Casey, M. A. (2000). *Focus groups: A practical guide for applied research* (3rd ed.). Thousand Oaks, CA: Sage.

Kumpfer, K. L., Alvarado, R., Smith, P., & Bellamy, N. (2002). Cultural sensitivity and adaptation in family-based prevention interventions. *Prevention Science, 3*, 241–246. doi:10.1023/A:1019902902119

Lau, A. S. (2006). Making the case for selective and directed cultural adaptations of evidence-based treatments: Examples from parent training. *Clinical Psychology: Science and Practice, 13*, 295–310. doi:10.1111/j.1468-2850.2006.00042.x

Lau, A. S. (2010). Physical discipline in Chinese American immigrant families: An adoptive cultural perspective. *Cultural Diversity and Ethnic Minority Psychology, 16*, 313–322. doi:10.1037/a0018667

Lau, A. S., Fung, J. J., Ho, L., Liu, L., & Gudino, O. (2011). Parent training with high-risk immigrant Chinese families: A pilot group randomized trial yielding practice-based evidence. *Behavior Therapy, 42*, 413–426. doi:10.1016/j.beth.2010.11.001

Lee, R. M., Choe, J., Kim, G., & Ngo, V. (2000). Construction of the Asian American Family Conflicts Scale. *Journal of Counseling Psychology, 47*, 211–222. doi:10.1037/0022-0167.47.2.211

Liebkind, K. (1996). Acculturation and stress. *Journal of Cross-Cultural Psychology, 27*, 161–180. doi:10.1177/0022022196272002

Lieh-Mak, F., Lee, P. W., & Luk, S. L. (1984). Problems encountered in teaching Chinese parents to be behavior therapists. *Psychologia: An International Journal of Psychology in the Orient, 27*, 56–64.

Lopez, S. R. (1997). Cultural competence in psychotherapy: A guide for clinicians and their supervisors. In C. E. Watkins (Ed.), *Handbook of psychotherapy supervision* (pp. 570–588). New York, NY: Wiley.

McCabe, K. M., Yeh, M., Garland, A. F., Lau, A. S., & Chavez, G. (2005). The GANA Program: A tailoring approach to adapting parent child interaction therapy for Mexican Americans. *Education & Treatment of Children, 28*, 111–129.

Miller, G. E., & Prinz, R. J. (1990). Enhancement of social learning family interventions for childhood conduct disorder. *Psychological Bulletin, 108*, 291–307. doi:10.1037/0033-2909.108.2.291

Miller, R. B. (1998). Epistemology and psychotherapy data: The unspeakable, unbearable, horrible truth. *Clinical Psychology: Science and Practice, 5*, 242–250. doi:10.1111/j.1468-2850.1998.tb00147.x

Park, M. S. (2001). The factors of child physical abuse in Korean immigrant families. *Child Abuse & Neglect, 25*, 945–958. doi:10.1016/S0145-2134(01)00248-4.

Portes, A., & Rumbaut, R. G. (2001). *Legacies: The story of the immigrant second generation.* Berkeley, CA: University of California Press.

Shelton, K. K., Frick, P. J., & Wootton, J. (1996). Assessment of parenting practices in families of elementary school-age children. *Journal of Clinical Child Psychology, 25*, 317–329. doi:10.1207/s15374424jccp2503_8

Webster-Stratton, C. (2011). *The Incredible Years parents, teachers, and children training series: Program content, methods, research and dissemination, 1980–2011.* Seattle, WA: Incredible Years.

Williams, C. L., & Berry, J. W. (1991). Primary prevention of acculturative stress among refugees: Application of psychological theory and practice. *American Psychologist, 46*, 632–641. doi:10.1037/0003-066X.46.6.632

Ying, Y.-W., Lee, P. A., Tsai, J. L., Lee, Y. J., & Tsang, M. (2001). Relationship of young adult Chinese Americans with their parents: Variation by migratory status and cultural orientation. *American Journal of Orthopsychiatry, 71*, 342–349. doi:10.1037/0002-9432.71.3.342

8

SABER ES PODER: THE CULTURAL ADAPTATION OF A TRAUMA INTERVENTION FOR LATINA WOMEN

FABIANA WALLIS, HORTENSIA AMARO, AND DHARMA E. CORTÉS

Clinicians who work with Latinas are keenly aware of the high level of traumatic experiences in this population. A recent survey of a national sample of 2,000 Latinas found that over 40% reported at least one experience of psychological trauma in their lifetime and that 61% of these women experienced more than one victimization (Cuevas, Sabina, & Picard, 2010). Polyvictimization was associated with increased clinically significant psychological distress. Despite the prevalence of psychological trauma, Latinas have been only minimally included in the development of evidence-based trauma interventions.

Many evidence-based treatments (EBTs) have not been developed for or had their efficacy tested in ethnocultural populations, and evidence-based practices have not always been adequately disseminated. Studies that document the efficacy of behavioral treatment approaches have been generally developed and tested with White Americans and therefore have limited generalizability to other populations. Few developers have in-depth knowledge of the specific ethnocultural populations with whom the treatment may be later used and therefore are not well equipped to offer suggestions for cultural adaptations. Finally, the conditions and context under which efficacy studies are often conducted differ greatly from those in many community-based settings in terms of language, resources, staff training, and other practical constraints. As a result, there is a serious gap between EBT scientific studies and service application needs, as well as deficiencies in the actual availability and relevance of EBTs for non-White Americans.

In an effort to bridge this gap, there has been an increased focus on tailoring EBTs to the specific populations and contexts in which they will be implemented. Although when compared with nonadapted efficacy and effectiveness studies, the number of ethnocultural adaptation interventions is small, three meta-analyses have been published to date (Griner & Smith, 2006; Huey & Polo, 2008; Smith, Domenech Rodríguez, & Bernal, 2011). Taken together, these studies support the growing consensus on the value of cultural adaptations and their efficacy (American Psychological Association Task Force on Evidence-Based Practices, 2006; Bernal, Jiménez-Chafey, & Domenech Rodríguez, 2009; Castro, Barrera, & Holleran Steiker, 2010).

In this chapter, we describe the theory and procedures used in the cultural adaptation of the trauma empowerment and recovery model (TREM; Harris, 1998) intervention for use with Latinas as an example that might assist others in approaching cultural adaptations. We also describe the changes that were derived from the adaptation process to inform clinical practice. This adaptation relies on a combination of theoretical, cultural, data-driven, and procedural models. It integrates emic and etic perspectives by retaining core trauma concepts while adding culture-specific constructs to meet culture-specific needs. First, the theoretical and cultural models provide a framework for what needs to be different and what needs to stay the same in cultural adaptations. Second, the data-driven and procedural models guide how the changes are made. Third, a review of specific changes illustrates the application of theory and procedure to clinical implementation. Finally, strengths, limitations, and next steps are outlined.

RATIONALE FOR CULTURAL ADAPTATIONS

The need for cultural adaptations has been critically examined. Arguments against cultural adaptations include costs of developing culture-specific programs, lack of empirical evidence that mainstream programs do *not* work for ethnocultural populations, and similarities in risk factors in both minority and nonminority groups (Dent, Sussman, Ellickson, Brown, & Richardson, 1996; Hansen, 1992; Tobler, 1992). In contrast, Castro, Barrera, and Martinez (2004) argued that adaptations are required when an intervention or program is culturally mismatched with a new target community. For example, when the original program is designed in consultation with White American consumers but the current target group is an ethnocultural minority, the intervention will lack community buy-in (resulting in low engagement and participation) and may conflict with the target group's beliefs, values, and norms, potentially resulting in high dropout rates and low efficacy.

Cultural adaptations are aimed at increasing ecological validity and the congruence between the client's experience and the elements of the treatment. Ecological validity is a concept that supports the need for culture-specific interventions. It is defined as the degree of congruence between the environment as experienced by the subject and the properties of the environment as assumed by the investigator (Bronfenbrenner, 1977). Since culture determines meaning, the cultural context is seen as an important starting point for the development of a treatment approach. Trauma is a type of experience where meaning making can have a critical impact on symptom development and response to treatment. For example, it is not uncommon in Latino cultures that the first disclosure of physical abuse from a male to a female partner is met with a response that minimizes the problem and over-emphasizes a woman's responsibility to keep the family together. Fawcett, Heise, Isita-Espejel, and Pick (1999) stated that this reaction to family violence or meaning making is typically passed down from one generation to the next by mothers and grandmothers. In our experience, it is not uncommon for group participants to describe receiving responses such as "And what did you think marriage was going to be like—all roses?" after they disclose being hit by their husband. In these situations, group participants will explain that they did not seek help because they were told it was their job to keep the family together. In response to this pattern, and aiming to interrupt this intergenerational socialization, one community-based intervention targeted family matriarchs for its domestic violence psychoeducational interventions (Fawcett et al., 1999). If evidence-based programs for mainstream groups lack cultural sensitivity, they can easily miss opportunities for effective interventions with a broad array of ethnocultural groups.

Scholars have varied perspectives on the issue of cultural adaptation of EBTs. Some have suggested that cultural adaptations may be warranted if an EBT is insufficiently successful in changing clinical outcomes for a cultural group or reveals that engagement is below previously established standards (Kumpfer, Alvarado, Smith, & Bellamy, 2002). Others have noted that a cultural adaptation may lead to otherwise unattainable goals and benefits. When a culture-specific element is added to an intervention to address a unique need in a community, it has the potential to add an outcome that would not have been otherwise possible (Barrera & Castro, 2006). For example, by addressing immigration as a potential source of trauma, symptoms associated with an immigration-related loss may be decreased or eliminated. In addition, a cultural adaptation may be necessary when a cultural group exhibits unique clinical problems based on a distinct set of risks or resilience factors (Lau, 2006).

The mental health literature provides strong evidence of cultural or race/ethnic differences in risk or protective factors for mental health outcomes. The *immigration paradox* posits that the longer immigrants live in the United States, the worse their health outcomes become, and this has been well documented among Latino immigrants. The reverse is true for Asian immigrants, whose health outcomes improve over time (Alegría, Takeuchi, et al., 2004). While exploring this effect further, Alegría et al. (2008) identified protective and risk factors for Latinos. Protective factors included foreign nativity (which varied by country of origin, disorder, and age of migration), strong family support networks, and religious involvement. Risk factors included discrimination, low social standing, cultural intergenerational conflict, unsafe neighborhoods, and unemployment. Recent research on Latino migrant farm workers revealed a negative impact of discrimination on both emotional and physical health (McClure et al., 2010). Other contextual factors affecting the mental health of Latinos include familism, acculturation, and enculturation (Alegría, Vila, et al., 2004). In addition, Latina immigrants may have unique traumatic experiences related to immigration—loss, separations (temporary or permanent), undocumented status and witnessing immigration raids, coercion and sexual harassment in the workplace, and acculturation stress—coupled with reduced access to services. Latinas may also have been exposed to war-related violence in their countries of origin. Although violence comes in many forms, in Puerto Rico, where there is no military unrest, residents have a higher risk of being exposed to violence in their lifetime than the mainstream U.S. population (Hough, Canino, Abueg, & Gusman, 1996). Similarly, Latinas in substance abuse and trauma treatment were more likely to have been exposed to community violence than White Americans, even after controlling for socioeconomic status (Amaro et al., 2005).

An often overlooked aspect of psychological trauma is exposure to ethnic and racial discrimination (Scurfield & Mackey, 2001). U.S.-born Latinas may face stressors such as increased exposure to discrimination (Pérez, Fortuna, & Alegría, 2008), including media coverage specifically on Latino immigrant communities. In the context of familism, they also may have a high risk of intergenerational conflict within the family system. More important, Latinas may experience unique symptoms in reaction to some types of trauma called *ataque de nervios* (Guarnaccia & Rogler, 1999) that require a unique clinical response to avoid misdiagnosis and inadequate treatment. A safe environment in which to promote recovery from these types of experiences may not occur as readily within programs developed for mainstream groups since those programs might overlook such sources and reactions to traumatic experiences. Moreover, although some risk factors and stressors may not be unique to Latinas, they are unique to Latina immigrants, for example, and are absent from mainstream interventions.

CULTURAL ADAPTATION MODELS AND PROCEDURES

Integrating Two Perspectives

Cultural adaptations of interventions can be conceptualized from two divergent viewpoints on the emic–etic paradigm (Brislin, 1986, as cited in Matías Carrelo et al., 2003). The emic perspective involves the study of phenomena from within the culture and its context—"from the inside" or particularist. It requires multiple linguistic and sociocultural factors to be considered for an adaptation, such as migration, acculturation, social position, discrimination, or acculturative stress (Alegría, Vila, et al., 2004). The etic perspective is "outside" the culture or universalist—it is fundamentally comparative and seeks to find equivalent phenomena across cultures. In the clinical setting, the integration of both perspectives means that the clinician balances universal norms, specific group norms, and individual norms while differentiating between normal and abnormal behavior (López et al., 1989). Specifically in the context of group clinical interventions, an emic approach increases relevance and identification with the material, whereas the etic perspective promotes group cohesiveness and provides common ground through universal psychological phenomena. Additional considerations are warranted when adapting interventions for broad ethnocultural groups, such as Latinos, given the range of within-group differences (Barrera, Castro, & Biglan, 1999), and therefore this intervention adaptation was designed to provide clinical opportunity for intragroup comparisons and exploration based on individual group membership. To incorporate emic perspectives in the adaptation process, we identified cultural considerations specific to the Latino community derived from two models developed by Bernal, Bonilla, and Bellido (1995) and Castro et al. (2004), both reviewed in Chapter 2 of this volume.

For the purposes of this adaptation, the cultural dimensions of both frameworks were combined with those that were similar across the models and are described as follows: (a) Language/cognitive information processing: Language is the "carrier" of culture (Bernal et al., 1995, p. 73); it must take into account the target group's literacy, age, and developmental level. (b) Persons: Cultural competence is required among program developers, program delivery staff, and the adaptation team. (c) Metaphors: Use of symbols and concepts such as refrains or *dichos*. (d) Content/deep structure: Cultural knowledge, core values, beliefs, norms, worldviews, lifestyles, customs, and traditions as the starting point and not the end result. (e) Concepts: Treatment constructs must be consonant with culture and conceptualized in a way that is consistent with the belief system of the clients to maximize treatment efficacy. (f) Goals/motivational characteristics: These must be matched with cultural values and traditions to reduce cultural conflict or behavioral resistance. (g) Methods/

delivery: Includes decisions regarding type of intervention, program location, materials, and presentation strategies. (h) Personal context/environment[1]: Includes a person's immediate environmental and sociocultural-historical contexts, ranging from acculturation and enculturation, acculturative stress, phases of migration, availability of social supports, and a person's relationship to country or culture of origin, to community readiness, infrastructure, and consultation.

The procedures guiding this adaptation were derived from Lau's (2006) data-driven approach embedded in Barrera and Castro's (2006) four-stage action model (see Chapter 2, this volume). It provided a framework to determine the balance between fidelity and fit (Backer, 2001; see Chapter 2, this volume) as adaptations strive to incorporate cultural aspects of the target population while trying to maintain core components of the original model.

Original Model and Parent Study

The TREM was developed by Maxine Harris (1998) at Community Connections in Washington, DC. TREM is a theory-based, manualized, 33-session, weekly, group-based intervention that draws on a combination of cognitive restructuring, psychoeducational, and skills-building techniques. It focuses on the clinical needs of women with trauma histories who also have substance abuse and mental health disorders. Each session provides a rationale for the session's topic, questions to guide discussion, and exercises or activities. Psychological trauma is defined broadly in this model; groups may include participants with different types of traumatic experiences. The 33-session curriculum, with a 24-session alternative, is divided into four parts: (a) empowerment, (b) trauma recovery, (c) advanced trauma recovery issues, and (d) closing rituals.

After review of the various manualized interventions available (Moses, Reed, Mazelis, & D'Ambrosio, 2003), TREM was selected for addressing the trauma history of program participants and implemented at the Boston Consortium model (BCM), one of the sites of the Women, Co-Occurring Disorders and Violence Study (WCDVS). A full description of the WCDVS study design is included in McHugo et al. (2005) and Giard et al. (2005). TREM was deemed the best match for the BCM client population and treatment settings given that it was developed for a similar clinical population of predominantly poor African American women. While we recognized TREM would need adaptation for Latinas, when compared with other trauma interventions, the population and clinical setting for which TREM was developed most closely approximated our client population. After an in-depth 3-day training and with ongoing supervision from the developers, TREM

[1]The context dimension in Bernal et al.'s (1995) model refers to the immediate and the broad context and is labeled *personal context* for the purposes of this chapter. It was combined with Castro et al.'s (2004) environment dimension because it also addresses the larger community context.

was implemented in English with White American, African American, and Latina participants at the Boston site's detoxification, outpatient, and residential substance abuse treatment settings. However, given the importance of match between the language used in the intervention and the language or linguistic context in which the traumatic experiences occurred (e.g., Nader, 2007), the clinical team identified the need to provide the trauma intervention in Spanish. Further, since Latina women had not been included in sufficient numbers in the development of TREM, the Boston site assessed its fit for this population, translated it, and introduced needed cultural adaptations.

CULTURAL ADAPTATION OF TRAUMA EMPOWERMENT AND RECOVERY MODEL

Participants

A total of 68 Latina women participated in the five cycles of the cultural adaptation process. Participants were primarily of Puerto Rican and Dominican background. Ages ranged from 19 to 53 years ($M = 31.87$, $SD = 7.97$); the majority (56%) were not married or partnered, and all were mothers, with an average of three children each. Most study participants reported being able to understand a conversation in English very well (82.4%), and over one fourth (29.4%) reported speaking only or mostly Spanish at home. All met criteria for the federal poverty level, and education level was on average below high school. Participants experienced a mean of 14.6 stressful events in their lifetime. In terms of types of abuse, the majority (85%) reported a history of physical abuse in childhood (50%) and adulthood (63.2%) and sexual abuse (86.8%). More women reported sexual abuse as a child (82%) than as an adult (51%). The sample's PTSD Symptom Scale scores are in the severe range (> 36), and Global Severity Index scores fell in the range for psychiatric outpatient and inpatient normative scores. Most of the women were in a residential treatment setting (81%), and 19% were in outpatient treatment. Addiction Severity Index alcohol and drug composite scores were .15 and .17, respectively, where severity ranges from 0 to 1. The average length of stay in treatment was 203 days, and 29 (42.6%) women had lengths of 271 days or more. Forty (58.8%) participants completed (i.e., attended 12 or more sessions) the trauma intervention, and the average number of sessions attended was 13 out of a total of 25 sessions ($M = 13.4$, $SD = 7.6$).

Measures

Data were collected via in-person interviews in the participant's preferred language. Information collected included demographic information (e.g., age, primary language, marital and relationship status, number of children), BCM services received, and five clinical outcome measures collected as part of the WCDVS (Giard et al., 2005; McHugo et al., 2005). Feedback forms were developed by members of the adaptation working group and completed by both participants and group leaders.

Procedures

Participants for the adaptation were recruited from the Boston site of the WCDVS study sample (described in McHugo et al., 2005). Eligibility was determined by the counselors. Women were included if they were at least 18 years of age, had a history of physical or sexual abuse, and met criteria for an Axis I mental health and substance abuse disorder. Eligible clients participated in the trauma group as part of their treatment plan. Group coleaders explained the purpose of the adaptation, and research staff collected feedback from participants.

Design

The TREM cultural adaptation process consisted of seven steps within Barrera and Castro's (2006) four-stage procedure model. During Phase I (information gathering), in consultation with TREM developer Maxine Harris, we created a working group (Step 1) consisting of bilingual Latina women. This group included a TREM-trained doctoral level psychologist, a doctoral level translator and literacy consultant, TREM-trained mental health clinicians and substance abuse counselors, researchers, and an agency administrator. Input from women in recovery was elicited throughout the adaptation process. A subset of this group conducted a review of existing literature (Step 2) to identify cultural adaptation models and cultural factors in treatment, and most were specific to adaptations for interventions with the Latino population. The primary source of "nonfit" between the original TREM and the target group was language. This step highlighted other discrepancies, such as types of traumatic events of target group and culturally relevant resources and materials, while issues of program delivery staff were already adequate.

During Phase II (preliminary adaptation design), the entire contents of the 24-session version of the TREM were translated into Spanish (Step 3) using a multistage method for translation and cross-cultural adaptation derived from the medical, sociological, and psychological literature (Beaton, Bombardier, Guillemin, & Ferraz, 2000; Brislin, Lonner, & Thorndike, 1973; Bullinger et al., 1998; Matías Carrelo et al., 2003; Wagner et al., 1998; World Health Organization, 1998). This approach involved collaboration among translators and experts on the content of the material being translated. For *Saber Es Poder* (SEP), two professional translators and bilingual clinicians worked together to ensure that the content of the TREM was adequately translated from a language use standpoint as well as relevant to the experiences of trauma of Latinas. The first step in this process involved translation of the TREM by a professional translator. A second independent translator reviewed the translated text and discussed proposed changes with the first translator. The translation version produced by these two steps was reviewed by a bilingual researcher and a clinician with expertise in the content area and Latino mental health who recommended changes that were incorporated. This revised version of the TREM was then implemented with participants, and the facilitator provided feedback on content and language issues stemming from the implementation of the intervention. Flip charts used during sessions to record participant input were also used during the adaptation process. These combined efforts resulted in the first draft of the adaptation. In addition, a subset of the group developed a group facilitator feedback form for each session and a client feedback form (Step 4).

During Phase III (preliminary adaptation tests), the first version of the translated TREM was piloted with Spanish-speaking clients (Step 5). Feedback forms were implemented at this time and reviewed by the working group. At the end of this first cycle, the working group identified areas to improve cultural fit, translation, and literacy issues.

During the last phase (adaptation refinement), we conducted four additional cycles with iterative adaptations in language and content until consensus was reached regarding cultural fit based on facilitator and client feedback (Step 6). We conducted a final review of the adaptation with the original TREM developer (Step 7).

CULTURALLY ADAPTED INTERVENTION: DOCUMENTATION OF CHANGES

The cultural adaptation resulted in a facilitator manual published entirely in Spanish that was given the name *Saber Es Poder* (Harris, Wallis, & Amaro, 2006). As a result of the adaptation process, changes were made to TREM's underlying assumptions, the content, and the facilitator training.

Underlying Assumptions

The TREM curriculum is guided by four basic assumptions (Harris, 1998): (a) Some current dysfunctional behaviors and/or symptoms may have originated as a legitimate coping response to trauma; (b) women who experience trauma in childhood are deprived of the opportunity to develop certain skills necessary for adult coping; (c) trauma severs core connections to one's family, to one's community, and ultimately to oneself; and (d) women who have been abused repeatedly may feel powerless and unable to advocate for themselves. These assumptions are based on the trauma literature that describes experiences of women across cultures (Renzetti, Edleson, & Kennedy Bergen, 2000) and are thus considered universal in the context of trauma. However, as a result of the data obtained through the cultural adaptation process and also to capture the intent and goal of the adaptation, a fifth assumption was necessary in SEP: Cultural realities may need to be effectively addressed during trauma recovery to maximize treatment gains for ethnocultural women. This assumption for the SEP adaptation is based on clinical observations that Latina women may have experienced unique traumatic events in unique contexts that require unique ways to address them.

Curriculum Content

Content changes were integrated throughout the curriculum instead of adding cultural factors in a separate session or sessions. In addition, changes were made in all areas of each session format: in session rationale, material, or questions for discussion with group members; in notes and instruction to facilitators; in new quotes from participants; and in exercises or activities. The following provides a description of the changes made across each of the eight cultural dimensions.

Language

The name of the cultural adaptation is a good example of the use of culturally syntonic language instead of a direct translation. *Saber es poder* translates as *knowing is power*; however, the term *poder* in Spanish also means *to be able to*, which implies action. Therefore, *saber es poder* implies that knowledge provides the power to act and, as such, stands as a definition of empowerment. The term *empowerment* in Spanish is a recent cultural import from U.S. psychology that is used almost exclusively in academic settings. As a result, it is a word that does not exist in the Spanish-language vocabulary of laypersons.

In addition, our attention to literacy issues resulted in a balance between familiarity and readability while taking advantage of the opportunity to enhance the participants' vocabulary. Instead of removing language that had created some confusion, such as the term *dynamics* when discussing relationships, we included a definition in the leaders' notes suggesting they explain how new terms are used in the context of a session. This provides an opportunity for women to feel empowered by gaining knowledge and new vocabulary.

Persons

The curriculum does not make assumptions about the cultural knowledge of Latina or bicultural facilitators. The instructions and SEP-specific training of facilitators provide information and resources to support group leaders' cultural competence. The adaptation process was led by a multinational working group comprised of Latina substance abuse treatment counselors, psychologists, social workers, and a literacy expert. This allowed for the nuances of language and culture to surface and to be addressed by representing either the lowest common denominator or by highlighting a tradition unique to a specific country.

Metaphors

Sayings or *dichos* can provide insight to cultural values associated with women, relationships, gender or role expectations, worldviews, and so on. During the TREM intervention, group participants are invited to share sayings that are reflective of their own country of origin. Discussing the meaning of sayings creates a safe way to simultaneously affirm and critically evaluate a cultural norm. For example, sayings such as *Porque te quiero te aporreo* (Because I love you, I beat you) and *Hay amores que matan* (Some love can kill) are typically used in the context of justifying the need for punishing or disciplining children, along the lines of the English expression "It's for your own good," which alludes to something bad that is necessary for a good purpose. However, people may use it to justify abusive or controlling behavior among adults. To take notice of such sayings, creatively discussing alternatives and identifying the original intent of the sayings, is a way to explore options within the confines of cultural norms and thus integrate the exploration of culturally derived metaphors in the treatment.

Content

Although the original TREM curriculum was developed with a diverse sample of White Americans, Black Americans, and some Asian American and Latina women, race and ethnicity were not explicitly addressed in the session content. In the adaptation, questions that guide each session discussion were added to include ethnicity:

TREM: When you think about being a woman, what are the first words or images that come to mind?

SEP: What is it like to be a Latina woman in the U.S.?

TREM: What role does forgiveness play, if any, in coming to terms with what happened to you?

SEP: What role do messages about "how a Latina should be" have in accepting what happened to you?

TREM: How much space do you need? What is a comfortable distance between you and others?

SEP: What are some cultural differences in terms of the personal space that we need?

Facilitators are encouraged to bring up these issues throughout the intervention to open up a space or to "give permission" to talk about race- and ethnicity-related stressors that are rarely addressed in mental health or substance abuse treatment. A more common practice is for programs to adopt a "color-blind" stance. The impact of this approach is twofold: On one hand, the experiences of women across ethnic groups are assumed to be the same, and the experiences of the majority become the "default," thus rendering invisible (and possibly invalid) the specific experiences of ethnic minority women; on the other hand, an opportunity is missed for women to have a safe space to talk about the impact of racial or ethnic discrimination and how it might amplify or complicate their trauma histories. At the same time, facilitators focus on positive aspects of being Latina to support the development or strengthening of women's cultural self-image.

When foreign-born or first- and second-generation immigrants are part of the group, it is important to open a discussion about immigration (e.g., loss, permanent separation from loved ones, inability to attend funerals), the trauma that may occur during the process of migration (e.g., extortion, sexual harassment, human trafficking), exposure to war-related trauma in their country of origin, and intergenerational conflicts that arise within families. Examples of intergenerational conflicts may include conflict between parents and U.S.-born or highly acculturated adolescents, between bilingual and monolingual members of the family, or when there is change in head of household, especially if it reverses expected gender roles. Again, paying attention to these unique circumstances contextualizes the treatment, reassures clients that the facilitators understand their past or current predicaments, and promotes the development of trust in the working alliance.

In a session focusing on psychological symptoms, the adaptation included information about a culture-bound syndrome common in Caribbean Latino cultures called *ataque de nervios* (Guarnaccia, Lewis-Fernández, & Rivera Marano, 2003), a nonpathological reaction to some types of trauma, such as the sudden death of a loved one. Similarly, in a session that explores the link between trauma and how women may feel about their bodies, we included a "stereotype check" regarding somatization and Latina women in the following facilitator instructions:

Given that it is a common assumption that the presence of physical pain among the Latino community is a cultural phenomenon, it is important to emphasize the importance to not attribute ALL physical pain to emotional issues. Therefore, it must be recommended that a physician examine symptoms of physical pain before attributing a psychological explanation. (Harris et al., 2006, p. 56)

Concepts/Deep Structure

This dimension is a particularly well-suited example of the integration of emic and etic perspectives. Deep structural changes are intended to produce changes in core concepts (Castro et al., 2004). In the SEP intervention, there are three core concept areas: trauma, substance abuse, and culture. As a result, the presence and absence of concept changes made during the adaptation process highlight core elements of each area. In the area of substance abuse, for example, the concept that these behaviors may have emerged as a way to cope with the impact of traumatic experiences is maintained unchanged. In the area of trauma, the etic concepts that focus treatment on personal strength or resilience, on the present, and on gender-specific experiences in promoting recovery are retained. However, they are balanced with emic concepts such as familism, personalism, respect, and collectivism. As a result, the adaptation is able to support a deeper discussion of family-orientation and gender-role values when addressing family violence or abuse by a family member. During the SEP-specific facilitator training (see the next section), we ensured that group leaders were familiar with these concepts and learned to apply them during mock group sessions. Instructions under "Leaders' Notes" in the manual also served as reminders for facilitators.

Goals/Motivation

To avoid the perception of conflict between goals of treatment and cultural values, the cultural value of *respeto* can be invoked when addressing issues of abuse from a family member or spouse to help clients understand the culturally consonant value of respect in human relations. Similarly, the valued role of Latina women as caregivers and mothers can be invoked to help clients understand how domestic violence is not only harmful to the woman herself but also to her children and thus align goals with cultural values. As Castro and colleagues (2004) suggested, approaching difficult issues from a familiar cultural perspective can minimize cultural conflict or behavioral resistance. Latinas in domestic violence situations frequently voice concerns that at the shelters the only thing they are told is to leave or divorce their partner and many times that goes against their beliefs. As a result, many Latinas decline or do not follow up with domestic violence shelter referrals.

Methods/Delivery

There are three ways in which SEP offers a different method and delivery of the intervention than the original TREM does. First, while TREM group leaders are encouraged to promptly redirect a participant's tangential material, SEP facilitators are trained to manage the content, process, and affect of the group in way that allows for some processing and some tangential material. Personalism, or "valuing interpersonal harmony and relating to others on a personal level" (Añez, Paris, Bedregal, Davidson, & Grilo, 2005, p. 224), is echoed in linguistic style by engaging in small talk and in circumstantial and tangential forms of expression. This is particularly true during the first several sessions, when participants are building cohesiveness as a group. Bernal and colleagues (1995) suggested balancing process and content for treatment effectiveness of cultural adaptations. However, this does not change the facilitators' role in providing containment of a potentially overwhelming disclosure of trauma history. The SEP facilitator training provided practice in this skill during mock groups.

SEP includes culturally specific literature, artwork, and resources. For example, Esmeralda Santiago's (1994) *Cuando Era Puertorriqueña, Latina Realities* by Oliva Espín (1997), *Nuestros Cuerpos, Nuestras Vidas* (Boston Women's Health Book Collective, 2000), and the *Sourcebook on Violence Against Women* (Renzetti et al., 2000) are suggested readings that provide perspectives on Latina and/or immigrant women. The use of literature is complemented by visual material in the form of artwork by Latina artist Frida Kahlo. Facilitators provide information about Kahlo's life and accomplishments and focus on either her history of physical pain or a psychologically abusive relationship as her traumatic experience. As a result, participants have a chance to identify with women from their own culture. Facilitators are given suggestions of appropriate paintings and are discouraged from using some more violent and/or graphic pieces of Kahlo's work. While looking at a painting, participants are asked to consider the question, "Why do you think she chose to express herself or her pain in this way?" There is only a brief silence before every single woman wants to share her thoughts. For example, we use the painting "The Little Deer" (Kahlo, 1946) for the session on the body called "The Body Remembers What the Mind Forgets." Participants typically access a deeper layer of analysis that was not reached during the question-guided discussion. Based on Kahlo's life experiences, the review of her other artwork often leads participants to make connections between trauma and infidelity, an event laden with cultural significance for many Latino immigrant families and typically avoided.

SEP introduced the use of culture-specific educational statements, in addition to TREM's trauma-specific education, as intervention methods (instead of exploration as follow-up to participants' disclosures or comments).

For example, a trauma-informed statement might be "Many women who experience trauma have difficulty trusting others," and a culture-specific statement might be "Many Latinas take pride in *aguantar* (or to endure). Have any of you ever felt this way?" Similarly, culture-specific information was provided in the notes for leaders. In the first session, for example, TREM suggests discussing the prevalence of trauma among women receiving services, while SEP suggests also discussing the high probability of exposure to traumatic events in some Latino communities (Hough et al., 1996). Cultural context can impact a person's exposure to trauma, his or her reactions, and, of course, treatment options. The culture-specific educational statements and questions are an additional intervention to understand the role of culture in recovery.

Two additional method and delivery strategies were unchanged from TREM. The structured format of the TREM curriculum was designed with the intention to provide predictability and safety as the context for trauma work. This strategy for trauma recovery has been widely documented in the literature (e.g., Herman, 1997) and was therefore maintained in the adaptation. The multimodal form of delivery was another strategy assessed as etic from a theoretical perspective and from provider and client feedback. The delivery includes oral, written, and experiential delivery as well as a written record of a participant's responses. Although TREM does not explicitly prescribe the use of narrative therapy approaches, this perspective can explain the power of recording a client's input on a flip chart during sessions. During a SEP group in Portland, Oregon, conducted in 2007 as we were nearing the end of the group, the members asked if they could keep the flip chart that had notes from the entire group. Fortunately, we found a volunteer to transcribe all the notes for them. The use of recoding the participants' input is a tool with a formidable capacity to empower.

Personal Context/Environment

As mentioned previously, Latina women have unique experiences according to the community they live in (e.g., rural vs. urban), their acculturation level (e.g., recent immigrant vs. U.S. born), their immigration status (e.g., whether they qualify for certain services or not), among other important contextual variables. While these experiences are not unique to Latinas, they lead to specific outcomes when they interface with immigration experiences and are therefore considered emic. Based on facilitator and client feedback, the absence of these issues in TREM produced a gap for our target group. Since these context variables can have an impact on recovery, we provided facilitators with the information and training to integrate these variables if appropriate to their specific group membership, and again, manual instructions serve as a reminder. Target community involvement in program development not only provides a better adaptation in terms of relevance and meaning but also provides the target community with a level of ownership that can promote participation once a program or curriculum is offered. Consumer input was used in both TREM and SEP.

Facilitator Training

The TREM curriculum has a corresponding facilitator training component. TREM developers designed the training to maximize the effectiveness of the intervention through trauma-specific clinical skills and fidelity to the model. They also provide training to TREM-trained facilitators to become trainers themselves. One of the authors (Wallis) received both trainings and developed a facilitator-training specific to SEP. An initial SEP training was piloted during the first TREM training with a day dedicated to SEP that was offered as a bilingual training in 2008 in Portland, Oregon. Almost three quarters of the trainees were bilingual and participated in the SEP portion of the training. This new training includes the adaptation changes and it consists of a 2-day agenda conducted entirely in Spanish. Some of the SEP-specific facilitator techniques that were discussed and/or practiced in mock groups included managing group process, appropriate use of culture-specific educational statements, effective use of artwork, cultural assumptions checks, and special issues in vicarious traumatization for minority clinicians.

LESSONS LEARNED FROM THE CULTURAL ADAPTATION OF TREM

The adaptation presented in this chapter aims to begin to narrow the gap in trauma-specific services for Latina women in the U.S. Latinas have extremely limited access to culturally competent, bilingual therapists trained in trauma-specific services—and this adaptation provides a culture-specific approach to trauma treatment. Clinicians who work with this population welcome the availability of much-needed specialized manualized interventions in the same language they will be implemented, as reported in data collected from SEP trainings. SEP participants also welcomed the intervention. In a recent TREM satisfaction survey conducted at the Boston site of the WCDVS, a review of 50 surveys conducted in Spanish revealed an overall satisfaction score of 3.28 (on a scale from 1 to 4, with 4 indicating the highest satisfaction). In addition, participants strongly endorsed recommending the group to other women in recovery (average score of 3.54). To our knowledge, this chapter describes the only cultural adaptation in the area of manualized trauma interventions. It addresses the needs of a specific subpopulation of Latina women with histories of psychological trauma, and the advantages of having a highly specific group are supported in the literature (Griner & Smith, 2006; Smith et al., 2011). Although the significance of language of origin has been emphasized only for Latinos with low acculturation levels or monolingual speakers (Castro et al., 2010), the language match between the context of traumatic events and that of trauma interventions may mediate outcomes (Nader, 2007). Therefore, this match may be a necessary component for both bilingual and monolingual participants in trauma treatment. This chapter also provides specific examples of changes based on culture that have direct implications for clinical practice. It also provides a contribution to the literature in terms of the role of clinical expertise in the development of evidence-based practices (American Psychological Association Task Force on Evidence-Based Practices, 2006). One of the challenges in developing this adaptation was integrating the emic perspective with a curriculum that would speak to the wide diversity within the Latino community. Facilitators are allowed to choose from the different questions and activity options and tailor the intervention within the limits of structured format and fixed topics. We believe that this flexibility helps achieve the balance between fidelity and fit.

Nonetheless, generalizability to other Latina subgroups may be a limitation of this adaptation. The adaptation sample consisted of urban Latinas of primarily Puerto Rican and Dominican origin. However, SEP was implemented with some success in Oregon with mostly Mexican-born Latinas from rural communities who had low incidence of substance abuse (Berdine, 2011). Further research may include more complex questions regarding the assessment of differences among Latinas: How different from each other are we really? Which are the differences that matter in the specific context of trauma, and which are not?

Attrition was also a challenging factor that needs further attention given that only 58% of the women completed the group during the adaptation. Although the adaptation completion rate is linked to sources of attrition within the overall program that may not be specific to SEP, there is a need to explore causes of attrition further and make modifications that could improve intervention completion rates. For example, clinicians recruited Latinas in an outpatient mental health setting for the 25-week SEP presenting it as three 8-week modules, and only one participant left the group after the first module, with no further attrition through the 25 weeks of intervention (L. V. Suárez, personal communication, April 14, 2011). It may be beneficial to test this strategy in outpatient substance abuse settings and assess its impact on attrition. A different use of modules was implemented successfully as part of a cultural adaptation with Latino families (D'Angelo et al., 2009). In this intervention, the adaptation converted sessions into modules to allow for more flexibility than that of a time-limited session. This approach emphasizes the content over the time to cover it, and D'Angelo et al. (2009) reported a 100% completion rate.

The treatment efficacy of the SEP intervention needs to be further evaluated. Research is needed to further assess whether the effects of the intervention are beneficial and satisfactory to Latinas who have experienced trauma and whether gains are maintained over time. SEP also needs to be evaluated with different subpopulations of Latinas who experienced trauma, for example, Latinas with varying levels of acculturation. Additionally, future research is needed to assess efficacy by comparing the adaptation to treatment as usual and identifying mediating variables.

More important, research methodologies such as community-based participatory research could address generalizability and external validity concerns. These include the participation of the target population in all stages of research and conducting research in the community instead of in a highly controlled research environment. Future research also needs to include community and contextual factors that occur during the evaluation of the adaptation since these can impact its effect (Castro et al., 2010). Similarly, studies with strong qualitative components can provide the depth of information required to capture the nuances of culture-specific clinical interventions. This depth of understanding of the intervention's impact is indispensable to providing clinicians with the necessary and specific tools to improve the lives of Latina women who have experienced trauma.

REFERENCES

Alegría, M., Canino, G., Shrout, P. E., Woo, M., Duan, N., Vila, D., . . . Meng, X.-L. (2008). Prevalence of mental illness in immigrant and non-immigrant U.S. Latino groups. *The American Journal of Psychiatry, 165,* 359–369. doi:10.1176/appi.ajp.2007.07040704

Alegría, M., Takeuchi, D., Canino, G., Duan, N., Shrout, P., Meng, X.-L., . . . Gong, F. (2004). Considering context, place and culture: The National Latino and Asian American Study. *International Journal of Methods in Psychiatric Research, 13,* 208–220. doi:10.1002/mpr.178

Alegría, M., Vila, D., Woo, M., Canino, G., Takeuchi, D., Vera, M., . . . Shrout, P. (2004). Cultural relevance and equivalence in the NLAAS instrument: Integrating epic and emic in the development of cross-cultural measures for a psychiatric epidemiology and services study of Latinos. *International Journal of Methods in Psychiatric Research, 13,* 270–288. doi:10.1002/mpr.181

Amaro, H., Larson, M. J., Gampel, J., Richardson, E., Savage, A., & Wagler, D. (2005). Racial/ethnic differences in social vulnerability among women with co-occurring mental health and substance abuse disorders: Implications for treatment services. *Journal of Community Psychology, 33,* 495–511. doi:10.1002/jcop.20065

American Psychological Association Task Force on Evidence-Based Practices. (2006). Evidence-based practices in psychology. *American Psychologist, 61,* 271–285. doi:10.1037/0003-066X.61.4.271

Añez, L. M., Paris, M., Jr., Bedregal, L. E., Davidson, L., & Grilo, C. M. (2005). Application of cultural constructs in the care of first generation Latino clients in a community mental health setting. *Journal of Psychiatric Practice, 11,* 221–230. doi:10.1097/00131746-200507000-00002

Backer, T. E. (2001). *Finding the balance—Program fidelity and adaptation in substance abuse prevention: A state-of-the-art review.* Rockville, MD: Center for Substance Abuse Prevention.

Barrera, M., Jr., & Castro, F. G. (2006). A heuristic framework for the cultural adaptation of interventions. *Clinical Psychology: Science and Practice, 13,* 311–316. doi:10.1111/j.1468-2850.2006.00043.x

Barrera, M., Jr., Castro, F. G., & Biglan, A. (1999). Ethnicity, substance use, and development: Exemplars for exploring group differences and similarities. *Development and Psychopathology, 11,* 805–822. doi:10.107/S0954579499002333

Beaton, D. E., Bombardier, C., Guillemin, F., & Ferraz, M. B. (2000). Guidelines for the process of cross-cultural adaptation of self-report. *Spine, 25,* 3186–3191. doi:10.1097/00007632-200012150-00014

Berdine, R. (2011). Evaluation of psycho-educational interventions in treating traumatized Latinas: Awareness, coping and behavior change (Unpublished doctoral dissertation). Pacific University, Forest Grove, OR.

Bernal, G., Bonilla, J., & Bellido, C. (1995). Ecological validity and cultural sensitivity for outcome research: Issues for the cultural adaptation and development of psychosocial treatment with Hispanics. *Journal of Abnormal Child Psychology, 23,* 67–82. doi:10.1007/BF01447045

Bernal, G., Jiménez-Chafey, M. I., & Domenech Rodríguez, M. M. (2009). Cultural adaptation of treatments: A resource for considering culture in evidence-based practice. *Professional Psychology: Research and Practice, 40,* 361–368. doi:10.1037/a0016401

Boston Women's Health Book Collective. (2000). *Nuestros cuerpos, nuestras vidas* [Our bodies, our lives]. New York, NY: Siete Cuentos Editorial.

Brislin, R. W. (1986). The wording and translation of research instruments. In W. L. Lonner & J. W. Berry (Eds.), *Field methods in cross-cultural research* (pp. 137–164). Newbury Park, CA: Sage.

Brislin, R. W., Lonner, W. E., & Thorndike, R. M. (1973). *Cross-cultural research methods.* New York, NY: Wiley.

Bronfenbrenner, U. (1977). Toward an experimental ecology of human development. *American Psychologist, 32,* 513–531. doi:10.1037/0003-066X.32.7.513

Bullinger, M., Alonso, J., Apolone, G., Leplège, A., Sullivan, M., Wood-Dauphinee, S., . . . Ware, J. E., Jr. (1998). Translating health status questionnaires and evaluating their quality: The IQOLA Project approach. *Journal of Clinical Epidemiology, 51*, 913–923. doi:10.1016/S0895-4356(98)00082-1

Castro, F. G., Barrera, M., Jr., & Holleran Steiker, L. K. (2010). Issues and challenges in the design of culturally adapted evidence-based interventions. *Annual Review of Clinical Psychology, 6*, 213–239. doi:10.1146/annurev-clinpsy-033109-132032

Castro, F. G., Barrera, M. Jr., & Martinez, C. R., Jr. (2004). The cultural adaptation of preventative interventions: Resolving tensions between fidelity and fit. *Prevention Science, 5*, 41–45. doi:10.1023/B:PREV.0000013980.12412.cd

Cuevas, C. A., Sabina, C., & Picard, E. H. (2010). Interpersonal victimization patterns in psychopathology among Latino women: Results from the SALAS study. *Psychological Trauma: Theory, Research, Practice, and Policy, 2*, 296–306. doi:10.1037/a0020099

D'Angelo, E. J., Llerena-Quinn, R., Shapiro, R., Colón, F., Rodriguez, P., Gallagher, K., & Beardslee, W. R. (2009). Adaptation of the Preventive Intervention Program for Depression for use with predominantly low-income Latino families. *Family Process, 48*, 269–291. doi:10.1111/j.1545-5300.2009.01281.x

Dent, C., Sussman, S., Ellickson, P., Brown, P., & Richardson, J. (1996). Is current drug abuse prevention programming generalizable across ethnic groups? *American Behavioral Scientist, 39*, 911–918. doi:10.1177/0002764296039007011

Espín, O. M. (1997). *Latina realities: Essays on healing, migration and sexuality.* Boulder, CO: Westview Press.

Fawcett, G. M., Heise, L. L., Isita-Espejel, L., & Pick, S. (1999). Changing community responses to wife abuse: A research and demonstration project in Iztacalco, Mexico. *American Psychologist, 54*, 41–49. doi:10.1037/0003-066X.54.1.41

Giard, J., Hennigan, K., Huntington, N., Vogel, W., Rinehart, D., Mazelis, R., . . . Veysey, B. (2005). Development and implementation of a multisite evaluation for the Women, Co-Occurring Disorders and Violence Study. *Journal of Community Psychology, 33*, 411–427. doi:10.1002/jcop.20060

Griner, D., & Smith, T. B. (2006). Culturally adapted mental health interventions: A meta-analytic review. *Psychotherapy: Theory, Research, Practice, Training, 43*, 531–548. doi:10.1037/0033-3204.43.4.531

Guarnaccia, P. J., Lewis-Fernández, R., & Rivera Marano, M. (2003). Toward a Puerto Rican popular nosology: *Nervios* and *ataques de nervios. Culture, Medicine and Psychiatry, 27*, 339–366. doi:10.1023/A:1025303315932

Guarnaccia, P. J., & Rogler, L. H. (1999). Research on culture-bound syndromes: New directions. *The American Journal of Psychiatry, 156*, 1322–1327.

Hansen, W. B. (1992). School-based substance abuse prevention: A review of the state of the art in curriculum, 1980-1990. *Health Education Research, 7*, 403–430. doi:10.1093/her/7.3.403

Harris, M. (1998). *Trauma recovery and empowerment model: A clinician's guide for working with women in groups.* New York, NY: Free Press.

Harris, M., Wallis, F., & Amaro, H. (2006). *Saber es poder: Modelo de trauma y recuperación para mujeres Latinas* [Knowledge is power: A model of trauma and recovery for Latina women]. Boston, MA: Boston Consortium of Services for Families in Recovery, Public Health Commission.

Herman, J. (1997). *Trauma and recovery.* New York, NY: Basic Books.

Hough, R. L., Canino, G. J., Abueg, F. R., & Gusman, F. D. (1996). PTSD and related stress disorders among Hispanics. In A. J. Marsella, M. J. Friedman, E. T. Gerrity, & R. M. Scurfield (Eds.), *Ethnocultural aspects of posttraumatic stress disorder: Issues, research and clinical applications* (pp. 301–338). Washington, DC: American Psychological Association. doi:10.1037/10555-012

Huey, S. J., Jr., & Polo, A. J. (2008). Evidence-based psychosocial treatments for ethnic minority youth. *Journal of Clinical Child and Adolescent Psychology, 37,* 262–301. doi:10.1080/15374410701820174

Kahlo, F. (1946). *The little deer* [Painting]. Houston, TX: Private collection.

Kumpfer, K. L., Alvarado, R., Smith, P., & Bellamy, N. (2002). Cultural sensitivity and adaptation in family-based prevention interventions. *Prevention Science, 3,* 241–246. doi:10.1023/A:1019902902119

Lau, A. S. (2006). Making the case for selective and directed cultural adaptations of evidence-based treatments: Examples from parent training. *Clinical Psychology: Science and Practice, 13,* 295–310. doi:10.1111/j.1468-2850.2006.00042.x

López, S. R., Grover, K. P., Holland, D., Johnson, M. J., Kain, C. D., Kanel, K., . . . Culkin, M. (1989). Development of culturally sensitive psychotherapists. *Professional Psychology: Research and Practice, 20,* 369–376. doi:10.1037/0735-7028.20.6.369

Matías Carrelo, L. E., Chávez, L. M., Negrón, G., Canino, G., Aguilar-Gaxiola, S., & Hoppe, S. (2003). The Spanish translation and cultural adaptation of five mental health outcome measures. *Culture, Medicine and Psychiatry, 27,* 291–313. doi:10.1023/A:1025399115023

McClure, H. H., Snodgrass, J. J., Martínez, C. R., Jr., Eddy, J. M., Jiménez, R. A., & Isiordia, L. E. (2010). Discrimination, psychosocial stress, and health among Latin American immigrants in Oregon. *American Journal of Human Biology, 22,* 421–423. doi:10.1002/ajhb.21002

McHugo, G. J., Caspi, Y., Kammerer, N., Mazelis, R., Jackson, E. W., Russell, L., . . . Kimerling, R. (2005). The assessment of trauma history in women with co-occurring substance abuse and mental disorders and a history of interpersonal violence. *The Journal of Behavioral Health Services & Research, 32,* 113–127. doi:10.1007/BF02287261

Moses, D., Reed, B., Mazelis, R., & D'Ambrosio, B. (2003). *Creating trauma services for women with co-occurring disorders: Experiences from the SAMHSA Women With Alcohol, Drug Abuse and Mental Disorders Who Have Histories of Violence Study.* Rockville, MD: Substance Abuse and Mental Health Administration, Centers for Substance Abuse Treatment, Mental Health and Substance Abuse Prevention.

Nader, K. (2007). Culture and the assessment of trauma in youth. In J. P. Wilson & C. S.-K. Tang (Eds.), *Cross-cultural assessment of psychological trauma and PTSD* (pp. 169–196). New York, NY: Springer US. doi:10.1007/978-0-387-70990-1_8

Pérez, D. J., Fortuna, L., & Alegría, M. (2008). Prevalence and correlates of everyday discrimination among U.S. Latinos. *Journal of Community Psychology, 36,* 421–433. doi:10.1002/jcop.20221

Renzetti, C. M., Edleson, J. L., & Kennedy Bergen, R. (Eds.). (2000). *Sourcebook on violence against women.* Thousand Oaks, CA: Sage.

Santiago, E. (1994). *Cuando era puertorriqueña* [When I was Puerto Rican]. New York, NY: Vintage Books.

Scurfield, R. M., & Mackey, D. W. (2001). Racism, trauma and positive aspects of exposure to race-related experiences: Assessment and treatment implications. *Journal of Ethnic & Cultural Diversity in Social Work, 10,* 23–47. doi:10.1300/J051v10n01_02

Smith, T. B., Domenech Rodríguez, M., & Bernal, G. (2011). Culture. *Journal of Clinical Psychology, 67,* 166–175. doi:10.1002/jclp.20757

Tobler, N. S. (1992). Drug prevention programs can work: Research findings. *Journal of Addictive Diseases, 11,* 1–28. doi:10.1300/J069v11n03_01

Wagner, A. K., Gandek, B., Aaronson, N. K., Acquadro, C., Alonso, J., Apolone, G., . . . Ware, J. E., Jr. (1998). Cross-cultural comparisons of the content of SF-36 translations across 10 countries: Results from the IQOLA Project. *Journal of Clinical Epidemiology, 51,* 925–932. doi:10.1016/S0895-4356(98)00083-3

World Health Organization. (1998). *Procedures for the development of new language versions of the WHO Composite International Diagnostic Interview (WHO-CIDI).* Geneva, Switzerland: Author.

9

INTEGRATING TOP-DOWN AND BOTTOM-UP APPROACHES TO CULTURALLY ADAPTING PSYCHOTHERAPY: APPLICATION TO CHINESE AMERICANS

WEI-CHIN HWANG

Research demonstrates that ethnic minorities are less likely to receive quality health services and to evidence worse treatment outcomes when compared with White Americans (Institute of Medicine, 1999; U.S. Department of Health and Human Services [USDHHS], 2001). Although considerable progress has been made in establishing and defining efficacious treatments for the general population, relatively little is known about the efficacy of evidence-based psychological practices (EBPPs) for people from diverse backgrounds (Bernal & Scharrón-del-Río, 2001; Hall, 2001).

As the demographics of the United States change, this critical lacuna in our knowledge, along with our underpreparedness to effectively treat ethnic minorities, will become more apparent. Asian Americans are proportionately the fastest growing immigrant group and number over 17 million (Humes, Jones, & Ramirez, 2011). Yet there continues to be a dearth of treatment research for this heterogeneous group. According to the Surgeon General's report titled *Mental Health: Culture, Race, and Ethnicity* (USDHHS, 2001),

This chapter was supported in part by National Institute of Mental Health (NIMH) Grant 1R34MH73545-01A2 and the Asian American Center on Disparities Research (NIMH Grant 1P50MH073511-01A2).

out of 9,266 participants involved in the efficacy studies forming the major treatment guidelines for bipolar disorder, schizophrenia, depression, and attention-deficit/hyperactivity disorder, only 11 were Asian Americans or Pacific Islanders. This lack of research is problematic because it can lead to uninformed assumptions that Western psychotherapies will be as effective for Asian Americans as for other groups, and it also offers little scientifically supported insight on how mental health services could be improved.

Despite many similarities across Asian Americans, more than 43 ethnic groups are encapsulated under this label, and they vary in experiences, beliefs, values, histories, migration patterns, religions, and languages (Lee, 1997). Even among Asian American groups encapsulated under the same ethnic label, there is great linguistic and cultural diversity. For example, among Chinese Americans, there is wide geographic diversity in immigration origins and histories, including sojourners from mainland China, Hong Kong, Taiwan, Singapore, Vietnam, and other places. Chinese Americans speak a variety of mutually incomprehensible languages, a small sampling of which includes Mandarin, Cantonese, Taiwanese, Toishanese, Hakka, Shanghainese, and Sichuanese. The diversity among Asian Americans is compounded by differences in acculturative status and immigration cohorts.

A recent review examining outcome research on evidence-based treatments (EBT) conducted with Asian Americans found very few treatment studies (Miranda et al., 2005). Among Asian American adults, only one study with a small sample ($N = 20$) using an 8-week cognitive behavior therapy (CBT) program for depressed Chinese Americans was found. This study had no control group or random assignment of patients (Dai et al., 1999). Regarding naturalistic studies, the extant literature indicates that Asian Americans are (a) less likely than other ethnic groups to seek treatment (Bui & Takeuchi, 1992; Hu, Snowden, Jerrell, & Nguyen, 1991; Snowden & Cheung, 1990; Sue, 1977; Sue, Fujino, Hu, Takeuchi, & Zane, 1991); (b) more likely to evidence more severe psychiatric impairment when they do seek services (Lin & Lin, 1978; Sue, 1977); and (c) less satisfied with treatment, evidence worse treatment outcomes, and drop out more prematurely than White Americans (Zane, Enomoto, & Chun, 1994). Although culturally adapted treatments have been found to be effective for other groups, there continue to be very few tested cultural adaptations of treatment for Asian Americans. There is some outcome research that suggests that treating clients in a more culturally sensitive manner (i.e., providing client–therapist ethnic matching and treatment at ethnic-specific services) can reduce premature treatment failure (Flaskerud & Liu, 1991; Sue et al., 1991; Takeuchi, Sue, & Yeh, 1995).

It is important to note that cultural competence and cultural adaptations of therapy are related but distinct concepts. Sue (1982) defined *cultural com-*

petence as the possession of cultural self-awareness, knowledge of other groups, and skills that facilitate the delivery of Western-based psychotherapy. Bernal, Jiménez-Chafey, and Domenech Rodríguez (2009) defined *cultural adaptation* as a systematic cultural modification of an EBT for use with a particular ethnocultural group.

Few models have been developed to help clinical researchers and practitioners systematically modify their treatment approaches when working with ethnic minority clientele. The purpose of this chapter is to discuss how a theoretically driven approach to adapting therapy can be used conjointly with a community-based formative approach. The top-down and bottom-up approaches that are integrated are the psychotherapy adaptation and modification framework (PAMF; Hwang, 2006b) and the formative method for adapting psychotherapy (FMAP; Hwang, 2009). These two approaches have been used to culturally adapt CBT for Chinese Americans.

In this chapter, a brief overview of each model is provided. Because recommendations for cultural adaptations that arose from these two models have been presented in previous publications (Hwang, 2006b, 2009), this chapter focuses more on illustrating the process of treatment development and providing readers with examples of discussions and questions that arise from integrating theory-driven and formative approaches. Further, it is impossible to fully address treatment issues associated with the incredible diversity encompassed under the label *Asian American* in one chapter. This chapter focuses on more recent Asian American immigrants and emphasizes values and similarities that are potentially generalizable across multiple Asian American groups.

THE PSYCHOTHERAPY ADAPTATION
AND MODIFICATION FRAMEWORK

The PAMF is a theoretically driven approach created by Hwang (2006b) to guide cultural adaptations to therapy. It was created to help support the EBPP movement and also serves as an important step in helping to develop EBTs. It is top-down in the sense that it is theory driven and utilizes information about the culture of interest to inform cultural adaptations. Existing research and clinical knowledge are used to drive adaptations. When working with different populations, practitioners make individual adjustments and modifications to work best with their clients (Hwang, 2006b; Hwang, Wood, Lin, & Cheung, 2006). The goal of a top-down and guided framework is to pool the collective knowledge of practitioners and researchers to target areas where adaptations may be most effective. In addition, the PAMF was developed to help practitioners thoroughly think through the reasons why they were making specific adaptations and to support these modifications with previous knowledge and cultural reasoning. It is important to note that many practitioners in the field have tremendous knowledge and experience in working with different cultural groups. Therapists are encouraged to use this collective knowledge in conjunction with their clinical style to individualize treatments for their clients. For beginning clinicians, the PAMF can support skills development in working with ethnically diverse clients.

The PAMF presents a three-tiered approach to making cultural adaptations. It consists of domains, principles, and rationales. *Domains* are general areas that practitioners should consider when modifying therapeutic approaches for their clients. *Principles* are more specific recommendations for adapting therapy for specific groups. *Rationales* are corresponding explanations for why these adaptations may be effective when used with the target population. This three-tiered approach was created for two purposes: (a) to serve as a guiding framework in which to make cultural adaptations to EBTs and the development of manualized treatments and (b) to help practitioners make the shift from the more abstract notion of being culturally competent to helping highlight and develop specific skills and strategies that can be effectively implemented when working with diverse clientele. Thus, the PAMF was created to help support the cultural competency movement as well as to help push the field ahead by improving the science of developing culturally adapted EBTs. Domains of the PAMF include (a) understanding dynamic issues and cultural complexities; (b) orienting clients to psychotherapy and increasing mental health awareness; (c) understanding cultural beliefs about mental illness, its causes, and what constitutes appropriate treatment; (d) improving the client–therapist relationship; (e) understanding cultural differences in the expression and communication of distress; and (f) addressing cultural issues specific to the population. Specific principles and rationales are detailed more fully in Hwang (2006b) and also discussed in relation to the bottom-up framework presented below.

THE FORMATIVE METHOD FOR ADAPTING PSYCHOTHERAPY

Community-based formative approaches are consumer oriented and often involve therapists, clients, and other community stakeholders and collaborators in the knowledge-generation process. Although theoretically driven approaches to cultural adaptation can provide a strong foundation for tailoring interventions, bottom-up or ground-up community-based approaches can also provide invaluable information by confirming theory-related adaptations, by generating ideas that more theory-driven approaches leave out, or by providing more specificity in the adaptations or examples offered. Another community-based approach is Domenech Rodríguez and Wieling's (2004) process model to cultural adaptations (see Chapter 2, this volume).

The FMAP framework is a community-based and bottom-up approach for culturally adapting psychotherapy (Hwang, 2009). The FMAP approach consists of five phases: (a) generating knowledge and collaborating with stakeholders, (b) integrating generated information with theory and empirical and clinical knowledge, (c) reviewing the initial culturally adapted clinical intervention with stakeholders and revising the culturally adapted intervention, (d) testing the culturally adapted intervention, and (e) finalizing the culturally adapted intervention. Unlike the PAMF, which was developed to help improve cultural competency of clinicians, support the EBPP movement, and contribute to the development of EBTs, the FMAP was developed specifically to aid in the design of culturally adapted EBTs. In doing so, it incorporates the top-down PAMF (Hwang, 2006b) to generate ideas for therapy adaptation, provide additional support for theoretically identified modifications, as well as to help flesh out and provide more specific and refined recommendations for increasing therapeutic responsiveness. The PAMF is explicitly integrated into Phases II and V of the FMAP to help generate knowledge and integrate extant knowledge with information generated from bottom-up processes. It can also be implicitly used in other phases (e.g., guiding and providing context for focus group discussions in Phases I and III). The information generated as part of the FMAP approach can also be used to strengthen the original knowledge base, thus creating a dynamic feedback loop and interplay between new and existing knowledge.

These frameworks have been used to guide cultural adaptations in a clinical trial funded by a National Institute of Mental Health R34 treatment development grant (I am the principal investigator). The clinical trial focused on creating a culturally adapted CBT manual for depressed Chinese Americans. The culturally adapted CBT manual is currently being tested against a non–culturally adapted CBT manual at two community mental health clinics. The PAMF and FMAP frameworks were used to guide adaptations and provided a heuristic to justify how adaptations would be made. The examples provided in the trial described below are not exhaustive and should be considered as one example of how the FMAP can be applied. In developing programs for specific populations, project leaders should make decisions about which consumers to involve to best meet project goals and needs. After describing the mechanics and implementation of the specific stages of the FMAP, I provide examples of various discussions and how they led to cultural adaptations and additional questions.

Phase I: Generating Knowledge and Collaborating With Stakeholders

According to the FMAP, there are six main categories of stakeholders: (a) mainstream health and mental health care agencies, (b) mainstream health and mental health care providers, (c) community-based organizations and agencies, (d) traditional and indigenous healers, (e) spiritual and religious organizations, and (f) clients (Hwang, 2009). In the current project, I invited (a) Asian-focused community mental health agencies (i.e., clinics that self-designate as specializing in serving predominantly Asian American populations), (b) mental health providers (psychiatrists, psychologists, social workers, marital family therapists), (c) traditional Chinese medicine (TCM) practitioners, and (d) Buddhist monks and nuns and both spiritual and religious Taoist masters. Specifically, I wanted to learn from agencies and practitioners who have expertise in treating Chinese American clients. Of course, eliciting client feedback is also important. An informed decision was made to do this later in the process for several reasons, including that many of the clients (a) had little to no exposure to mental health services, (b) were ill and could potentially lose confidence in treatment if project staff ask them for treatment advice, and (c) had minimal ability to differentiate types of treatments offered before receiving them. Client feedback was more extensively elicited in Phases IV and V.

To help ensure that the treatment program that was developed would be sustainable, mental health clinics that specialized in providing treatment to Asian clients were included because I wanted to make sure that the intervention developed could be feasibly implemented in the parameters of real-world settings (e.g., frequency of sessions, staffing and assignment of caseloads, hours of operation, billing and financial limitations). Seven Asian-focused clinics, two of which served as primary clinical trial sites and five as focus group collaborators, were incorporated. Several clinics were involved to ensure that clinic biases and a range of different clinic beliefs, assumptions, and notions of best practice would be included. Focus groups were not held at clinical trial sites to ensure that the treatment conditions for a subsequent clinical trial at these clinics would not be compromised.

Fourteen focus groups were conducted at community mental health clinics located in California, with multiple focus groups conducted at larger clinics. Agencies involved included Asian Americans for Community Involvement in San Jose, Asian Community Mental Health Services in Oakland, Asian Pacific Counseling and Treatment Center in Los Angeles, Asian Pacific Mental Health Services in Gardena, and Chinatown North Beach Service Center in San Francisco. Mental health care providers working in the agencies were asked to participate because they were experts in the field and had insights and expertise in working with depressed Asian American clients. Because I wanted to create an intervention that could be more easily modified for other Asian groups in the future, focus groups included staff who treated Chinese American and other Asian Americans. Each focus group consisted of four to six mental health practitioners with a range of clinical experiences, which helped facilitate both breadth and depth of discussions. Two sets of focus groups were conducted.

The first 4 hours involved general discussions of cultural adaptation, review of an EBT manual (Miranda et al., 2006), and discussion of other treatment approaches, books, and manuals that clinicians may have previously used. Another advantage of having practitioners participate in the development of the treatment is to facilitate buy-in to the treatment because they would be the ones to potentially use it once it was developed. The second set of focus groups was conducted in Phase III and is described further below.

In addition to focus groups, interviews were conducted with several Buddhist monks and nuns, spiritual and religious Taoist masters, and TCM practitioners. These traditions and practices have strongly influenced Chinese culture for thousands of years and have greatly influenced Chinese notions of self, health, and well-being. Interview data helped maximize understanding of existing healing practices and how they interface with Chinese cultural customs, traditions, and beliefs.

Focus group collaborations helped reduce personal, clinician, and agency-specific biases. Collaborating with traditional healers also helped ensure that cultural adaptations were grounded in client belief systems and helped generate ideas of how Western mental health treatment and traditional medicines can be integrated or mutually supportive. Because not all of the stakeholders possessed similar opinions of which therapeutic interventions or modifications would be most beneficial to the clients, the most recurrent themes were used. For this project, I made the final decision on what adaptations to include.

Phase II: Integrating Generated Information With Theory and Empirical and Clinical Knowledge

The second phase of the FMAP involved integrating information generated from bottom-up processes (e.g., community-based focus groups, interviews) with top-down theoretical, scientific, and clinical knowledge (e.g., the PAMF, my own clinical experience) to inform adaptations. Specifically, I reviewed the extant empirical and clinical literature on treating Chinese Americans, reflected upon discussions and issues that arose during focus groups and interviews, and integrated my own clinical experiences to write a new culturally adapted treatment manual.

Phase III: Review of Culturally Adapted Clinical Intervention by Stakeholders and Further Revision

The third phase of the FMAP involved consumer-based discussions and focus groups on the culturally adapted treatment before it was implemented. After the treatment manual was written, focus groups were conducted with the same groups of therapists at each agency. Initial impressions of the new intervention (English and Chinese versions) and feedback for improvement were elicited (Hwang, 2008b, 2008c). Overall, therapists were excited to see the newly developed intervention and believed that it would make significant contributions to improving the treatment of Chinese Americans. They believed that the manual would be effective in treating depressed Chinese Americans and that the patients would be responsive to this culturally adapted treatment. This phase was largely confirmatory, and the discussion primarily focused on wording changes to help ensure that ideas, words, and concepts would translate properly into different Chinese languages.

The intervention was then translated and back-translated by a team of four master's level therapists, one postdoctoral fellow, and myself. To help strengthen language equivalence, the manual was written with translations in Chinese in mind. In addition, during the translation process, the English version was also modified to increase language equivalence. Feedback from 15 undergraduate students, three master's level therapists, one postdoctoral fellow, and four graduate students was elicited. Because written Chinese may have differences based on regional and linguistic variability of expression, translated materials were reviewed by lay community participants from different Chinese regions (e.g., mainland China, Taiwan, and Hong Kong) to ensure comprehensibility of materials.

Phase IV: Testing the Culturally Adapted Intervention

The fourth phase of the FMAP involved testing the culturally adapted intervention and using the feedback from therapists and clients who participated in the clinical trial to further inform revisions. The intervention developed is a 12-session depression treatment program intended to be implemented across 12 weeks (Hwang, 2008b, 2008c). A variety of clinical and cultural outcome measures from clients, therapists, and independent assessors were used to test the efficacy of the interventions, including symptom reduction; treatment satisfaction; premature dropout; working alliance formation; and adherence, receipt, and enactment of treatment. Clinical trial sites included Richmond Area Multi-Services in San Francisco and Asian Pacific Family Center in Los Angeles. Assessments were conducted at baseline and at Sessions 4, 8, and 12 of treatment, as well as 3 months posttreatment. Therapy sessions were recorded to check for treatment fidelity. I provided weekly group supervision to all therapists participating in the program. Although having one supervisor for both conditions could potentially lead to allegiance biases, the use of different supervisors could also lead to a supervisor effect. On the basis of the FMAP model, having one supervisor was the best option because supervision information gathered could be used to further refine the treatment after the trial was completed.

Phase V: Synthesizing Stakeholder Feedback and Finalizing the Culturally Adapted Intervention

The fifth phase of the FMAP involves conducting interviews with consumers (clients and therapists) about their experiences participating in the treatment program. This phase has not yet been completed. Clients will be asked to discuss whether the program helped them feel less depressed and more effective in dealing with their life problems. Therapists will be asked whether they felt the program helped their clients feel less depressed and deal with their life problems. Moreover, both groups will be asked to provide feedback on which aspects of the program were most beneficial and will also be asked for recommendations for improving the program. The knowledge acquired through the different phases will be used to further refine and finalize the culturally adapted treatment. Adaptations retained and generated will be highlighted and integrated into the three-tiered PAMF. Rationales and source for adaptations will be made explicit (e.g., whether the modifications are supported by theory, research, prior clinical knowledge, or information generated from the FMAP clinical trial). The information generated as part of the bottom-up FMAP approach will then be used to strengthen the PAMF and help contribute to the extant knowledge base.

EXAMPLES OF CULTURAL ADAPTATIONS GENERATED BY THE PAMF AND FMAP

It is important to underscore the iterative process of revision and re-revision when developing culturally adapted therapies. Currently, the culturally adapting CBT for Chinese Americans project is in Phase IV, but the adaptations that were developed were the result of a continual back and forth exchange between theory and community knowledge. Phases I through III generated useful information that supported the development of the first version of the culturally adapted treatment manual. Specific examples of the issues that arose throughout the first four phases are provided below. To provide the discussion with more structure, illustrations are framed in reference to the different domains of the PAMF model and the different phases of the FMAP. Special attention is given to illustrating how an iterative approach to therapy adaptation can lead to concrete results and specific recommendations.

Cultural Complexities and Dynamic Sizing

The first domain of the PAMF framework involves what Hays (2001) called *cultural complexities*, or the recognition that clients have multiple identities that may be even more salient than their ethnic identities, and what Sue (1998) called *dynamic sizing*, or knowing when to generalize cultural and potentially stereotypical knowledge and when to individualize the treatment for the client. In Phase I of the FMAP, focus groups discussed the different types of problems that depressed Asian Americans and Chinese Americans encounter. Various themes emerged, such as immigration stressors, citizenship problems, marital conflict, late life issues, housing issues, and family conflict. These issues are consistent with patient reports in Phase IV (clinical trial). The focus groups also provided evidence that a treatment for Chinese Americans needed to address the breadth of problems that this group encounters, including cultural issues such as migration-related stresses, as well as universal issues such as relationship problems. The focus groups also provided evidence that Chinese Americans are a diverse group. Practitioners need to individualize treatments for their patients and not stereotype. For example, rather than saying, "Family is really important to Chinese people," say, "You seem to really care a lot about your family." This helps clients feel validated rather than stereotyped. In addition, rather than making stereotypical assumptions such as "Thought records don't work with Asian Americans," it may be better to be even more specific if one is to stereotype at all—for example, "Thought records work better with more educated and more acculturated Asian Americans."

Nevertheless, as noted by some therapists in Phase I focus groups, making general statements about Chinese Americans can be helpful in increasing feelings of camaraderie and understanding. On the basis of this information, I decided to add the words *Chinese Americans* in some parts of the manual but not in others. Specifically, generalized statements were added into sections that might help improve the feeling that the program was developed for Chinese Americans, areas that might help normalize beliefs and experiences (e.g., stigma, stereotypes about mental health treatment), and sections that might draw on specific cultural strengths and healing practices (e.g., cultural symbols, philosophies, teachings). Therapists in Phase III focus groups reaffirmed that such statements would be helpful when used appropriately, and clients reacted positively to them during the clinical trial in Phase IV. It is important to note that all of the therapists providing treatment in the clinical trial were Chinese Americans. Because of cultural complexities associated with cross-race patient–therapist dyads, non-Chinese American therapists may need to be more cautious about making these types of statements because there is a greater chance of clients feeling stereotyped, especially in the absence of a strong working relationship.

Another interesting discussion centered on the use of cultural symbols that can have both philosophical and religious meaning. For example, the Tai Qi diagram (often referred to as the yin and yang diagram) has a religious association with Taoism but also has cultural meaning because it has been an integral part of Chinese culture and TCM for thousands of years. As part of Phase I, I learned more about TCM, religious and philosophical schools of Taoism, and Buddhism. The Tai Qi diagram teaches people that they need to have balance in life and energy or Qi (dark and light sides of the picture), about the principle of impermanence (as represented by the curvy line in the middle, which symbolizes the ups and downs of life), and about polarities (e.g., no matter how bad things are, something good is likely to happen and vice versa—as represented by the small dark and light dots in the light and dark regions of the diagram). In Phase II, I decided to integrate this diagram into the manualized treatment and also incorporate healthy activities that may strengthen one's Qi (which is also a basic part of TCM and Chinese culture).

During Phase III therapist focus groups, an interesting discussion began on whether Chinese Americans who were Christian would be offended by the Tai Qi diagram and its religious connotations, or whether they would be able to focus on the philosophical and cultural meaning of the symbol. After discussing the issue, the groups decided that Christian Chinese Americans would be able to understand and relate to its meanings, just as many non-Asians can relate to other Asian healing and healthy activities (e.g., yoga, martial arts, Tai Qi). However, it was recommended that therapists who implement the manual should be flexible in applying the symbolic meaning of these teachings to other symbols that Christian Chinese Americans may relate to, such as a cross. This is also an example of how a cultural adaptation made for one Asian American group (i.e., Chinese Americans) may not be able to be stereotypically applied or may not be as meaningful to other Asian American groups (i.e., Filipino Americans, who tend to be more Christian than Taoist). In Phase IV (the clinical trial), the majority of Chinese Americans treated in the study responded positively to the Tai Qi diagram. Although this issue is included under the PAMF domain of cultural complexities and dynamic sizing, it is also applicable to the cultural beliefs domain.

During Phase I interviews with TCM doctors, it was reiterated that in TCM, depression is related to having too much Yin Qi (the dark side of the Tai Qi diagram—also known as the more feminine or moon energy) and not enough Yang Qi (the light side of the diagram—also known as the more masculine or sun energy). During Phase II, I developed a "Sitting in the Sun" exercise that asks clients to practice sitting in the sun for a few minutes during the week and to image the sunlight warming their mind, body, and spirit. Whether a client believes in Qi or not, this exercise can be helpful because it also serves as a form of behavioral activation. Therapists in Phase III felt that this exercise would help their clients. In Phase IV, clients responded very well to the Sitting in the Sun exercise. It is interesting, however, that the exercise was modified for some Chinese American women who feared getting a tan because in more traditional or conservative Chinese culture being lighter is associated with greater beauty and higher social status. For these clients, the exercise was modified so they could sit in the shade or next to running water. Sitting next to running water can be especially helpful for women experiencing "angry depression," which in TCM is tied to family conflict and anger toward spouse and children.

Orientation to Therapy

Given the Western origins of psychotherapy, Chinese Americans may be less familiar with mental health treatment and Western conceptualizations of mental illness (Hwang, 2006b). The topic of therapy orientations was introduced in Phase I focus groups, specifically the questions of how much therapy orientation is needed and whether therapy orientations and education about mental illness interfere would with the treatment approach of different theoretical orientations. In Phase I, the cognitive–behavioral, solution-focused, and psychodynamic/psychoanalytic therapists generally believed that therapy orientations would be helpful. During Phase II, I developed a comprehensive therapy orientation program that focused on discussing why and how the program was developed, structural orientation to therapy (e.g., meeting length and time), facts and fallacies about therapy, roles and responsibilities of therapists and client, probable course of therapy, preventing premature dropout, setting goals for therapy, and addressing emergency issues. During the focus groups in Phase III, therapists reaffirmed that a comprehensive therapy orientation would be beneficial, and patients responded positively to it in Phase IV.

When I introduced a discussion about diagnosis and discussing diagnoses with patients during Phase I, mixed reactions arose. Some therapists felt it would be beneficial to talk about diagnosis and that patients have a right to know their diagnosis. Other therapists felt that knowing one's diagnosis was less important and that some Chinese American patients would not be able to tolerate being labeled with a diagnosis. An emphasis on addressing and reducing symptoms was favored by this group. In Phase II, I decided to incorporate psychoeducation regarding depression but also to place an emphasis on addressing symptoms. Rather than listing in order the nine symptoms of major depression according to the *Diagnostic and Statistical Manual of Mental Disorders* (American Psychiatric Association, 1994), physical and mental symptoms were separated. In addition, a checkbox was placed next to each symptom, and therapists were trained to introduce the items in the checklist as problems that people sometimes struggle with and to ask the client if he or she experienced similar problems. Afterward, the client was told that when people experienced a significant number of these symptoms, it is called major depression. Clients were then asked if they thought they had major depression. During Phase III, focus group therapists reaffirmed that this stigma reduction and self-realization approach to diagnosis would be effective. They also noted that the separation of mental and physical symptoms would be helpful. They were also pleased to find that their recommendations to include additional somatic symptoms and social functioning checklists were incorporated.

During Phase IV, patients responded warmly to therapy and depression orientation. None reacted adversely to talking about their diagnosis, which is contrary to the stereotype that Chinese Americans would not be able to tolerate having a mental illness diagnosis. They were able to identify and accept their diagnosis. The majority of therapists reported that depression was a more acceptable diagnosis than more severe psychopathologies such as schizophrenia (see Hwang, 2008a, for a more detailed review of diagnostic issues with Chinese Americans).

Cultural Beliefs

For adaptations to therapy to be effective, the adaptations must make clinical sense and also align with the cultural belief system of the client. Cultural bridging can help relate therapy concepts to client belief systems (Ham, 1989; Hong, 1993; Hwang et al., 2006). For example, clients can be told that cultivating healthy cognitions and increasing healthy behaviors can help improve one's balance in the Chinese notion of energy or Qi (Hwang, 2006b). This bridging technique helps align the goals and techniques of CBT with Chinese notions of health and medicine, which can also help facilitate adherence to treatment and align client and therapy goals. Focus group discussions during Phase I confirmed that cultural bridging is important, and the techniques derived from my research in Phase II were thought to be effective by therapists in Phase III. In Phase IV, patients responded well to bridging therapy concepts to Chinese cultural notions of health and energy.

Another method of adapting therapy to client belief systems is to integrate cultural metaphors (Bernal, Bonilla, & Bellido, 1995; Costantino, Malgady, &

Rogler, 1986). Hwang et al. (2006) discussed using Chinese sayings known as *chengyu* to help clients reframe their thinking and engage in healthier activities. *Chengyu* are metaphorical sayings that can help teach ethics, highlight morals, provide inspiration, and influence behaviors. Because the PAMF model highlights the use of *chengyu*, therapists in Phase I were asked if they used them with clients and whether they could help generate a list of *chengyu* that might be helpful in therapy. Some therapists used *chengyu* when treating their clients, but the majority did not. Those who did not already use them in their clinical practice agreed that doing so could be effective. In Phase III, therapists liked the *chengyu* that served as the theme of the manual created in Phase II. The *chengyu* was 山不轉路轉;路不轉人轉;人不轉心轉, literally meaning "If a mountain is blocking your path, find a road around it. If the road doesn't take you where you want to go, make your own way. If the approach you take doesn't help you reach your goal, then change your mind-set and do something different." I felt that this saying represented the essence of psychotherapy and CBT. The *chengyu* that was chosen from the end of the manual was 山窮水盡疑無路,柳暗花明又一村, which talks about coming to an edge of a cliff and river and not seeing any path to follow, but following the shade of willow tree blossoms to find another village. This *chengyu* conveys the meaning that no matter how bad things are, things are sure to get better, which is similar to an old African saying, "No matter how long the night, the day is sure to come."

Another cultural adaptation was to make a play on words. The title of the culturally adapted treatment manual is *Improving Your Mood: A Culturally Responsive and Holistic Approach to Treating Depression in Chinese Americans*. One of the graduate students on the project recommended putting the fifth character of the Chinese title of the manual in brackets, brackets, 提升您心[晴]指數: 反映文化與綜觀整合的華裔美國人憂鬱治療. By putting brackets around the fifth character, the fourth and fifth characters, whose original meaning was "mood," develop an alternative additional meaning (i.e., brightening one's day or clearing up the darkness). Clients responded positively to these adaptations.

Client–Therapist Relationship

There are many ways to improve the client–therapist relationship (Norcross, 2011). Changing the vocabulary that one uses to deliver the language of therapy is one method to improve the therapeutic alliance and can lead to differential experiences in therapy. For example, during Phase I focus groups, one therapist recommended making a comparison between physical therapy and psychotherapy as a way to improve the working alliance, help reduce stigma, and help clients understand therapeutic tasks and homework assignments. The discussion proceeded, and it was concluded that using the words *exercise* and *practice* rather than *homework* would be more appropriate and help support this comparison. Another therapist half-jokingly stated that Chinese people have such high academic pressure and do too much homework while growing up so that they may have an aversive reaction to hearing the word as an adult. Clients responded well to this type of vocabulary change during Phase IV.

Another method of strengthening the working alliance is to help clients better understand therapeutic tasks and goals. For example, an exercise called "Chaining," which was in the non–culturally adapted CBT treatment manual (Miranda et al., 2006), was modified. Chaining involves listing the problem or situation that the client is experiencing on the middle of a piece of paper. The client is then asked to list four thoughts, behaviors, or communication statements above and below the stated problem that might improve or worsen their mood. The focus on emotional goals in Western therapeutic homework assignments is also evident in other manuals (e.g., "thought records" in *Mind Over Mood;* Greenberger & Padesky, 1995). Because of the goal-oriented nature of Chinese culture as well as the emphasis on cause and effect (*Yin* = Cause; *Guo* = Effect—part of the Tai Qi diagram; Hwang et al., 2006), I changed the homework assignment and called it the "Climbing the Mountain" exercise, and put a space for goal at the top of the chaining assignment and also put a space for consequence at the bottom. This highlights how thoughts, behaviors, and communication statements can help clients achieve not only emotional goals but also concrete goals and consequences. In addition, the vertical structure of the worksheet was changed to an ascending and descending stairway, which goes along with the exercise and practice theme. Mountains were drawn around the stairway because of the emphasis on mountains in Chinese culture and because there are five Great Mountains in Taoism and four Sacred Mountains in Buddhism. Climbing mountains is believed to be good for a person's mind, body, and spirit, and this integration aligns with Chinese cultural strengths. Therapists in Phase III focus groups believed the Climbing the Mountain exercise would help clients. Many clients have enjoyed the exercise during Phase IV clinical trial thus far.

Cultural Differences in Expression and Communication

When working with clients from a different cultural background, therapists need to have a good understanding of communication styles and nuances. As mentioned in the Orientation to Therapy section, an effort was made to include a discussion of both somatic and psychological expression of distress. Another adaptation topic that was purposefully introduced in Phase I focus groups was whether standard communication trainings that focus on being direct and assertive would be appropriate or sufficient for Chinese Americans. Specifically, Chinese culture places a greater emphasis on nonverbal and indirect communication (Sue, 1990). Examples for communication effectiveness had to be modified to include implications, physical gestures, and even communicating through extended family members, all methods that are sometimes used in Chinese culture. In addition, two types of communication styles, more Western direct approaches (e.g., saying that you love someone and care about them) as well as examples of indirect Chinese approaches (e.g., showing somebody that you care about them by making a nice meal or bringing them a cup of tea), are discussed in the manual.

Another issue that was discussed was whether 12 sessions would be enough in treating depressed Chinese Americans. Some therapists believed that Chinese American clients felt less comfortable in expressing their feelings and talking in therapy. They thought that clients needed more time to acclimate to the culture of psychotherapy and receive its benefits. Because the study focused on running a clinical trial comparing culturally adapted and non-culturally adapted CBT, the treatment length was kept at 12 sessions to make the treatments comparable. However, I made an effort to reduce the amount of material covered in each session and to reduce the amount of materials covered under key points. For example, instead of educating clients about a dozen different types of maladaptive cognitions, half as many were covered to make learning of materials less overwhelming.

Cultural Issues of Salience

Integrating issues pertinent to the cultural background of the client can improve outcomes (Hwang, 2006b). For example, addressing the unique roles, needs, and situations of immigrants as a culture in transition is important in treating Chinese Americans. The immigrant history of the client is important contextual information for therapists to better address client needs. Highlighting acculturative stressors, such as linguistic limitations that inhibit the chances of getting jobs, citizenship worries, and separation from friends and family, can improve the treatment process. A session was created to address how acculturation-related processes can affect family relations and mental health in Chinese Americans. Specifically, Acculturative Family Distancing (AFD) was covered in one session of the manual (Hwang, 2006a; Hwang & Wood, 2009).

AFD is defined as the distancing that occurs between parents and youth as a result of communication difficulties and cultural value incongruence that are a consequence of different rates of acculturation among parents and children. These communication and value differences may serve to increase family conflict and lead to increased risk for depression and other psychological problems. The session that was developed in Phase II was reviewed by therapists in Phase III. Therapists reported that directly discussing AFD would be important, and Phase IV clients who experienced intergenerational family conflict with their children stated that addressing AFD was important.

CONCLUSION

In this chapter, an integrated top-down and bottom-up approach to adapting psychotherapy was introduced. Given that the majority of the world is not accustomed to Western-based psychotherapy, developing culturally effective therapeutic interventions is an important and necessary goal. An "as-is" approach to psychotherapy may be insufficient for treating clients from different cultural backgrounds because of differences in belief systems, customs, and experiences. Establishing scientific support for the use of evidence-based adapted interventions with ethnocultural populations, as well as empirical support for culturally adapted EBTs, will be important in improving the mental health care of ethnocultural minorities and will help advance our understanding of intervention science.

REFERENCES

American Psychiatric Association. (1994). *Diagnostic and statistical manual of mental disorders* (4th ed.). Washington, DC: Author.

Bernal, G., Bonilla, J., & Bellido, C. (1995). Ecological validity and cultural sensitivity for outcome research: Issues for the cultural adaptation and development of psychosocial treatments with Hispanics. *Journal of Abnormal Child Psychology, 23*, 67–82. doi:10.1007/BF01447045

Bernal, G., Jiménez-Chafey, M. I., & Domenech Rodríguez, M. M. (2009). Cultural adaptation of treatments: A resource for considering evidence-based practice. *Professional Psychology: Research and Practice, 40*, 361–368. doi:10.1037/a0016401

Bernal, G., & Scharrón del Río, M. (2001). Are empirically supported treatments valid for ethnic minorities? Toward an alternative approach for treatment research. *Cultural Diversity and Ethnic Minority Psychology, 7*, 328–342. doi:10.1037/1099-9809.7.4.328

Bui, K. V., & Takeuchi, D. T. (1992). Ethnic minority adolescents and the use of community mental health care services. *American Journal of Community Psychology, 20*, 403–417. doi:10.1007/BF00937752

Costantino, G., Malgady, R. G., & Rogler, L. H. (1986). Cuento therapy: A culturally sensitive modality for Puerto Rican children. *Journal of Consulting and Clinical Psychology, 54*, 639–645. doi:10.1037/0022-006X.54.5.639

Dai, Y., Zhang, S., Yamamoto, J., Ao, M., Belin, T. R., Cheung, F., & Hifumi, S. S. (1999). Cognitive behavioral therapy of minor depressive symptoms in elderly Chinese Americans: A pilot study. *Community Mental Health Journal, 35*, 537–542. doi:10.1023/A:1018763302198

Domenech Rodríguez, M., & Wieling, E. (2004). Developing culturally appropriate, evidence-based treatments for interventions with ethnic minority populations. In M. Rastogi & E. Wieling (Eds.), *Voices of color: First person accounts of ethnic minority therapists* (pp. 313–333). Thousand Oaks, CA: Sage.

Flaskerud, J. H., & Liu, P. Y. (1991). Effects of an Asian client-therapist language, ethnicity, and gender match on utilization and outcome of therapy. *Community Mental Health Journal, 27*, 31–42. doi:10.1007/BF00752713

Greenberger, D., & Padesky, C. (1995). *Mind over mood: Change how you feel by changing the way you think.* New York, NY: Guilford Press.

Hall, G.C.N. (2001). Psychotherapy research with ethnic minorities: Empirical, ethical, and conceptual issues. *Journal of Consulting and Clinical Psychology, 69*, 502–510. doi:10.1037/0022-006X.69.3.502

Ham, M. D. (Ed.). (1989). Immigrant families and family therapy [Special issue]. *Journal of Strategic & Systemic Therapies, 8(2)*.

Hays, P. (2001). *Addressing cultural complexities in practice: A framework for clinicians and counselors.* Washington, DC: American Psychological Association. doi:10.1037/10411-000

Hong, G. K. (1993). Synthesizing Eastern and Western psychotherapeutic approaches: Contextual factors in psychotherapy with Asian Americans. In J. L. Chin, J. H. Liem, M. A. D.-C. Ham, & G. K. Hong (Eds.), *Transference and empathy in Asian American psychotherapy: Cultural values and treatment needs* (pp. 77–90). Westport, CT: Praeger.

Hu, T. W., Snowden, L. R., Jerrell, J. M., & Nguyen, T. D. (1991). Ethnic populations in public mental health: Services choice and level of use. *American Journal of Public Health, 81*, 1429–1434. doi:10.2105/AJPH.81.11.1429

Humes, K. R., Jones, N. A., & Ramirez, R. R. (2011). *Overview of race and Hispanic origin: 2010* (Report No. C2010BR-02, pp. 1–23). Washington, DC: U.S. Bureau of the Census.

Hwang, W. (2006a). Acculturative family distancing: Theory, research, and clinical practice. *Psychotherapy: Theory, Research, Practice, Training, 43*, 397–409. doi:10.1037/0033-3204.43.4.397

Hwang, W. (2006b). The Psychotherapy Adaptation and Modification Framework (PAMF): Application to Asian Americans. *American Psychologist, 61*, 702–715. doi:10.1037/0003-066X.61.7.702

Hwang, W. (2008a). Diagnostic nondisclosure of schizophrenia to Chinese American patients: Are we being culturally sensitive or feeding into cultural misconceptions? *Asian Journal of Counselling, 15*, 1–31.

Hwang, W. (2008b). *Improving your mood: A culturally responsive and holistic approach to treating depression in Chinese Americans* (Client manual—Chinese and English versions). Unpublished copyrighted treatment manual.

Hwang, W. (2008c). *Improving your mood: A culturally responsive and holistic approach to treating depression in Chinese Americans* (Therapist manual—Chinese and English versions). Unpublished copyrighted training manual.

Hwang, W. (2009). The Formative Method for Adapting Psychotherapy (FMAP): A community-based developmental approach to culturally adapting therapy. *Professional Psychology: Research and Practice, 40,* 369–377. doi:10.1037/a0016240

Hwang, W., & Wood, J. J. (2009). Acculturative family distancing (AFD) in immigrant families: A structural model of linkages with mental health outcomes among young adults. *Child Psychiatry and Human Development, 40,* 123–138. doi:10.1007/s10578-008-0115-8

Hwang, W., Wood, J., Lin, K., & Cheung, F. (2006). Cognitive-behavioral therapy with Chinese Americans: Research, theory, and clinical practice. *Cognitive and Behavioral Practice, 13,* 293–303. doi:10.1016/j.cbpra.2006.04.010

Institute of Medicine. (1999). *Unequal treatment: Confronting racial and ethnic disparities in health care.* Washington, DC: National Academies Press.

Lee, E. (Ed.). (1997). *Working with Asian Americans: A guide for clinicians.* New York, NY: Guilford Press.

Lin, T. Y., & Lin, M. C. (1978). Service delivery issues in Asian-North American communities. *The American Journal of Psychiatry, 135,* 454–456.

Miranda, J., Bernal, G., Lau, A., Kohn, L., Hwang, W., & LaFramboise, T. (2005). State of the science on psychosocial interventions for ethnic minorities. *Annual Review of Clinical Psychology, 1,* 113–142. doi:10.1146/annurev.clinpsy.1.102803.143822

Miranda, J., Woo, S., Lagomasino, I., Hepner, K. A., Wiseman, S., & Muñoz, R. (2006). *Group cognitive behavioral therapy for depression: Thoughts, activities, people and your mood.* Unpublished manuscript, San Francisco General Hospital.

Norcross, J. (2011). *Psychotherapy relationships that work: Evidence-based responsiveness.* New York, NY: Wiley/Blackwell. doi:10.1093/acprof:oso/9780199737208.001.0001

Snowden, L. R., & Cheung, F. K. (1990). Use of inpatient mental health services by members of ethnic minority groups. *American Psychologist, 45,* 347–355. doi:10.1037/0003-066X.45.3.347

Sue, D. W. (1982). Position paper: Cross-cultural counseling competencies. *The Counseling Psychologist, 10,* 45–52. doi:10.1177/0011000082102008

Sue, D. W. (1990). Culture-specific strategies in counseling: A conceptual framework. *Professional Psychology: Research and Practice, 21,* 424–433. doi:10.1037/0735-7028.21.6.424

Sue, S. (1977). Community mental health services to minority groups: Some optimism, some pessimism. *American Psychologist, 32,* 616–624. doi:10.1037/0003-066X.32.8.616

Sue, S. (1998). In search of cultural competence in psychotherapy and counseling. *American Psychologist, 53,* 440–448. doi:10.1037/0003-066X.53.4.440

Sue, S., Fujino, D., Hu, L. T., Takeuchi, D. T., & Zane, N. W. (1991). Community mental health services for ethnic minority groups: A test of the cultural responsiveness hypothesis. *Journal of Consulting and Clinical Psychology, 59,* 533–540. doi:10.1037/0022-006X.59.4.533

Takeuchi, D. T., Sue, S., & Yeh, M. (1995). Return rates and outcomes from ethnicity-specific mental health programs in Los Angeles. *American Journal of Public Health, 85,* 638–643. doi:10.2105/AJPH.85.5.638

U.S. Department of Health and Human Services. (2001). Mental health: Culture, race, and ethnicity (Suppl. to *Mental health: A report of the Surgeon General*). Rockville, MD: U.S. Department of Health and Human Services, Public Health Service, Office of the Surgeon General.

Zane, N., Enomoto, K., & Chun, C. (1994). Treatment outcomes of Asian- and White-American clients in outpatient therapy. *Journal of Community Psychology, 22,* 177–191.

III

NEW FRONTIERS

10

CULTURAL ADAPTATION FOR AMERICAN INDIAN CLIENTS

JACQUELINE S. GRAY

Most indigenous approaches to psychotherapy begin with the *relationship*, knowing a person, developing trust, and respect for the individual, which fits very well with Western interpersonal approaches. Indigenous approaches are centered in indigenous values, which include the person and the community (e.g., family, clan, band, tribe). Unfortunately, there exists no Western research to determine the efficacy of this method with indigenous populations. This chapter addresses the lack of culturally adapted, evidence-based approaches to therapy with American Indian adults and children, some of the reasons for and issues in developing evidence-based approaches with this population, and recommendations of cultural practices to consider in making cultural adaptations that have been collected from mental health providers throughout Indian Country.[1] The cultural practices and their potential to inform cultural adaptations are discussed as they apply to American Indian values and practices to make treatment more appropriate for this population. Promising ways to adapt treatment for American Indian clients are presented, primarily addressing trauma and loss, which are prevalent in all areas

---

[1] *Indian Country* is defined in federal law to mean reservations, allotments, and dependent Indian communities. Thirty-five U.S. states have areas that meet this definition.

of Indian Country. Specific techniques are presented that integrate American Indian culture into a positive therapeutic approach, for example, the use of balloon sculpture to utilize the American Indian value of giving gifts that are made for an individual to gain rapport and engage children in therapy. This chapter also includes some approaches to grief work with traditional American Indian adults.

Before addressing evidence-based practices (EBPs) with American Indians, it is important to understand a few basic issues, including the diversity among American Indians and their special status with the U.S. government. The small population numbers (1.7% of the U.S. population), the many tribes and villages across the nation, the sovereignty of tribes, and the comorbidity of diagnoses for those in treatment all make research on treatment with American Indians very difficult.

SOCIAL, HISTORICAL, AND CULTURAL CONTEXT

The 2010 U.S. Census indicated there were approximately 5.2 million American Indian/Alaska Native people in the United States (Humes, Jones, & Ramirez, 2011). There may be as many as 20 million people in the United States with "Indian blood"; however, there is no single definition of who is Indian. For example, the U.S. Census defines an American Indian by self-identification, but tribal groups have their own criteria, from descendancy (i.e., proving one is a descendent of a person on the tribal roll) to establishing the "degree of blood" of the tribe in which they are enrolling for membership (Utter, 2001). American Indians who are eligible for services provided by the tribe or the government receive a card indicating their Certificate of Degree of Indian Blood, tribal membership, and eligibility for services (Utter, 2001). Although the general perception is that American Indians live on reservations primarily in the Western part of the United States, approximately 61% of American Indians live in urban areas (Urban Indian Health Institute, 2007). Urban Indians vary a great deal from reservation Indians in their cultural identity, bicultural competence, and assimilation (Aragon, 2006).

There are currently 564 federally recognized American Indian tribes and Alaska Native villages in the United States (Bureau of Indian Affairs, 2009). This number can fluctuate because of the ability of the Bureau of Indian Affairs to recognize or not recognize tribes, much as the president and Congress can choose to recognize or not recognize other governments (Utter, 2001). This number does not include state-recognized tribes or tribes that are not recognized by a state or federal government. These are legal relationships based on treaties establishing tribes as having *domestic sovereign nation* status and certain inherent rights, powers, and entitlements to certain benefits and services on the basis of the tribal relationship with the federal government (Utter, 2001).

The cultures of these tribes vary greatly, but there are no truly traditional Native cultures left in the United States (Utter, 2001). O'Brien (1989) described 10 broad cultural regions across the North American continent based on geographical influence, family and kinship systems, seasonal life, economic structure, and other factors prior to colonization by Europeans. O'Brien's 10 regions are Northeast, Southeast, Great Plains, Plateau, Great Basin, Southwest, California, Northwest Coast, Sub-Arctic, and Arctic.

Some Native cultures are philosophically very close to their traditional past and may often be referred to as *traditional*, whereas others may be closer to the dominant Western culture of the United States, or *assimilated*. Individual tribe members may fall anywhere along the continuum between traditional and assimilated; others may be bicultural, or "walk in two worlds"; and still others may be marginalized and not identify with either culture. Many who may have grown up with Western or no cultural identity may choose as adults to rediscover their Native cultural roots and find teachers to help them learn more about their cultural heritage. The variability in cultures across regions and within individuals and the adherence to the cultures underline the importance for the therapist of carefully examining how an American Indian client may relate to culture and identity.

CULTURAL VALUES

The history of the indigenous cultures in the United States provides an additional layer to the cultural aspects that affect clients. Each tribe has its own history with the federal government, although each may consider how the government policy of assimilation has impacted historical trauma and cultural identity within their tribe. The policy of relocation to reservations resulted in many tribes being removed from their ancestral lands. Forty-two tribes were relocated to Oklahoma, ranging from the Ottawa in Canada in the North to the Kickapoo of Texas in the South and from the Seminole of Florida in the Southeast and the Delaware of the Northeastern United States to the Modoc of Northern California in the West (Utter, 2001).

In the late 1880s, the policies moved to forced assimilation into the dominant society by changing the dress, customs, language, religion, and philosophy of American Indians to those of Western culture. Children were taken from their homes and families and sent across the country to boarding schools, where all signs of their homes, language, and culture were stripped away. Clothes children wore on the trip were taken away, and "White" clothes were provided, their hair was cut, they were allowed to speak only English, and none of their customs, foods, dances, or spiritual practices were allowed. Boarding schools relished providing before-and-after pictures of the students to illustrate how they "civilized the savage" (National Archives and Records Administration, 2011). Systemic influences across history included (a) dispossession of lands and belongings, (b) biological warfare, including smallpox, (c) disruption of culture, (d) Indian wars, (e) federal and religious boarding schools, (f) termination, (g) relocation, and (h) modern influences (Brave Heart & DeBruyn, 1998). The culture was not passed on from the elders to the children. The values were not taught through the traditional stories. Abuse, death, and demoralization abounded through these policies (Utter, 2001).

Traditional values vary from tribe to tribe and region to region. For example, the Oyate, or Lakota, have four cardinal values, five virtues, and seven aspects of the Lakota way of life: (a) values—bravery, fortitude, generosity, and wisdom; (b) virtues—courage, respect, humility, patience, and tolerance; and (c) Lakota way of life—prayer, respect, compassion, honesty, generosity, humility, and wisdom (Salway, 2011). In contrast, the Ojibwe have seven traditional values or teachings: love, respect, courage, honesty, wisdom, humility, and truth (Eshkakogan, 2011). In considering core values with respect to American Indians, some generalizations are made, but there are exceptions, so it is important to allow for individual differences (BigFoot & Braden, 1998).

The Native perspective of some dominant society values may be somewhat different from the Western perspective of the same values. One extremely important value is cooperation, which is viewed as harmony, respect, and noninterference (BigFoot & Braden, 1998). Cooperation is also seen as having a more personal orientation, and is used not to control others but to respect dignity and autonomy. The Western perspective is generally more focused on accomplishing the task at hand (Kohls, 1984).

Acknowledgement of conflict is usually indirect in indigenous cultures, focusing on social harmony rather than being obvious, overt, and direct, as is usually seen in Western society. Personal relationships are emphasized within indigenous cultures rather than the task orientation of Western culture. There is a great respect for dignity and autonomy, but shame and dishonor are considered serious violations against a person, the family, the clan, and the tribe (BigFoot & Braden, 1998). Competition is seen as positive when it benefits the whole or common good, rather than being simply competition between members of the group. Improving by competing against one's past performance is good, but boasting about performance is discouraged (BigFoot & Braden, 1998).

Generosity, ownership, focus on the present, and courtesy are also indigenous values. Generosity and sharing are greatly valued among indigenous cultures. Possessions are a means for helping others, whereas contributing and ownership are seen as possession at the present time. Conversely, stinginess or greed is discouraged (BigFoot & Braden, 1998). A person from the Western culture may feel that he or she has loaned an indigenous person something, but the indigenous person may view it as a gift that does not require repayment or return (Kohls, 1984). Materialism and ownership of things are not as important as being a good person. Status and getting ahead, which are valued in Western society, are not highly prized in indigenous cultures. Saving, putting away for the future, amassing large quantities of food or possessions, or financial security are not considered important among indigenous cultures. In the past, nature provided all that was needed. Typically, excess goods are acquired to give away during ceremonies. What one needs is in the present, and the future will take care of itself (BigFoot & Braden, 1998).

The aspect of focusing on the present, the here and now, as opposed to dwelling on the future or the past, is a key concept in understanding indigenous culture. The past and future are appreciated, but it is more important to be than to become. Present orientation is also related to the concept of time (BigFoot & Braden, 1998; Kohls, 1984). Time is considered fluid rather than something to be controlled or managed. Native people were conscious of time and marked it by natural phenomena, such as the sun, moon, and seasons. American Indians are not influenced by the same Puritan work ethic of the dominant culture, just as they do not have the same view of property and self-sufficiency as the majority culture. Most American Indians understand the need for work, but it is interwoven with spirituality, balance, and harmonious lifestyles (BigFoot & Braden, 1998; Kohls, 1984).

Courtesy has always been considered important and is defined as being generous, respectful, polite, courteous, and hospitable toward others. Lack of direct eye contact is a sign of respect rather than evasiveness (BigFoot & Braden, 1998; Kohls, 1984). Socially, American Indians tend to speak in a soft, slow, deliberate manner, stressing the emotions more than the content. American Indians are very expressive of emotions but can be very reserved if they have a history of hostility or distrust of others. Speech is usually an expression secondary to behavior. Silence is especially valued, and most Natives are comfortable with silence.

American Indians value wisdom, which comes with age and experience, rather than the dominant society's value of youth (BigFoot & Braden, 1998). Elders are respected for their wisdom, which comes from greater experience and a broader perspective. The American Indian extended family may seem quite confusing to those with little experience with the culture because family relationships are defined beyond blood relatives and apply to friends and other tribal and clan members, who are bestowed a family title (e.g., brother, sister, son, daughter, grandchild) based on the closeness and role they play in one another's lives. These relationships are an important part of the social, religious, and spiritual life of the family. These relationships also reflect the interdependence and effective child-rearing practices observed (BigFoot & Braden, 1998).

Spirituality permeates all areas of Natives' lives. They do not believe in forcing their beliefs on others. Spirituality is considered a part of the person and their relationship to all that surrounds them, not a religion. All things in nature are viewed as for the good of all and cannot be owned by individuals. One should live in balance and cooperation with nature, using what is needed to live, rather than trying to control it or own it (BigFoot & Braden, 1998; Hodge, Limb, & Cross, 2009).

Finally, criticism is communicated indirectly through another person or in storytelling using examples of right and wrong rather than through the direct confrontation favored by Western culture (BigFoot & Braden, 1998; Kohls, 1984). Criticism can be communicated through humor, for example, by making a comment about sleeping all day to someone who gets up late or giving someone a humorous "Indian name" based on a behavior that is outside the norm of the society. However, humor as an indirect communication is also used to convey acceptance. For example, teasing indicates trust and acceptance and is used after relationships have been established. Interpersonal relationships hold a great deal of importance among American Indians (BigFoot & Braden, 1998).

MENTAL HEALTH RESEARCH WITH AMERICAN INDIAN AND ALASKA NATIVES

When examining research related to mental health practices with American Indians/Alaska Natives, no known results related to evidence-based treatment (EBT) modalities with American Indian or Alaska Native populations were found to have been published or listed in dissertation abstracts. The only outcome studies have included substance abuse treatment and prevention programs. Most comprehensive services for American Indians/Alaska Natives are provided through Indian Health Service and tribal mental health and substance abuse services. These services are focused on the mental health and substance abuse services needed by those eligible in a specific area and not on research of approaches. Gone and Alcántara (2007) identified only nine outcome studies that addressed work with American Indians or Alaska Natives, and just two of those studies used control group comparisons. Both of the control group studies were for prevention approaches rather than therapeutic interventions (LaFromboise & Howard-Pitney, 1995; Manson & Brenneman, 1995). Of the other outcome studies identified that used no untreated group comparison and pre- and post-intervention assessments, two used epidemiological data obtained annually to show a decrease in suicidal gestures and attempts. Two other studies used samples of four Native children, one for a school-based early intervention with children for antisocial disorders and the other for a pharmacological approach with children diagnosed with attention-deficit/hyperactivity disorder and fetal alcohol syndrome (Diken & Rutherford, 2005; Gone & Alcántara, 2007; Oesterheld et al., 1998).

The challenges to conducting this research include difficulty recruiting a large enough sample to test treatment modalities, difficulty obtaining a sample with a single diagnosis because of the large proportion of two or more comorbid conditions, and definition of who is Indian to describe participants by tribe, region, urban, reservation, enrollment, descendancy, or self-identification (Noe et al., 2006; Safran et al., 2009). Another barrier to conducting outcome research with American Indian/Alaska Native populations may be the lack of assessments validated with these populations that can measure the outcomes of treatment (Safran et al., 2009). In 2005, Miranda et al. found that although there were limited outcome studies of psychosocial treatments of minorities, studies addressing treatment with American Indians/Alaska Natives were missing. More commonly found in practice with American Indians/Alaska Natives are practice-based treatments and EBP rather than EBT (Gone, 2009). Kazdin (2008) described evidence-based practice as the clinical activities that are "informed by evidence about interventions, clinical expertise, and patient needs, values, and preferences" (p. 147) and described evidence-based treatment as "interventions or techniques that have produced therapeutic change in controlled trials" (p. 147).

American Indians/Alaska Natives lead the nation in many health disparities, having many times the national average levels of tuberculosis (850%), alcoholism (650%), motor vehicle crashes (330%), diabetes (290%), unintentional injuries (250%), and suicide (170%), to name a few (Centers for Disease Control and Prevention, 2007). Most of the research conducted has focused on prevention efforts targeted to youth and school-based interventions or preliminary assessment of acceptance of EBP conception (Dixon et al., 2007; Jackson, Wenzel, Schmutzer, & Tyler, 2006; Miranda et al., 2005). Finally, research has shown that American Indians tend to drop out of treatment earlier than other groups and are more likely to terminate treatment after the first session (LaFromboise, Trimble, & Mohatt, 1998; Sue, Allen, & Conaway, 1978). This could be due to a lack of cultural competence and sensitivity on the part of the therapist or to mistrust of non-Native, Western approaches among those receiving treatment (Trimble & Gonzalez, 2007).

Some Western EBTs, such as cognitive behavior therapy, do not fit with the culture and traditions of many American Indians because these treatments focus on the individual rather than the family, extended family, and community (Johnson, 2006; Speck & Attneave, 1973). Group therapy has been a proven approach when American Indian culture, values, and traditions are incorporated, as with the talking circle[2] (Edwards & Edwards, 1984). Other factors that should be included are tribal identification, differences in values, and level of acculturation (Johnson, 2006). It is important to know how these factors affect the client.

AN EMERGING MODEL FOR ADAPTING EVIDENCE-BASED PRACTICES WITH AMERICAN INDIANS

Research on EBPs with American Indians is in its infancy. Many practitioners in Indian Country have made cultural adaptations of various therapies within their own practices, but little has been done to evaluate and document the efficacy of these adaptations. Most times, there is no model or theoretical underpinning for these adaptations. Hall (2001) described these adaptations, or *culturally sensitive therapies* (CSTs), in a discussion of EBT and EBP. CSTs address divergent experiences of ethnic minority groups as compared with the mainstream culture. Gone (2009) tried to bridge the gap between EBT and CSTs by studying treatment of historical trauma from residential boarding school experiences in a Canadian First Nations healing lodge. Themes from the study included emotional burdens, cathartic disclosure, self-as-project reflexivity, and impact of colonization. He found that healing was more important than treatment in aboriginal therapeutic services. Gone concluded that healing discourse helped bridge the gap between EBT and CSTs and, further, suggested that EBT be adapted in increments for culturally diverse populations.

Although many practitioners in the field make cultural adaptations to treatments as they see fit, in most cases, models or theoretical frameworks are not utilized in considering those adaptations. The work of utilizing adaptations based on informed models is just beginning. There are indications that cultural adaptations may be useful in developing treatments for American Indians. At least two known models exist that suggest how adaptations may be culturally integrated: Johnson's (2006) model of Native healing and Big-Foot and Schmidt's (2009) honoring children–mending the circle (HC-MC)

---

[2]A *talking circle* involves a group of people sitting in a circle for discussion. An American Indian object, such as a *talking feather* or *talking stick*, is passed from one person to another, and the person holding the object is the only one allowed to speak. Others are only allowed to make faint noises of agreement, such as grunts. Even if a person requires several minutes to collect their thoughts before speaking, if they hold the object, the time is theirs. In true talking circles, prayers may also be a part of the time, including passing of tobacco and making of prayer ties that will be offered later (Standley, 2012).

model. The medicine wheel and the four directions are the basis for both models. The medicine wheel illustrates balance in one's life and is used as a symbol of the circle of life, balance in mental, physical, emotional, and spiritual health. All areas must be nourished, exercised, and nurtured for a person to be his or her best. The medicine wheel is recognized by many Native cultures. Johnson focused on a medical model with her medicine wheel to address the downward spiral into trauma resulting from the events that have impacted American Indians. The West in Johnson's model of Native healing represents Western and EBTs. She indicated that values and traditions are critical in adapting Western EBPs for use with American Indians and that these values and traditions must be incorporated at the individual, family, and community levels. BigFoot and Schmidt developed a well-being model, the HC-MC model, based on the medicine wheel. The HC-MC model includes extended family, practices of respect, beliefs regarding the Circle, and interconnectedness of spirituality and healing as its foundation in a more positivist approach to prevention and treatment.

In Figure 10.1, the models have been integrated into an American Indian medicine wheel model of wellness, balance, and healing: the four directions wellness model. This integrated model shows the inverted triangle in the circle to illustrate the trauma and disruptions to community, family, and individual that bring "dis-ease" and unbalance into the system. The four sections of the medicine wheel connect through the central spiritual hub of the wheel demonstrating the interconnectedness of the physical, social, emotional, and mental quadrants through the spiritual core. The four directions model exemplifies the need to keep all aspects in balance around the spiritual core. The animals of each direction represent the values that are important in maintaining the wellness related to that aspect. The types of activities included in helping the individual, family and community maintain balance are located in each direction. The eagle comes from the sunrise to the east and represents illumination, humility, acknowledgement, spontaneity, joy, and prudence. The cougar is in the sun's highest point and represents physical strength, heart, generosity, loyalty, and sacrifice. The bear sleeps and dreams in the night and represents introspection, harmony, ascension, testing, power, perseverance, and practice. Finally, the buffalo from the cold and snow of the North represents wisdom, honesty, acceptance, synthesis, analysis, interpretation, and prayer of the elders (Bopp, 1985).

As the model is examined, the interconnectedness and overlap among the quadrants of the wheel become clearer. The model demonstrates how any healing needs to incorporate all aspects into the healing process to perpetuate wellness and balance, or as the Lakota say in Indian Country, "Mitakuye oyasin!" [We are all related!]. The four directions model can be used to adapt

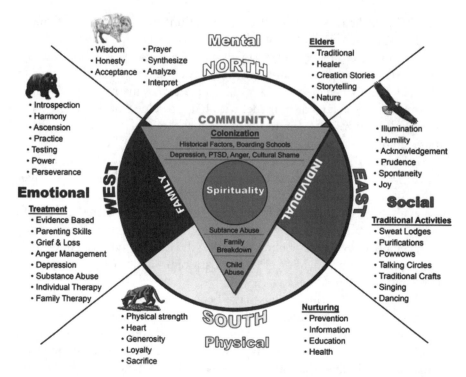

Figure 10.1. American Indian medicine wheel model of wellness, balance, and healing. From *Mental Health Care for Urban Indians: Clinical Insights From Native Practitioners* (p.190), by. T. M. Witko, 2006, Washington DC: American Psychological Association, Copyright 2006 by the American Psychological Association.

treatment approaches in a culturally sensitive way. Following the adaptation, evaluation is necessary to establish practices that work, do not work, and need further adaptation within the culture. It must be applied with caution because there are over 700 tribal groups in the United States, and each may have variations in their ceremonies, traditions, and stories that must be taken into account for the individual client (Dancing Feather & Robinson, 2003).

APPLICATION OF THE FOUR DIRECTIONS WELLNESS MODEL TO CULTURAL ADAPTATIONS

The four directions wellness model is intended as a guide to therapists and researchers seeking to advance practice, theory, or research with American Indian populations. Because this population is tremendously heterogeneous, adaptations need to be carefully considered and selected by way of close collaboration with the group with which they will be used. Which adaptations are considered and what specific form each takes will depend on identity considerations, problem definition, therapist issues in the treatment context, therapy environment in the treatment context, treatment modality, and work with children.

Identity Considerations

When adapting a treatment approach, the therapist must consider aspects of tribal identification, differences in values, and acculturation of the client. When all this is taken into consideration in a cultural worldview, the appropriate healing approach can be determined. It is important to avoid clashes in values. One story of how American Indian values and traditions can be generalized with negative outcomes involves a person who wanted to give a Native painting to an American Indian speaker as a gift. The picture depicted an owl in flight beautifully crafted by a prominent local Native artist. The person who selected the painting did not know that the owl was an omen of death in the tribal culture of the speaker. When the painting was presented, the speaker's face registered distress, and the person presenting the gift did not understand why. Neither party came away from the situation feeling good about what was meant by the other, and the gift fell short of the goal. Some time spent learning about the speaker's tribe and interests or going with a standard traditional gift (e.g., Star quilt, Pendleton blanket, or other Pendleton gift) would have left all feeling truly honored.

Problem Definition

When assessing the history and cultural context of clients, it is important to understand their perspective on the problem that brought them to therapy (Spierings, 2004). How would their problem be explained within their understanding of their culture? Is the problem within a medical, magical, religious, spiritual, biographical, or educational context? How would it be treated by traditional healers within their culture? What is necessary to return to a sense of balance? It is important to collaborate with traditional healers if this is important to the client. It is good to know what practices—such as sweat lodges, ceremonies, and traditional medicines—they use, but it is important to respect that ceremonies and treatments may be kept private within the culture and that it is impolite to intrude without invitation or to pursue the information if the client is hesitant to provide it.

The therapist may want to ask about traditional practices in a way that provides clients an opportunity to give only as much information as they may be comfortable providing, such as, "I know your ceremonies and traditional ways are sacred, but it would help me to know what you can tell me about the practices you observe" (Barnard, 2007). It is important here to note that food and water are considered medicine in many Native cultures and serve a purpose for keeping the life in balance. Another approach to learning would be to ask the client, "If there were an elder in the family, what would that elder tell you about your problem? How would the elder tell you your problem should be treated?" This approach also helps get to the values or influences of elders and family. It is also important to understand how clients express emotions. Asking how men or women in their culture express feelings, such as anger, shame, guilt, sadness, fear, disgust, and joy, provides an emotional cultural context. This would be followed by asking how the therapist would recognize these feelings in the client's expressions. It may also be necessary to access how the emotions may be expressed in the client's family or tribe.

Therapist Issues in the Treatment Context

The therapist's attitude and the therapeutic environment are paramount and should include a willingness to self-disclose, tell stories, and collaborate with the client in addition to demonstrating regard and respect for the client. A collaborative stance may be communicated by an acknowledgement that therapists know their field but clients are experts on their culture. Therapists can clearly communicate a desire to learn and invite clients to share and teach the therapist. This creates equality in the relationship and a respect for the therapist's willingness to admit to not knowing everything. Regard and respect can be established by asking about traditional greetings, such as a soft, gentle handshake as opposed to the Western expectation of a firm handshake. It is also helpful for Native people to have something to do with their hands, such as beading, clay, journey stick, crafts, or other projects, while they listen or talk. Dolores Subia BigFoot explains in her training that having something to do with the hands helps focus attention and also addresses the need to look somewhere other than at the speaker or listener. Check to see if clients have words from their culture for how they wish to be addressed, such as Lakota or Oyate instead of American Indian, Native American, or Sioux. Would they like to have certain grasses or herbs present in their sessions, such as sage, sweetgrass, or cedar? How do clients say certain greetings in their traditional language? Do they know any of their traditional language? Treat their answers and teachings as important information and act on the information. The more you show that you value and appreciate the beauty in the client's culture, the more you build trust and open up sharing (Tumani, 2004).

Therapy Environment in the Treatment Context

Sage and sweetgrass can make the physical surroundings of therapy more welcoming. Burning of sage can create a positive, culturally friendly environment for many American Indian clients because sage is used for blessing and purifying and is utilized in many cultures throughout the United States today. Use of sage also communicates an acceptance of the culture and openness to making a difficult experience as comfortable as possible. In many buildings today, however, burning anything, including sage, sweetgrass, tobacco, or scented candles, may not be permitted. Alternatives to this may be to smudge outside the building or to provide dried sage that the client can take to breathe in the scent and sprinkle over them instead of smudging with the smoke of the burning sage. Sage oil can also be used to provide the olfactory anchor to a positive and peaceful experience. These suggestions were made by Mary Ann Black Bull, cultural instructor at Cankdeska Cikana Community College in Fort Totten, North Dakota. A braid of sweetgrass or bundle of sage can be important, as can a cup of water in a therapeutic setting. Offering water to the client can also be considered "providing medicine," as Native cultures see anything that contributes to the health and wellness of the individual as medicine, including food and water. Displaying some American Indian art, including paintings, pottery, dolls, dream catchers or beadwork, can demonstrate an appreciation and acceptance within the therapist's environment. Most important is making the space warm and inviting with an air of acceptance for the culture of the client.

Treatment Modality

It may be important to be deliberate about the selection of group or individual treatment. For example, with one tribe, there was need for a group therapy process to address grief over the loss of a number of young people in a single accident. Because of the number of people within the tribe who were affected, it seemed groups would be best approach. When working with grief issues, it is important to know the taboos, traditions, and practices within the culture. Within this tribe, the names of the deceased were not to be spoken because doing so pulled them back from the spirit world and did not let them move forward on their journey. Instead of focusing on the discourse, the group focused on an artistic expression to honor the people and their lives and mourn their passing. Talking also occurred within the group but in a context that allowed the clients to respect their culture as they processed the loss. This approach was developed in consultation with Bernadette St. Clair and Linda Large, social workers at the Fort Washakie Indian Health Service. The decision to include or exclude family, extended family, spiritual healers, or others integral to the client must be carefully considered within the cultural context. Whether or not it is appropriate for the therapist to be part of the ceremonies conducted by a spiritual healer is a factor that challenges Western ethical teachings about boundaries. The therapist's willingness to be a part of such activities may be critical to the progress of the therapy and should be discussed with the client, the participating extended family, and the healer.

Work With Children

Sometimes, engaging children, whether they are traditional or more assimilated, can be difficult in indigenous communities. Even children who are assimilated appreciate and respect their cultural traditions and values. Balloon sculpture can be used to quickly engage children and integrate values of generosity, respect, and the value of interpersonal relationship while building rapport with the child. This process also helps in engaging the parents by demonstrating the therapist's commitment to their cultural values. This adaptation for Native practice was presented at an Indian Health Service Mental Health Conference by Vincen Barnes, a psychologist with the Aberdeen Area of the Indian Health Service in South Dakota. He provided practical lessons from his work in Indian Country.

When Native children are depressed and meeting someone of authority who is new to them, it is common for there to be no eye contact and very little verbal response. The therapist engages children by bringing out something most children identify with fun—balloons—even if the children are depressed. The children are invited to pick a color and, within the therapist's abilities, an animal, hat, or other sculpture they would like their therapist to make or that they would like to have. This encourages interaction with the therapist immediately and can move the rapport building forward. Be aware that in Native communities, therapists will receive requests for buffalo, horses, eagles, and wolves, so it is good to have some practice at making more complex animals as soon as possible. The children are then given their sculpture to take with them when they leave the office. This expresses respect by giving the children the choices of colors and objects and values the children's input. It expresses generosity and value by giving the children something the therapist has made himself or herself just for the child, and the children can take their balloon sculpture away with them as a bond with the therapist. The balloon sculptures also present teachable moments. If a balloon breaks during the twisting and forming, the therapist can address what you do when the unexpected happens or when things blow up in your face. If the sculpture comes undone (untwisted), the therapist can talk about how sometimes you think you are finished with something only to find out it may have to be redone or fixed.

When engaging in play or imaginative activities in therapy with indigenous children, it can be very useful to include animals (e.g., puppets, stuffed animals, drawings) that are meaningful in cultural stories. For example, coyote, wolf, bear, buffalo, eagle, and horse are very popular. Stories that focus on these animals are wonderful teaching tools that include the cultural aspects of people's relationship to all things. Stories were how children were taught by the elders. *American Indian Stories* and *Indian Fairy Tales* are public domain literature available to download for free with Kindle. The Internet can also be a rich resource with many stories provided on tribal sites (e.g., http://www.ewebtribe.com/NACulture/stories.htm; http://www.apples4theteacher.com/native-american/short-stories/; http://minnesotahumanities.org/resources/amikoonse). These stories can also be very helpful in therapy. I think of the story of the Cherokee grandfather who was teaching his grandchildren about life. He said to them,

> A fight is going on inside me. . . . It is a terrible fight, and it is between two wolves. One wolf represents fear, anger, envy, sorrow, regret, greed, arrogance, self-pity, guilt, resentment, inferiority, lies, pride, and superiority. The other wolf stands for joy, peace, love, hope, sharing, serenity, humility, kindness, benevolence, friendship, empathy, generosity, truth, compassion, and faith. This same fight is going on inside of you and every other person too.

The grandchildren thought about it for a minute, and then one child asked his grandfather, "Which wolf will win?" The old Cherokee simply replied, "The one I feed."

A PROMISING TREATMENT MODALITY FOR AMERICAN INDIANS

One treatment modality used worldwide to address trauma in culturally sensitive ways is eye movement desensitization and reprocessing (EMDR; Shapiro, 2005). Although there are no specific studies of EMDR with American Indians, the approaches to adaptation in international cultures apply to indigenous cultures. The EMDR International Association's international trauma work emphasizes the importance of establishing the emotional constructs of culture, culture-related characteristics, ways of expression, and symptoms (Tumani, 2004). This would also be important for Native cultures inside the United States. EMDR is utilized with treatment of unresolved traumas, whether a small embarrassment or a major life trauma. American Indians have suffered many traumas throughout history (e.g., boarding school experiences, loss of culture, loss of language, genocide; Gone, 2007) and in their lives today, from extreme poverty to the many deaths of young people from suicide and homicide and traumatic deaths from accidents, fires, drowning, and weather (Centers for Disease Control and Prevention, 2007). EMDR is usually implemented with a visual object, such as a hand, light, or pen, for clients to follow with their eyes. Within cultures where there has been a great deal of abuse, waving a hand (or fingers) can be perceived as threatening. American Indians may find it preferable to use a prayer feather so that the client focuses on something that is culturally and spiritually significant to him or her rather than the fingers or something that may have an unknown negative association. This suggestion was made by EMDR trainer William Harrar from his interaction with a medicine man from a Northern Plains tribe during training. The feather provides a symbol of peace, strength, and freedom; however, it is important to note that prayer feathers are usually eagle feathers or white turkey feathers painted to look like eagle feathers. To use a feather from an unknown bird or one that could be offensive to the client could have the opposite of the desired effect. To avoid potential pitfalls, the therapist can ask the client to bring a treasured object. With children, finger puppets can be used, and with indigenous children, animal puppets, especially those used in the cultural stories, may be particularly powerful. Allowing clients to choose the object can empower them as partners in their own treatment. The internal processing of the trauma without having to find words to communicate the experience provides a powerful process. American Indians in some areas have been trained with EMDR, but most are focused on practice and providing their clients with what they need rather than on building research evidence.

Within Native cultures, treatments of historical trauma developed by Brave Heart (2004) and the White Bison Wellbriety Movement (Coyhis, 2009) utilize Native culture, healing, ceremonies, and symbolism combined with facilitators trained in both traditional and Western approaches. The stories and illustrations provide meaning for Natives attending the groups. They focus on history, trauma, and forgiveness within the community as a whole. They also work within traditional values and beliefs to facilitate a healing, positive approach that is cross-generational and cross-gender in nature.

CONCLUSION

In summary, there is an absence of research in the area of EBPs with American Indian clients. Many therapeutic practices may integrate culturally sensitive aspects, but it is unclear whether the culture is truly integrated into the practices. Although clinicians believe these adaptations are beneficial in working with indigenous clients, there has been no research to examine their actual effectiveness. Assessments that are used to measure the effectiveness of treatments have rarely been examined to determine their reliability, validity, and norms within American Indian populations. If we do not know if the measure is accurate, how can we know if there is a difference in treatment? In addition to Western practices with indigenous populations, research needs to include traditional cultural healing practices to determine their efficacy with indigenous populations. Evaluation of a culturally integrated model that allows for the interconnectedness of all parts to achieve balance and wellness needs to occur to begin building evidence of traditional and Western models of treatment. The four directions model may provide an opportunity to engage systematic cultural adaptations in a manner that facilitates competent treatment as well as evaluation of and research on adapted therapies that will contribute to the literature on EBPs with American Indians and Alaska Natives.

The small numbers of American Indians compared with the total U.S. population, the large numbers of tribes with diverse cultures, the lack of culturally appropriate validated outcome measures, the high comorbidity rates of mental health diagnoses, and the low retention rate of American Indian clients in therapy are major barriers to efficacy research. It is very difficult to obtain a large enough sample in a geographical area to test outcomes. A clinical trial within a tribal community will also have difficulty keeping participants from sharing information with the control group because of the closeness and interactions within the community.

EBPs from research with the general population are applied in tribal and Indian Health Service behavioral health clinics without testing or evaluation to determine if they are effective or should be used in this population. Therapists use local culture and traditions in adaptations for their clients, but these are primarily culturally sensitive practices that are passed orally from one therapist to another at Indian Health Service meetings or other gatherings of providers for indigenous people. Clinicians in the Indian Health Service and other indigenous settings are focused on providing services, and time is not allowed for research. These clinicians do not have the time or resources to examine the effectiveness of their treatments and, instead, continue using approaches on the basis of what seems to work in their practices or what is provided in training of Western models. Approaches like the balloon sculpture may be shared with other therapists as clinical presentations when a practice becomes known to someone on the planning committee.

Most research on efficacy and outcomes has been conducted with prevention programs, such as American Indian Life Skills Curriculum (LaFromboise, 1996) and Sources of Strength (LoMurray, 1998) for suicide prevention and other programs for substance abuse prevention (Dixon et al., 2007). These programs are currently seen as promising practices because not enough research has been conducted to determine their effectiveness. Most of the studies are conducted within school settings where a larger number of participants are in a closed environment and the program is implemented as part of the curriculum.

To address the need for models and adaptations of evidence-based research in treatment, partnerships need to be developed with providers in

Indian Country. Psychologists' traditional ways of testing practices in large urban areas and university centers are not available in most American Indian communities, nor are they practical for gathering American Indian participants. Data that may be collected in urban settings may only have enough American Indian participants if studies are pooled. It is important to examine how we conduct the research to reach those who do not fit into the Western model. If a method for listing needed research in Indian Country could be developed that students looking for thesis and dissertation topics might consult, this could lead to more small studies from different tribes and regions related to a treatment modality. Such studies could provide better answers as to what works and what does not work with Native communities and clients.

There is a great deal of work yet to be done. Examination of assessments for their utility in outcome research is important before their efficacy can actually be determined. Establishing clinical trials with treatment modalities in Indian Country requires time to build relationships with the Indian Health Service and providers in American Indian communities. Examination of traditional approaches requires training traditional healers as coresearchers and partnering with them to examine the utility in the traditional approaches. It is time to choose a place to begin and start the work.

REFERENCES

Aragon, A. M. (2006). A clinical understanding of urban American Indians. In T. M. Witko (Ed.), *Mental health care for urban Indians: Clinical insights from Native practitioners* (pp. 19–31). Washington, DC: American Psychological Association. doi:10.1037/11422-001

Barnard, A. G. (2007). Providing psychiatric-mental health care for Native Americans: Lessons learned by a non-Native American PMHNP. *Journal of Psychosocial Nursing and Mental Health Services, 45(5),* 30–35.

BigFoot, D. S., & Braden, J. (1998). *On the back of a turtle.* Oklahoma City, OK: University of Oklahoma Health Sciences Center.

BigFoot, D. S., & Schmidt, S. (2009). *Project making medicine.* Oklahoma City, OK: University of Oklahoma Health Sciences Center.

Bopp, J. (1985). *The sacred tree: Reflections on Native American spirituality* (3rd ed.). Twin Lakes, WI: Lotus Light.

Brave Heart, M. Y. H. (2004). The historical trauma response among Natives and its relationship to substance abuse: A Lakota illustration. *Journal of Psychoactive Drugs, 35,* 7–13. doi:10.1080/02791072.2003.10399988

Brave Heart, M. Y. H., & DeBruyn, L. M. (1998). The American Indian holocaust: Healing historical unresolved grief. *Journal of American Indian Alaska Native Mental Health Research, 8(2),* 60–82. doi:10.5820/aian.0802.1998.60

Bureau of Indian Affairs, U.S. Department of the Interior. (2009). *Indian affairs.* Retrieved from http://www.bia.gov/index.htm

Centers for Disease Control and Prevention. (2007, May 29). *CDC injury center.* Retrieved from http://www.cdc.gov/ncipc/factsheets/nativeamericans.htm

Coyhis, D. (2009). *Healing the legacy of the boarding schools: 1879–2009 Wellbriety journey for forgiveness.* Aurora, CO: Author.

Dancing Feather, F., & Robinson, R. (2003). *Exploring Native American wisdom: Lore, traditions, and rituals that connect us all.* Franklin Lakes, NJ: Career Press.

Diken, I. H., & Rutherford, R. B. (2005). First step to success early intervention program: A study of effectiveness with Native American children. *Education & Treatment of Children, 28,* 444–465.

Dixon, A. L., Yabiku, S. T., Okamoto, S. K., Tan, S. S., Marsiglia, F. F., Kulis, S., & Burke, A. M. (2007). The efficacy of a multicultural prevention intervention among urban American Indian youth in the Southwest. *Journal of Primary Prevention, 28,* 547–568. doi:10.1007/s10935-007-0114-8

Edwards, E., & Edwards, M. (1984). Group work practice with American Indians. *Social Work With Groups, 7,* 7–21. doi:10.1300/J009v07n03_03

Eshkakogan, D. (2011). *Nishinaabe Bimiiadziwin Kinoomaadwinan: Teachings of the medicine wheel: Teachings of the seven grandfathers.* Retrieved from http://www.umich.edu/ojibwe/lessons/semester-two/seven-grandfathers/

Gone, J. P. (2007). "We never was happy living like a Whiteman": Mental health disparities and the postcolonial predicament in American Indian communities. *American Journal of Community Psychology, 40,* 290–300. doi:10.10007/s10464-007-9136-x

Gone, J. P. (2009). A community-based treatment for Native American historical trauma: Prospects for evidence-based practice. *Journal of Consulting and Clinical Psychology, 77,* 751–762. doi:10.1037/a0015390

Gone, J. P., & Alcántara, C. (2007). Identifying effective mental health interventions for American Indians and Alaska Natives: A review of the literature. *Cultural Diversity and Ethnic Minority Psychology, 13,* 356–363. doi:10.1037/1099-9809.13.4.356

Hall, G. C. N. (2001). Psychotherapy research with ethnic minorities: Empirical, ethical, and conceptual issues. *Journal of Consulting and Clinical Psychology, 69,* 502–510. doi:10.1037/0022-006X.69.3.502

Hodge, D. R., Limb, G. E., & Cross, T. L. (2009). Moving from colonization toward balance and harmony: A Native American perspective on wellness. *Social Work, 54,* 211–219. doi:10.1093/sw/54.3.211

Humes, K. R., Jones, N. A., & Ramirez, R. R. (2011). Overview of race and Hispanic origin 2010: U.S. Census briefs 2010 (Publication No. C2010BR-02). Retrieved from http://www.census.gov/prod/cen2010/briefs/c2010br-02.pdf

Jackson, L. C., Wenzel, A., Schmutzer, P. A., & Tyler, J. D. (2006). Applicability of cognitive–behavior therapy with American Indian individuals. *Psychotherapy: Theory, Research, Practice, Training, 43,* 506–517. doi:10.1037/0033-3204.43.4.506

Johnson, C. L. (2006). Innovative healing model: Empowering urban Native Americans. In T. M. Witko (Ed.), *Mental health care for urban Indians: Clinical insights from Native practitioners* (pp. 189–204). Washington, DC: American Psychological Association. doi:10.1037/11422-010

Kazdin, A. E. (2008). Evidence-based treatment and practice: New opportunities to bridge clinical research and practice, enhance the knowledge base, and improve patient care. *American Psychologist, 63,* 146–159. doi:10.1037/0003-066X.63.3.146

Kohls, L. R. (1984). *The values Americans live by.* Washington, DC: Meridian House International.

LaFromboise, T. D. (1996). *Adolescent life skills development.* Madison, WI: University of Wisconsin Press.

LaFromboise, T. D., & Howard-Pitney, B. (1995). The Zuni life skills development curriculum: Description and evaluation of a suicide prevention program. *Journal of Counseling Psychology, 42,* 479–486. doi:10.1037/0022-0167.42.4.479

LaFromboise, T. D., Trimble, J. E., & Mohatt, G. V. (1998). Counseling intervention and American Indian tradition: An integrative approach. In D. R. Atkinson, G. Morten, & D. W. Sue (Eds.), *Counseling American minorities* (5th ed., pp. 137–158). New York, NY: McGraw-Hill.

LoMurray, M. (1998). *Sources of strength.* Bismarck, ND: Mental Health Association in North Dakota.

Manson, S. M., & Brenneman, D. L. (1995). Chronic disease among older American Indians: Preventing depressive symptoms and related problems of coping. In D. K. Pagett (Ed.), *Handbook on ethnicity, aging, and mental health* (pp. 284–303). Westport, CT: Greenwood.

Miranda, J., Bernal, G., Lau, A., Kohn, L., Hwang, W., & LaFromboise, T. (2005). State of the science on psychosocial interventions for ethnic minorities. *Annual Review of Clinical Psychology, 1,* 113–142. doi:10.1146/annurev.clinpsy.1.102803.143822

National Archives and Records Administration. (2011). *Records of the Bureau of Indian Affairs (BIA): 1793–1989: 75.10.2. Records of the Educational Division, records of the Industries Section, photographic prints and negatives; 75.20. Records of Indian Schools; 75.29. Still pictures 1968–1979.* Retrieved from http://www.archives.gov/research/guide-fed-records/groups/075.html#75.29

Noe, T. D., Manson, S. M., Croy, C. D., McGough, H., Henderson, J. A., & Buchwald, D. S. (2006). In their own voices: American Indian decisions to participate in health research. In J. E. Trimble & C. B. Fisher (Eds.), *The handbook of ethical research with ethnocultural populations and communities* (pp. 77–92). Thousand Oaks, CA: Sage. doi:10.4135/9781412986168.n5

O'Brien, S. (1989). *American Indian tribal governments.* Norman, OK: University of Oklahoma Press.

Oesterheld, J. R., Kofoed, L., Tervo, R., Fogas, B., Wilson, A., & Feichtner, H. (1998). Effectiveness of methylphenidate in Native American children with fetal alcohol syndrome and attention deficit/hyperactivity disorder: A controlled pilot study. *Journal of Child and Adolescent Psychopharmacology, 8*, 39–48. doi:10.1089/cap.1998.8.39

Safran, M. A., Mays, R. A., Jr., Huang, L. N., McCuan, R., Pham, K. P., Fisher, S. K., & Trachtenberg, A. (2009). Mental health disparities. *American Journal of Public Health, 99*, 1962–1966. doi:10.2105/AJPH.2009.167346

Salway, L. (2011). *Outline of Lakota Culture 109: The medicine wheel: Values, virtues and ceremonies which keep the sacred hoop strong.* Rapid City, SD: Life Initiatives. Retrieved from http://lifeinitiativesinc.org/trainingculture109.html

Shapiro, R. (2005). *EMDR solutions: Pathways to healing.* New York, NY: Norton.

Speck, R. V., & Attneave, C. L. (1973). *Family networks.* New York, NY: Random House.

Spierings, J. (2004). *Multi-Cultural EMDR.* Hamden, CT: EMDR Humanitarian Assistance Programs.

Standley, S. J. (2012). *Native American talking circles.* Retrieved from http://www.drstandley.com/nativeamerican_talking_circles.shtml

Sue, S., Allen, D. B., & Conaway, L. (1978). The responsiveness and equality of mental health care to Chicanos and Native Americans. *American Journal of Community Psychology, 6*, 137–146. doi:10.1007/BF00881035

Trimble, J. E., & Gonzalez, J. (2007). Cultural considerations and perspectives for providing psychological counseling for Native American Indians. In P. Pederson, J. Draguns, W. Lonner, & J. E. Trimble (Eds.), *Counseling across cultures* (6th ed., pp. 93–111). Thousand Oaks, CA: Sage.

Tumani, V. (2004). Intercultural competence. In J. Spierings (Ed.), *Multi-Cultural EMDR* (pp. 6–8). Camden, CT: EMDR Humanitarian Assistance Program.

Urban Indian Health Institute. (2007). *Fact sheet: Health status for urban American Indians and Alaska Natives.* Retrieved from http://www.snahc.org/documents/02_UrbanIndianHealth.pdf

Utter, J. (2001). *American Indians: Answers to today's questions.* Norman, OK: University of Oklahoma Press.

11

TOWARD CULTURAL ADAPTATION OF INTERPERSONAL PSYCHOTHERAPY FOR DEPRESSED AFRICAN AMERICAN PRIMARY CARE PATIENTS

CHARLOTTE BROWN, KYAIEN O. CONNER,
AND MICHELLE McMURRAY

Major depression is a common and debilitating illness, and it is estimated that it occurs in 6% to 10% of primary care patients (Katon & Schulberg, 1992; Stafford, Ausiello, Misra, & Saglam, 2000). Psychosocial treatments for depression have been developed and found to be effective as a first-line treatment for depression alone and in combination with medication (Agency for Health Care Policy and Research Depression Guideline Panel, 1993). One of these treatments, interpersonal psychotherapy (IPT), was developed more than 30 years ago as a brief treatment for major depression by Gerald L. Klerman and colleagues (see Weissman et al., 1979), who manualized the intervention and evaluated its efficacy in randomized acute and maintenance treatment studies in the 1970s (for a review, see Weissman & Markowitz, 1994). IPT is a time-limited intervention that focuses on problems within the patient's current interpersonal relationships related to unresolved grief, role transitions, interpersonal role disputes, and interpersonal skills deficits (Klerman, Weissman, Rounsaville, & Chevron, 1984; Weissman, Markowitz, & Klerman, 2000).

In the 3 decades since its development, numerous studies have documented the efficacy of IPT with adolescent, adult, and geriatric populations (Weissman et al., 2000). In a recent meta-analysis of 38 randomized trials of

IPT for depression, Cuijpers et al. (2011) found IPT to be more effective than control conditions (e.g., usual care, waiting list, placebo), with a moderate to large effect size in acute treatment of depression. However, the efficacy of IPT was comparable with, but not superior to, with other psychotherapies, and it was less effective than pharmacotherapy. However, IPT combined with pharmacotherapy was more effective in preventing relapse than pharmacotherapy alone. Despite the demonstrated effectiveness of IPT for treatment of depression, relatively few studies have explored the effectiveness of this psychotherapy with adult populations in primary care settings (Wolf & Hopko, 2008). Even fewer have examined IPT's effectiveness with ethnocultural groups. This represents a missed opportunity to address health disparities, given that racial and ethnic minority adults and older adults are more likely to receive treatment for depression in primary care settings (Alvidrez, 1999; Miranda et al., 2003). Therefore, it is important to examine the evidence base for psychosocial treatments that might be provided in these settings. In this chapter, we review the published studies of IPT in primary care settings, cultural adaptations made to IPT, and findings on its use with African Americans and older adults suffering from depression. On the basis of this review and findings from our own work, we also provide recommendations for adaptations to IPT in its delivery to African Americans that may improve treatment engagement, retention, and outcomes.

COMPARISON OF IPT, PHARMACOTHERAPY, AND USUAL CARE IN ADULT PRIMARY CARE PATIENTS

We identified only two published randomized clinical trials of IPT delivered to primary care patients less than 60 years of age. Neither of these studies adapted IPT for use in the primary care setting. Schulberg et al. (1996) randomized 275 adult patients (18–64 years of age; 43% African American, 57% White American) to IPT, pharmacotherapy (nortriptyline), or the primary care physician's usual care for the treatment of major depression in four academically affiliated primary care centers in Pittsburgh, Pennsylvania. IPT was administered weekly, for 16 weeks, by a clinical psychologist. Overall, individuals who received IPT and pharmacotherapy experienced a more rapid decrease in depressive symptoms than those who were randomized to usual care. At 8 months, 70% of the individuals who received IPT or treatment with medication had recovered, compared with only 20% of the usual care patients. Additionally, when participants were severely depressed, IPT and treatment with nortriptyline were similarly effective in reducing depressive symptoms. This study provides compelling evidence for the use of IPT as a first-line treatment in the care of patients with major depression in primary care settings.

In contrast, the findings of Browne et al. (2002) do not support the use of IPT as an independent treatment for dysthymia in primary care. This study examined the effectiveness of IPT alone and in combination with the medication sertraline for the treatment of dysthymia in a university-affiliated primary care center in Ontario, Canada. Adults 18 to 74 years of age ($N = 707$; race/ethnicity of sample not reported) were randomized to receive either IPT alone, sertraline alone, or sertraline plus IPT and then were followed for an additional 18 months after the initial 6 months of acute treatment. In this study, 15 master's level therapists with 10 to 20 years of counseling experience, who received 2 weeks of IPT training, delivered IPT. Participants were offered 12 one-hour sessions that were scheduled flexibly over that time frame, with individuals completing 10 sessions on average. After 6 months of treatment with IPT alone, sertraline alone, or combination treatment, patients who received either sertraline alone or sertraline plus IPT had significantly greater symptom reduction than those who received IPT alone. The difference in treatment effectiveness was maintained at 2-year follow-up.

As previously noted, ethnocultural groups are more likely to receive mental health care from their primary care physician (Alvidrez, 1999) and less likely to accept referral to mental health specialists (Miranda et al., 2003). Most studies demonstrate lower rates of treatment for depression in younger and older African Americans than in White Americans (Richardson, Anderson, Flaherty, & Bell, 2003; Snowden, 2001). Even when these patients are recognized and treated, they are more likely to drop out of mental health treatment prematurely (Areán, Alvidrez, Nery, Estes, & Linkins, 2003). Although the studies described above provide some evidence that IPT is an effective treatment in primary care, either alone and/or in combination with antidepressant medication, there is an absence of information regarding the impact of racial or ethnic differences on clinical outcomes.

In a post hoc analysis of the initial study by Schulberg et al. (1996), Brown, Schulberg, Sacco, Perel, and Houck (1999) examined whether there were racial differences in clinical outcomes and treatment retention in participants treated for major depression. This study observed that African American and White American participants reported similar symptom reduction when treated with either psychotherapy (IPT) or pharmacotherapy. However, African Americans had poorer functional outcomes than White Americans.

Overall, there were no significant racial differences in retention in Brown et al.'s (1999) full acute and continuation phase treatment protocol. However, racial differences in retention were evident in different phases of depression treatment. Thus, although there were no significant differences in the proportions of White Americans and African Americans who completed the acute phase of pharmacotherapy (61% vs. 45%, respectively) or psychotherapy (54% vs. 41%, respectively), there was a statistically significant difference by race in completion of the continuation phase of both the pharmacotherapy (35% of African Americans vs. 71% of White Americans) and psychotherapy (100% of African Americans vs. 76% of White Americans) arms. This finding is contrary to prior work, which documents lower retention rates in psychotherapy among African Americans and suggests that IPT may be acceptable to minority patients.

Brown et al. (1999) acknowledged that the available data did not permit examination of whether cultural context might have influenced the impact of IPT on functional outcomes or overall treatment participation. Unfortunately, to date, this is the only published report of the effectiveness of IPT that evaluates racial differences in clinical outcomes. We found no published studies of IPT with depressed primary care patients of other racial/ ethnic backgrounds.

IPT WITH OLDER ADULTS

Older adults of all races have higher rates of medical comorbidity and are also more likely to be diagnosed and treated for depression in the primary care sector. Therefore, there has been increasing focus on addressing the depression treatment needs of this population with IPT. Consistent with some of the findings for younger adults, several studies attest to the effectiveness of IPT in the treatment of depression in older adults. Among the latter, the most common problem areas are grief and role transitions; therefore, the goal of IPT with older adults is to begin to overcome these conflict areas through active dialogue with a trained clinician.

The majority of well-designed studies examining the efficacy and effectiveness of IPT among older adults have been randomized controlled trials comparing IPT plus placebo with antidepressants (nortriptyline and paroxetine). Although the majority of these studies support the use of IPT in acute and continuation phase treatment of major depression and find IPT to be generally efficacious as compared with pharmacologic treatments, results are not consistent. Overall, findings indicate that IPT is most effective in treating geriatric depression when combined with antidepressant medication, particularly when the patient presents with a chronic and recurrent course of depression (Reynolds et al., 1999).

IPT Is as Effective as Antidepressants

The Prevention of Suicide in Primary Care Elderly: Collaborative Trial (PROSPECT; Bruce et al., 2004) used a collaborative care approach to treatment and found that individuals who received either medication alone or IPT experienced a greater decrease in depression severity and were more likely to have a remission at 4 months than the usual care group. Joo, Morales, De Vries, and Gallo (2010) reported on racial differences in treatment attendance between African Americans and White Americans. African Americans and White Americans with major depression had similar psychotherapy attendance rates. However, African Americans with minor depression attended fewer sessions than Whites with this disorder. They concluded that reducing barriers to psychotherapy by colocating services in primary care offices was only partially effective.

Sloane, Staples, and Schneider (1985) examined IPT compared with nortriptyline and pill placebo in a sample of 24 older adults with depression. This study found that IPT was as effective as nortriptyline in reducing symptoms of depression. These results suggest that IPT is as effective as antidepressants in treating geriatric depression and, therefore, should be considered a first-line treatment.

IPT Plus Antidepressant Is Effective in Preventing Relapse, Treating Grief-Related Depression, and Treating Partial Responders to Antidepressant Medication

In the Maintenance Therapy in Late-Life Depression (MTLD) study (Reynolds et al., 1999), researchers used a randomized controlled trial design with 187 older adults (58+ years of age; 91% White American) and examined longer term outcomes of IPT and medication. During acute phase treatment, participants were treated with IPT and an antidepressant. When patients had achieved remission, researchers then tested the efficacy of IPT plus placebo compared with IPT plus nortriptyline or nortriptyline alone in the maintenance phase of therapy. Results indicated that among geriatric patients with recurrent depression, the combined treatment of IPT plus nortriptyline was more effective in preventing relapse than IPT plus placebo or nortriptyline alone. Reynolds et al. (2010) also found that IPT and depression care management had comparable effectiveness in treating depression to remission in older adults who had previously had a partial response to an antidepressant. In a study of grief-related major depression, Reynolds et al. (1999) examined acute treatment of late life depression. With a sample of 80 older adults, they found that the combination of IPT plus nortriptyline was associated with a significantly higher rate of remission when compared with nortriptyline alone, pill placebo alone, or pill placebo with IPT. These studies suggest that when considering relapse prevention and grief-related depression, the combination treatment of IPT with an antidepressant is the most efficacious treatment strategy.

IPT Is Less Effective With Severely Ill Older Adults

Using data from the MTLD study (Reynolds et al., 1999), Taylor et al. (1999) found that severely depressed older adults were more likely to relapse when they received IPT alone. This research suggests that older adults with lower levels of depressive symptoms at baseline can remain well with monthly maintenance IPT alone and that the maintenance efficacy of IPT alone is greatest for patients who show a full recovery through the acute and continuation phases of combined treatment (IPT and an antidepressant).

Dombrovski et al. (2007) evaluated the effectiveness of maintenance treatments for late life depression in patients who had demonstrated a clinical response to an open trial of paroxetine and IPT. With a sample of 116 older adults (70+ years of age; 93% White American), they found that pharmacotherapy was superior to placebo in preserving overall well-being, social functioning, and role limitations due to emotional problems. However, IPT did not preserve health-related quality of life better than clinical management. Dombrovski et al. have suggested that these results may have been due to the more significant medical illness found in this sample compared with other study samples of older adults with depression. Thus, IPT may be more effective in treating depression in older adults with less severe physical illness, cognitive impairment, and disability.

Limitations of the Research on IPT With Older Adults

Although the majority of these studies suggest that IPT is an efficacious treatment for depression, the absence of racial and ethnic minority patients in this research is extremely concerning. The generalizability of research findings examining the efficacy of IPT is significantly limited because it has been evaluated in primarily healthy, ambulatory, White American patients with major depressive disorder (Areán & Cook, 2002). Although there are no data to suggest IPT would be ineffective for racial minority older adults, and research conducted with younger African Americans has shown IPT to be effective at engaging and retaining African Americans and Latinos in treatment and significantly reducing their depressive symptoms (Grote, Zuckoff, Swartz, Bledsoe, & Geibel, 2007), additional research examining the effectiveness and of IPT with racial/ethnic minority older adults is necessary.

Also, several studies in older adults evaluated the effectiveness of IPT plus placebo when compared with antidepressants. It is important to note that IPT plus placebo cannot be considered equivalent to IPT alone (Areán & Cook, 2002). Clients taking a placebo in addition to receiving IPT may have different outcomes from those not taking the placebo because of different expectations about recovery. Therefore, the long-term effectiveness of IPT as a standalone therapy in the treatment of late life depression is difficult to judge on the basis of the current state of this research (Areán & Cook, 2002).

Modifications to IPT for Older Adults

Modifications to IPT for older adults include IPT for older adults in primary care (IPT-PC) and IPT for older adults with cognitive impairments (IPT-CI). IPT-PC is very similar to traditional IPT but is adapted to better meet the needs of older adults being treated in the primary care setting (Bruce et al., 2004). The primary adaptation of IPT-PC is that it is informed by a psychoeducation orientation where patients are shown an educational video about depression, the rationale behind IPT, and the importance of treatment adherence. A unique feature of IPT-PC is that it was adapted to be delivered by telephone, thereby making the intervention more accessible to more frail older adults. IPT-PC is a newly adapted intervention for older primary care patients, and its efficacy is not yet well-established; however, IPT-PC may be a promising intervention for older adults who have difficulty traveling to appointments or who are homebound because of physical disability (Bruce et al., 2004).

IPT-CI was adapted to better meet the needs of older adults who are cognitively impaired in addition to being depressed (M. D. Miller & Reynolds, 2007). The main adaptations of IPT-CI include two components: (a) an active therapist and (b) the integration of a family caregiver into the therapeutic process. M. D. Miller and Reynolds (2007) stated that often older adults with cognitive impairment have difficulty remembering things discussed in the therapy session. They suggested that older adults with cognitive impairment are better able to stay connected in the therapeutic process if the clinician provides more directives and actively jogs the client's memory instead of waiting for the client to bring up important issues.

M. D. Miller and Reynolds (2007) also suggested that including family caregivers into the therapeutic process is critical to the success of IPT with older adults with cognitive impairment. The addition of family caregivers into IPT is compatible with the IPT model because while the client is going through role transitions from a greater to a less functional state, family members are often going through role transitions of their own (e.g., from family member to caregiver), and they may benefit from the therapy sessions themselves. Clinicians, however, must use clinical judgment when deciding how to integrate a caregiver into the therapeutic process. It is often most beneficial to bring them into treatment from the beginning. However, in some cases, meeting with the client and his or her caregiver simultaneously may not be in the client's best interest. In such cases, the clinician should work with the caregiver in his or her own individual sessions or by phone.

In addition to focusing on helping clients move past former roles, IPT-CI emphasizes helping clients to focus on areas of function that remain intact and to accept the necessary dependency on others (M. D. Miller & Reynolds, 2007). IPT-CI is a relatively new adaptation to IPT and has yet to be formally tested. However, a preliminary case study by M. D. Miller and Reynolds suggests that IPT-CI may be a useful adaptation for the treatment of depression among older adults with cognitive impairment.

Strengths and Weaknesses of IPT for Geriatric Depression

Identified barriers to the use of IPT in treating geriatric depression are predominately practical in nature. The provision of IPT requires a significant time commitment by the client and necessitates the availability of an IPT-trained clinician (M. D. Miller & Reynolds, 2007). Stigma, financial restraints, transportation to weekly sessions, and insurance restrictions may also become barriers to treatment; however, these are often barriers to any psychological intervention and need to be addressed. One way to alleviate the burden of transportation and stigma is the integration of mental health treatment and primary care. In the PROSPECT study, clinicians delivered IPT to their clients in the primary care setting (Bruce et al., 2004). This collaborative care model, however, was unable to continue after the project's funding ended. Therefore, research studies that address the feasibility and sustainability of providing IPT to older adults are needed.

Despite these limitations, using IPT to treat depression in late life has a number of strengths. One of the primary strengths is the ability to effectively treat geriatric depression without the use of antidepressants. Research suggests that many older adults, particularly African American older adults, prefer counseling over medication. In fact, some African American older adults are vehemently against taking antidepressants (Conner et al., 2010). Also, it is not uncommon for persons with depression to believe that antidepressants are addictive or habit forming (Brown et al., 2005). Therefore, IPT is an effective intervention that can be offered to older adults who are averse to taking antidepressants.

Research suggests that IPT is an efficacious intervention for late life depression and that its positive effects endure over long periods of time. As a standalone treatment, however, the ability of IPT to effectively treat patients at highest risk remains inconsistent. The benefits of IPT for the treatment of geriatric depression, either alone or in combination with another treatment, cannot be ignored. The time-limited focus of IPT, as well as its emphasis on functional outcomes, makes it an attractive treatment option for this population. In addition, the emphasis of IPT on discourse and the exchange of ideas may be more consistent with the treatment preferences of racial and ethnic minority older adults. Moreover, IPT's focus on role transitions and prolonged grief reactions make it particularly complementary to the life changes and stressors commonly seen in older adults with depression.

SUGGESTED CULTURAL ADAPTATIONS TO IPT FOR AFRICAN AMERICAN PRIMARY CARE PATIENTS

Although hundreds of studies have evaluated the efficacy and effectiveness of IPT for the treatment of depression (Weissman & Markowitz, 1994; Weissman et al., 2000), a limited number have focused on depression in primary care patients. There is a dearth of literature examining the effectiveness of IPT for racial and ethnic minorities. With the exception of the work conducted by Brown et al. (1999), none of the published studies of IPT in depressed primary care patients enrolled sufficient number of racial/ethnic minority patients to address this issue. Brown et al.'s (1999) findings are promising regarding IPT's effectiveness in alleviating depressive symptoms. However, although IPT focuses explicitly on role functioning, the fact that African Americans did not achieve improvement in functioning comparable with White Americans is concerning. This possibly suggests that specific cultural adaptations that are responsive to the racial/ethnic minority cultural and psychosocial context are needed if we are to (a) provide this psychotherapy effectively in diverse populations (Bernal, Jimenez-Chafey, & Domenech Rodriguez, 2009) and (b) distinguish between adaptations to evidence-based treatments (EBTs)—such as those made to IPT for treatment of older adults as well as older adults with cognitive impairment—and cultural adaptation procedures. Bernal et al. (2009) defined the latter as the "systematic modification of an EBT or intervention protocol to consider language, culture, and context in such a way that it is compatible with the client's cultural patterns, meanings and values" (p. 362).

The focus of IPT on interpersonal role functioning may be particularly appealing to depressed persons from racial/ethnic groups that have a more collectivist as opposed to individualist orientation (Brown, Abe-Kim, & Barrio, 2003). To learn more about African Americans' beliefs about depression and its treatment, we conducted three focus groups with 41 African American adults (23–70 years of age; 35% male and 65% female) who had experienced at least one episode of depression in the preceding 6 months. Focus groups were audiotaped and transcribed. Through the process of content analysis (Patton, 1990), we used line-by-line coding of the transcripts to identify salient themes and broader categories of themes (i.e., experiences with depression, barriers to seeking treatment, and strategies used to cope with depression).

Findings from these focus groups (Brown et al., 2001) support the importance of social relationships in the help-seeking process. The nature and impact of relationships were the most dominant themes in the focus groups. Participants discussed relationships as causes of depression, their value in helping one to cope with depression, and also how significant others might serve as deterrents to getting appropriate treatment. Trusting therapeutic relationships were also viewed as a key element in effective treatments for depression.

Participants' emphasis on relationships is congruent with cultural collectivism, an important value among contemporary African Americans. For those who hold this value, interdependence and collective responsibility are emphasized, and the individual is encouraged to look beyond his or her personal needs and to consider the needs of the group (Akbar, 1985). Our findings suggest that many participants struggled with ways to incorporate these values in ways that enabled them to maintain important social network ties while also acknowledging that professional help was necessary for effective management of depression. Unfortunately, for many participants, this conflict resulted in not discussing depression with anyone, whereas others were able to develop alliances with people who could be supportive of their efforts to get treatment.

One focus group participant (Brown, Taylor, Lee, Thomas, & Ford, 2001) described her experience as follows:

> My girlfriend, when she found out that I had admitted myself to the hospital, she came down and said, "What are you doing in here? You don't need to be in here . . . you're not crazy!" I was like, "Well, I'm not here because I'm crazy. I'm here because I need help for myself. I want to make myself better." That is one of the things that keeps people from getting help. They are afraid of what somebody else is going to say or think. (p. 10)

Cultural adaptations to IPT for African Americans might therefore focus on the role of perceived stigma associated with depression (Brown et al., 2010; U.S. Department of Health and Human Services, 1999, 2001) and its impact on interpersonal role functioning, particularly with respect to reaching out for professional support. Additionally, engagement in treatment may also be problematic for African Americans. For example, in the recent National Comorbidity Survey Replication (Wang et al., 2005), racial and ethnic minorities and those with low incomes who suffered from psychiatric disorders were more likely to remain untreated than White Americans. Grote and colleagues (Grote, Swartz, & Zuckoff, 2008; Grote et al., 2007) developed an adaptation to a briefer version of IPT (an eight-session version developed by Swartz et al., 2006) for low-income pregnant women, which included adding a pretreatment engagement session. Their pilot work has demonstrated improved treatment engagement in participants who received the pretreatment engagement session (Grote et al., 2007). Several of the adaptations developed by Grote and colleagues might be useful to evaluate in larger trials with depressed African American primary care patients. The briefer version of IPT developed by Swartz et al. (2006) was designed to address practical barriers to care, including time constraints and financial limitations. The treatment is more focused, with the initial phase of treatment limited to two instead of three sessions and focused on current relationships only. Also, only one problem area (instead of one to two) is addressed, and the area of interpersonal deficits is avoided. Brief IPT also uses behavioral activation strategies.

A key feature of Grote et al.'s (2008, 2007) adaptation is the pretreatment engagement session, which focuses on the individual's perceptions of his or her problems and specific obstacles to participating in treatment through the use of techniques derived from ethnographic interviewing (Schensul, Schensul, & LeCompte, 1999) and motivational interviewing (W. R. Miller & Rollnick, 2002). These strategies are particularly relevant for helping the therapist to understand the perspectives, experiences, and values of clients from a different culture and to address practical psychological and cultural barriers and treatment ambivalence.

Our qualitative work supports the importance of this type of pretreatment engagement (Brown et al., 2001). Even when the need for treatment was recognized, focus group participants expressed concerns about therapists' cultural sensitivity and ability to relate to them, as exemplified in the following statement:

> Sometimes the people that we go to for treatment don't know enough about us, our culture, in a reality-based way . . . really have some experience or exposure enough to help us. Because you're really asking people to bare their souls when they come in, whether you're getting medication or in therapy, you're asking people to share some sensitive stuff. . . . (Brown et al., 2001, p. 12)

Grote et al.'s (2007) ethnographic approach acknowledges that there are likely to be cultural differences and encourages the therapist to assume the role of an interested learner who is able to relinquish control and invite the client to be the expert or teacher, regarding his or her perceptions, culture, and experiences.

Another possible focus for cultural adaptation within the area of interpersonal role conflicts involves exploring perceived experiences of discrimination on the basis of race. It is important that therapists recognize that role disputes may involve perceptions of discrimination. Research has demonstrated that African Americans frequently report experiencing discrimination on the basis of race, and this can contribute significantly to psychological distress and physiological stress responses (Paradies, 2006; Pascoe & Smart Richman, 2009). In our focus group discussions, both depressed clients and providers concurred that although experiences of racism and discrimination typically had a significant impact on the psychological well-being of African Americans, mental health services are often not provided in a manner that facilitates discussion of these issues. Providers may lack sufficient awareness of the impact of discrimination and/or not have adequate training and skills to address it. Clinicians can be helpful to clients by actively listening to their experiences of perceived discrimination or racism, thereby providing validation for their emotional reactions to often demoralizing experiences. Like any experience that creates distress, clients benefit from the therapist's assistance in learning to evaluate and adapt their expectations, learning and using problem-focused coping skills, and managing emotional distress.

From this review of IPT in primary care settings, this treatment appears to be promising for African Americans and possibly other racial/ethnic minority groups. However, the research does not strongly demonstrate comparable outcomes for White Americans and racial/ethnic minorities (e.g., attendance, psychosocial functioning). Clinicians using this approach should ensure that they are aware of the barriers that may attenuate engagement and response to treatment when treating racial and ethnic minority clients. Clinicians must take responsibility for providing culturally competent care, which at a minimum should include knowledge of their client's cultural background, practical barriers to treatment, experiences of discrimination, and their capacity for developing effective coping strategies. It is critical that future randomized controlled trials include racial and ethnically diverse participants in sufficient numbers to conduct subanalyses before we can conclude that empirically validated treatments are really effective for these groups. In addition, future work might usefully incorporate cultural adaptations such as the engagement strategies developed by Grote et al. (2008, 2007) and address content such as the impact of stigma and racial discrimination in role conflicts. Continued research in this area may ultimately lead to the provision of additional psychosocial treatment options for depressed African Americans, who are more likely to seek care in the primary care setting.

REFERENCES

Agency for Health Care Policy and Research Depression Guideline Panel. (1993). *Depression in primary care: Vol. 2. Treatment of major depression: Clinical practice guideline, No. 5* (AHCPR Publication No. 93-0551). Washington, DC: Government Printing Office.

Akbar, N. (1985). Our destiny, authors of a scientific revolution. In H. Pipes & J. McAdoo (Eds.), *Black children: Social, educational, and parental environments* (pp. 17–31). Thousand Oaks, CA: Sage.

Alvidrez, J. (1999). Ethnic variations in mental health attitudes and service use among low-income African American, Latina, and European American young women. *Community Mental Health Journal, 35*, 515–530. doi:10.1023/A:1018759201290

Areán, P. A., Alvidrez, J., Nery, R., Estes, C., & Linkins, K. (2003). Recruitment and retention of older minorities in mental health services research. *The Gerontologist, 43*, 36–44. doi:10.1093/geront/43.1.36

Areán, P. A., & Cook, B. L. (2002). Psychotherapy and combined psychotherapy/pharmacotherapy for later life depression. *Biological Psychiatry, 52*, 293–303. doi:10.1016/S0006-3223(02)01371-9

Bernal, G., Jimenez-Chafey, M., & Domenech Rodriguez, M. (2009). Cultural adaptation of treatments: A resource for considering culture in evidence-based practice. *Professional Psychology: Research and Practice, 40*, 361–368. doi:10.1037/a0016401

Brown, C., Abe-Kim, J., & Barrio, C. (2003). Depression in ethnically diverse women: Implications for treatment in primary care settings. *Professional Psychology: Research and Practice, 34*, 10–19. doi:10.1037/0735-7028.34.1.10

Brown, C., Battista, D., Bruehlman, R., Sereika, S. S., Thase, M. E., & Dunbar-Jacob, J. (2005). Beliefs about antidepressant medication in primary care patients: Relationship to self-reported adherence. *Medical Care, 43*, 1203–1207. doi:10.1097/01.mlr.0000185733.30697.f6

Brown, C., Conner, K. O., Copeland, V. C., Grote, N., Beach, S., Battista, D., & Reynolds, C. F., III. (2010). Depression stigma, race, and treatment seeking behavior and attitudes. *Journal of Community Psychology, 38*, 350–368. doi:10.1002/jcop.20368

Brown, C., Schulberg, H. C., Sacco, D., Perel, J. M., & Houck, P. R. (1999). Effectiveness of treatments for major depression in primary medical care practice: A post hoc analysis of outcomes for African American and White patients. *Journal of Affective Disorders, 53*, 185–192. doi:10.1016/S0165-0327(98)00120-7

Brown, C., Taylor, J., Lee, B. E., Thomas, S. B., & Ford, A. (2001). *Managing depression in African Americans: Consumer and provider perspectives.* Pittsburgh, PA: Mental Health Association of Allegheny County.

Browne, G., Steiner, M., Roberts, J., Gafni, A., Byrne, C., Dunn, E., . . . Kraemer, J. (2002). Sertraline and/or interpersonal psychotherapy for patients with dysthymic disorder in primary care: 6-month comparison with longitudinal 2-year follow-up of effectiveness and costs. *Journal of Affective Disorders, 68*, 317–330. doi:10.1016/S0165-0327(01)00343-3

Bruce, M. L., Ten Have, T. R., Reynolds, C. F., III, Katz, I. I., Schulberg, H. C., Mulsant, B. H., . . . Alexopoulos, G. S. (2004). Reducing suicidal ideation and depressive symptoms in depressed older primary care patients: A randomized controlled trial. *JAMA, 291*, 1081–1091. doi:10.1001/jama.291.9.1081

Conner, K. O., Lee, B., Mayers, V., Robinson, D., Reynolds, C. F., III, Albert, S., & Brown C. (2010). Attitudes and beliefs about mental health among African American older adults suffering from depression. *Journal of Aging Studies, 24*, 266–277. doi:10.1016/j.jaging.2010.05.007

Cuijpers, P., Geraedts, A. S., van Oppen, P., Andersson, G., Markowitz, J. C., & van Straten, A. (2011). Interpersonal psychotherapy for depression: A meta-analysis. *The American Journal of Psychiatry, 168*, 581–592. doi:10.1176/appi.ajp.2010.10101411

Dombrovski, A. Y., Lenze, E. J., Dew, M. A., Mulsant, B. H., Pollock, B. G., Houck, P. R., & Reynolds, C. F., III. (2007). Maintenance treatment for old-age depression preserves health-related quality of life: A randomized, controlled trial of paroxetine and interpersonal psychotherapy. *Journal of the American Geriatrics Society, 55*, 1325–1332. doi:10.1111/j.1532-5415.2007.01292.x

Grote, N. K., Swartz, H. A., & Zuckoff, A. (2008). Enhancing interpersonal psychotherapy for mothers and expectant mothers on low incomes: Adaptations and additions. *Journal of Contemporary Psychotherapy, 38*, 23–33. doi:10.1007/s10879-007-9065-x

Grote, N. K., Zuckoff, A., Swartz, H. A., Bledsoe, S. E., & Geibel, S. (2007). Engaging women who are depressed and economically disadvantaged in mental health treatment. *Social Work, 52*, 295–308. doi:10.1093/sw/52.4.295

Joo, J. H., Morales, K. H., De Vries, H. F., & Gallo, J. J. (2010). Disparity in use of psychotherapy offered in primary care between older African American and White adults: Results from a practice-based depression intervention trial. *Journal of the American Geriatrics Society, 58*, 154–160. doi:10.1111/j.1532-5415.2009.02623.x

Katon, W., & Schulberg, H. (1992). Epidemiology of depression in primary care. *General Hospital Psychiatry, 14*, 237–247. doi:10.1016/0163-8343(92)90094-Q

Klerman, G., Weissman, M., Rounsaville, B., & Chevron, E. (1984). *Interpersonal psychotherapy of depression.* New York, NY: Basic Books.

Miller, M. D., & Reynolds, C. F., III. (2007). Expanding the usefulness of interpersonal psychotherapy (IPT) for depressed elders with co-morbid cognitive impairment. *International Journal of Geriatric Psychiatry, 22*, 101–105. doi:10.1002/gps.1699

Miller, W. R., & Rollnick, S. (2002). *Motivational interviewing: Preparing people for change.* New York, NY: Guilford Press.

Miranda, J., Chung, J. Y., Green, B. L., Krupnick, J., Siddique, J., Revicki, D. A., & Belin, T. (2003). Treating depression in predominantly low-income young minority women: A randomized controlled trial. *JAMA, 290*, 57–65. doi:10.1001/jama.290.1.57

Paradies, Y. (2006). A systematic review of empirical research on self-reported racism and health. *International Journal of Epidemiology, 35*, 888–901. doi:10.1093/ije/dyl056

Pascoe, E. A., & Smart Richman, L. (2009). Perceived discrimination and health: A meta-analytic review. *Psychological Bulletin, 135*, 531–554. doi:10.1037/a0016059

Patton, M. (1990). *Qualitative research and evaluation methods.* Beverly Hills, CA: Sage.

Reynolds, C. F., III, Dew, M. A., Martire, L. M., Miller, M. D., Cyranowski, J. M., Lenze, E., . . . Frank, E. (2010). Treating depression to remission in older adults: A controlled evaluation of combined escitalopram with interpersonal psychotherapy versus escitalopram with depression care management. *International Journal of Geriatric Psychiatry, 25,* 1134–1141. doi:10.1002/gps.2443

Reynolds, C. F., III, Miller, M. D., Pasternak, R. E., Frank, E., Perel, J. M., Cornes, C., . . . Kupfer, D. J. (1999). Treatment of bereavement-related major depressive episodes in later life: A controlled study of acute and continuation treatment with nortriptyline and interpersonal psychotherapy. *The American Journal of Psychiatry, 156,* 202–208.

Richardson, J., Anderson, T., Flaherty, J., & Bell, C. (2003). The quality of mental health care for African Americans. *Culture, Medicine, and Psychiatry, 27,* 487–498. doi:10.1023/B:MEDI.0000005485.06068.43

Schensul, S. L., Schensul, J. J., & LeCompte, M. D. (1999). *Essential ethnographic methods: Observations, interviews, and questionnaires (Ethnographer's Toolkit 2).* Walnut Creek, CA: Alta Mira Press.

Schulberg, H. C., Block, M. R., Madonia, M. J., Scott, C. P., Rodriguez, E., Imber, S. D., . . . Coulehan, J. L. (1996). Treating major depression in primary care: Eight-month clinical outcomes. *Archives of General Psychiatry, 53,* 913–919. doi:10.1001/archpsyc.1996.01830100061008

Sloane, R., Staples, F., & Schneider, L. (1985). Interpersonal therapy versus nortriptyline for depression in the elderly. In G. Burrows, T. Norman, & L. Dennerstein (Eds.), *Clinical and pharmacological studies in psychiatric disorders* (pp. 344–346). London, England: John Libbey.

Snowden, L. R. (2001). Barriers to effective mental health services for African Americans. *Mental Health Services Research, 3,* 181–187. doi:10.1023/A:1013172913880

Stafford, R. S., Ausiello, J. C., Misra, B., & Saglam, D. (2000). National patterns of depression treatment in primary care. *Primary Care Companion to the Journal of Clinical Psychiatry, 2,* 211–216. doi:10.4088/PCC.v02n0603

Swartz, H. A., Zuckoff, A., Frank, E., Spielvogle, H. N., Shear, M. K., Fleming, D., & Scott, J. (2006). An open-label trial of enhanced brief interpersonal psychotherapy in depressed mothers whose children are receiving psychiatric treatment. *Depression and Anxiety, 23,* 398–404. doi:10.1002/da.20212

Taylor, M. P., Reynolds, C. F., III, Frank, E., Cornes, C., Miller, M. D., Stack, J. A., . . . Kupfer, D. J. (1999). Which elderly depressed patients remain well on maintenance interpersonal psychotherapy alone? Report from the Pittsburgh Study of Maintenance Therapies in Late-Life Depression. *Depression and Anxiety, 10,* 55–60. doi:10.1002/(SICI)1520-6394(1999)10:2<55::AID-DA3>3.0.CO;2-F

U.S. Department of Health and Human Services. (1999). *Mental health: A report of the Surgeon General.* Retrieved from http://www.surgeongeneral.gov/library/mentalhealth/pdfs/front.pdf/

U.S. Department of Health and Human Services. (2001). Mental health: Culture, race, and ethnicity. A supplement to Mental Health: A Report of the Surgeon General. Retrieved from http://www.surgeongeneral.gov/library/mentalhealth/cre/sma-01-3613.pdf

Wang, P. S., Lane, M., Olfson, M., Pincus, H. A., Wells, K. B., & Kessler, R. C. (2005). Twelve-month use of mental health services in the United States: Results from the National Comorbidity Survey Replication. *Archives of General Psychiatry, 62*, 629–640. doi:10.1001/archpsyc.62.6.629

Weissman, M. M., & Markowitz, J. C. (1994). Interpersonal psychotherapy: Current status. *Archives of General Psychiatry, 51*, 599–606. doi:10.1001/archpsyc. 1994.03950080011002

Weissman, M. M., Markowitz, J. C., & Klerman, G. (2000). *Comprehensive guide to interpersonal psychotherapy*. New York, NY: Basic Books.

Weissman, M. M., Prusoff, B. A., DiMascio, A., Neu, C., Goklaney, M., & Klerman, G. L. (1979). The efficacy of drugs and psychotherapy in the treatment of acute depressive episodes. *American Journal of Psychiatry, 136*, 555–558

Wolf, N. J., & Hopko, D. R. (2008). Psychosocial and pharmacological interventions for depressed adults in primary care: A critical review. *Clinical Psychology Review, 28*, 131–161. doi:10.1016/j.cpr.2007.04.004

12

EVIDENCE-BASED TREATMENT IN PRACTICE-BASED CULTURAL ADAPTATIONS

ANÉ M. MARÍÑEZ-LORA AND MARC S. ATKINS

Much about how clinicians use and interpret evidence-based treatments (EBTs) in their clinical practice is unknown. The scarce research in this area suggests that clinicians adapt psychosocial interventions to meet the needs of the populations they serve (e.g., Hill, Maucione, & Hood, 2007). This chapter introduces a systematic adaptation model developed to examine and support clinicians' cultural adaptations using the current research literature on Latino immigrants. The systematic model presented was developed as a guide for using the empirical literature available to make adaptations on EBTs that reflect the cultural values, norms, and experiences of Latinos in the United States. The chapter begins with a brief overview of EBTs and cultural adaptation of EBTs, in particular, behavioral parent training (BPT), and continues with a brief description of our recent work with the application of BPT programs in community-based mental health agencies.

The ideas presented in this chapter were developed in part while both authors were supported on a Substance Abuse and Mental Health Services Administration grant (SM54483-01-1) and while the first author was supported on a National Institute of Mental Health career development grant (K23MH083049).

EVIDENCE-BASED TREATMENTS

The historic Surgeon General's report on mental health highlighted an increasing number of efficacious treatments for most mental health disorders and underscored the disconnect between research and clinical practice (U.S. Department of Health and Human Services [USDHHS], 1999). Another seminal report called attention to the importance of culture and context and the underrepresentation of ethnic–racial minorities in the mental health research providing the evidence base for these treatments (USDHHS, 2001). The underrepresentation of minorities in clinical trials underlines the disconnect between research and practice and has resulted in a debate about whether EBTs are effective or generalize to ethnic–racial minorities (e.g., Bernal & Scharrón-del-Río, 2001; Hall, 2001; Lau, 2006; Miranda, Nakamura, & Bernal, 2003; Quintana & Atkinson, 2002). This debate on the appropriateness of employing EBTs with ethnocultural youths is part of the larger debate about how to narrow the efficacy–effectiveness gap (e.g., outcomes in controlled trials vs. outcomes in typical practice settings). Community-based service providers are underrepresented in these clinical trials (Weisz, Sandler, Durlak, & Anton, 2005), and the dissemination and implementation of evidence-based practices in routine mental health care settings has been slow and challenging (Corrigan, McCraken, & Blaser, 2003; USDHHS, 1999).

CULTURAL ADAPTATION OF EVIDENCE-BASED TREATMENTS

The debate about whether EBTs are effective and whether they generalize to ethnocultural populations has generated concern about the cultural sensitivity of EBTs. In turn, concerns about the cultural sensitivity of EBTs have resulted in efforts to adapt them for different ethnocultural groups to improve treatment engagement and outcomes (e.g., Bernal, 2006; Bernal & Scharrón-del-Río, 2001; Lau, 2006). In this chapter, *adaptation* refers to the "systematic modification of an EBT or intervention protocol to consider language, culture, and context in such a way that it is compatible with the client's cultural patterns, meanings and values" (Bernal, Jiménez-Chafey, & Domenech Rodríguez, 2009, p. 361).

Adaptations of EBTs, although perceived as helping to bridge if not narrow the efficacy–effectiveness gap, are also perceived as compromising the fidelity and effectiveness of rigorously studied interventions (Castro, Barrera, & Martinez, 2004). Critics of cultural adaptation of EBTs advise caution and underscore that the evidence linking fidelity to outcomes is stronger than that linking adaptation to outcomes (Elliott & Mihalic, 2004). Although no known studies have examined fidelity in culturally adapted treatments, recent meta-analyses have provided support for cultural adaptations (Benish, Quintana, & Wampold, 2011; Smith, Domenech Rodríguez, & Bernal, 2011).

EVIDENCE-BASED BEHAVIORAL PARENT TRAINING

The use of the parent behavioral or management training model to address externalizing behavior difficulties in children and adolescents is supported by substantial empirical evidence (e.g., Eyberg, Nelson, & Boggs, 2008; Kaminski, Valle, Filene, & Boyle, 2008; Kazdin, 1997; Maughan, Christiansen, Jenson, Olympia, & Clark, 2005; Taylor & Biglan, 1998; Webster-Stratton, Reid, & Hammond, 2004). BPT has been found to be successful in addressing a wide variety of child behaviors ranging from conduct, oppositional, and attentional problems to health-related behaviors such as enuresis and encopresis (Graziano & Diament, 1992; Maughan et al., 2005). BPT interventions have also been found to reduce children's problem behaviors and negative parent–child interactions, increase parental competence (Webster-Stratton, 1998), improve marital functioning (Ireland, Sanders, & Markie-Dadds, 2003), and reduce parental stress (Pisterman et al., 1992). Moreover, BPT interventions have been found to have long-term effects (Long, Forehand, Wierson, & Morgan, 1994) and to be more cost-effective than individual child therapy (Bourke & Nielsen, 1995; Wright, Stroud, & Kennan 1993). Consequently, it is not surprising that parent management training is widely used and that there is an array of empirically validated BPT programs currently available (e.g., Boggs et al., 2004: parent–child interaction therapy; Forgatch & DeGarmo, 1999: The Oregon Social Learning Center's Parenting Through Change Program; McMahon & Forehand, 2003: Helping the Noncompliant Child; Sanders, Markie-Dadds, Tully, & Bor, 2000: The Triple P-Positive Parenting Program; Webster-Stratton et al., 2004: The Incredible Years).

Common across BPT interventions is the use of a social learning theory framework, applied behavior modification, and a triadic indirect-service model as well as a focus on behavioral changes both in parents and in children, although the child is most often the identified client (Graziano & Diament, 1992; Maughan et al., 2005; Medway, 1989). A primary assumption of BPT is that parents are active change agents and that clinicians indirectly treat children by training their parents to use behavioral modification strategies (Graziano & Diament, 1992). Hence, a BPT intervention acts as a moderating variable and creates targeted changes in parents that result in the desired targeted changes in the child (Graziano & Diament, 1992; Maughan et al., 2005). Typically, a therapist delivers the BPT intervention individually or in a group format (e.g., Gross, Fogg, et al., 2003; McMahon & Forehand, 2003), using a variety of methods or instructional tools, such as handouts, live modeling by clinician accompanied by rehearsals, self-administered videotaped modeling or videotaped modeling combined with clinician consultation, and self-administered interactive CD-ROM programs (Kacir & Gordon, 1999; McMahon & Forehand, 2003; O'Dell et al., 1982; Webster-Stratton, 1990). Progress with BPT interventions is typically documented via observations of parent–child interactions and/or parent reports.

A recent meta-analysis identified the components of parent training programs associated with successful outcomes in children ages 0 through 7 (Kaminski et al., 2008). Increasing positive parent–child interactions, improving emotional communication skills, teaching time out, emphasizing the importance of parental consistency, and requiring parents to practice new parenting strategies during the clinical session were associated with larger effect sizes (Kaminski et al., 2008). Teaching parents problem-solving skills; teaching them how to promote children's cognitive, academic, or social skills; and including additional services (e.g., stress management, anger management) were associated with lower effect sizes (Kaminski et al., 2008).

BPT With Diverse Populations

Although the internal validity of BPT interventions has been substantially supported, their external validity has not, in particular with ethnocultural groups (Forehand & Kotchick, 1996). For example, the research on the effectiveness of BPT with Latino immigrant parents is very limited (Dumka, López, & Jacobs Carter, 2002). However, the limited empirical evidence supporting the utility of EBTs with ethnocultural groups (Miranda et al., 2005) combined with available research suggests that there are more similarities than differences in parenting practices across different cultural groups (Fox & Solís-Cámara, 1997; Julian, McKenry, & McKelvey, 1994; Solís-Cámara & Fox, 1995).

Research conducted on diverse ethnocultural groups within the United States suggests culture-general or universal parenting attitudes, behaviors, and involvement practices, particularly with young children (e.g., Fox & Solís-Cámara, 1997; García Coll, 1990; Julian et al., 1994; Solís-Cámara & Fox, 1995). Moreover, BPT interventions have more empirical support in their use with diverse ethnocultural groups than other EBTs do. For example, parent–child interaction therapy (PCIT) was found to reduce physically abusive parent behavior (Chaffin et al., 2004), and the Incredible Years program was found to reduce children's behavioral difficulties in White American, Latino, African American, and Asian American participants (Reid, Webster-Stratton, & Beauchaine, 2001). By contrast, empirical support for differences in BPT outcomes across ethnocultural groups has also been documented. For example, Caughy, Miller, Genevro, Huang, and Nautiyal (2003) found that outcomes from the Healthy Steps program in the area of inductive/authoritative discipline suggested that the program was beneficial for White American parents but had negative effects for Latino and African American parents; Latino and African American parents' inductive/authoritative discipline scores were lower than those obtained by their corresponding control groups. In the Fast Track intervention, ethnocultural children made less improvement in teacher-rated aggressive oppositional behavior than White American children did (Conduct Problems Prevention Research Group, 2002). Gross, Fogg, et al. (2003) also found that the Incredible Years program reduced problematic parenting behavior and attitudes—as it had with a sample composed of predominantly White American families (Webster-Stratton, 1998) and a sample composed of parents in five ethnic–racial categories, of which White Americans were the largest group (Webster-Stratton, Reid, & Hammond, 2001). Unlike in these studies, it did not reduce children's behavioral difficulties at postintervention or 1-year follow-up in a sample of predominantly low-income, urban African American and Latino parents. Hence, although there is empirical support for the efficacy of standard BPT with ethnocultural parents, there is also evidence suggesting culture-specific experiences, parenting practices, and responses to treatment.

Evidence of Culture-Specific Parenting Practices in Latinos

Research has highlighted evidence of culture-specific parenting practices in Latinos that may influence their response to BPT programs. Latino parents have been found to endorse different beliefs, developmental goals, and attitudes, suggesting different parenting patterns from those of White Americans (e.g., Domenech Rodríguez, Donovick, & Crowley, 2009; García Coll, 1990; Julian et al., 1994). For example, there is evidence that Latino parents emphasize children exercising self-control more than White American parents do (Julian et al., 1994) and that Latino parents differ from White American parents in their understanding of child development and their beliefs about their children's developmental timetables (e.g., the age at which children can start to plan and participate in different activities; Savage & Gauvain, 1998). Mexican American parents use the teaching strategies of modeling, visual cues, directives, and negative physical control more than White American mothers do (Zayas & Solari, 1994). When compared with Asian American and White American parents, Latino parents have been found to emphasize obedience ("doing what he or she was asked"), self-control, and getting along with others more, and to report praising their children less (Julian et al., 1994). Latino parents have also been found to endorse monitoring their children's behavior and encouraging conformity in their children more than White American and Asian American parents do (Okagaki & Frensch, 1998).

The available research also highlights notable parenting differences between Latino subgroups. For example, Dominican American mothers and mainland Puerto Rican mothers have been found to differ in their endorsement of authoritative parenting, even after controlling for demographic variables such as acculturation, marital status, and parental educational level (Calzada & Eyberg, 2002). Immigrant Mexican parents and first-generation Mexican Americans differ in the teaching strategies they use with their children (Delgado-Gaitan, 1994). More acculturated Latino mothers are more similar to White American parents than to less acculturated Latino mothers in their beliefs about children's developmental timetables (Savage & Gauvain, 1998). Highly acculturated Mexican American mothers of higher socioeconomic status used greater complexity in their parental reasoning with their children than less acculturated Mexican American mothers of equal socioeconomic status did (Gutierrez, Sameroff, & Karrer, 1988). These examples support the conclusion that parenting is a culturally influenced configuration of behaviors, beliefs, attitudes, and goals.

INTRODUCING EVIDENCE-BASED TREATMENTS TO COMMUNITY-BASED PRACTICE

Underlying the increasing emphasis on developing, testing, and using EBTs is a commitment to the provision of high-quality effective services to those in need (e.g., Patel, Butler, & Wells, 2006; USDHHS, 1999). However, EBTs are typically developed to adhere to highly specified research guidelines that do not consider the context of service delivery (Hoagwood, Burns, Kiser, Ringeisen, & Schoenwald, 2001). In the past 20 years, although much knowledge has been gained about treatments that work under highly controlled situations, little knowledge has been gained about how the context of service delivery and culture influence the efficacy of EBTs, and this has resulted in a research-to-practice gap (Forehand & Kotchick, 1996; Hoagwood et al., 2001; Ringeisen, Henderson, & Hoagwood, 2003). Next, we describe two efforts to narrow the research-to-practice gap and bring evidence-based practices to community settings. In the past 4 years we have collaborated with the Illinois Department of Mental Health (DMH) in two programs to bring evidence-based practices to community settings, with the second author as consultant and the first author as co-consultant and/or clinical supervisor to participating community-based agencies.

Program 1

Our first experience as evidence-based practices consultants was to a collaborative effort between the Illinois DMH and the Chicago Public Schools on a systems of care grant, funded by the Substance Abuse and Mental Health Services Administration (SAMHSA), examining a model of mental health consultation to urban schools. Part of our work was to identify and provide a series of trainings on EBTs and practices to a small clinical team—typically composed of two mental health providers (MHPs) and one or two parent outreach workers—from each of the eight community-based social service agencies participating in the project. The MHPs were typically master's level clinicians, and the parent outreach workers were required to have at minimum a high school diploma or the equivalent.

Following an assessment of the needs of the clinical teams, training was provided in several evidence-based intervention strategies and programs, including a video-based BPT program delivered using a group format (Gross, Julion, & Garvey, 2003). The behavioral management strategies included in the curriculum of the program used included special time focused on child, effective commands, planned ignoring, logical consequences, positive and negative reinforcement, and time out (Gross, Julion, & Garvey, 2003: The Chicago Parent Program). Training of the clinical teams on the BPT program was conducted by one of the developers of the program and the first author. Two of the eight clinical teams—one working primarily with African Americans and one working primarily with Latino immigrant children and families—attended this training. Both teams identified and prioritized parent training as an area of need in the community they served.

The training on the BPT program was provided in four interdependent steps. First, the clinical teams received didactic information on the strategies covered in the program to improve the quality of parent–child interactions and help parents modify their children's behavior, guidance and modeling on how to use the manual and the video vignettes to teach the core behavioral management strategies, and several question-and-answer sessions addressing clinical teams' concerns about the program's responsiveness to the low-income African American and Latino immigrant families they served. These concerns ranged from addressing scheduling challenges and providing child care for parents during group sessions to supporting parents in their consistent use of the strategies they learn. Second, the first author and the clinical team serving Latinos immigrants of Mexican background worked closely to translate the parenting terms and key concepts for the group discussion and the parent handouts of the parent program for conceptual and semantic equivalence (Bravo, Woodbury-Farina, Canino, & Rubio-Stipec, 1993).

The third step involved field-testing the adapted intervention for Latino families. The first author and the lead team MHP co-led the 12-session group predominantly in Spanish, with the other members of the clinical team (one clinician and two parent outreach workers) helping parents understand the English-language video vignettes when needed. The fourth step involved discussions after each group session between the first author and the lead MHP regarding their perception of the reception of the program by parents, challenges encountered in covering the information targeted for a particular session, and ideas for different strategies to increase parent engagement and buy-in of the usefulness of the strategies and to clarify the different concepts and strategies for parents. In addition to running the group and providing materials in parents' preferred language (Spanish), the first author and the lead MHP identified culturally congruous and contextually sensitive strategies to supplement the program in response to what appeared to be a need for adaptation based on parents' contributions to group discussions. Parents' contributions reflected Mexican immigrant children and families' distinctive sociocultural context of risk and resilience. For example, the program's group discussions were supplemented with discussions about (a) parents' immigration-related experiences (e.g., reasons for migrating, the immigration journey, acculturation) and stressors and how these affected family functioning and parent—child interactions and relationships; (b) how the strategies parents were learning could be used to help them recover from the negative impact their immigration experience had on family functioning and parent—child interactions; and (c) parents' discomfort using rewards and allowing the child to take the lead when playing with their children.

Program 2

In 2006 the second author was asked by the Illinois DMH to develop and lead a yearlong BPT program as part of the first statewide effort in Illinois to test the feasibility of bringing evidence-based practices to community-based settings. The project is presently in its 5th year, with three to five agencies participating each year. Agencies apply to be part of the project and agree to release a small clinical team composed of two or three master's level MHPs and their clinical supervisors from some of their responsibilities so that they can participate in the yearlong training on BPT. The first author has been part of this project since its inception as a consultant clinical supervisor to participating agencies.

During the first 4 years of the project the BPT program developed for community-based MHPs included eight full-day workshops that provided didactic information and continued professional development and biweekly supervision, support, and technical assistance. The workshops reviewed specific strategies and principles of BPT (e.g., special time focused on child, effective commands, positive and negative reinforcement, punishment, time out, functional analysis of behavior) and included the application of content through case examples, interactive group discussions, and role play. The supervision sessions provided the MHP teams the opportunity to review individual cases and discuss the barriers and constraints to implementing the BPT strategies. The primary learning objectives of the program were to develop and increase clinicians' (a) understanding of the fundamental principles across different BPT programs, (b) skills in implementing BPT strategies, (c) competence in providing parents the support they need to implement BPT strategies with their children, and (d) skills in identifying barriers to implementation and problem solving with parents to address these barriers.

Two of the MHP teams participating in the Illinois DMH BPT program served an increasing Mexican immigrant population. Services to participating families were delivered at the agency or in clients' homes. The program used a combination of individual sessions with parents and family sessions that included the parents, the targeted child, and other relatives living in the home.

The translation of materials and the delivery of services in parents' preferred language (Spanish) were the first steps in engaging families. The biweekly supervision focused as much on technical assistance on the proper implementation of the strategies as on how to use the collective knowledge and understanding of the consulting clinical supervisor and the members of the MHP teams of Mexican culture and the experiences of Mexican immigrants in the United States. This collective knowledge and understanding of Latino and, in particular, Mexican culture guided and scaffolded how the teams presented and reinterpreted the parenting strategies for parents and how they understood and addressed the barriers to implementation presented by parents. The first author, who served as consulting clinical supervisor for these agencies, used the literature on the Latino immigration experience and available data on Latino parenting values as guides and references for these adaptations. For example, the understanding of the distinctive sociocultural experience of parent–child separation during the migration journey and reunification years later, particularly prevalent in the Mexican immigrant population (Mitrani, Santisteban, & Muir, 2004; Suárez-Orozco, Todorova, & Louie, 2002), was used to engage a mother struggling with the noncompliant behavior of her child and the child's reactions to her behavioral expectations. The treatment goals and the purpose and function of the behavioral strategies were reinterpreted to reflect this mother's cultural values. In addition, the motivational interviewing strategies (Miller & Rollnick, 2002) and the stages of change approach (Prochaska & DiClemente, 1983) used were infused with this cultural knowledge and influenced the clinical teams' work with parents at each phase of treatment (e.g., relationship building, identification of behaviors of concern, understanding purpose and function of target behavior, identification of parenting strategies to address behavior, implementation, evaluation).

Lessons Learned

The two programs described above were developed and implemented to narrow the research-to-practice gap and bring evidence-based practices to community settings. One key component to narrowing this gap appeared to be the consideration and incorporation of knowledge and understanding of the culture of the Latino parents receiving the BPT and the context in which they lived. Translation of the parent training material, such as parent handouts for conceptual and semantic equivalence, was not sufficient to engage parents. That is, parents appeared to struggle to find some of the content reflective of their experiences even when it was presented in their native language. Instead, it appeared that consideration of different dimensions of culture and the experiences of Latinos was critical to (a) engaging MHPs and families, (b) making the behavioral management strategies relevant to them, and (c) understanding the barriers encountered in implementation and maintenance of the strategies. In the next section, we describe the combined model that was influenced by the work described above and developed by the first author to understand MHPs' use, interpretation, and adaptation of EBTs when working with Latino immigrant families.

COMBINED MODEL TO UNDERSTAND CLINICIANS' CULTURAL ADAPTATIONS

Good clinical practice involves tailoring psychosocial interventions to meet the needs of the populations served, which suggests sensitivity to the experiences and concerns of different groups (Miranda et al., 2005). Although the research studying what MHPs do is scarce, a recent qualitative study of facilitators' fidelity to the Strengthening Families Program for Parents and Youth, an empirically supported substance abuse prevention program, found that most reported adapting the program (Hill et al., 2007). Seventy percent of these adaptations were deletions and additions to program content, games, and activities (Hill et al., 2007).

Although little is known about the adaptations clinicians make to EBTs, even less is known about how they make decisions to adapt. The methodical use of data to identify and prioritize the adaptation needs for a given EBT is a critical step in developing a science of cultural adaptation.

Toward that end, Lau's (2006) framework for cultural adaptation and Bernal, Bonilla, and Bellido's (1995) framework for ecological validity were combined to understand and inform the clinical work reported above and better explicate the need for cultural adaptation for Latinos and clinicians' adaptation decisions (Maríñez-Lora, 2007). This combined model was developed as a supervisory tool both to understand and guide clinicians' self-reported adaptations and clinical judgments when implementing a BPT program and to provide clinicians with a structure for making adaptations that were guided by the empirical literature. Below we briefly describe the combined model to evidence-informed clinical work.

Lau's Framework for Cultural Adaptation

Lau's (2006) framework for identifying the need for cultural adaptation and for using research to inform adaptation and strengthen community engagement and contextual relevance provides an evidence-driven, systematic approach to translational research (see Chapter 2, this volume). Two types of research evidence assist in isolating or selecting the target problems: (a) evidence of distinctive sociocultural context of risk and resilience and (b) evidence of threats to the social validity of EBTs. For example, differential outcomes across ethnic groups when an EBT is delivered with fidelity may highlight the need to focus on group-specific risk processes. On one hand, knowledge about sociocultural context and group-specific risk processes can lead to the identification and inclusion of specific culturally informed instrumental goals that set the stage for the original outcome goal of improved functioning. On the other hand, not reaching optimal dosage due to group-specific factors or barriers constraining treatment receptiveness and engagement provides evidence of low social validity. Knowledge of attitudes about seeking mental health treatment, acceptability, and feasibility of the therapeutic procedures used, combined with participants' perceptions of relevance, effectiveness, and demands placed on them, can help identify specific barriers to engagement with an EBT and its component parts.

Once the areas in need of adaptation are selected, a directed approach is used to develop one of two types of treatment adaptations while maintaining fidelity to the original EBT model: (a) contextualizing EBT content or (b) enhancing participant engagement in the EBT. Contextualizing content includes the addition of treatment components and changing of content to better address differences in symptom presentation in a particular group. Enhancing engagement includes contextualizing content to be more reflective of participants' experiences and reframing the purpose of treatment to one that is more culturally acceptable (e.g., educational vs. therapeutic). The design of the cultural adaptation is focused on improving the EBT–target group fit. See Chapter 7 by Lau in this volume for further details on her framework.

Ecological Validity Framework

Lau (2006) provided a two-step, data-driven framework for identifying and prioritizing cultural adaptation needs for any EBT in a target community. However, due to its general approach, the framework does not provide guidance on how to operationalize adaptations to improve the EBT–target group fit or dimensions in which to ground them. Bernal et al.'s (1995) framework for culturally sensitive clinical research with Latinos both complements and gives greater specificity to Lau's notion of a selective (Step 1) and, in particular, a directed approach (Step 2) to adaptation. Bernal et al.'s (1995) framework is composed of eight overlapping dimensions: language, persons, metaphors, content, concepts, goals, methods, and context. See Chapter 2 of this volume for a description of this framework.

Combined Cultural Adaptation Model for Latinos

Ethnicity is a limited and distal marker of an individual's cultural context (Lau, 2006; Sue, 1999). In order to understand the link between cultural variables and psychological processes, one must evaluate the cultural dimensions assumed to distinguish one cultural group from another (Betancourt & López, 1993). The dimensions in Bernal et al.'s (1995) framework, combined with the evidence-based procedural structure provided by Lau's (2006) framework, allow for the methodological identification of proximal explanatory concepts responsible for group differences and, as a result, adaptation needs for Latinos (Sue, 1999). The combination of these frameworks is illustrated in Figure 12.1 (Maríñez-Lora, 2007). At each of Lau's steps, Bernal et al.'s (1995) dimensions provide the culturally informed scaffolding to (a) isolate or select the target problems in a target group (i.e., evidence of distinctive sociocultural context of risk and resilience and/or evidence of threats to an EBT's social validity) and (b) direct or focus the adaptation to contextualizing EBT content or to enhancing participant engagement in the EBT (Step 2; see Figure 12.1). That is, Bernal et al.'s (1995) dimensions provide the sociocultural knowledge both to isolate and identify the distinctive context of risk and resilience and to operationalize the adaptations for Latinos. Presented next are three case examples illustrating how the combined model can be used to inform culturally sensitive, evidence-based adaptations to BPT programs when working with Latino families. The first author provided supervision in the form of technical support to MHPs and used the combined model as an evidence-based approach to adaptation. Different strategies were dis-

Step 1:
•Identify areas of poor fit and reasons why (selective adaptation)

•Use dimensions to operationalize the target areas that need adaptation

Step 2:
•Identify types of necessary adaptations (directed adaptations)

•Use dimensions to operationalize the adaptations

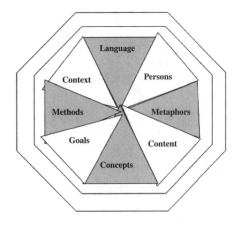

Figure 12.1. Combined cultural adaptation model for working with Latino children and families.

cussed during supervision, and MHPs were guided toward using strategies and approaches with empirical support.

Case 1: Separation and Reunification

A low-income Mexican immigrant single mother of two requested mental health services to address her 7-year-old son's noncompliant and oppositional behavior toward herself and aggressive behavior toward his younger sister. The mother–son dyad had been separated for 4 years due to the mother's immigration to the United States. The son joined the mother and younger sister in the United States at the age of 6½. The mother reported expecting her son to be very happy about their reunion. She expressed hurt that he wanted to return to Mexico and struggled with the idea that her child might be experiencing strong mixed emotions about the reunification. She described feeling simultaneously guilty, insecure, angry, and resentful and interpreting her son's behavioral difficulties as a rejection of her and as ingratitude and disrespect toward her sacrifice of immigrating to better provide for him.

The combined model described above was used to consult the relevant literature, which confirmed parent–child separation during the immigration journey as a distinctive social–cultural context of risk particularly prevalent in the Mexican immigrant population (e.g., Mitrani et al., 2004; Suárez-Orozco et al., 2002). Due to the prominence of the parent–child separation and reunification in this case, the absence of the immigration experience in the BPT program was considered a possible threat to the social validity of the

EBT for this family. Therefore, adaptations were determined necessary to contextualize the content to be more responsive to the mother–son dyad's experience. Bernal et al.'s (1995) dimensions were used to operationalize the target areas requiring adaptation and the adaptations themselves. The dimensions of content (i.e., knowledge of the Mexican immigration experience and the cultural values and norms interacting with that experience) and context (i.e., family separation and reunification as a result of immigrating to the United States) were used to identify the distinctive social–cultural context of risk and resilience in the first step of Lau's (2006) framework. The dimensions of content, context, language (treatment was delivered in Spanish), method (i.e., treatment modality and role of therapist), and goals (i.e., parent's specific goals for treatment, child-rearing goals) were used both to contextualize the BPT and to enhance this family's participation in treatment, the second step in Lau's (2006) framework.

The BPT was delivered as part of a family therapy treatment plan with the purpose of helping the family adjust to its reunification. The relevant literature highlighted the successful inclusion of the impact of the immigration experience into the family therapy context (e.g., Coatsworth, Pantin, & Szapocznik, 2002; Pantin, Coatsworth, et al., 2003; Pantin, Schwartz, Sullivan, Coatsworth, & Szapocznik, 2003). Using the context of the immigration experience within the treatment modality of family therapy, the therapist presented BPT as a set of tools to assist the mother in rebuilding and strengthening her nuclear family in a foreign land. The therapist normalized the family's experience, as common among families experiencing reunification, and took on the role of the mother's coach in her efforts to rebuild and strengthen her relationship with her son and do the groundwork to increase the frequency of positive interactions among her children.

Adaptations did not replace the core components of the BPT program but supplemented them with knowledge about the negative impact of immigration on the parent–child relationship and reframed the purpose and function of the core components to be more reflective of and responsive to parent's goals for the child. For example, the strategy of special time focused on the child was reframed as an opportunity for the mother to get to know her son again and to make up for lost intimate time with him.

Case 2: Teaching Instrumental Competencies

The work with a low-income Cuban immigrant single mother and her 7-year-old daughter had come to a standstill. The mother was reporting inconsistent use of some BPT strategies (i.e., implementing a predictable routine for child, home rules, rewards). The mother reported that when used, the strategies were effective, but she was reluctant to use two strategies deemed important: (a) a set daily time when she focused on her daughter and, using only reflective commenting, allowed the daughter to take the lead in play and (b) the planned ignoring of some behaviors that did not put anyone's safety at risk. Special time focused on the child was recommended to provide the child with more positive attention from her mother. Planned ignoring was recommended because this mother struggled with identifying things that her daughter was doing well and had developmentally unrealistic behavioral expectations (i.e., caring for her 4-year-old sister, knowing without being told the behaviors that her mother wanted to see). When asked about her difficulties using planned ignoring and special time focused on the child, the mother expressed concern that by using the former she would appear weak in her daughter's eyes and that the latter strategy felt awkward and unnatural to her. The mother described her parenting style as very firm and responsive to the child's behavioral infractions, with the purpose of protecting the child from the negative influences of the poor urban neighborhood where they lived and raising her to be *bien educada* (obedient, courteous, deferential, and respectful). She perceived the daughter's being *bien educada* as a characteristic or an instrumental competency that would assure her the support and familial commitment of the extended family and the goodwill of other adults in her life (i.e., teachers).

With the combined model used as a guide, this mother's difficulties with special time focused on the child and planned ignoring suggest culturally specific beliefs and caregiving practices that threatened the social validity of these strategies, highlighting the need for adaptation. Bernal et al.'s (1995) content, concepts, goals, methods, and context dimensions were used to guide the research literature review and to operationalize and understand the culturally specific beliefs and caregiving practices threatening the social validity of the EBT. The relevant literature drew attention to Latino parents endorsing different developmental goals (e.g., García Coll, 1990; Julian et al., 1994), emphasizing that Latino children exercise more self-control (Julian et al., 1994), conform more, and receive more parental monitoring than White American children do (Okagaki & Frensch, 1998). In addition, more recent research on first-generation, low-income Latino parents suggests that they adhere to a protective parenting style (see Domenech Rodríguez et al., 2009). A protective parenting style is characteristically high on parental warmth (i.e., supportive interest, involvement, and engagement in child's activities), high on demandingness (i.e., direct parental control over child's behavior), and low on autonomy granting (i.e., child autonomy and individual expression within the family; Domenech Rodríguez et al., 2009). Special time focused on the child was reintroduced as a parenting strategy that could be flexibly incorporated into typical daily activities with the child and as a protective strategy to increase the frequency of positive parent–child interactions, strengthen the parent–child bond, and monitor the child's interests.

Planned ignoring was tactically paired with the parenting strategy of redirecting, both to support the mother in explicitly teaching the child the behaviors she wants to see more of and to reduce the number of behaviors that she ignores. In addition, meetings with the mother were supplemented with discussions of developmentally appropriate behavioral expectations and what is reasonable to expect of a 7-year-old who is *bien educada*.

Case 3: Co-Parenting

A mixed-generation Latino couple (first-generation Mexican immigrant father and second-generation Mexican American mother) with an 8-year-old son presenting with oppositional, inattentive, and disorganized behaviors at home and at school appeared to be very interested in learning about different parenting strategies. In the clinic, engagement was high, and both parents practiced the strategies (e.g., special time with child, social rewards, time out) with their child during the sessions with their clinician. However, reports from parents indicated little progress in the target child behaviors (i.e., compliance, completing tasks). Exploration of contextual barriers revealed that the paternal grandparents, who lived with them and provided child care, strongly disapproved of the parents' decisions to seek mental health services to parent their child.

The work with this family included using the aforementioned combined framework to identify and address threats to the notion of receiving formal help (i.e., services at a local community mental health services agency) in general and receiving help on parenting, specifically, at different stages of the treatment process. The grandparents' disapproval of mental health services suggested beliefs that threatened the social validity of seeking formal help. Bernal et al.'s (1995) dimensions of content and goals were instrumental in identifying that the cultural value of *familismo* (familism) and the interdependence it implies appeared to be at the root of the conflict between the grandparents and parents around how to address the child's challenging behaviors. Familismo "refers to feelings of loyalty, reciprocity, and solidarity toward members of the family as well as the notion of the family as an extension of the self" (Cortés, 1995, p. 249). Three attitudinal dimensions of familismo appeared to be influencing the conflict between grandparents and parents and preventing the implementation of the parenting strategies at home: perceived support from the family, familial obligations, and the family as behavioral and attitudinal referents (Sabogal, Marín, Otero-Sabogal, Marín, & Perez-Stable, 1987). Grandparents appeared to struggle with parents' decision to seek formal help for their son when they did not advise it and had never sought formal mental health services. Parents appeared to interpret grandparents' negative reaction to their decision to seek formal help for their child and their refusal to use the parenting strategies at home as refusal to fulfill the familial obligation of providing emotional and instrumental support. In addition, the mother, who was more acculturated than the father, was overall less willing to use the grandparents as referents when making decisions about how to help her son with his behavioral difficulties.

Although the grandparents and the parents could not agree on the decision to seek formal services for child, they did agree that the child's difficulties and the conflict about how to best address these difficulties were negatively impacting their everyday interactions as a close-knit family. All adult members of the family endorsed a commitment to increased frequency of positive adult–child interactions and to parenting consistency as a strategy to improve the emotional climate of the home for all family members. The grandparents were able to agree that the parents had decided to seek formal help with the best of intentions to help their son. The grandparents agreed to support the parents by learning and implementing the behavioral parenting strategies. The parents agreed to consult closely with the grandparents to determine which strategies were resulting in the desired behavioral changes. The treatment plan included periodic revisiting of how the parenting strategies contributed to the positive functioning of the family unit and problem-solving sessions to address the challenges the parents and grandparents encountered in negotiating and implementing the strategies.

CONCLUSION

The literature suggests that clinicians make adaptations to EBTs to better meet the needs of the populations they serve (e.g., Hill et al., 2007; Miranda et al., 2005). This suggests that the research-to-practice gap can also be understood as a gap between evidence-based practices and practice-based adaptations, on which there is little or no research. Little is known and understood about the frequency and quality of the adaptations that clinicians make and whether these adaptations accommodate to the unique needs of clients or, alternatively, detract from the effectiveness of practices by deviating from core principles of evidence-based practices. The combined systematic model presented here has the potential of informing both research and clinical practice about the quality of the cultural adaptations clinicians make to EBTs when working with Latino immigrants and the cultural rationale behind their decisions to adapt, as well as providing theoretically informed guidelines to clinicians to encourage effective adaptations to meet the needs of the increasingly diverse clinical population served in community mental health practice. As illustrated in the case examples provided in this chapter, the research literature, although not expansive, can guide clinicians and supervisors to make thoughtful and evidence-informed adaptations that are consistent with cultural norms.

REFERENCES

Benish, S.G., Quintana, S., & Wampold, B.E. (2011). Culturally adapted psychotherapy and the legitimacy of myth: A direct-comparison meta-analysis. *Journal of Counseling Psychology, 58,* 279–289. doi:10.1037/a0023626

Bernal, G. (2006). Intervention development and cultural adaptation research with diverse families. *Family Process, 45,* 143–151. doi:10.1111/j.1545-5300.2006.00087.x

Bernal, G., Bonilla, J., & Bellido, C. (1995). Ecological validity and cultural sensitivity for outcome research: Issues for the cultural adaptation and development of psychosocial treatments with Hispanics. *Journal of Abnormal Child Psychology, 23,* 67–82.

Bernal, G., Jiménez-Chafey, M.I., & Domenech Rodríguez, M.M. (2009). Cultural adaptation of treatments: A resource for considering culture in evidence-based practice. *Professional Psychology: Research and Practice, 40,* 361–368. doi:1037/a0016401

Bernal, G., & Scharrón-del-Río, M.R. (2001). Are empirically supported treatments valid for ethnic minorities? Toward an alternative approach for treatment research. *Cultural Diversity and Ethnic Minority Psychology, 7,* 328–342. doi:10.1037/1099-9809.7.4.328

Betancourt, H., & López, S.R. (1993). The study of culture, ethnicity, and race in American psychology. *American Psychologist, 48,* 629–637. doi:10.1037/0003-066X.48.6.629

Boggs, S.R., Eyberg, S.M., Edwards, D.L., Rayfield, A., Jacobs, J., Bagner, D., & Hood, K. K. (2004). Outcomes of Parent–Child Interaction Therapy: A comparison of treatment completers and study dropouts one to three years later. *Child & Family Behavior Therapy, 26,* 1–22. doi:10.1300/J019v26n04_01

Bourke, M.L., & Nielsen, B.A. (1995). Parent training: Getting the most effective help for the most children. *Journal of Psychological Practice, 1,* 142–152.

Bravo, M., Woodbury-Farina, M., Canino, G. J., & Rubio-Stipec, M. (1993). The Spanish translation and cultural adaptation of the Diagnostic Interview Schedule (DISC) for children in Puerto Rico. *Culture, Medicine and Psychiatry, 17,* 329–344.

Calzada, E.J., & Eyberg, S.M. (2002). Self-reported parenting practices in Dominican and Puerto Rican mothers of young children. *Journal of Clinical Child and Adolescent Psychology, 31,* 354–363. doi:10.1207/S15374424JCCP3103_07

Castro, F.G., Barrera, M., & Martinez, C.R. (2004). The cultural adaptation of prevention interventions: Resolving tensions between fidelity and fit. *Prevention Science, 5,* 41–45. doi:10.1023/B:PREV.0000013980.12412.cd

Caughy, M.B., Miller, T.L., Genevro, J.L., Huang, K., & Nautiyal, C. (2003). The effects of Healthy Steps on discipline strategies of parents of young children. *Journal of Applied Developmental Psychology, 24,* 517–534. doi:10.1016/j.appdev.2003.08.004

Chaffin, M., Silovsky, J. F., Funderburk, B., Valle, L. A., Brestan, E. V., Balachova, T., . . . Bonner, B. L. (2004). Parent–child interaction therapy with physically abusive parents: Efficacy for reducing future abuse reports. *Journal of Consulting and Clinical Psychology, 72*, 500–510. doi:10.1037/0022-006X.72.3.500

Coatsworth, J. D., Pantin, H., & Szapocznik, J. (2002). Familias unidas: A family-centered ecodevelopmental intervention to reduce risk for problem behavior among Hispanic adolescents. *Clinical Child and Family Psychology Review, 5*, 113–131. doi:10.1023/A:1015420503275

Conduct Problems Prevention Research Group. (2002). Predictor variables associated with positive Fast Track outcomes at the end of the third grade. *Journal of Abnormal Child Psychology, 30*, 37–52. doi:10.1023/A:1014227031125

Corrigan, P., McCraken, S., & Blaser, B. (2003). Disseminating evidence-based mental health practices. *Evidence-Based Mental Health, 6*, 4–5. doi:10.1136/ebmh.6.1.4

Cortés, D. E. (1995). Variations in familism in two generations of Puerto Ricans. *Hispanic Journal of Behavioral Sciences, 17*, 249–255. doi:10.1177/07399863950172008

Delgado-Gaitan, C. (1994). Socializing young children in Mexican-American families: An intergenerational perspective. In P. M. Greenfield & R. R. Cocking (Eds.), *Cross-cultural roots of minority child development* (pp. 1–37). Hillsdale, NJ: Erlbaum.

Domenech Rodríguez, M. M., Donovick, M. R., & Crowley, S. L. (2009). Parenting styles in a cultural context: Observations of "protective parenting" in first-generation Latinos. *Family Process, 48*, 195–210. doi:10.1111/j.1545-5300.2009.01277.x

Dumka, L. E., López, V., & Jacobs Carter, S. (2002). Parenting interventions adapted for Latino families: Progress and prospects. In J. M. Contreras, A. M. Neal-Barnett, & K. A. Kerns (Eds.), *Latino children and families in the United States* (pp. 203–231). Westport, CT: Greenwood/Praeger Press.

Elliott, D. S., & Mihalic, S. (2004). Issues in disseminating and replicating effective prevention programs. *Prevention Science, 5*, 47–53. doi:10.1023/B:PREV.0000013981.28071.52

Eyberg, S. M., Nelson, M. M., & Boggs, S. R. (2008). Evidence-based psychosocial treatments for children and adolescents with disruptive behavior. *Journal of Clinical Child and Adolescent Psychology, 37*, 215–237. doi:10.1080/15374410701820117

Forehand, R., & Kotchick, B. A. (1996). Cultural diversity: A wake-up call for parenting. *Behavior Therapy, 27*, 187–206. doi:10.1016/S0005-7894(96)80014-1

Forgatch, M. S., & DeGarmo, D. S. (1999). Parenting through change: An effective prevention program for single mothers. *Journal of Consulting and Clinical Psychology, 67*, 711–724. doi:10.1037/0022-006X.67.5.711

Fox, R. A., & Solís-Cámara, P. (1997). Parenting of young children by fathers in Mexico and the United States. *Journal of Social Psychology, 137*, 489–495. doi:10.1080/00224549709595465

García Coll, C. T. (1990). Developmental outcome of minority infants: A process-oriented look into our beginnings. *Child Development, 61,* 270–289. doi:10.2307/1131094

Graziano, A. M., & Diament, D. M. (1992). Parent behavioral training: An examination of the paradigm. *Behavior Modification, 16,* 3–38. doi:10.1177/01454455920161001

Gross, D., Fogg, L., Webster-Stratton, C., Garvey, C., Julion, W., & Grady, J. (2003). Parent training of toddlers in day care in low-income urban communities. *Journal of Consulting and Clinical Psychology, 71,* 261–278. doi:10.1037/0022-006X.71.2.261

Gross, D., Julion, W., & Garvey, C. (2003). *The Chicago Parent Program of Rush University.* Unpublished manuscript.

Gutierrez, J., Sameroff, A. J., & Karrer, B. M. (1988). Acculturation and SES effects on Mexican-American parents' concepts of development. *Child Development, 59,* 250–255. doi:10.2307/1130407

Hall, G. C. N. (2001). Psychotherapy research with ethnic minorities: Empirical, ethical, and conceptual issues. *Journal of Consulting and Clinical Psychology, 69,* 502–510. doi:10.1037/0022-006X.69.3.502

Hill, L. G., Maucione, K., & Hood, B. K. (2007). A focused approach to assessing program fidelity. *Prevention Science, 8,* 25–34. doi:10.1007/s11121-006-0051-4

Hoagwood, K., Burns, B. J., Kiser, L., Ringeisen, H., & Schoenwald, S. K. (2001). Evidence-based practice in child and adolescent mental health services. *Psychiatric Services, 52,* 1179–1189. doi:10.1176/appi.ps.52.9.1179

Ireland, J. L., Sanders, M. R., & Markie-Dadds, C. (2003). The impact of parent training on marital functioning: A comparison of two group versions of the Triple P-Positive Parenting Program for parents of children with early-onset conduct problems. *Behavioural and Cognitive Psychotherapy, 31,* 127–142. doi:10.1017/S1352465803002017

Julian, T. W., McKenry, P. C., & McKelvey, M. W. (1994). Cultural variations in parenting: Perceptions of Caucasian, African American, Hispanic and Asian American parents. *Family Relations, 43,* 30–37. doi:10.2307/585139

Kacir, C. D., & Gordon, D. A. (1999). Parenting adolescents wisely: The effectiveness of an interactive videodisk parent training program in Appalachia. *Child & Family Behavior Therapy, 21,* 1–22. doi:10.1300/J019v21n04_01

Kaminski, J. W., Valle, L. A., Filene, J. H., & Boyle, C. L. (2008). A meta-analytic review of components associated with parent training program effectiveness. *Journal of Abnormal Child Psychology, 36,* 567–589. doi:10.1007/s10802-007-9201-9

Kazdin, A. E. (1997). Parent management training: Evidence, outcomes, and issues. *Journal of the American Academy of Child & Adolescent Psychiatry, 36,* 1349–1356. doi:10.1097/00004583-199710000-00016

Lau, A. S. (2006). Making the case for selective and directed cultural adaptations of evidence-based treatments: Examples from parent training. *Clinical Psychology: Science and Practice, 13,* 295–310. doi:10.1111/j.1468-2850.2006.00042.x

Long, P., Forehand, R., Wierson, M., & Morgan, A. (1994). Does parent training with young noncompliant children have long-term effects? *Behaviour Research and Therapy, 32,* 101–107. doi:10.1016/0005-7967(94)90088-4

Maríñez-Lora, A. M. (2007, June). *A framework to evaluate parenting programs for Latino immigrants.* In N. Chavez (Chair), *Parent–child relationships in Latino immigrant families: Theory, research and intervention.* Symposium conducted at the biennial conference of the Society for Community Research and Action, Division 27 of the American Psychological Association, Pasadena, CA.

Maughan, D. R., Christiansen, E., Jenson, W. R., Olympia, D., & Clark, E. (2005). Behavioral parent training as a treatment for externalizing behaviors and disruptive behavior disorders: A meta-analysis. *School Psychology Review, 34,* 267–286.

McMahon, R. J., & Forehand, R. (2003). *Helping the noncompliant child: Family based-treatment for oppositional behavior* (2nd ed.). New York, NY: Guildford Press.

Medway, F. J. (1989). Measuring the effectiveness of parent education. In M. J. Fine (Ed.), *The second handbook on parent education: Contemporary perspectives* (pp. 237–255). San Diego, CA: Academic Press.

Miller, W. R., & Rollnick, S. (2002). *Motivational interviewing: Preparing people for change* (2nd ed.). New York, NY: Guilford Press.

Miranda, J., Bernal, G., Lau, A., Kohn, L., Hwang, W., & LaFromboise, T. (2005). State of the science on psychosocial interventions for ethnic minorities. *Annual Review of Clinical Psychology, 1,* 113–142. doi:10.1146/annurev.clinpsy.1.102803.143822

Miranda, J., Nakamura, R., & Bernal, G. (2003). Including ethnic minorities in mental health intervention research: A practical approach to a long-standing problem. *Culture, Medicine and Psychiatry, 27,* 467–486. doi:10.1023/B:MEDI.0000005484.26741.79

Mitrani, V. B., Santisteban, D. A., & Muir, J. A. (2004). Addressing immigration-related separations in Hispanic families with a behavior-problem adolescent. *American Journal of Orthopsychiatry, 74,* 219–229. doi:10.1037/0002-9432.74.3.219

O'Dell, S. L., O'Quin, J. A., Alford, B. A., O'Briant, A. L., Bradlyn, A. S., & Giebenhain, J. E. (1982). Predicting the acquisition of parenting skills via four training methods. *Behavior Therapy, 13,* 194–208. doi:10.1016/S0005-7894(82)80063-4

Okagaki, L., & Frensch, P. A. (1998). Parenting and children's school achievement: A multiethnic perspective. *American Educational Research Journal, 35,* 123–144.

Pantin, H., Coatsworth, D., Feaster, D. J., Newman, F. L., Briones, E., Prado, G., . . . Szapocznik, J. (2003). Familias unidas: The efficacy of an intervention to promote parental investment in Hispanic immigrant families. *Prevention Science, 4,* 189–201. doi:10.1023/A:1024601906942

Pantin, H., Schwartz, S. J., Sullivan, S., Coatsworth, J. D., & Szapocznik, J. (2003). Preventing substance abuse in Hispanic immigrant adolescents: An ecodevelopmental, parent-centered approach. *Hispanic Journal of Behavioral Sciences, 25,* 469–500. doi:10.1177/0739986303259355

Patel, K. K., Butler, B., & Wells, K. B. (2006). What is necessary to transform the quality of mental health care. *Health Affairs, 25,* 681–693. doi:10.1377/hlthaff.25.3.681

Pisterman, S., Firestone, P., McGrath, P., Goodman, J. T., Webster, I., Mallory, R., & Goffin, B. (1992). The effects of parent training on parenting stress and sense of competence. *Canadian Journal of Behavioural Science/Revue canadienne des sciences du comportement, 24,* 41–58. doi:10.1037/h0078699

Prochaska, J. O., & DiClemente, C. C. (1983). Stages and processes of self-change of smoking: Toward an integrative model of change. *Journal of Consulting and Clinical Psychology, 51,* 390–395. doi:10.1037/0022-006X.51.3.390

Quintana, S. M., & Atkinson, D. R. (2002). A multicultural perspective on principles of empirically supported interventions. *Counseling Psychologist, 30,* 281–291. doi:10.1177/0011000002302005

Reid, M. J., Webster-Stratton, C., & Beauchaine, T. P. (2001). Parent training in Head Start: A comparison of program response among African American, Asian American and Hispanic mothers. *Prevention Science, 2,* 209–227. doi:10.1023/A:1013618309070

Ringeisen, R., Henderson, K., & Hoagwood, K. (2003). Context matters: Schools and the "research to practice gap" in children's mental health. *School Psychology Review, 32,* 153–168.

Sabogal, F., Marín, G., Otero-Sabogal, R., Marín, B. V., & Perez-Stable, E. J. (1987). Hispanic familism and acculturation: What changes and what doesn't? *Hispanic Journal of Behavioral Sciences, 9,* 397–412. doi:10.1177/07399863870094003

Sanders, M. R., Markie-Dadds, C., Tully, L. A., & Bor, W. (2000). The Triple P-Positive Parenting Program: A comparison of enhanced, standard, and self-directed behavioral family intervention for parents of children with early onset conduct problems. *Journal of Consulting and Clinical Psychology, 68,* 624–640. doi: 10.1037/0022-006X.68.4.624

Savage, S. L., & Gauvain, M. (1998). Parental beliefs and children's everyday planning in European-American and Latino families. *Journal of Applied Developmental Psychology, 19,* 319–340. doi:10.1016/S0193-3973(99)80043-4

Smith, T. B., Domenech Rodríguez, M., & Bernal, G. (2011). Culture. *Journal of Clinical Psychology, 67,* 166–175. doi:10.1002/jclp.20757

Solís-Cámara, P., & Fox, R. A. (1995). Parenting among mothers with young children in Mexico and the United States. *Journal of Social Psychology, 135,* 591–599.

Suárez-Orozco, C., Todorova, I. L. G., & Louie, J. (2002). Making up for lost time: The experience of separation and reunification among immigrant families. *Family Process, 41,* 625–643. doi:10.1111/j.1545-5300.2002.00625.x

Sue, S. (1999). Science, ethnicity, and bias: Where have we gone wrong? *American Psychologist, 54,* 1070–1077. doi:10.1037/0003-066X.54.12.1070

Taylor, T. K., & Biglan, A. (1998). Behavioral family interventions for improving child-rearing: A review of the literature for clinicians and policy makers. *Clinical Child and Family Psychology Review, 1,* 41–60. doi:10.1023/A:1021848315541

U.S. Department of Health Human Services. (1999). *Mental health: A report of the Surgeon General*. Rockville, MD: Author.

U.S. Department of Health and Human Services. (2001). *Mental health: Culture, race, and ethnicity. A supplement to Mental health: A report of the Surgeon General*. Rockville, MD: Author.

Webster-Stratton, C. (1990). Enhancing the effectiveness of self-administered videotape parent training for families with conduct-problem children. *Journal of Abnormal Child Psychology, 18*, 479–492.

Webster-Stratton, C. (1998). Preventing conduct problems in Head Start children: Strengthening parenting competencies. *Journal of Consulting and Clinical Psychology, 66*, 715–730. doi:10.1037/0022-006X.66.5.715

Webster-Stratton, C., Reid, J., & Hammond, M. (2001). Preventing conduct problems, promoting social competence: A parent and teacher training partnership in Head Start. *Journal of Clinical Child Psychology, 30*, 283–302. doi:10.1207/S15374424JCCP3003_2

Webster-Stratton, C., Reid, M. J., & Hammond, M. (2004). Treating children with early-onset conduct problems: Intervention outcomes for parent, child, and teacher training. *Journal of Clinical Child and Adolescent Psychology, 33*, 105–124. doi:10.1207/S15374424JCCP3301_11

Weisz, J. R., Sandler, I. N., Durlak, J. A., & Anton, B. S. (2005). Promoting and protecting youth mental health through evidence-based prevention and treatment. *American Psychologist, 60*, 628–648. doi:10.1037/0003-066X.60.6.628

Wright, L., Stroud, R., & Kennan, M. (1993). Indirect treatment of children via parent training: A burgeoning form of secondary prevention. *Applied and Preventive Psychology, 2*, 191–200. doi:10.1016/S0962-1849(05)80089-7

Zayas, L. H., & Solari, F. (1994). Early childhood socialization in Hispanic families: Context, culture, and practice implications. *Professional Psychology: Research and Practice, 25*, 200–206. doi:10.1037/0735-7028.25.3.200

IV
THE FUTURE OF CULTURAL ADAPTATIONS

13

BRIDGING THE GAP BETWEEN RESEARCH AND PRACTICE IN A MULTICULTURAL WORLD

MELANIE M. DOMENECH RODRÍGUEZ AND GUILLERMO BERNAL

Taking cultural context into account when developing interventions for populations outside of those for whom they were developed is considered competent (American Psychological Association [APA] Presidential Task Force on Evidence-Based Practice, 2006), ethical (APA, 2010), and effective psychological practice (Benish, Quintana, & Wampold, 2011; Griner & Smith, 2006; Smith, Domenech Rodriguez, & Bernal, 2011). How practitioners engage in the process of taking cultural context into account can vary widely from idiosyncratic to highly systematic adaptation. In-the-moment adaptations are typically based on the unique needs of the client or clients present in a given psychotherapeutic encounter. In contrast, systematic adaptations are typically informed by the literature and follow a particular cultural adaptation model (see Chapter 2, this volume). Highly systematic adaptations may also be evaluated by carefully calibrated measures (e.g., where measurement equivalence has been established). Our present practice and our practice-based research have been informed by decades of psychotherapy theory development, intervention development, and evolutions in how treatments are understood to be effective and valid for broad dissemination. There is no single, correct way to make cultural adaptations to evidence-based treatments (EBTs). Rather than focusing on one model or one approach, this chapter first provides general and specific guidelines for psychologists wishing to engage in state-of-the-art cultural adaptation of EBTs. Following this, we turn to questions regarding the future of cultural adaptations.

The development and evolution of theories of psychotherapy, psychotherapy practice with ethnocultural groups (ECGs), and the evidence-based psychotherapy movement combined bring us logically to cultural adaptation of EBTs. In short, psychotherapy theories provide the specification of mechanisms for change that are presumed to lead to positive mental health outcomes. Psychotherapy practice in general allowed for the verification, in the field, of these theories. Psychotherapy practice with ECGs allowed for the gathering of some evidence regarding the generalizability of those psychotherapy theories to groups other than those for whom they were generated. The evidence-based movement has pushed researchers and practitioners to consider evidence broadly, opening the door to bidirectional influence between "mainstream psychology" and "multicultural psychology." Indeed, the lines between psychological researchers who conduct implementation studies and applied practitioners can be quite difficult to distinguish because researchers are expected to take clinical expertise into account and applied practitioners are expected to consider "the best available evidence" in implementing psychotherapeutic treatments (APA Presidential Task Force, 2006).

CONSIDERATIONS IN CULTURAL ADAPTATIONS

In proceeding with recommendations, we give guidance in three major areas: whether to adapt treatments (i.e., evaluation guidelines), general considerations in cultural adaptation, and specific recommendations when culturally adapting. The process begins with a careful selection of the EBT.

Selecting a Treatment

We draw on Ford and Urban's (1998) framework to understand commonalities across theories of psychotherapy. They suggested that all theories of psychotherapy contain three essential components: (a) a propositional model that stipulates the basic thesis of how the variables (or constructs in the model) are associated with a beneficial outcome, (b) a procedural (or practice) model or models that guide the therapist in a set of actions, and (c) underlying philosophical assumptions about the model. If we embed these essential components in a particular context of culture, then we can ask: What is the fit between the components (propositional model, procedural model, and underlying assumptions) of a particular evidence-based psychotherapy developed in one cultural group and its applicability or transportability to a different cultural group. Thus, a standard EBT's propositional, procedural, and/or assumptive models (or a combination of these) may fit or may not fit the particular cultural group of interest.

The analysis of fit will change according to the target of intervention, the persons affected, the expertise of those involved in the analysis, and the resources available to address the issues at hand, among many other variables. Rather than present an exhaustive list of variables, an example is presented here based on the work of the first author using parent management training with Latino families (e.g., Domenech Rodriguez, Baumann, & Schwartz, 2011). In the case of the Oregon model of parent management training (PMTO), interventions and therapist training practices are based on social interaction learning theory (Patterson, Forgatch, & DeGarmo, 2010). Simply stated, the theory posits that contexts exert their influence on child outcomes through their effect on parenting practices. As such, interventions are aimed at supporting the skills development of parents because these practices are believed to be the most proximal determinant of child outcomes. The theory specifies effective parenting practices (i.e., positive involvement, problem solving, effective discipline, skills building, monitoring) and the mechanisms through which ineffective practices are established, maintained, and exacerbated (i.e., negative reciprocity, escalation, negative reinforcement).

When considering the fit between the propositional model and the beliefs, values, and/or practices of Latino parents, many stated assumptions of the model emerge. One of the many can be summarized as "ineffective parenting practices lead to undesirable child behavior such as tantrums." The literature on Latino parenting (e.g., Calzada, 2010) reflects the congruence between the theory's stated assumption (propositional model) and Latino parents' parenting practices (procedural model). This specific evidence reflects Latino parents' understanding that it is their responsibility to teach children appropriate behaviors and that tantrums are undesirable. As the chapters in this volume reflect, there are important questions in this domain about which evidence (e.g., literature, focus groups, surveys), from whom (e.g., clinicians, parents), and about what (e.g., acceptability of the specific treatment, general parenting issues) is best used to address the propositional model assumptions.

An examination of the fit of the PMTO procedural model with Latino cultures can also generate many considerations. One procedure that might be examined is *time out*, which is a mild consequence of child misbehavior. Time out is a relatively complicated practice to establish for parents across cultural groups and may be perceived by some parents as "American parenting" (Domenech Rodríguez et al., 2011). There is no evidence that the procedure itself is unacceptable; however, care may need to be taken in explaining the rationale for its use in a manner that is relevant to Latino parents, and procedures may need to be put in place to support parents' success (e.g., role plays).

Finally, attention to underlying assumptions is of great importance from a multicultural perspective, where making the invisible "visible" is key to multicultural competence. In the case of PMTO, parents are seen as primary agents of change in child behavior; an argument may be made that the theory parts from an assumption of the self as independent from context (e.g., parents as ultimately responsible for child-rearing). This is consistent with the individualistic orientation that characterizes that cultural context from which the theory emerged. An individualistic orientation contrasts with Latinos' collectivism and could present challenges in the selection of the particular EBT. However, there is no evidence that PMTO limits "parenting" to only biological parents. On the contrary, PMTO research has demonstrated the importance of other child-rearing agents, such as stepparents (Bullard et al., 2010) and foster parents (DeGarmo, Chamberlain, Leve, & Price, 2009).

The analysis may or may not lead to a definitive answer regarding the fit of an EBT with a particular ECG; however, the thoughtful process of considering the common dimensions of EBTs may lead to greater or lesser certainty about the potential for fit. As Trimble, Scharrón-del-Río, and Hill (Chapter 3, this volume) suggest, treatment providers and intervention researchers alike may thoughtfully engage a cultural adaptation process and learn that the best option is to develop an entirely new treatment. For those who do find an EBT, the question then turns to whether or not to culturally adapt the treatment.

Evaluation Guidelines on the Need for Cultural Adaptation

In the debate of whether or not to culturally adapt, it does not seem wise or warranted to provide a definitive response. Rather, it seems that practitioner–scholars might best serve their clients and their science by determining when they should adapt a treatment. To that end, we offer some specific evaluation guidelines (EGs) for making a determination of whether to culturally adapt an EBT.

EG1. Are There Evidence-Based Treatments for the Presenting Problem?

EBTs have been in place for some time, yet there are not EBTs for every presenting concern. This is especially true in cases where presenting problems are comorbid (e.g., Kazdin & Whitley, 2006). There is also a dearth of EBTs for culture-bound syndromes. In gathering the best possible research evidence, researchers and practitioners may find that there is little guidance in specific domains. In these cases, to develop a promising treatment, practitioners and researchers alike may need to combine general knowledge of psychological change predictors (e.g., cognitions, behaviors) with findings from the relevant literature on the disturbances in the specific ECG. Cultural adaptation models may help in determining what contexts to attend to in treatment development.

EG2. Are the Evidence-Based Treatments Accessible to Treatment Providers?

A present-day challenge in the dissemination of EBTs is to make them available to treatment providers. Even in cases where manuals and articles may be accessible, training to attain competence in the delivery of the EBT may be difficult, if not impossible, because of cost and time requirements (see Herschell, Kolko, Baumann, & Davis, 2010). In addition, once attained, competence must be maintained, requiring continued access to experts, therapist time (away from clients, protected for training and development), and therapist and/or agency resources (Herschell et al., 2010). The same is true for university-based researchers who may not have the financial resources or protected time to engage in specialized training away from their academic duties. Where EBTs may not be feasibly applied, therapists and researchers may find that they can most feasibly engage in the development of new treatments as outlined in EG1.

EG3. Does the Evidence-Based Treatment Target the Appropriate Mechanisms for Good Outcomes in the Population of Interest?

In the case where there is an EBT, the next logical step is to determine whether it has been used with the ECG of interest to the treatment provider or researcher. If the case has not been made through theoretical or empirical contributions, the treatment provider must determine whether the EBT is viable for use with the ECG of interest. The evidence for the factors that explain the development of conditions or symptoms of anxiety, depression, and other disorders in specific ECGs such as African Americans, Latinos, Asian Americans, and American Indians serves as a basis on which to decide whether a cultural adaptation is warranted. For example, if there is evidence that anxious or depressive behavior is predicted by the same variables across groups, then an adaptation may not be indicated. However, there may be a history of trauma and loss for some ECGs that may be connected to the experience of depression and anxiety (see Chapter 10, this volume).

There is evidence that the experience of immigration for some groups is closely linked to crisis, loss, and intergenerational and cultural value conflicts, with implications for treatment (see Chapter 8, this volume). In these cases, a cultural adaptation may be indicated. Similarly, in some parent training approaches, positive involvement and effective discipline predict positive outcomes in child behavior problems. However, in diverse ECGs, ethnic and racial socialization may be operating in such a way that what is usually understood as "positive involvement" and "effective discipline" may require changes to the parent training model. Evidence for the applicability of treatments to cultural groups includes studies suggesting that the same predictors operate in the same way across populations.

EG4. Is the Evidence-Based Treatment Acceptable to the Ethnocultural Group?

A treatment may target the correct mechanism but in a manner that is not acceptable to the ECG with whom a provider is working. *Ecological validity* refers to congruence between the patient's and the therapist's views of the psychotherapy environment, such that both perceive interpersonal processes, healing methods, and the theory of change as important ingredients of the healing context. If a treatment is ecologically valid, then no adaptation is necessary. We consider that evidence for ecological validity is present in findings of engagement in therapy, retention in treatment, and client reports of treatment acceptability. In other words, if there is evidence that attrition from treatment is high, the treatment or intervention is not acceptable, and there are specific barriers (environmental, social, or psychological) to the treatment, then a cultural adaptation may be considered. Alternatively, if the evidence on outcomes suggests that patients fare well across different population or groups, then a cultural adaptation may not be indicated. Moreover, if studies of mediators show that the same mediators work in the same way with ECGs, then it is additional evidence that an adaptation may not be needed.

EG5. Are Other Treatment-Related Procedures Valid?

Will procedures for engagement and evaluation of treatments be appropriate for the population of interest? Engagement in and evaluation of treatment are complex. The success of any treatment study depends on successful engagement and retention. The procedures used may need to be revised for use with populations that are diverse in language, socioeconomic status, ethnicity, gender, sexual preferences, disability, and so forth. In practice and mental health services contexts, the issue is quite similar. The point is whether the same strategies of engagement and retention work in the same way with all groups.

Similarly, the instruments used in the evaluation of diverse groups vary greatly. The language of the evaluation, the instruments used, as well as their validity and reliability, should be considered. There is growing evidence that calls into question what is being measured and how when investigating constructs as common as symptoms of depression. For example, the measurement models of commonly used instruments for depression (e.g., Center for Epidemiologic Studies Depression Scale; Radloff, 1977) are different for particular ECGs (Rivera-Medina, Caraballo, Rodriguez-Cordero, Bernal, & Dávila-Marrero, 2010), and different cutoff scores for depression may be required (Rivera-Medina, Bernal, & Rosselló, 2010). Such findings call into question the measurement validity of instruments used in evaluations. The question is whether the same evaluation process and instruments work in the same way for the population of interest. Evidence for the validity of engagement procedures includes the finding that similar engagement strategies and procedures are effective for diverse populations. Evidence for the validity of evaluation procedures includes published findings on the equivalence of measures and evaluation procedures used.

EG6. Are Fidelity and Fit United by "And" or "Versus"?

There has been much discussion of the "fidelity versus fit" debate in cultural adaptations. The so-called tension has been described as the degree to which a cultural adaptation modifies the original EBT in such a way that the essential components linked to positive outcomes are changed (Castro, Barrera, & Holleran Steiker, 2010). The concern is that changing the key components of an EBT through a cultural adaptation may compromise the effectiveness of the treatment (Elliott & Mihalic, 2004). This assessment is essential to treatment selection. Where fitting an EBT to a particular ECG is met with tension (i.e., fidelity vs. fit), this may be a good indicator that the EBT is not the best fit for a particular ECG. When the fidelity of the treatment is easily maintained in the context of fitting the treatment to an ECG, it is good evidence for the selection of that EBT. Providers have tailored treatments for use across contexts with a great deal of success (e.g., PMTO for divorced mothers, stepfamilies, foster care caregivers, teachers; Patterson et al., 2010). Evidence of flexibility in the application of core intervention components across situations may provide some indication of degree of flexibility for fitting to ECGs.

General Guidelines for Cultural Adaptation

There are myriad models to inform cultural adaptations of EBTs (see Chapter 2, this volume). Some models privilege fidelity (e.g., Kumpfer, Melo, & Whiteside, 2008), whereas others privilege fit (e.g., Bernal, Bonilla, & Bellido, 1995). A recent meta-analysis (Smith et al., 2011) showed that culturally adapted treatments result in superior outcomes compared with nonadapted treatments. Indeed, a recent report (Norcross, 2011) concluded that adapting the therapy relationship to client or patient characteristics such as culture enhances the effectiveness of treatment. Culture was found to be a "demonstrably effective" method of adapting psychotherapy. However, there is no evidence that any one model of cultural adaptation is superior to another. What we see across models is a certain degree of convergence on underlying values (e.g., providing a benefit to persons from diverse ethnocultural communities) and observable procedures (e.g., gathering local qualitative observations). When proceeding with cultural adaptations of an EBT, we recommend the following general guidelines (GGs): identify a conceptual framework, document all adaptations, evaluate the outcome and integrity, refine the treatment, and reevaluate the outcome in an iterative process.

GG1. Use a Conceptual Adaptation Framework to Identify Key Elements in the Adaptation

Although some a posteriori adaptations will be necessary if existing models are followed, we believe following a particular cultural adaptation structure a priori is key to the successful implementation of an EBT with ethnocultural populations. It is wise to select a conceptual framework or model that has already been implemented with good results. The a priori preparation serves to organize concepts and procedures that can identify the types of adaptations needed. For example, whether the adaptation is oriented to individual characteristics (e.g., disorder or diagnosis, age, population, language) or cultural processes (e.g., values, beliefs, cultural norms, worldview, lifestyle), changes may be required in terms of the fit with the treatment's theory of change or its procedural model. In addition, advance preparation sets the stage for the essential preliminary work that may entail a review of the literature or the use of focus groups or in-depth interviews with community participants, providers, and therapists who can inform the adaptation.

There is no known cultural adaptation model that prescribes the placement of specific adaptations. For some, changes will be made to existing sessions to attune the content as needed. In other cases, sessions will be added. For example, Brown, Conner, and McMurray (Chapter 11, this volume) included pretreatment engagement sessions in her implementation of interpersonal psychotherapy with older African Americans with depression. Both may be useful and warranted (Parra-Cardona et al., 2012); it is up to the interventionist to make a thoughtful plan for where adaptations are needed.

GG2. Carefully Document All Adaptations

Documenting all cultural adaptations is essential so that one can determine what areas of an EBT need to be changed and for whom and in what circumstances. A conceptual framework can help in identifying the categories in which changes may be needed. The documentation can also serve to identify whether the nature and magnitude of the changes resulted in a cultural adaptation or a different treatment or intervention.

GG3. Evaluate Outcomes of the Culturally Adapted Evidence-Based Treatment

Once the treatment has been adapted, the next step is to evaluate its feasibility, acceptability, and outcomes. This is usually done in a pilot study with a small sample size or in a series of case studies to test the treatment (this volume includes several examples of such evaluations). Tests of efficacy and effectiveness are optimal, but they are complex, time consuming, and costly. Nevertheless, even in a practice setting, baseline and posttreatment measures can be administered, and benchmarks can be used to determine whether the outcomes achieved are equivalent to those found in the literature. Evaluations can also be conducted using qualitative research strategies to investigate outcomes in terms of acceptability, feasibility, and engagement of ECGs with the culturally adapted treatment.

GG4. Evaluate the Integrity of the Original Treatment Model Vis-à-Vis the Adapted Version

As noted earlier, a central concern is the degree to which the adapted intervention maintains its integrity to the original model. The issue of fidelity versus fit is central. The first question to ask is whether the adaptation altered the propositional model. If so, then the theory of change was altered, and the result is a different treatment with distinctly different assumptions as to what causes change. If the propositional model or theory of change remained the same, then fidelity was maintained. The second question to ask is whether the adaptation altered the procedural model. If it did not, then again, integrity was achieved. However, if some components of the intervention were changed, their sequence rearranged, or other procedures were introduced, then the integrity of the procedural model may be compromised. Here again, there may be a new treatment resulting from a different set of procedures.

Other nuances are involved in whether a particular cultural adaptation maintains its integrity to the original model. For example, if both the propositional model and the procedural model were significantly changed, then, clearly, the result of the adaptation was a different treatment. Similarly, if the propositional model was changed and new mediators are now posited, in theory, the treatment also changed, and the integrity of the original treatment is compromised. The third question to consider is whether the propositional model remained intact but the procedural model was changed. In this scenario, integrity is achieved at the theoretical level but not with regard to the procedural model. The treatment developers of some intervention models accept the notion that procedures and process can be changed to fit populations and contexts, whereas others believe that altering any component of the intervention represents a loss of fidelity.

GG5. Reevaluate Outcomes of the Refined Adapted Evidence-Based Treatment

Once there is positive evidence on outcomes, feasibility, acceptability, and fidelity, the treatment can be further refined in preparation for a test of efficacy or effectiveness. The key is to establish the efficacy of the culturally adapted intervention for particular ECGs with solid outcome data. An important design question is how to further evaluate outcomes. The conventional strategy is to compare the adapted treatment with that used with a control group (i.e., waiting list, treatment as usual, placebo) or to compare the culturally adapted treatment with a "standard" unadapted treatment. If one has gone through the process outlined in the guidelines described earlier, then the need or indications for a cultural adaptation have been established on the basis of the best available evidence. The rationale for another test of whether a cultural adaptation is superior to a nonadapted EBT is redundant at best and, at worst, foolish. Furthermore, such an approach usually entails large sample sizes because one is comparing two active conditions. Instead of the standard test of *absolute efficacy* (i.e., comparing an active treatment against a control), the more rigorous test of *relative efficacy* (i.e., comparing two active treatments) does not seem warranted unless there is a persuasive theoretical issue. In addition, the costs for such a test are so high that it is unlikely than any funding source would support it. Thus, our recommendation is to use treatment as usual or waiting-list group comparisons as tests of efficacy for culturally adapted treatments.

A less conventional strategy is to use benchmarks based on published trials to test for equivalence of the results. The design here might entail evaluating outcomes at baseline, posttreatment, and follow-up with no control group and comparing the effect size changes from pre- to posttreatment with those of other studies with similar samples using standard nonadapted interventions on which benchmarks are developed. For example, in a study that evaluated the adaptation of cognitive behavior therapy (CBT) to a school-based intervention, outcomes were benchmarked in relation to results of efficacy trials (Shirk, Kaplinski, & Gudmundsen, 2009). The results showed that the treatment responses of the school-based CBT were comparable to those of efficacy trials. The authors concluded that their adapted treatment was robust. Such benchmarking strategies can be an important resource for testing cultural adaptations and establishing the equivalence of adaptation using existing efficacy trials as a point of comparison.

Specific Guidelines for Cultural Adaptation

Next, we present a set of recommendations for gathering data on which to base cultural adaptations. In this volume, a number of chapters provide examples on specific steps and procedures. We draw from these models to provide a set of specific guidelines (SGs).

SG1. Involve the Target Population

Procedures to involve the target population in the process of adapting EBTs need to be developed. There are a number of ways to ensure participation; these generally entail qualitative techniques such as in-depth interviews, focus groups, and the use of opinion leaders. These techniques can determine the acceptability of the treatment. Participants can also be quite helpful in suggesting how useful or relevant certain constructs (that are central to the treatment) are to the target population. As an example, focus group participants may be given a treatment manual and asked to comment on its clarity, usefulness, and likely acceptability by the target population. Another technique is to survey the population of interest to develop a set of questions aimed at increasing the ecological validity of the treatment or intervention. Thus, questions about cultural and language preferences, cultural values and practices, barriers to treatment, among others, can inform cultural adaptations to the protocol.

SG2. Involve Treatment Providers Who Are Knowledgeable About the Target Population

Involving members from the community of therapists and treatment providers and any personnel involved in the delivery of mental health services is invaluable in conducting cultural adaptations of treatments. These individuals are usually experienced in the day-to-day issues of providing treatment to a wide range of populations and have probably been engaging in cultural adaptations. Therapists and other providers of EBTs are generally knowledgeable about the target population and are an invaluable source of information on what modifications may be needed. Here again, techniques include in-depth interviews, focus groups, and surveys.

One of the benefits of involving therapists and treatment providers in the design for modifying a therapy or intervention is that participants in this process often develop a sense of ownership of the project. Meaningful participation can go a long way in developing partnerships with community organizations that can lead to the sustainability of EBTs in community settings. In the end, the sustainability of treatments makes it possible for effective interventions to be available and delivered to those in need.

SG3. Planning the Adaptation of the Treatment or Intervention

Planning the cultural adaptation of a treatment or intervention presupposes that a cultural adaptation is indicated and supported by the best available evidence. Planning the adaptation entails using a top-down or a bottom-up approach, or a combination of these (e.g., Hwang, Chapter 9, this volume). For example, a top-down approach might start with a review of the literature identifying problems in engagement, retention, and dropout rate, or with worldviews and values that do not appear to fit with aspects of the identified EBT. A bottom-up approach would entail using strategies to involve potential participants or treatment providers and learn from their experience and through a systematic use of qualitative techniques what might need to be adapted. The other alternative is to use a combination of top-down and bottom-up strategies.

In the planning, a strategy is first selected and a plan carefully laid out. If focus groups are to be used, then questions to guide the discussion are developed and a plan for the analysis of the results is defined. If a survey is to be used, a similar process of defining the questions and selecting a population to survey followed by an analysis of the results is used. After these data are collected, the process of adapting the treatment or intervention begins. In some cases, modifications are made to engagement strategies. Structural changes may also be made to overcome barriers that limit or impede access (e.g., language, child care, transportation) to services. If there is a detailed session-by-session manual, that document is subjected to careful scrutiny on the basis of these results; this could result in a language translation and a rephrasing of material to be more attuned with cultural values, ensuring that metaphors and cultural beliefs or worldviews are included in the document and that the goals, methods, and content of the material do not contradict the values and worldviews of the target population. As noted earlier, it is important to carefully document all adaptations made and why they were made.

SG4. A Preliminary Pilot Study on the Acceptability and Feasibility of the Treatment Intervention

Once the adaptation has been completed, a preliminary pilot study on the acceptability and feasibility of the treatment or intervention is in order. Here there is a range of options that may include case studies, pretreatment to posttreatment single groups studies, and small trials comparing the culturally adapted treatment with a no-treatment control. The side benefit of measuring outcomes and carefully documenting the process of delivering the intervention is that this information can be used to further refine the cultural adaptation. There are useful models for intervention development (e.g., the stage model for behavioral therapies; Rounsaville, Carroll, & Onken, 2001) and for cultural adaptations (Bernal, 2006; see also Chapters 2, 4–10, this volume).

SG5. Reviews of the Literature on Issues, Themes, and Constructs With the Barriers to Treatment With the Particular Population

A comprehensive literature review is necessary to document a priori the themes, issues, concepts, and constructs related to engagement, barriers to treatment, and beliefs about treatment of the particular population. For example, notions about the self versus the family, the group, or the collective may play a central role in groups that are less assimilated to Western norms and values. A review of these issues is informative in planning cultural adaptations. For practitioners, comprehensive literature reviews, decade reviews, or meta-analyses are feasible ways to review the relevant literature in a reasonable amount of time.

SG6. Consider Specific Details of Delivery

From the chapters in this volume, the following important questions emerge: (a) Should the intervention be delivered in group, individual, or another format? (b) Who should be a part of the intervention? Only the people experiencing distress? Their caretakers? Others? (c) How should the intervention be presented (e.g., psychoeducation, psychotherapy)? (d) What structures can be put in place to support the intervention delivery (e.g., a community advisory board)? These are a few of the questions that can be posed regarding the specific details of delivery; each presents opportunities for gathering knowledge in practice and in research contexts.

THE FUTURE OF CULTURAL ADAPTATIONS

This volume has focused on the cultural adaptation of EBTs. This focus is warranted by the relatively scant attention paid to treatment compared with therapist characteristics in the multicultural psychology literature. There is ample literature on the importance of delivering treatments in a culturally competent manner. As we end this volume, we address some of the challenges that lie ahead for cultural adaptations in practice and research.

Culture Processes and Common Factors

Psychotherapy approaches have grown remarkably in the past 5 decades. The growth in distinct theories increased from about 60 in the 1960s to over 200 by the early 1980s and more than 400 by 1986. There are more than 400 different psychotherapy approaches (Garfield, 1994). Indeed, a cultural adaptation raises the specter of an exponential proliferation of culturally adapted approaches. Does it make sense to adapt so many treatments, even if we limit these to only EBTs? If we follow Gordon Paul's (1967) dictum of "What treatment, by whom, is most effective for this individual, with that specific problem, and under which set of circumstances" (p. 111), cultural adaptations are simply a further refinement or customization of treatments to the client's individual needs.

An important next step in developing research and practice in cultural adaptation is to examine how cultural processes are part of all aspects of the treatment (i.e., engagement, assessment, diagnosis, treatment, maintenance, follow-up, and outcome). As an example, the proliferation of psychotherapy approaches has led to comparative analyses of psychotherapy (e.g., Ford & Urban, 1998; Frank & Frank, 1991) and to studies of change processes. Studies have identified 12 change processes (e.g., Prochaska, 1979; Prochaska & DiClemente, 1992; Prochaska, Velicer, DiClemente, & Fava, 1988) and common factors (e.g., Tracy, Lichtenberg, Goodyear, Claiborn, & Wampold, 2003). The field is moving toward identifying important commonalities across seemingly different treatments. In addition, integrative approaches (Goldfried, 2010; Norcross & Goldfried, 2005) have evolved that promote a theoretical framework for integrating common elements of treatment and that serve as important models. When we are within our own cultural frame, we only have an insider's view of processes (*emic*). A meta-level of culture or cultures or a perspective from outside the culture (*etic*) can serve to develop a frame from which to conceptualize common multicultural processes in psychotherapy.

For example, meta-analytic findings of outcome studies (Baskin, Tierney, Minami, & Wampold, 2003; Norcross, 2011; Norcross & Wampold, 2011) have suggested that extratherapeutic factors (40%), common factors (30%), specific techniques (15%), and expectancy (15%) contribute in varying degrees to positive outcomes. The future of cultural adaptations may well be determined by studies that examine how culture intersects with each of these sets of factors. The so-called common factors are usually composed of the therapy relationship, which is fundamentally cultural, and expectancy (i.e., the belief that psychotherapy will help). An important avenue for cultural adaptation research and practice is the exploration of how cultural variables intersect or influence outcome and process. The debate in the field has centered on the false dichotomy of fidelity versus fit, when fidelity should be seen as a complement or an ally of fit. Moreover, the focus should be on viewing the whole enterprise of psychotherapy as a cultural phenomenon and on examining the cultural features that are part of both the process and the outcome.

Evaluation of Culturally Adapted Treatments

Recently, several scholars have suggested that the moment is ripe for testing culturally adapted evidence-based treatments (CA-EBTs) against the original EBT (Barrera, Castro, Strycker, & Toobert, 2012; La Roche & Christopher, 2009). The rationale is based on the idea that, first, there are now a number of conceptual frameworks that can guide such studies and, second, that most CA-EBTs have only been tested against no-treatment control conditions instead of against the unchanged condition. The rationale is that only a direct comparison between a culturally adapted and the original EBT can yield definitive proof of the benefits of the adaptation. Although it may be empirically interesting to conduct comparative efficacy trials of CA-

EBTs against the unchanged original version, methodological, conceptual, and ethical issues warrant a more careful consideration.

Cardemil and collegues (2010) eloquently pointed out some of the methodological challenges in comparative efficacy trials of CA-EBTs versus standard treatments, noting that such comparisons are likely to result in negative findings. First, the positive effects of the standard treatment together with those of the CA-EBT will likely produce a ceiling effect on additional gains on outcome. Second, because randomized clinical trials (RCTs) have been notoriously poor in recruiting ethnic minorities, in part because of poor engagement strategies, some kind of procedure should be put in place to engage these groups. Thus, a cultural component, at least in the engagement phase of the treatment, would have to be incorporated, most probably changing "the very nature of the standard intervention so that it is functioning as a cultural adaptation" (Cardemil et al., 2010, p. 16).

There are other serious challenges to such head-to-head comparisons. In RCTs, there is a notable difference in the sample size needed to detect differences between groups (i.e., power) in studies of relative efficacy as compared with studies of absolute efficacy. The latter require a large sample size because two active treatments are being compared. Thus, the cost of the study is much higher and unlikely to get support from funding sources, particularly when these tests are proposed as pilot studies. The large sample size and its related cost would make it impractical to conduct a pilot study, unless there were sound theoretical reasons for the comparison (i.e., questions regarding mediators and moderators of change). However, for a study that entails mediators and moderators, the treatment effects need to be well documented because it usually makes little sense to evaluate the process if the efficacy is in question. Thus, investigators interested in such comparisons are in a catch-22 situation.

Furthermore, relative efficacy trials of standard versus CA-EBTs would require blind experimental procedures and the assurance that therapists administering the experimental intervention would reduce the likelihood of being able to discern a difference in the treatment condition (Cardemil et al., 2010). These procedures are almost impossible to implement. Even if it were possible to suspend cultural competence, a practitioner would be tasked with questioning the ethics of the approach. Asking therapists to suspend tailoring treatments for clients from diverse cultural contexts would result in delivering, at best, a culturally inappropriate treatment and, at worst, a culturally incompetent treatment.

A central methodological concern about comparing CA-EBTs with a standard treatment is that these designs may violate the equipoise in RCTs (Friedman, Furberg, & DeMets, 2010). *Equipoise* refers to the "uncertainty principle" that is essential in a randomized trial: Investigators in all aspects of the study adhere to a position in which participants are enrolled in a trial only if there is true uncertainty about which of the trial conditions is most likely to benefit the participant (Friedman et al., 2010). Thus, if we eliminate central aspects of the therapy encounter, such as preferred language, attention to culture, and context, it is highly likely that the deck is being stacked in favor of the CA-EBT, thus violating equipoise. Yet, putting the question of equipoise aside, to compare a culturally sensitive treatment with a standard treatment would necessitate that therapists not insert in the therapy culturally sensitive elements because doing so would reduce the likelihood of identifying an effect, as Cardemil et al. (2010) pointed out. In theory, this might be possible, but in practice, it raises other conceptual and ethical issues.

If psychotherapy is viewed as a cultural phenomenon (see Chapter 1, this volume), stripping the culture from treatment is a logical impossibility. Psychotherapy and EBTs are cultural products and processes. The history of psychotherapy shows that it has evolved by responding to varying contexts and well as to the cultural values and beliefs of the times. To attempt to eliminate culture experimentally from a treatment condition in order to compare it with a culturally sensitive comparison condition makes little sense except in the myopic view of crass empiricism. A more sensible approach might be to compare degrees of cultural adaptation in a particular treatment. However, here again, the question of violating equipoise might very well resurface.

In terms of ethics, Principle E of the APA "Ethical Principles of Psychologists and Code of Conduct" (APA, 2010) regarding the respect for people's dignity and rights stipulates that

> Psychologists are aware of and respect cultural, individual, and role differences, including those based on age, gender, gender identity, race, ethnicity, culture, national origin, religion, sexual orientation, disability, language, and socioeconomic status and consider these factors when working with members of such groups. Psychologists try to eliminate the effect on their work of biases based on those factors, and they do not knowingly participate in or condone activities of others based upon such prejudices.

Thus, to establish a treatment condition that at best ignores and at worst deliberately eliminates the consideration of factors such as language, race, ethnicity, and culture would seem to be an ethical violation. As Trimble and Fisher (2005) pointed out, a key ethical consideration in working across ECGs is developing and maintaining trust-based relationships as well as exercising respect with the participants and communities. Sensitivity to diverse worldviews and practices is fundamental in working with ECGs. To take cultural context out of the development or delivery of an intervention seems to go against minimal competence (APA Presidential Task Force, 2006), ethics (APA, 2010), and effective psychological practice (Benish et al., 2011; Smith et al., 2011). Clearly, the field needs new methods of inquiry to develop the science of treatment research with ethnic minorities (Lau, Chang, & Okazaki, 2010).

Cultural Competence and Cultural Adaptation

As we end this volume, we realize that there is a nearly inseparable relationship between cultural competence and cultural adaptation. We understand that cultural adaptations apply to treatments, whereas cultural competence refers to the therapist. Indeed, in many chapters, authors make statements regarding the importance of the therapist as an agent of change, implicating cultural competence in the delivery of culturally adapted treatments. A culturally competent psychotherapist without the proper tools (i.e., treatments) to effect change may be likened to a skilled carpenter without the tools of the trade. Similarly, a carefully adapted intervention that is not delivered by a skilled and multiculturally competent clinician can languish or, worse yet, be misused. Definitions of multicultural competence vary in label and scope and include culturally responsive, culturally centered, culturally oriented, and culturally sensitive components, in addition to multicultural competency. We include them here to clarify the use of these terms and the distinction between cultural competence and cultural adaptation.

Cultural Responsivity

Hays and Iwamasa (2006) defined the development of a *culturally responsive* approach to CBT as relying on the therapist. For a therapist to be culturally responsive, she or he must begin with self-awareness of biases and knowledge gaps. These authors described the process as personal and ongoing. Rather than arriving at cultural competence, a therapist makes a commitment to developing a "cultural schema" that will facilitate his or her ability to understand the cognitive, social, and emotional contexts of culturally diverse clients. Hays and Iwamasa gave specific recommendations for developing cultural responsiveness: (a) obtain cultural information from culture-specific sources, (b) attend cultural celebrations and other public events, (c) obtain supervision from a person who belongs to and is knowledgeable about a minority culture, (d) consult with a culturally diverse professional group, (e) read from the wealth of multicultural counseling research, and (f) develop relationships with people of diverse cultures (p. 8).

Culture Centeredness

APA's (2003) "Guidelines on Multicultural Education, Training, Research, Practice, and Organizational Change for Psychologists" define *culture centeredness* in a similar fashion as cultural responsivity. The definition stresses the psychologist's awareness and consideration of culture: "In culture-centered practices, psychologists recognize that all individuals, including themselves, are influenced by different contexts, including the historical, ecological, sociopolitical, and disciplinary" (p. 380). In contrast to and Iwamasa's (2006) cultural responsiveness, culture centeredness calls for self-awareness of the therapist as a culturally rooted being.

Cultural Orientation

Fouad and Arredondo (2007) used the term *culture centered* in their work and promoted a *cultural orientation* on the part of psychologists. The authors specified that psychologists must attend to "role of culture" in their multiple professional roles, including clinical practice, teaching, research, and organizational practice. They cited market and ethical considerations in doing so. Specifically, they warned that psychologists who do not become culturally oriented might simply become unemployed and unemployable.

Cultural Sensitivity

López et al. (1989) proposed an integration of emic (i.e., within the culture, particular) and etic (i.e., outside the culture, universal) perspectives as fundamental to their culturally sensitive frame for developing culturally sensitive psychotherapists. Specifically, they view *cultural sensitivity* as a skill related to the "clinician's ability to balance a consideration of universals norms, specific groups norms, and individual norms in (a) differentiating between normal and abnormal behavior, (b) considering etiology factors, and (c) implementation of appropriate interventions" (p. 370).

In addition, Ridley and Kliner (2003) defined cultural sensitivity as "the ability of counselors to acquire, develop, and actively use an accurate cultural perceptual schema in the course of multicultural counseling. Such a schema must be realistic, plastic, and receptive of many modes of stimulus input." (p. 130). Ridley and Kliner laid out three steps in this information processing model in which therapists (a) focus on cultural stimuli possibly pertinent to the cognitive schema; (b) structure information to better understand cultural processes in psychotherapy that may be related to goals, methods, and relationship aspects of the treatment; and (c) use the conceptual frame to inform treatment goals and make the intervention more culturally responsive.

In an interesting operationalization, Castro (1998) placed cultural sensitivity on a continuum of cultural capacity that ranged from the undesirable "cultural destructiveness" category to more desirable ratings of cultural openness/sensitivity (+1), cultural competence (+2), and cultural proficiency (+3). Following this model, cultural sensitivity is achieved on the way to competence and, ultimately, proficiency.

Multicultural Competence

Perhaps one of the more robustly described and studied concepts in this general area of inquiry is *multicultural competence*. Many definitions have been offered of this construct (cf. Ridley & Kliner, 2003). Multicultural competence definitions typically include three domains: self-awareness, knowledge of the cultural group of interest, and an effective skill set for intervening with that group. It is important to note that the field has not arrived at one single definition of multicultural competence; nor is there agreement about whether there should be one uniform definition (Ridley & Kliner, 2003). As such, it is therapist centered but includes specific intervention components. Trimble (2003) stated that "to achieve multicultural competence, one must be consciously willing to learn and explore other cultural groups; without a conscious intent and desire, the achievement and realization of multicultural competence is not likely to occur" (p. x). Relevant to our discussions on cultural adaptations, Trimble expressly stated that a multiculturally competent psychologist need not discard existing knowledge in psychology.

Across definitions of cultural competence and cultural adaptation, two themes emerge. Both of these are iterative processes. A person does not arrive at cultural competence, nor does the ideal manual for the specific population emerge. Rather, treatment providers and treatments are continually responding to local and current contexts. Similarly, both cultural competence and cultural adaptation require that those engaged in them build on prior knowledge and experiences, gathering from ample sources to best understand the questions of interest. Ultimately, the goal of engaging cultural competence and cultural adaptations is to benefit clients. These benefits will more likely arrive if both the professional and the tools of the trade are as fine-tuned as possible, given current knowledge and experience.

CONCLUSION

The best available evidence suggests that the more cultural adaptations performed on an EBT, the better the outcomes (Smith et al., 2011). Furthermore, an interdivisional task force on EBT relationships concluded that customizing, tailoring, or adapting the therapy to client characteristics beyond diagnosis improves its effectiveness (Norcross, 2011). Adaptations in general, and cultural adaptations in particular, are the future of psychotherapy and intervention research and practice. This is particularly so in a multicultural society. The flow of ideas and cultural contact through time and space is common in our globalized world, requiring the adoption of views, theories, and approaches that are transcultural and cross-border to better appreciate the meaning of cultural life (Moran & Keane, 2009). Because the fundamental work of psychotherapy is the cultural life of the individual and the family, cultural adaptations are an essential resource for research and practice in contemporary multicultural societies.

REFERENCES

American Psychological Association. (2003). Guidelines on multicultural education, training, research, practice, and organizational change for psychologists. *American Psychologist, 58,* 377–402. doi:10.1037/0003-066X.58.5.377

American Psychological Association. (2010). *Ethical principles of psychologists and code of conduct: 2010 Amendments.* Retrieved from http://www.apa.org/ethics/code/index.aspx

American Psychological Association Presidential Task Force on Evidence-Based Practice. (2006). Evidence-based practice in psychology. *American Psychologist, 61,* 271–285. doi:10.1037/0003-066X.61.4.271

Barrera, M., Jr., Castro, F. G., Strycker, L. A., & Toobert, D. J. (2012). Cultural adaptations of behavioral health interventions: A progress report. *Journal of Consulting and Clinical Psychology.* Advance online publication. doi:10.1037/a0027085

Baskin, T. W., Tierney, S. C., Minami, T., & Wampold, B. E. (2003). Establishing specificity in psychotherapy: A meta-analysis of structural equivalence of placebo controls. *Journal of Consulting and Clinical Psychology, 71,* 973–979. doi:10.1037/0022-006X.71.6.973

Benish, S. G., Quintana, S., & Wampold, B. E. (2011). Culturally adapted psychotherapy and the legitimacy of myth: A direct-comparison meta-analysis. *Journal of Counseling Psychology, 58,* 279–289. doi:10.1037/a0023626

Bernal, G. (2006). Intervention development and cultural adaptation research with diverse families. *Family Process, 45,* 143–151. doi:10.1111/j.1545-5300.2006.00087.x

Bernal, G., Bonilla, J., & Bellido, C. (1995). Ecological validity and cultural sensitivity for outcome research: Issues for the cultural adaptation and development of psychosocial treatments with Hispanics. *Journal of Abnormal Child Psychology, 23,* 67–82. doi:10.1007/BF01447045

Bullard, L., Wachlarowicz, M., DeLeeuw, J., Snyder, J., Low, S., Forgatch, M., & DeGarmo, D. (2010). Effects of the Oregon model of Parent Management Training (PMTO) on marital adjustment in new stepfamilies: A randomized trial. *Journal of Family Psychology, 24,* 485–496. doi:10.1037/a0020267

Calzada, E. J. (2010). Bringing culture into parent training with Latinos. *Cognitive and Behavioral Practice, 17,* 167–175. doi:10.1016/j.cbpra.2010.01.003

Cardemil, E. V., Kim, S., Davidson, T., Sarmiento, I. A., Ishikawa, R. Z., Sanchez, M., & Torres, S. (2010). Developing a culturally appropriate depression prevention program: Opportunities and challenges. *Cognitive and Behavioral Practice, 17,* 188–197. doi:10.1016/j.cbpra.2010.01.005

Castro, F. G. (1998). Cultural competence training in clinical psychology: Assessment, clinical intervention, and research. In A. S. Bellack & M. Hersen (Eds.), *Comprehensive clinical psychology: Sociocultural and individual differences* (Vol. 10, pp. 127–140). Oxford, England: Pergamon Press.

Castro, F. G. I., Barrera, M., & Holleran Steiker, L. K. (2010). Issues and challenges in the design of culturally adapted evidence-based interventions. *Annual Review of Clinical Psychology, 6*, 213–239. doi:10.1146/annurev-clinpsy-033109-132032

DeGarmo, D. S., Chamberlain, P., Leve, L. D., & Price, J. (2009). Foster parent intervention engagement moderating child behavior problems and placement disruption. *Research on Social Work Practice, 19*, 423–433. doi:10.1177/1049731508329407

Domenech Rodriguez, M. M., Baumann, A. A., & Schwartz, A. L. (2011). Cultural adaptation of an evidence based intervention: From theory to practice in a Latino/a community context. *American Journal of Community Psychology, 47*, 170–186. doi:10.1007/s10464-010-9371-4

Elliott, D. S., & Mihalic, S. (2004). Issues in disseminating and replicating effective prevention programs. *Prevention Science, 5*, 47–53. doi:10.1023/B:PREV.0000013981.28071.52

Ford, D. H., & Urban, H. B. (1998). *Contemporary models of psychotherapy: A comparative analysis* (2nd ed.). Hoboken, NJ: Wiley.

Fouad, N. A., & Arredondo, P. (2007). *Becoming culturally oriented: Practical advice for psychologists and educators.* Washington, DC: American Psychological Association. doi:10.1037/11483-000

Frank, J. D., & Frank, J. B. (1991). *Persuasion and healing: A comparative study of psychotherapy* (3rd ed.). Baltimore, MD: Johns Hopkins University Press.

Friedman, L. M., Furberg, C. D., & DeMets, D. L. (2010). *Fundamentals of clinical trials.* New York, NY: Springer. doi:10.1007/978-1-4419-1586-3

Garfield, S. L. (1994). Eclecticism and integration in psychotherapy: Developments and issues. *Clinical Psychology: Science and Practice, 1*, 123–137. doi:10.1111/j.1468-2850.1994.tb00015.x

Goldfried, M. R. (2010). The future of psychotherapy integration: Closing the gap between research and practice. *Journal of Psychotherapy Integration, 20*, 386–396. doi:10.1037/a0022036

Griner, D., & Smith, T. B. (2006). Culturally adapted mental health intervention: A meta-analytic review. *Psychotherapy: Theory, Research, Practice, Training, 43*, 531–548. doi:10.1037/0033-3204.43.4.531

Hays, P. A., & Iwamasa, G. Y. (Eds.). (2006). *Culturally responsive cognitive-behavioral therapy: Assessment, practice, and supervision.* Washington, DC: American Psychological Association. doi:10.1037/11433-000

Herschell, A. D., Kolko, D. J., Baumann, B. L., & Davis, A. C. (2010). The role of therapist training in implementation of psychosocial treatment: A review and critique with recommendations. *Clinical Psychology Review, 30*, 448–466. doi:10.1016/j.cpr.2010.02.005

Kazdin, A. E., & Whitley, M. K. (2006). Comorbidity, case complexity, and effects of evidence-based treatment for children referred for disruptive behavior. *Journal of Consulting and Clinical Psychology, 74,* 455–467. doi:10.1037/0022-006X.74.3.455

Kumpfer, K. L., Pinyuchon, M., de Melo, A. T., & Whiteside, H. O. (2008). Cultural adaptation process for international dissemination of the strengthening families program. *Evaluation & the Health Professions, 35,* 226–239. doi:10.1177/0163278708315926

La Roche, M. J., & Christopher, M. S. (2009). Changing paradigms from empirically supported treatment to evidence-based practice: A cultural perspective. *Professional Psychology: Research and Practice, 40,* 396–402. doi:10.1037/a0015240

Lau, A. S., Chang, D. F., & Okazaki, S. (2010). Methodological challenges in treatment outcome research with ethnic minorities. *Cultural Diversity and Ethnic Minority Psychology, 16,* 573–580. doi:10.1037/a0021371

López, S. R., Grover, K. P., Holland, D., Johnson, M., Kain, C. D., Kanel, K., . . . Rhyne, M. C. (1989). Development of culturally sensitive psychotherapists. *Professional Psychology, Research and Practice, 20,* 369–376. doi:10.1037/0735-7028.20.6.369

Moran, A., & Keane, M. (2009). *Cultural adaptation.* New York, NY: Routledge.

Norcross, J. C. (2011). *Psychotherapy relationships that work* (2nd ed.). New York, NY: Wiley/Blackwell.

Norcross, J. C., & Goldfried, M. R. (2005). *Handbook of psychotherapy integration* (2nd ed.). New York, NY: Oxford University Press.

Norcross, J. C., & Wampold, B. E. (2011). Evidence-based therapy relationships: Research conclusions and clinical practices. *Psychotherapy: Theory, Research, & Practice, 48,* 98–102. doi:10.1037/a0022161

Parra-Cardona, J. R., Domenech Rodríguez, M., Forgatch, M., Sullivan, C., Bybee, D., Tams, L., . . . Bernal, G. (2012). Culturally adapting an evidence-based parenting intervention for Latino immigrants: Preliminary implications for family therapy practice and research. *Family Process, 51,* 56–72. doi:1111/j.1545-5300.2012.01386.x

Patterson, G. R., Forgatch, M. S., & DeGarmo, D. S. (2010). Cascading effects following intervention. *Development and Psychopathology, 22,* 949–970. doi:10.1017/S0954579410000568

Paul, G. L. (1967). Strategy of outcome research in psychotherapy. *Journal of Consulting Psychology, 31,* 109–118. doi:10.1037/h0024436

Prochaska, J. O. (1979). *Systems of psychotherapy: A transtheoretical analysis.* Oxford, England: Dorsey.

Prochaska, J. O., & DiClemente, C. C. (1992). The transtheoretical approach. In J. C. Norcross & M. R. Goldfried (Eds.), *Handbook of psychotherapy integration* (pp. 300–334). New York, NY: Basic Books.

Prochaska, J. O., Velicer, W. F., DiClemente, C. C., & Fava, J. (1988). Measuring processes of change: Applications to the cessation of smoking. *Journal of Consulting and Clinical Psychology, 56,* 520–528. doi:10.1037/0022-006X.56.4.520

Radloff, L. S. (1977). The CES-D scale: A self-report depression scale for research in the general population. *Applied Psychological Measurement, 1,* 385–401. doi:10.1177/014662167700100306

Ridley, C. R., & Kliner, A. J. p. (2003). Multicultural counseling competence: History, themes, and issues. In D. B. Pope-Davis, H. L. K. Coleman, W. M. Liu, & R. L. Toporek (Eds.), *Handbook of multicultural competencies in counseling & psychology* (pp. 3–20). Thousand Oaks, CA: Sage.

Rivera-Medina, C., Bernal, G., & Rosselló, J. (2010). Predictive validity of the Child Depression Inventory items for major depression disorder in Latino adolescents. *Hispanic Journal of Behavioral Sciences, 32,* 232–258. doi:10.1177/0739986310361919

Rivera-Medina, C. L., Caraballo, J. N., Rodriguez-Cordero, E. R., Bernal, G., & Dávila-Marrero, E. (2010). Factor structure of the CES-D and measurement invariance across gender for low-income Puerto Ricans in a probability sample. *Journal of Consulting and Clinical Psychology, 78,* 398–408. doi:10.1037/a0019054

Rounsaville, B. J., Carroll, K. M., & Onken, L. S. (2001). A stage model of behavioral therapies research: Getting started and moving on from stage I. *Clinical Psychology: Science and Practice, 8,* 133–142. doi:10.1093/clipsy.8.2.133

Shirk, S. R., Kaplinski, H., & Gudmundsen, G. (2009). School-based cognitive-behavioral therapy for adolescent depression: A benchmarking study. *Journal of Emotional and Behavioral Disorders, 17,* 106–117. doi:10.1177/1063426608326202

Smith, T. B., Domenech Rodriguez, M., & Bernal, G. (2011). Culture. In J. C. Norcross (Ed.), *Psychotherapy relationships that work.* New York, NY: Wiley/Blackwell.

Tracey, T. J. G., Lichtenberg, J. W., Goodyear, R. K., Claiborn, C. D., & Wampold, B. E. (2003). Concept mapping of therapeutic common factors. *Psychotherapy Research, 13,* 401–413. doi:10.1093/ptr/kpg041

Trimble, J. E. (2003). Foreword. In D. Pope-Davis & H. L. K. Coleman, (Eds.), *Handbook of multicultural competencies* (2nd ed., pp. x–xiii). Thousand Oaks, CA: Sage.

Trimble, J. E., & Fisher, C. G. (2005). *Handbook of ethical and responsible research with ethnocultural populations and communities.* Thousand Oaks, CA: Sage.

INDEX

Personalism, 170
Personality, 8, 26
Personalized interventions, 127
Persons (EVF dimension)
    of ecological validity framework, 25
    in TEPSI, 103
    in trauma intervention adaptation,
        161, 167
Pharmacotherapy, 224–226
Phiri, P., 33
Physical abuse, 159
Physical activity, 116–117, 122
Pick, S., 159
Pilot study
    for acceptability and feasibility of
        treatment, 276
    of adaptation for parent training,
        149–152
    of MLP adaptation, 123–125, 128
    of TEPSI intervention, 101
Pinyuchon, M., 32
Planning, 275–276
Play, child-directed, 137–138, 145, 150
Play therapy, 25, 214
PMTO (parent management training),
    267–268
Podorefsky, D. L., 34
Poling, K., 75–76
Positive outcomes, 269–270
Positivist paradigm, 23
Postmenopausal women, 116
Posttreatment change, 125
Practice gaps, 244–248, 255
Pragmatist tradition, 23–24
Praise
    barriers to implementing strategy of,
        145, 150–151
    beliefs about, 138–139
    and Chinese immigrant parents, 135,
        144–145, 151–152
    in parent training, 138–140
Prayer feather, 216
Preliminary adaptations, 120–125,
    164–165
the present, 204–205
Presenting problem, 268–269
Presumptive truth fallacy, 9–10
Pretreatment change, 125
Pretreatment engagement, 233
Prevention interventions, 217

Prevention of Suicide in Primary Care
    Elderly: Collaborative Trial
    (PROSPECT), 226–227
Primary care
    ITP for older adults in, 229
    older adults in, 231–234
    physicians, 225
Principled cultural sensitivity, 46
Principles, 182
Privileges, 143–144
Problem definition, 211–212
Problem solving, 122
Procedural model
    fidelity of adaptation to, 273
    psychotherapy as, 5
    in treatment selection, 266–267
Procedures
    for informed consent, 121
    for MLP adaptation, 121–122
    for Saber es Poder curriculum, 164
    for trauma interventions, 161–163
    for validity, 270–271
Processes
    cultural, 277–278
    defined, 24
    variation in, 265–266
Propositional model
    fidelity of adaptation to, 273
    psychotherapy as, 5
    in treatment selection, 266–267
PROSPECT (Prevention of Suicide
    in Primary Care Elderly:
    Collaborative Trial), 226–227
Protective factors, 160
Psychoanalysis, 7
Psychodynamic approaches, 5–6
Psychoeducation
    for Chinese immigrant parents, 139
    on ecological validity framework, 79
    for family members, 92–93
    for high-risk urban population, 34
    intervention focus on, 97, 100
    for parents, 100–101, 103–104
    in parent training, 148–149
    trauma- and culture-specific, 170–171
Psychosis, 33
Psychosocial interventions, 114–115
Psychotherapy
    changes and adaptations in, 7–9
    client-centered, 8

culturally responsive, 24–25
and culture, 4, 280
definitions of, 5
with ethnocultural groups, 266
historical adaptations of, 5–10
role of culture in, 38
as vehicle for oppression, 9–10
Psychotherapy adaptation and
    modification framework (PAMF)
    cultural adaptations generated by,
        187–195
    and FMAP, 183
    overview of, 181–182
    as top-down approach, 31–32
PT. *See* Parent training
Puerto Ricans
    adolescents, 75, 94
    parents, 244
    in TEPSI intervention, 97, 101–106
Pumariega, A. J., 72
Pumariega, J. B., 72
Punitive discipline, 148–149

Qi, 189–190

Randomized clinical trials (RCTs), 101,
    279–280
Rathod, S., 33
Rationales, 182
Realism, 36, 55–56
Red pedagogy, 60
Reevaluation, 273–274
Refinement. *See* Adaptation refinement
Reinforcement, differential, 141–142, 145
Relapse, 227
Relationships
    in American Indian cultures, 204–206
    child–parent, 137–144, 251–254
    client–therapist, 192–193
    collaborative, 49–50, 184–185
    with ethnocultural communities, 56
    in help-seeking process, 232
    indigenous approaches to, 201
    therapeutic, 152, 192–193
Religious beliefs, 189–190
Renzetti, C. M., 159
Reparation, 59
Research
    with American Indians, 48, 206–208
    on Asian Americans, 179–181

with cultural sensitivity framework,
    27
ethical considerations for, 52–61
on ethnic minorities, 47–49
gap between practice and, 244–248,
    255
on IPT with older adults, 228–229
marketing, 39–40
partnerships, 47–49, 61, 77
skills in Western academia, 59
Resiliency, 34
Resnicow, K., 27, 29
Respect, 280
Responders, partial, 227
Response cost, 143–145
Responsitivity, cultural, 281
Restructuring, cognitive, 148
Retention, 225–226
Reunification, 251–252
Revision process, 187–188
Rewards, 135, 140–141
Reyes-Rodríguez, M., 97, 100
Reynolds, C. F. III, 227, 229–230
Rhode, P., 92
Ridley, C. R., 282
Rights, 280
Risk factors
    contextual, 160
    for depression, 72
    for diabetes, 113–114, 119
    with parenting, 148–149
    race or ethnic differences in, 160
Rodgers, A., 93–94
Rogers, Carl, 8
Rogers, E. M., 39
Rogler, L. H., 12
Role functioning, 231–232
Rosselló, J., 26, 94
Rothe, E., 72

Saber es Poder (Saber es Poder), 165–172
Sacco, D., 225–226
Sáez-Santiago, E., 94, 100
Sage (herb), 212–213
St. Clair, Bernadette, 213
SAMHSA (Substance Abuse and
    Mental Health Services
    Administration), 245
Sander, J. B., 93
Santiago, E., 170

ABOUT THE EDITORS

Guillermo Bernal, PhD, is professor of psychology and director of the Institute for Psychological Research at the University of Puerto Rico. His work has focused on training, research, and the development of mental health services responsive to ethnocultural groups. Dr. Bernal has over 150 scholarly publications. He has received the American Family Therapy Academy Distinguished Contribution to Family Systems Research award (2009) and has been honored as an Elder of the National Multicultural Conference and Summit (2013). He obtained his doctorate from the University of Massachusetts, Amherst (1978), and is a fellow of the American Psychological Association (Divisions 45, 12, 27).

Melanie M. Domenech Rodríguez, PhD, is an associate professor of psychology at Utah State University. Her work has focused on research, teaching, practice, and training with diverse populations. For her clinical research and training, she has specialized in the Parent Management Training-Oregon (PMTO) model, and evidence-based parenting intervention. She has also made substantive contributions to teaching, research, and training in professional ethics. Dr. Domenech Rodríguez obtained her doctoral degree at Colorado State University (1999) and was a postdoctoral fellow with the Family Research Consortium-III. She is a fellow of American Psychological Association (Division 45).